Early Christianity at Amheida (Egypt's Dakhla Oasis), A Fourth-Century Church

Volume 1
The Excavations

(Amheida VII)

Nicola Aravecchia

Institute for the Study of the Ancient World
NYU Press

New York
2024

© 2024 Institute for the Study of the Ancient World
New York University Press

ISBN
Hardcover: 9781479813506
Ebook (consumer): 9781479813490
Ebook (library): 9781479813544

Library of Congress Control Number: 2024935729

Suggested citation for this volume:
Nicola Aravecchia. *Early Christianity at Amheida (Egypt's Dakhla Oasis), A Fourth-Century Church: Volume 1, The Excavations* (Amheida VII) (2024)

Design by Katerina Boukala-Karkagianni

Printed in the United States

ISAW Monographs

ISAW Monographs publishes authoritative studies of new evidence and research into the texts, archaeology, art history, material culture, and history of the cultures and periods representing the core areas of study at NYU's Institute for the Study of the Ancient World. The topics and approaches of the volumes in this series reflect the intellectual mission of ISAW as a center for advanced scholarly research and graduate education whose aim is to encourage the study of the economic, religious, political, and cultural connections between ancient civilizations, from the Western Mediterranean across the Near East and Central Asia, to China.

Roger S. Bagnall and Giovanni R. Ruffini, *Ostraka from Trimithis, Volume 1* (Amheida I) (2012)

George Hatke, *Aksum and Nubia: Warfare, Commerce, and Political Fictions in Ancient Northeast Africa* (2013)

Jonathan Ben-Dov and Seth Sanders (eds.), *Ancient Jewish Sciences and the History of Knowledge in Second Temple Literature* (2014)

Anna L. Boozer, *A Late Romano-Egyptian House in the Dakhla Oasis: Amheida House B2* (Amheida II) (2015)

Roger S. Bagnall, Nicola Aravecchia, Raffaella Cribiore, Paola Davoli, Olaf E. Kaper, and Susanna McFadden, *An Oasis City* (2016)

Roger S. Bagnall, Roberta Casagrande-Kim, Cumhur Tanrıver, *Graffiti from the Basilica in the Agora of Smyrna* (2016)

Rodney Ast and Roger S. Bagnall, *Ostraka from Trimithis, Volume 2* (Amheida III) (2016)

Nicola Aravecchia, *'Ain el-Gedida: 2006–2008 Excavations of a Late Antique Site in Egypt's Western Desert* (Amheida IV) (2019)

Roger S. Bagnall and Alexander Jones, *Mathematics, Metrology, and Model Contracts: A Codex From Late Antique Business Education (P.Math.)* (2020)

Clementina Caputo, *The House of Serenos, Part I: The Pottery* (Amheida V) (2020)

Jonathan Valk and Irene Soto Marín (eds.), *Ancient Taxation: The Mechanics of Extraction in Comparative Perspective* (2021)

Hélène Cuvigny, *Rome in Egypt's Eastern Desert* (2021)

Paola Davoli, *The House of Serenos, Part II: Archaeological Report on a Late-Roman Urban House at Trimithis* (Amheida VI) (2022)

Sofie Schiødt, Amber Jacob, and Kim Ryholt (eds.), *Scientific Traditions in the Ancient Mediterranean and Near East* (2023)

Antonis Kotsonas, *The Sanctuary of Hermes and Aphrodite at Syme Viannou VII: The Greek and Roman Pottery* (2024)

Maria Grazia Masetti-Rouault, Ilaria Calini, Robert Hawley and Lorenzo d'Alfonso (eds.), *Between the Age of Diplomacy and the First Great Empire: Ancient Western Asia Beyond the Paradigm of Collapse and Regeneration (1200-900 BCE)* (2024)

Nicola Aravecchia, *Early Christianity at Amheida (Egypt's Dakhla Oasis), A Fourth-Century Church: Volume 1, The Excavations* (Amheida VII) (2024)

To Roger S. Bagnall: a mentor, a colleague, a friend

Table of Contents

List of Figures	xiii
Foreword	xxv
Preface	xxvii

Chapter 1: Introduction
- 1.1. Overview of the Amheida Church Project — 1
- 1.2. The Dakhla Oasis — 3
- 1.3. History of the Amheida Project — 8
- 1.4. Topography of the Site and Main Excavated Features — 9
- 1.5. Methodology of Excavation, Documentation, and Conservation — 19

Chapter 2: Early Christianity in the Great Oasis
- 2.1. Archaeological Evidence from Dakhla — 25
  - 2.1.1. The Churches of Dakhla — 26
  - 2.1.2. Christian Cemeteries in Dakhla — 37
- 2.2. Documentary Evidence from Amheida — 39
- 2.3. Early Christian Sites and Monuments in Kharga — 42

Chapter 3: Area 2.3: The Church
- 3.1. The Excavation of Building 7 — 57
- 3.2. Room 1 — 59
- 3.3. The Foundations of Room 1 — 99
  - 3.3.1. Test Trench 1 — 100
  - 3.3.2. Test Trench 2 — 106
- 3.4. Tombs 1–4 and 17 in Room 1 — 120
- 3.5. Rooms 14–16 — 137

Chapter 4: Survey and Excavations to the South the Church
- 4.1. Introduction — 141
- 4.2. Room 5 — 146
- 4.3. Room 6 — 158
  - 4.3.1. Tomb 5 in Room 6 — 171
- 4.4. Room 7 — 175
- 4.5. Room 8 — 189

4.6. Room 9	197
4.7. Room 10	207
4.8. Rooms 11 and 13	214
4.8.1. Test Trench 3 in Room 13	229
4.9. Room 12	236

Chapter 5: The Underground Funerary Crypts

5.1. The Excavation of Rooms 2–4	245
5.2. Room 2	246
5.2.1. Tombs 6–9 in Room 2	269
5.3. Room 3	282
5.3.1. Tombs 10–16 in Room 3	299
5.3.2. Test Trench 4 to the East of Room 3	313
5.4. Room 4	319
5.5. Building 7 as a Funerary Church	337
5.5.1 Crypts in Early Christian Churches of Egypt	345

Chapter 6: The Painted Ceiling of the Church

6.1. Introduction	353
6.2. Excavation and Conservation of the Fragments	357
6.3. The Polychrome Decoration of the Ceiling	358
6.4. Discussion	365

Chapter 7: Discussion of the Archaeological Evidence

7.1. The Development of the Church Complex	373
7.2. A pulpit?	375
7.3. Rooms 5, 11, and 13: A Double Staircase?	378
7.4. Remarks on the Chronology of Building 7	380
7.4.1. The Ostraka from Area 2.3	385
7.5. Building 7 within the Amheida Cityscape	389
7.6. Parallels	393

Chapter 8: Epilogue

8.1. Significance of the Discovery of the Church and Funerary Crypts	403
8.2. Considerations for Future Work in Area 2.3 (and Beyond)	405

Table of Chronology	409
Bibliography	411
Index	437

List of Figures

Chapter 1

Fig. 1.1: Map of Egypt
Fig. 1.2: Map of Dakhla's roads and caravan routes
Fig. 1.3: Map of Dakhla Oasis
Fig. 1.4: Site plan of Amheida (2023)
Fig. 1.5: Remains of the *temenos* on the temple's hill (Area 4)
Fig. 1.6: View of the necropolis at the south end of Amheida
Fig. 1.7: View of the Roman pyramid (following restoration) at the southeast end of the site
Fig. 1.8: View of the baths of Amheida (B6), showing the pillared hall (in the background) and a round pool (in the foreground)
Fig. 1.9: Plan of Serenos's house (B1)
Fig. 1.10: Detail of a painted scene on the east wall of room 1 inside Serenos's house, showing the personification of the *polis* of Trimithis/Amheida (at the far left) and, to her right, a procession of Olympian deities witnessing the adultery of Aphrodite and Ares
Fig. 1.11: Rhetorical exercises in a schoolroom (B5) at Amheida
Fig. 1.12: Aerial view of house B2 at Amheida

Chapter 2

Fig. 2.1: Plan of buildings on mound I at ʿAin el-Gedida
Fig. 2.2: Aerial view (to northeast) of the church complex of ʿAin el-Gedida
Fig. 2.3: Plan of the East Churches at Kellis
Fig. 2.4: Plan of the West Church at Kellis
Fig. 2.5: Plan of the church at ʿAin el-Sabil
Fig. 2.6: Plan of the church (and adjacent structures) at Deir Abu Matta
Fig. 2.7: Plan of the church of Deir el-Molouk
Fig. 2.8: Block from the temple area at Amheida, bearing a Greek inscription with a dedication to Ammon
Fig. 2.9: Map of Kharga Oasis showing the location of early Christian sites
Fig. 2.10: Plan of the church in the temple of Hibis, Kharga Oasis
Fig. 2.11: Plan of the church of ʿAin el-Turba
Fig. 2.12: The Christian necropolis at El-Bagawat

Fig. 2.13: View (to northeast) of building 180 at El-Bagawat

Fig. 2.14: View (to south) of the monastic complex of Deir Mustafa Kashef (left) in relation to Deir el-Bagawat (right)

Fig. 2.15: View (to southeast) of the church and monastic complex of ʿAin Zaaf East

Fig. 2.16: Plan of the church of ʿAin Zaaf West

Fig. 2.17: Plan of ʿAin el-Gallal (North and South)

Fig. 2.18: Plan of the churches surveyed at Umm el-Dabadib (a) and at ʿAin el-Tarakwa (b)

Fig. 2.19: Plan of the church of Dush

Fig. 2.20: Plan of the church of Shams el-Din

Fig. 2.21: View (to east) of the church of Shams el-Din

Chapter 3

Fig. 3.1: Aerial view (to southwest) of the church before excavation began

Fig. 3.2: Plan of building 7

Fig. 3.3: Aerial view (to northeast) of the church at the end of the 2012 season

Fig. 3.4: Plan of room 1

Fig. 3.5: View of the southwest corner of room 1, with walls exposed at foundation level

Fig. 3.6: View (to south) of the preserved top of F1 (east wall of room 1)

Fig. 3.7: View (to east) of the south half of wall F1

Fig. 3.8: Profile of the doorway, set in wall F1, opening from room 1 into room 16

Fig. 3.9: View (to southeast) of platform F19

Fig. 3.10: View (to east) of platform F19

Fig. 3.11: View of the north (a) and south (b) sets of steps in platform F19

Fig. 3.12: View (from above) of remains of rectangular base (F12)

Fig. 3.13: View (to south) of remains of rectangular base and semi-column (F2)

Fig. 3.14: View (to southwest) of room 1's south wall (F13) and mud-brick *mastaba* (F18)

Fig. 3.15: View (to south) of the east half of south wall F13 and *mastaba* F18

Fig. 3.16: Profile of the doorway, set in wall F13, connecting room 1 with the south annex

Fig. 3.17: Remains of *mastaba* F18, abutting wall F13, near the southwest corner of room 1 (view to south)

Fig. 3.18: View (to south) of the church's west wall (F14)

Fig. 3.19: Aerial view (to east) of room 1

Fig. 3.20: View (to southwest) of F9, the foundation wall of the church's north colonnade

Fig. 3.21: F10, a fragmentary column and base of the north colonnade

Fig. 3.22: Remains of heart-shaped pillar and square base (F11) at the east end of the north colonnade

Fig. 3.23: Remains of F26, likely a pulpit

Fig. 3.24: View (to northeast) of foundation wall F8, forming the church's west return aisle

Fig. 3.25: View (to west) of foundation wall F30

Fig. 3.26: View (to northeast) of F7, the foundation wall of the church's south colonnade

Fig. 3.27: View (to north) of remains of square bases and columns F4–F5 along the south colonnade

Fig. 3.28: Remains of heart-shaped pillar and square base (F3) at the east end of the south colonnade

Fig. 3.29: Drawing of heart-shaped pillar and square base F3

Fig. 3.30: View (from above) of column+base F4

Fig. 3.31: View (from above) of column+base F5

Fig. 3.32: View (from above) of column+base F6

Fig. 3.33: Aerial view (to east) of room 1, showing the remains of floor levels in its eastern half

Fig. 3.34: Outline of floor levels in the central nave and in the east half of room 1

Fig. 3.35: View (to west) of remains of floor F21 in the northeast corner of room 1

Fig. 3.36: View (to south) of remains of floor F20 in the northeast area of room 1

Fig. 3.37: View (to west) of patches of floors F23 and F27 in the southeast corner of room 1

Fig. 3.38: View (to northeast) of remains of floor F22 in the nave of room 1

Fig. 3.39: N–S profile (looking east) of the stratigraphy of room 1 in the area of the nave (showing the extent of floor F22)

Fig. 3.40: Mosaic of photogrammetric images of the church at Amheida, following the 2023 excavations

Fig. 3.41a–b: Harris Matrix of room 1

Fig. 3.42: View (to northeast) of collapse DSU2 in room 1

Fig. 3.43: View (to south) of collapse DSU6 in room 1

Fig. 3.44: Large fragment of plaster from DSU6 (likely from a doorway)

Fig. 3.45: View (to west) of DSU7 in the south aisle (after partial removal)

Fig. 3.46: View (from above) of wall collapse DSU9 in the south aisle

Fig. 3.47: Fragments of painted plaster, from the collapsed ceiling of room 1, retrieved in DSU5

Fig. 3.48: Illustrated ostrakon (inv. 15851) from DSU10 in room 1

Fig. 3.49: View (from above) of test trench 1 after excavation

Fig. 3.50: View of north face of F16

Fig. 3.51: Drawing of north profile of F16

Fig. 3.52: View of top of F16 (foundation of pillar or column)

Fig. 3.53: View of south face of F17 (foundation of pillar or column)

Fig. 3.54: Drawing of south profile of F17

Fig. 3.55: View of top of F17 (foundation of pillar or column)

Fig. 3.56: View of wall F14's east face inside test trench 1

Fig. 3.57: View (from above) of DSU18

Fig. 3.58: View (from above) of DSU8

Fig. 3.59: View (from above) of DSU20 (at foundation level of F16–17)

Fig. 3.60: Aerial view (to southeast) of building 7

Fig. 3.61: N–S section of walls F15 and F9 in test trench 2

Fig. 3.62: View of east face of wall F14 in test trench 2

Fig. 3.63: View of northwest corner of room 1, with lump of mortar above ledge of walls F14–15

Fig. 3.64: View (from above) of foundation trench F28

Fig. 3.65: View of south face of wall F15 in test trench 2 (west part)

Fig. 3.66: View of south face of wall F15 in test trench 2 (central part)

Fig. 3.67: View (from above) of foundation trench F29

Fig. 3.68: View of north face of wall F9 in test trench 2

Fig. 3.69: East profile of test trench 1

Fig. 3.70: View of east profile of test trench 1

Fig. 3.71: View (to east) of stratigraphy in test trench 2

Fig. 3.72: Plan of test trench 2 at the end of the 2012 season

Fig. 3.73: View (to east) of DSU30 in test trench 2

Fig. 3.74: View (to south) of DSU3 in the northwest corner of the central nave (after partial excavation)

Fig. 3.75: View of excavation of tomb 1

Fig. 3.76: View (to west) of human remains (FN127) in tomb 1

Fig. 3.77: Aerial view (to southwest) of building 7, showing the location of tombs 2–4 along the north wall of room 1

Fig. 3.78: View (to west) of burial pit F24 and superstructure F25 of tomb 2

Fig. 3.79: Plan of tomb 2 in room 1

Fig. 3.80: View (to west) of human remains (FN139) in tomb 2

Fig. 3.81: View (to west) of burial pit F31 and superstructure F34 (lower level) of tomb 3

Fig. 3.82: Plan showing superstructure F34 (upper level) of tomb 3 and superstructure F32 of tomb 4

Fig. 3.83: Plan showing superstructure F34 (lower level) of tomb 3

Fig. 3.84: View (to west) of human remains (FN12) in tomb 3

Fig. 3.85: Aerial view (to south) of building 7 after surface clearance in 2012

Fig. 3.86: View (to west) of burial pit F33 and superstructure F32 of tomb 4

Fig. 3.87: Partial view of pit fill DSU45 and of human remains (FN13) in tomb 4

Fig. 3.88: Aerial view (to east) of tomb 17 in room 1 (during excavation)

Fig. 3.89: Plan showing superstructure F112 and outline of pit (F113) of tomb 17

Fig. 3.90: View (to west) of superstructure F112 and outline of pit (F113) of tomb 17

Fig. 3.91: View (to east) of coffin (inv. 17098) inside tomb 17

Fig. 3.92: View from above of human remains (FN55) in tomb 17

Fig. 3.93: Aerial view (to northeast) of the area of the sanctuary and *pastophoria* (before excavation of the crypts)

Fig. 3.94: Photogrammetric mosaic of rooms 14–16 (above rooms 2–4 respectively)

Fig. 3.95: View (to west) of remains of room 16. Photograph taken during the first day of excavation of the underground crypt (room 4)

Chapter 4

Fig. 4.1: View (to southeast) of building 7's south annex (before excavation)

Fig. 4.2: Aerial view (to southwest) of excavated rooms to the south of the church

Fig. 4.3: Plan of rooms 5–13

Fig. 4.4: View of south face of wall F40

Fig. 4.5: Aerial view (to south) of room 5

Fig. 4.6: View (to east) of wall F37 in room 5

Fig. 4.7: View (to north) of wall F13 in room 5, with threshold into room 1

Fig. 4.8: Drawing of upper surface of doorway between rooms 1 and 5

Fig. 4.9: View (to east) of threshold between rooms 5 and 6

Fig. 4.10: Sketch of hole in wall F13 (room 5)

Fig. 4.11: View (to south) of staircase F35 in room 5

Fig. 4.12: Drawing of staircase F35

Fig. 4.13: N–S section of staircase F35 (looking E), reconstructed

Fig. 4.14: View (to east) of patches of floors F38 and F46 in room 5

Fig. 4.15: Harris Matrix of room 5

Fig. 4.16: View (to northwest) of DSU35 (wall collapse) in room 5

Fig. 4.17: View (to south) of DSU47–48 in room 5

Fig. 4.18: Aerial view (to south) of room 6

Fig. 4.19: View (to north) of wall F13 in room 6

Fig. 4.20: View (to east) of wall F36 in room 6

Fig. 4.21: View of wall F40 (north face), wall F41 (east face), and platform F47 in the southwest corner of room 6
Fig. 4.22: View (to south) of threshold between room 6 and the (unexcavated) area south of building 7
Fig. 4.23: Sketch of doorway within wall F40 (into room 6)
Fig. 4.24: View (to west) of wall F41 in room 6
Fig. 4.25: Plan of room 6, showing the outline of the preserved patches of floors F50–51
Fig. 4.26: View (to southwest) of floors F50–51 in room 6
Fig. 4.27: View (to south) of platform F47 in room 6
Fig. 4.28: Plan of platform F47 in room 6
Fig. 4.29: Harris Matrix of room 6
Fig. 4.30: View (to southwest) of room 6 before excavation
Fig. 4.31: View (to southeast) of DSU36–37 in room 6
Fig. 4.32: View (to north) of tomb 5 in room 6
Fig. 4.33: Plan of tomb 5 in room 6
Fig. 4.34: Remains of palm-rib mat (inv. 17011) below the superstructure of tomb 5
Fig. 4.35: Human remains (FN5) inside tomb 5
Fig. 4.36: Aerial view (to south) of room 7
Fig. 4.37: View (to north) of wall F42 in room 7
Fig. 4.38: Sketch of wall F42 (south face)
Fig. 4.39: View (to west) of wall F43 in room 7
Fig. 4.40: View (to east) of wall F41 in room 7
Fig. 4.41: Sketch of wall F41 (west face)
Fig. 4.42: View (to south) of wall F40 in room 7
Fig. 4.43: View (to east) of upper floor F62 in room 7
Fig. 4.44: View (to northwest) of stove F61 in room 7
Fig. 4.45: Plan of stove F61 in room 7
Fig. 4.46: Harris Matrix of room 7
Fig. 4.47: View (to south) of collapse DSU32 in room 7
Fig. 4.48: View (to east) of collapse DSU80 in the doorway of room 7
Fig. 4.49: View (to southwest) of DSU82 in room 7
Fig. 4.50: Aerial view (to east) of room 8
Fig. 4.51: View (to north) of wall F13 in room 8
Fig. 4.52: View (to south) of wall F42 in room 8
Fig. 4.53: Plan showing the preserved extent of floors F50, F51, and F54 in rooms 6 and 8–9

Fig. 4.54: View (to southeast) of floors F50–51 in room 8 (room 6 is in the background)

Fig. 4.55: Remains of floor F54 in rooms 8–9 (view to southwest)

Fig. 4.56: Harris Matrix of room 8

Fig. 4.57: View (to south) of collapse DSU38 in room 8

Fig. 4.58: View (to west) of DSU38 in room 8

Fig. 4.59: Large fragment of mud plaster with palm reed impression (and white plaster on the opposite side), found in room 8

Fig. 4.60: View (to southeast) of room 9 in the south annex

Fig. 4.61: View (to north) of wall F13 in room 9

Fig. 4.62: View (to west) of wall F44 in room 9

Fig. 4.63: View (to south) of wall F40 in room 9

Fig. 4.64: View (to east) of wall F43 in room 9

Fig. 4.65: View (to east) of doorway between room 9 and room 7

Fig. 4.66: View (to northeast) of preserved patches of floors F54–55 in room 9

Fig. 4.67: View of the southeast corner of room 9, with post-abandonment installations

Fig. 4.68: View (to southeast) of stove F45 in room 9

Fig. 4.69: Plan of stove F45 in room 9

Fig. 4.70: Harris Matrix of room 9

Fig. 4.71: Aerial view (to northwest) of the church complex, showing the location of room 10

Fig. 4.72: View (to north) of wall F39 in room 10

Fig. 4.73: View (to south) of wall F40 in room 10

Fig. 4.74: View (to west) of floors F48–49 in room 10

Fig. 4.75: Harris Matrix of room 10

Fig. 4.76: View (to west) of collapse DSU46 in room 10

Fig. 4.77: View (to west) of collapse DSU57 in room 10

Fig. 4.78: Aerial view (to south) of rooms 5 and 11–13.

Fig. 4.79: View (to north) of room 11 and test trench 3 in room 13 (after the removal of wall F57)

Fig. 4.80: View (to northwest) of wall F37 in rooms 11 and 13

Fig. 4.81: View (to north) of wall F58 in rooms 11 and 13

Fig. 4.82: Sketch of mortar and plaster areas on the west surface of wall F58

Fig. 4.83: View (to south) of wall F40 in room 11

Fig. 4.84: View (to north) of wall F13 in room 13

Fig. 4.85: View of the north face of wall F57 (in room 13)

Fig. 4.86: Prospect of the north face of wall F57

Fig. 4.87: View of the south face of wall F57 in room 11

Fig. 4.88: View (from above) of the top of wall F57

Fig. 4.89: Harris Matrix of room 11

Fig. 4.90: View (to north) of DSU74 and DSU75 in room 11

Fig. 4.91: View (to north) of DSU76–78 in room 11

Fig. 4.92: View (to north) of DSU85 (= DSU98 below wall F57) in room 11

Fig. 4.93: View (to north) of DSU94

Fig. 4.94: Plan of rooms 11 and 13, showing the extent of DSU94 and DSU97–98

Fig. 4.95: View from above of room 13 after excavation

Fig. 4.96: Harris Matrix of room 13

Fig. 4.97: View (from above) of DSU96–97 in test trench 3 inside room 13

Fig. 4.98: Prospect of south face of wall F13 in room 13

Fig. 4.99: Detail of ledge at the bottom of wall F13 (south face) in room 13

Fig. 4.100: View (to north) of upper surface of wall F40 in room 12

Fig. 4.101: View of north half of wall F58 (east face) in room 12

Fig. 4.102: Sketches (not to scale) of wooden elements above ledge of wall F58 (a) and of cavity inside the same wall (b) in room 12

Fig. 4.103: View of north half of wall F76 (west face) in room 12

Fig. 4.104: Sketch of wooden elements against wall F76 (west face) in room 12

Fig. 4.105: View (to north) of wall F13 in room 12

Fig. 4.106: View (to south) of room 12 during excavations

Fig. 4.107: Harris Matrix of room 12

Chapter 5

Fig. 5.1: Aerial view (to southwest) of building 7 during the 2023 excavation season, with the three crypts (room 2–4) in the foreground

Fig. 5.2: Plan of rooms 2–4

Fig. 5.3: 3D model of underground crypts (rooms 2–4)

Fig. 5.4: Aerial view (to southwest) of room 2 (north crypt) before excavation

Fig. 5.5: Plan of room 2 before excavation, with features visible at the level of the vault

Fig. 5.6: Remains of vaulted ceiling above room 2 (view to north)

Fig. 5.7: View (to southwest) of platform F68 above the vault of room 2

Fig. 5.8: View (to north) of wall F15 inside room 2

Fig. 5.9: View (to west) of wall F1 inside room 2

Fig. 5.10: View (to east) of wall F59 inside room 2

List of Figures

Fig. 5.11: View (to south) of wall F64 inside room 2

Fig. 5.12: Sketch of doorway in wall F64, connecting rooms 2 and 3

Fig. 5.13: View from above (to south) of floor F75 and burials inside the north crypt (room 2)

Fig. 5.14: Aerial view (to north) of room 2, showing the extent of the earlier floor level (F108+F111)

Fig. 5.15: Plan of room 2 at the end of the 2023 season

Fig. 5.16: View of foundations of wall F15 within tomb 9 (room 2)

Fig. 5.17a–b: Harris Matrix of room 2

Fig. 5.18: View (to southwest) of DSU15 below F65 (west portion of room 2's vault)

Fig. 5.19: Plan of room 2 showing the extent of DSU99–101

Fig. 5.20: View (to southwest) of collapse DSU102

Fig. 5.21: View from above (to northeast) of collapse DSU103 and sand layer DSU101 in room 2

Fig. 5.22: Detail of DSU105 in the northeast corner of room 2

Fig. 5.23: View (to north) of cooking pot (inv. 30129) *in situ*

Fig. 5.24: View (to west) of tombs 6–8, at the end of the 2013 season

Fig. 5.25: Plan of tombs 6–9 in room 2 before excavation

Fig. 5.26: Hypothetical reconstruction of room 2 (view to southwest)

Fig. 5.27: View (to west) of tomb 6

Fig. 5.28: View (to north) of lower mud-brick covering (F79) inside tomb 6 (room 2)

Fig. 5.29: View of human remains (FN23) inside tomb 6 (room 2)

Fig. 5.30: View (to southwest) of tombs 7–8

Fig. 5.31: View (to west) of human remains (FN24) inside tomb 7 (room 2)

Fig. 5.32: View (to west) of human remains (FN27) inside tomb 8 (room 2)

Fig. 5.33: View (from above) of burial cut F81 of tomb 9 (room 2)

Fig. 5.34: View (to north) of coffin (inv. 17039) inside tomb 9

Fig. 5.35: View of the coffin being lifted out of the north crypt

Fig. 5.36: Coffin (inv. 17039) from tomb 9 after conservation

Fig. 5.37: Bronze object (inv. 17038) from tomb 9 after conservation

Fig. 5.38: Aerial view of human remains (FN26) inside tomb 9 (room 2)

Fig. 5.39: Aerial view (to west) of room 3 at the end of the 2023 season

Fig. 5.40: View (to south) of doorway opening from room 3 into room 4

Fig. 5.41: View (to northeast) of doorway opening from room 3 into room 2

Fig. 5.42: View (to south) of doorways leading from room 2 (in the foreground) into room 3 and room 4

Fig. 5.43: View (to north) of remains of vaulted roof of room 3

Fig. 5.44: Plan of room 3 at the beginning of excavations

Fig. 5.45: Prospects of walls of room 3

Fig. 5.46: Aerial view (to south) of tombs 10–16 in room 3 after excavation

Fig. 5.47: Plan of tombs 10–16 in room 3 after excavation

Fig. 5.48: Detail of foundations of room 3's north wall (F64) inside tomb 11

Fig. 5.49: Detail of foundations of room 3's east wall (F59) inside tomb 12

Fig. 5.50: Detail of foundations of room 3's south wall (F78) inside tomb 13

Fig. 5.51: Detail of foundations of room 3's west wall (F1) inside tomb 10

Fig. 5.52: Reconstructed section of room 3's stratigraphy (facing north)

Fig. 5.53a–b: Harris Matrix of room 3

Fig. 5.54: View (to north) of DSU110 and DSU112

Fig. 5.55: View (to south) of a cluster of mudbricks (DSU131) in the southwest corner of room 3

Fig. 5.56: East-west section (facing south) of tomb 12 in room 3

Fig. 5.57: Plan of tombs 10–15 before their excavation

Fig. 5.58: View (to north) of mud-brick superstructure F86 (partially missing) above tomb 10

Fig. 5.59: View (to west) of tomb 10

Fig. 5.60: View of southwest corner of burial pit F87, showing east-west wall F98

Fig. 5.61: Profile (looking south) of wall F98 (inside pit F87 of tomb 10)

Fig. 5.62: Aerial view (to west) of human remains (FN43) inside tomb 10 (room 3)

Fig. 5.63: View (from above) of human remains (FN49) inside tomb 11 (room 3)

Fig. 5.64: View (from above) of human remains (FN47) inside tomb 12 (room 3)

Fig. 5.65: View (to south) of superstructure F92 of tomb 13 (room 3)

Fig. 5.66: View (from above) of human remains (FN40) inside tomb 13 (room 3)

Fig. 5.67: View (to east) of burial cuts F97 of tomb 14 (in the background) and F99 of tomb 15 (in the foreground)

Fig. 5.68: View (from above) of superstructure F96 of tomb 14 (room 3)

Fig. 5.69: View (from above) of human remains (FN41) inside tomb 14 (room 3)

Fig. 5.70: View (from above) of human remains (FN42) inside tomb 15 (room 3)

Fig. 5.71: View (to west) of burial cut F106 of tomb 16 (room 3)

Fig. 5.72: East-west section (facing south) of tomb 16 in room 3

Fig. 5.73: View (to west) of human remains (FN47) inside tomb 16 (room 3)

Fig. 5.74: View (to south) of test trench 4

Fig. 5.75: Plan of test trench 4

Fig. 5.76: Harris Matrix of test trench 4

List of Figures

Fig. 5.77: View (to east) of collapsed wall with painted plaster (DSU172) in test trench 4

Fig. 5.78: Partial view (to northwest) of room 4, showing the doorway opening onto room 3 to the north and (in the background) the doorway leading into room 2

Fig. 5.79: Prospects of walls of room 4

Fig. 5.80: Plan of room 4 showing the features and deposits at the top of the crypt

Fig. 5.81: View of west wall F1 of room 4, showing remains of vault segment F105

Fig. 5.82: View of south wall F13 of room 4, showing the curvature of the original barrel-vaulted roof

Fig. 5.83: View (to southwest) of room 4's west wall, showing the shaft (F82) that once led from the church's ground floor into the underground crypts

Fig. 5.84: View (from above) of shaft F82

Fig. 5.85: View (from above, to southeast) of shaft F82

Fig. 5.86: Hypothetical reconstruction of room 16 (view to northwest), showing the trapdoor leading into the underground crypts

Fig. 5.87: View (to south) of DSU120 and (below) DSU134 with visible remains of wooden fragments

Fig. 5.88: View (from above, to west) of upper floor F85 in room 4

Fig. 5.89: Plan of room 4 showing lower floor F107

Fig. 5.90: View (from above, to south) of lower floor F107 in room 4, showing circular imprints in the southeast corner

Fig. 5.91a–b: Harris Matrix of room 4

Fig. 5.92: Half-complete basin (inv. 30538) with coin attached to it (inv. 17037), found within DSU118 in room 4

Fig. 5.93: Half-complete basin (inv. 30538) with coin attached to it (inv. 17037), from DSU118 in room 4

Fig. 5.94: View (to south) of vault collapse DSU120+DSU121 in room 4

Fig. 5.95: Plan of room 4 with wall collapse DSU126

Fig. 5.96: View (to west) of wall collapse DSU126 in room 4

Fig. 5.97: View (from above, to south) of room 4 at the end of the excavations

Fig. 5.98: Plan of room 4 at the end of the excavations

Fig. 5.99: Plan of the church with crypts at Tell el-Makhzan, near Pelusium

Fig. 5.100: Plan of the church at the "Eastern gate" of Antinoopolis, including the burials in the nave

Chapter 6

Fig. 6.1: Fragment of wall with painted decoration from the area near the apse (room 15)

Fig. 6.2: Large patch of wall plaster (FN82) from room 1, with traces of graffiti and inscriptions (line drawing superimposed)

Fig. 6.3: Dorothea Schulz working on fragments of collapsed painted ceiling in room 1

Fig. 6.4: Large fragments of collapsed ceilings in the church's east and north aisles, with imprints of palm ribs still visible

Fig. 6.5: Fragment of purple, yellow, and dark yellow band, with traces of a wavy vegetal motif

Fig. 6.6: Reconstruction of the purple, yellow, and dark yellow band motif

Fig. 6.7: Fragment of the painted ceiling, with triangle-, lozenge-, and square-pattern

Fig. 6.8: Reconstruction of triangle-, lozenge-, and square-pattern

Fig. 6.9: Fragment of pentagon- and hexagon-pattern

Fig. 6.10: Hypothetical reconstruction of pentagon- and hexagon-pattern

Fig. 6.11: Fragment of painted ceiling with octagons

Fig. 6.12: Fragment of painted ceiling with eight-lozenge star

Fig. 6.13: Reconstruction of pattern with octagons, squares, and eight-lozenge stars

Fig. 6.14: Hypothetical reconstruction of the interior of the church at Amheida at night

Fig. 6.15: Painted geometric decoration from Mausoleum 25 at El-Bagawat

Chapter 7

Fig. 7.1: View (to north) of the stepped podium and of the wall sealing the central doorway inside the church of ʿAin el-Gedida

Fig. 7.2: Direction (conjectural) of the staircase in rooms 5, 11, and 13

Fig. 7.3: *O.Trim.* 2.532, found in DSU85 (foundation fill of room 11)

Fig. 7.4: View (to east) of building 7

Fig. 7.5: Hypothetical isometric view of the church at Amheida

Fig. 7.6: N–S hypothetical section of the church at Amheida

Fig. 7.7: E–W hypothetical section of the church at Amheida

Chapter 8

Fig. 8.1: Plan of the south area of Amheida, showing the church (B7) and (in the red circle) visible remains of what may be another church at the southwest edge of the site

Foreword

The combination of a dry environment with an absence of medieval and modern settlement on top of many ancient sites has made the exploration of the oases of Egypt's Western Desert extraordinarily fruitful over the last several decades. Among the finds have been many early churches, largely of the fourth century and thus of the half-century after Constantine's victory over Licinius that brought Christianity into clear public view as a visible institution. Many of these sites still await full publication, and some have not yet been excavated. The full publication of one such early church is therefore of great interest. The church at ancient Trimithis published in this volume is important even beyond that inherent value, however, because it was not only excavated stratigraphically, but also extensively below floor level, revealing a considerable number of burials. These, as so often, raise more questions than they settle, and they particularly lead one to ask whether deeper excavations at other oasis churches would also produce burials. We as yet have no way of distinguishing churches that followed the doctrinal tenets and organizational rules of the Alexandrian episcopate from those one might identify as Meletian or Arian, let alone structures that might have belonged to Manichaean communities, which we know to have existed in the Dakhla Oasis. The Trimithis church is therefore still just a step toward understanding fourth-century Christianity in the oases, but it is an important step.

Roger S. Bagnall

Preface

This volume is an archaeological, historical, and art historical study of a remarkable basilica-church excavated between 2012 and 2013, and in 2023, at Amheida (ancient Trimithis) in Dakhla Oasis (Egypt's Western Desert). The project, sponsored by New York University, was directed by Roger Bagnall (David M. Ratzan since 2023), with Paola Davoli as the archaeological field director at Amheida in 2012–2013 and Nicola Aravecchia as the field director of the church's excavations (and field director at Amheida since 2023).[1] Some aspects of the work included in the present report were published in 2015, 2016, and 2020.[2]

The primary goal of this report is to offer a thorough presentation and discussion of the archaeological evidence from the three excavation seasons at the Amheida. My organization of the material is intended to make it accessible to both scholars and a broader interested audience, with chapters more densely focused on the archaeological data paired with others that provide a contextualization of the evidence. My hope is that such an approach will allow the reader not only to learn about our work at Amheida, but also to appreciate the significance of the discovery of the church for the study of the Christianization of Egypt's Western Desert.

The church discovered at Amheida dates to the fourth century CE and is therefore one of the earliest churches in Egypt; it has, moreover, the oldest set of Christian funerary crypts ever found in the country. It thus offers a wealth of new data on early Christianity in Egypt, the origins of Christian art and architecture, and early Christian burial customs.

---

1. The other members of the 2012–2013 and 2023 missions that were involved in the excavations at the church were: Stefania Alfarano (2023), Roberta Casagrande-Kim (2023), and Dorota Dzierzbicka (2012–2013), senior archaeologists; Yasser Farouq (2023), Nancy Highcock (2012–2013), and Ahmed Abdalla Said (2023), archaeologists; Sa'ad Bakhit (2023), archaeologist and illustrator; Kechu Huang (2023) and Harper Tooch (2023), assistant archaeologists; David M. Ratzan (2012–2013 and 2023), numismatist; Vicente Barba Colmenero (2023), Clementina Caputo (2012–2013 and 2023), Yael Chevalier (2013), Julie Marchand (2012–2013), and Irene Soto Marín (2012–2013), ceramicists; Paola Vertuani (2023), illustrator; Marina M. S. Nuovo (2012–2013 and 2023) and Océane Henri (2012–2013), registrars; Daniela Villa (2023), registrar and archaeologist; Roger S. Bagnall (2012–2013 and 2023), papyrologist; Tosha Dupras (2013), Peter G. Sheldrick (2023), and Lana Williams (2013), bioarchaeologists; Leonardo Davighi (2023) and Fabrizio Pavia (2012–2013), topographers; Bruno Bazzani (2012–2013 and 2023), database management, computer operations, and photographer; Bahaa Gomaa (2012), Mahmoud Samir Hussein (2023), and Mohamed Ahmed Sayed Mustafa (2012–2013), conservators; Dorothea Schulz (2012), conservator of painted fragments; Ashraf Barakat (2012–2013 and 2023), assistant to the director; Gaber Murad (2012–2013 and 2023), house manager; Christina Chopra, Marek Dospěl, Matthew Firpo, and Mary Van Dempsey, student assistants in 2012. The inspectors of the Ministry of State for Antiquities were Nasr Abd-el Razek Mohamed Senussi in 2012, Sayyida Hamdy Mohamed in 2013, and El-Zahraa Kamal, Azzaz Nasr, and Abdallah Nasr Eldeen in 2023.

2. See Aravecchia 2015a; Aravecchia et al. 2015; Ast and Bagnall 2016; Aravecchia 2020b.

The present volume is structured into eight chapters. Chapter 1 is an introduction to the Dakhla Oasis and situates Amheida as an important *polis* (city) of rural Egypt in the fourth and fifth centuries. The chapter includes a brief history of the research project and a section on the methodology of excavation and documentation that was adopted at Amheida.

Chapter 2 provides an overview of the emergence of Christianity as a flourishing religion in late antique Dakhla. It then analyzes the available sources attesting to the existence of a thriving Christian community at Amheida in the fourth century.

Chapters 3 and 4 present and discuss the archaeological data collected during the survey and two seasons of excavations at the church of Amheida. These chapters also highlight the contribution that the study of the evidence makes to a fuller understanding of the building's construction and use.

Chapter 5 examines the underground funerary crypts excavated below the sanctuary, within the context of the church's overall layout and construction history. It also raises questions connected to the overall extent of the crypts and their spatial relationship to the church above and the nearby cemetery.

Chapter 6 provides an art historical discussion of the fragments of polychrome geometric decoration from the collapsed ceiling of the church. It highlights the popularity and longevity of this decorative style in Egypt, from the Ptolemaic period to late antiquity, as well as in the artistic tradition of the wider Mediterranean region.

Chapter 7 touches upon issues of chronology and the development of the church complex. It also considers the church within the topographical context of the surrounding built environment.

Chapter 8 assesses the architectural and historical significance of the discovery of the church at Amheida, including its funerary crypts. It also offers considerations for future investigations within the church and the area surrounding the complex.

A second volume will follow, written by specialists of the Amheida research team on the different types of objects that were retrieved during the excavation of the church's complex. These include: ceramics and terracotta figurines (Clementina Caputo); coins and inscriptions (David M. Ratzan);[3] human remains (Tosha L. Dupras, Lana Williams, and Peter G. Sheldrick); and small finds (Marina M. S. Nuovo, Stefania Alfarano, Roberta Casagrande-Kim, Francesca Cozza, and Cesare Iezzi).[4]

I would like to thank first and foremost Roger S. Bagnall, who invited me to join the Amheida team in 2005 and has played since then an essential role in my professional development: this volume is dedicated to him. I am very grateful to Paola Davoli, from whose expertise, skills, and friendship I have greatly benefited since I began working in Egypt. I am also obliged to all members of the Amheida church team for their tireless efforts and invaluable

---

3. The ostraka that were found in the church complex were published in the third volume of the *Amheida* series: Ast and Bagnall 2016.

4. I am grateful to several of these colleagues for offering preliminary data, which were included in the present volume, in particular David M. Ratzan (coins), Clementina Caputo and Irene Soto-Marín (ceramics), Marina M. S. Nuovo (other categories of small finds), and Peter G. Sheldrick (human remains).

contribution to this project, in particular Dorota Dzierzbicka, Stefania Alfarano, and Roberta Casagrande-Kim.

The writing of this book was made possible in large part by a Dumbarton Oaks fellowship in the Spring of 2021. Several friends and colleagues contributed by reading early versions of the manuscript and by offering precious feedback, especially David Ratzan, who spent countless hours helping me with this project. The volume also benefited from the skills and expertise of Kristen DeMondo and Cecilia Fosen, who retraced most plans and drawings ahead of publication, Caleb Ullendorff, who created hypothetical views and sections of the church, and Katerina Boukala, who designed the book. Particular thanks go to Bruno Bazzani, who helped with photography and indexing, and to Stefania Alfarano, the current Assistant Field Director, who edited and elaborated many of the figures in this volume for final publication with the eye of an experienced archaeologist.

I would like to acknowledge all my colleagues at Washington University in St. Louis, in particular Tim Moore and Cathy Keane (Classics) and Liz Childs and Bill Wallace (Art History and Archaeology), for their strong support of my research project.

Finally, I owe a tremendous depth of gratitude to my family and friends, who always supported my work and encouraged me throughout the ups and downs of life. And above all, I thank my mother, who first instilled in me an abiding love and passion for the ancient world.

Chapter 1

Introduction

1.1. Overview of the Amheida Church Project

The conversion of the Roman empire to Christianity brought changes that still affect us today. Understanding the origins of this phenomenon, therefore, has a relevance that reaches beyond the study of late antiquity. While written sources provide a large amount of information on the origins of Christianity, the archaeological evidence also plays an indispensable role. Some of the most precious evidence comes from Egypt's Western Desert, in particular the oases of Dakhla and Kharga. The recent discovery of a late antique church at Amheida has added a significant new source of information to what was known about the flourishing of Christianity in the region during the fourth century.

In studying the archaeological evidence from the church, three questions were key to our understanding of early Christianity, both in Egypt and in the wider Mediterranean world: What was the chronological, cultural, and socio-economic context in which Christianity flourished at Amheida in the early fourth century? How were distinctive features of Christian art and architecture disseminated to the most remote regions of the late Roman empire, such as Dakhla? Finally, how did the appearance of Christianity transform the built landscape of the Mediterranean world?

From its inception, the Amheida church project has approached these broad inquiries through a set of more precise research questions. Some of these concern relative and absolute chronology and touch upon issues, such as the coexistence of polytheism and Christianity at Amheida (and in Dakhla Oasis) during the fourth century, as well as the seeming abandonment of the city by the early fifth century. The goal in tackling these questions was to gain a deeper understanding of fourth-century Egyptian Christianity, an understanding that we could hardly get in other ways.

Other questions address the architecture of the site. Which pre-existing traditions, both architectural and artistic, shaped the development of the earliest-known churches in Egypt? How did they reach even the most remote oases of the Western Desert? How do they compare with models of Christian places of cult in other regions of the Mediterranean? This investigation has enriched our knowledge of the networks through which new architectural forms and artistic idioms were disseminated in late antiquity. It has shed light on a "globalized" world in which even geographically remote regions, like the oases of Egypt's Western Desert, were quickly exposed to new beliefs, ideas, and trends.

Furthermore, the site of Amheida offers a privileged vantage point from which to consider issues concerning the "Christianization" of Egypt's physical landscape in late antiquity. This study investigates the church in the context of the site's topographical layout. It explores how the construction of the church took place within an already densely built environment and how the city underwent significant alterations. The aim was to investigate the earliest stages of a phenomenon that is widely attested in Egypt (both in the larger centers of the Nile Valley and in the more distant oases of the Western Desert) and throughout the Mediterranean world in late antiquity.

From its very conception, the Amheida church project was designed to be interdisciplinary in nature, in order to benefit from the interaction and cooperation of experts in several disciplines, including ceramology, numismatics, and physical anthropology. Of particular importance in the project's final stages were methods derived from the fields of digital humanities, history, cultural anthropology, and art history. The author of this volume (as well as the authors of the forthcoming companion volume about the small finds) had access to an online archaeological database that the Amheida team members have compiled since the beginning of the excavations. The data were studied and compared with the evidence gathered at other early Christian churches excavated in Dakhla, as well as in further regions.

The team also viewed the Amheida church through a historical and anthropological lens, considering especially its function as a funerary complex. There are several important questions that we considered, such as: What can be said about the identity of the individuals buried in the church and their place in the local social hierarchy? Why were they not interred in the necropolis located at the southern end of the city? Furthermore, is it possible to establish any correlation between the social position of the deceased and the proximity of their burial to the sanctuary of the church? Our examination of much of the archaeological evidence was also informed by an art historical perspective, as we considered stylistic approaches and idioms recognizable in the church's architectural features, as well as the evidence of painted geometric decoration from the collapsed ceiling.

In sum, our hope is that this collaborative and multidisciplinary study can offer a holistic picture of the emergence of Christianity at a fourth-century *polis* of Egypt's Western Desert.

1.2. The Dakhla Oasis

Dakhla lies in the Western Desert of Egypt, roughly 800 km southwest of Cairo and about 300 km west of Luxor (fig. 1.1). It is one of the five major oases that dot the desertic region to the west of the Nile Valley, comprising Siwa, Bahariya, Farafra, Dakhla, and Kharga.[1]

Dakhla stretches from northwest to southeast, to the south of an escarpment, 300–400 m high, that separates the oasis depression from the northern Libyan plateau.[2] The oasis measures about 80 km from east to west and ca. 30 km from north to south and extends over an area of ca. 410 km. Today, the area encompassed by the oasis does not consist entirely of irrigated land, but rather of several small oases that are separated from each other by desert sand. The west edge of Dakhla is marked by the dunes of the Great Sand Sea, while to the south the oasis ends in a desert expanse that reaches Sudan. Desert land also defines the east border of Dakhla, separating it from Kharga Oasis, which lies about 190 km further east. The depression of the oasis is at a height ranging between 92 and 140 m above sea level; it is generally flat, with only small outcroppings, as well as spring mounds, dotting the landscape. Apart from the northern escarpment, the only mountain of the oasis is Gebel Edmondstone, situated toward its northwest end.[3]

Dakhla lies in the east half of the Libyan Desert, which is one of the driest regions on earth; thus, its natural environment is particularly harsh, with average temperatures that soar above 40°C during summer.[4] Particularly in winter months, the temperature drops drastically at night. Rains are a rare sight and often of no particular intensity when they occur. Northern winds are common and very fierce, often causing sandstorms that cloud the sky and force any human activity to a halt, leaving sand dunes behind.[5] The latter pose a significant threat to life in Dakhla, as they can move over time and obliterate houses as well as cultivated fields.[6]

In antiquity, an elaborate network of roads and caravan routes linked Dakhla with Asyut on the west bank of the Nile, the neighboring oases of Farafra (via the escarpment) and Kharga (via the desert or the escarpment), as well as remote sites in the southwest of Egypt, including Gilf Kebir and Gebel Uweinat (fig. 1.2).[7] Numerous passes were identified on the northern escarpment, allowing people (and animals) to climb from the bed of the oasis up

---

1. The Fayyum is often considered an oasis as well, but since it is connected to the Nile via the Bahr Yussef, it should rather be considered a pseudo-oasis. The list does not include Wadi el-Natrun, a depression located west of the Nile Delta.

2. Geological phenomena that occurred since the Early Cretaceous shaped the region in which Dakhla lies. Large parts of the oasis seem to have been once covered by water, as indicated by evidence gathered during surveys carried out in Dakhla and dated from the Late Cretaceous to the Quaternary Eras. Subsequently, major environmental changes brought about the desertification of the region, leading to the disappearance of the existing prehistoric fauna and flora, as well as of the first human settlements in Dakhla: Kleindienst et al. 1999.

3. See Kleindienst et al. 1999 for data on the geology and geomorphology, as well as the palaeobotany and palaeozoology, of Dakhla Oasis. See also Mills 1999, 171 and Kimura 2021.

4. Kleindienst et al. 1999, 3; Giddy 1987, 3.

5. This happens particularly during the months from March to June: see Kleindienst et al. 1999, 3.

6. Kaper 2012, 718.

7. Vivian 2008, 180–81; Giddy 1987, 10–11; Paprocki 2019, 219–23, 256–61, 263; Förster 2007. Cf. also Ikram 2019 on the routes between Dakhla and Kharga.

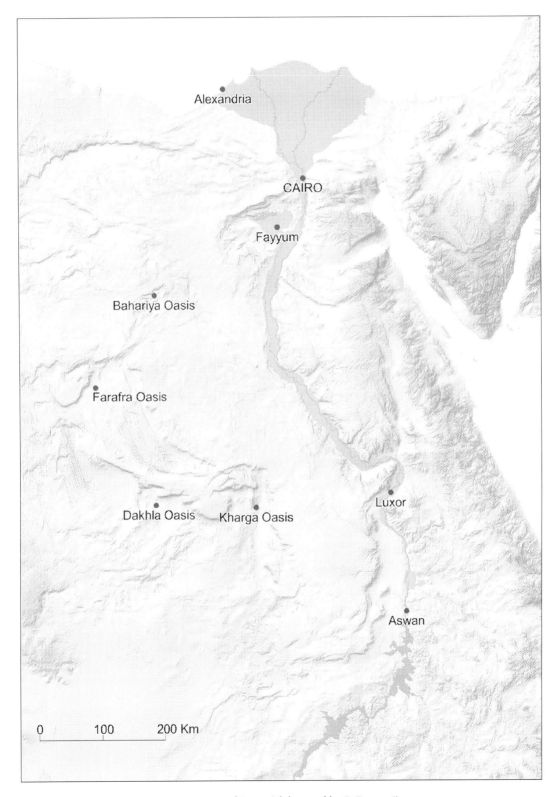

Fig. 1.1: Map of Egypt (elaborated by B. Bazzani).

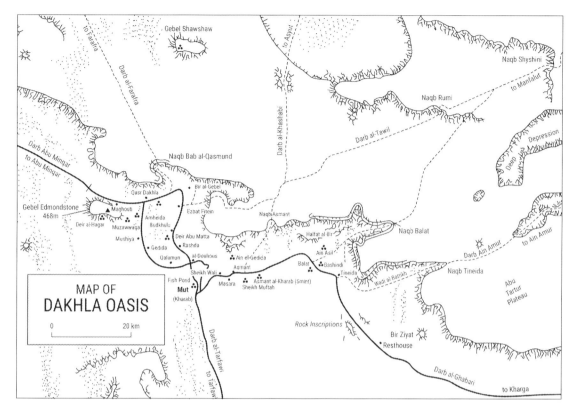

Fig. 1.2: Map of Dakhla's roads and caravan routes (after Vivian 2008, 174; tracing by K. DeMondo).

onto the Libyan plateau and travel northwest to Farafra, northeast to the Nile Valley, and east to Kharga.[8]

A wealth of water, and easy access to it, has allowed life to flourish in Dakhla since antiquity.[9] Thanks to the low elevation of the depression in which the oasis lies, humans could utilize the water stored in aquifers under the oasis's sandstone bed.[10] Dakhla is dotted with several springs of water that is rich in sulfur and iron and reaches the surface thanks to artesian pressure. Hundreds of wells, many of which were in use in the Roman period, are also spread throughout the land and were a source of significant wealth in the oasis;[11]

---

8. Vivian 2008, 180.
9. Bagnall and Tallet 2019, 6; Ast 2019, 105; Bravard 2019.
10. See Schild and Wendorf 1977, 10 for more details about the type of sandstone attested in Dakhla. On ground water in the oasis, and its possible origin, see Giddy 1987, 29–31. Cf. Ball 1927a–b, Hellström 1949, and Murray 1952 on phreatic layers underneath Egypt's Western Desert.
11. Mills 1999, 177; Bagnall 2015; Bravard 2019.

The cultivated fields are irrigated with water that is extracted from the wells, nowadays by means of mechanical pumps.[12]

The geographical location of the oasis, at a considerable distance from the inhabited centers of the Nile Valley, inevitably entailed a high degree of isolation from the rest of Egypt. Nevertheless, archaeological and documentary evidence testifies to the fact that Dakhla established and maintained close ties with the inhabitants of the Valley. Dakhla and its neighboring oases were areas of strategic importance already in the Pharaonic period, due to their location on the way to Nubia. They were also regions of great economic significance.[13] Dakhla continued to be inhabited during the Ptolemaic period; until recent years, evidence of Ptolemaic phases of occupation in the oasis was relatively scarce, especially in comparison with that from the Roman period.[14] However, recent fieldwork at the site of Mut el-Kharab, in the center of Dakhla, and broad ceramic surveys in the region have begun to redress this imbalance.[15]

Following the Roman conquest of Egypt in 30 BCE, the oasis witnessed agricultural expansion on a scale not experienced before, with a focus on the production of wine, olives, and grapes.[16] The available documentary, as well as archaeological, evidence also points to a dramatic increase in population size for Dakhla following the Roman conquest of Egypt.[17] The new conquerors were attracted to the oases of Dakhla and Kharga by their agricultural potential, as well as their strategic liminal location at the southern border of the Roman empire and along important caravan routes. These geo-political, as well as economic, factors may have contributed to the decision by the Romans to establish, in Dakhla and especially in Kharga, several forts and military outposts.[18]

Archaeological and documentary evidence indicate that Dakhla was densely inhabited in the Byzantine period as well (ca. 300–700 CE).[19] Administratively, Dakhla and Kharga in this

---

12. See Mills 1999, 173 on the irrigation methods employed in Dakhla in ancient and modern times. In recent years, evidence for ancient installations that may be identified as *qanats* (Arabic plural *qanawat*) were found in Dakhla by a mission of the Egyptian Ministry of State for Antiquities: see Youssef 2012. The *qanat* was an ancient irrigation system consisting of a tunnel that was gently sloping and brought water from its underground source at a higher elevation to lower ground. The tunnel was accessible by means of vertical shafts placed at regular intervals, allowing construction and maintenance of the aqueduct. On ancient *qanats* see, among others, English 1968 and Briant 2001. A wealth of evidence for *qanats*, dated to the Persian period and still in use in Roman times, was found and investigated in Kharga Oasis: see Grimal 1995, 572–74; Wuttmann 2001; Rossi and Ikram 2018, 510–21. The evidence of *qanats* in Dakhla still awaits excavation and publication.

13. Giddy 1987, 51–52. Numerous migrants and settlers from the Nile Valley possibly moved to Dakhla around 2300 BCE, as part of a process of agricultural exploitation of its cultivable lands: Mills 1999, 174.

14. For information on the oases of Egypt's Western Desert in the Graeco-Roman period, see Wagner 1987.

15. See Gill 2012 and Gill 2016.

16. Kaper and Wendrich 1998, 2. The Romans may have also been interested in the extraction of alum, which existed in Dakhla: see Giddy 1987, 5. The agricultural exploitation of the land in the region received a considerable impetus from the invention, in the Ptolemaic period, of the waterwheel (*saqiya* in Arabic): cf. Hairy 2009, 558–60. This device made it possible to extract water up to higher elevations, thus allowing for less reliance on more complex systems like *qanats*: Kaper 2012, 718.

17. Bagnall and Rathbone 2004, 249; 262; Kaper 2012, 718.

18. Boozer 2007, 65–66. See also Reddé 1999; Rossi 2012; Rossi and Ikram 2018, 429–51 on military outposts in Kharga. On the Roman *castrum* in El-Qasr in northwest Dakhla, to be identified as the base of a Roman military unit stationed at Trimithis/Amheida, see Kucera 2012. For the available documentary evidence on the Roman garrison of Trimithis, see Ast and Bagnall 2015.

19. Churcher and Mills 1999, 263–64; Kaper 2012, 718.

period were known as the "Great Oasis," with its capital at Hibis (in Kharga).[20] Documentary evidence from the beginning of the fourth century CE attests that, at that time, the unit was split into two nomes (administrative districts), known as the Mothite nome (Dakhla, with Mut as its capital) and the Hibite nome (Kharga, with its capital at Hibis).[21] Around the end of the fourth and the early fifth century, however, one detects the signs of economic decline, as well as partial or full abandonment of numerous settlements including Amheida and Kellis.[22] The reasons for such a population decline in late antique Dakhla (as well as Kharga) are still being debated by scholars, but decreased availability of water, combined with the encroaching of sand dunes on the built and natural landscape, are likely to have been a key—or at least contributing—factor.[23]

Dakhla continued to be populated in the Arab period, without ever experiencing full abandonment of all its sites. However, European knowledge of the oasis was lost until it was "re-discovered" at the beginning of the nineteenth century, when travelers reached Dakhla and began to disseminate information about its people, customs, and extant archaeological remains.[24]

The degree of preservation of ancient sites, monuments, and artifacts in Dakhla is often excellent, and generally higher than that of the archaeological evidence from the Delta or the Nile Valley;[25] among the possible reasons are the geographical isolation and its natural environment of the oasis, as well as a dry climate that favors the preservation of organic remains (especially in comparison with the Nile Delta).[26] Nevertheless, Dakhla's archaeological heritage did not raise noteworthy scholarly interest until the middle of the twentieth century, with the work of the Egyptian archaeologist Ahmed Fakhry.[27] In 1977, the Institut Français d'Archéologie Orientale (IFAO) began excavations in Dakhla, establishing an enduring presence in the oasis that continues today. The following year, the Dakhleh Oasis Project (DOP), an international and multidisciplinary research project, was founded and is still active today.[28]

---

20. Bagnall and Tallet 2019, esp. 83–100. In Egyptian, Dakhla and Kharga were known as *Knmt*, or Southern Oasis: see Kaper 2012, 718.

21. Kaper 2012, 718–19. The modern Arabic toponyms of Kharga and Dakhla match exactly the Greek names, i.e., ἐξωτέρω ("exterior") and ἐσωτέρω ("interior"), which were used for the two oases respectively in the fifth century CE: Wagner 1987, 131.

22. Bagnall et al. 2015, 7. On Amheida, see Davoli 2015d and Bravard 2019, 27. On Kellis, see Hope 2001 and, most recently, Hope and Bowen 2022a.

23. Kaper 2012, 718; Bravard et al. 2016. Growing insecurity may also have been an important factor: see Hope and Bowen 2022a, 396–97. See also Bagnall and Caputo 2021.

24. Starkey 2001; Kleindienst et al. 1999, 7–8; Boozer 2013, with relevant bibliography.

25. Kaper 2012, 718.

26. As pointed out by O. E. Kaper (2012, 718), settlement patterns in the oases of the Western Desert were different than in the Nile Valley (or the Delta); for example, decreased availability of water in the oases often led to the complete abandonment of sites. Very often, these were not built over but were buried below a thick coat of sand, which hid and protected their remains for centuries.

27. Fakhry 1982; see also Mills 1985.

28. The DOP was established with the goal to investigate the environment of the oasis, its longer-term diachronic changes, and the effect of the latter on the development of life and human settlement in the region: Thurston 2003, 17–22.

DOP teams carry out research that spans chronologically from prehistory to the modern era; the various missions work independently but adopt a collaborative approach, aiming at the exchange of data and knowledge among the different disciplines.[29]

1.3. History of the Amheida Project

The current research project at Amheida began in 2001, under the direction of R. S. Bagnall of Columbia University (New York University since 2008) and the sponsorship of Columbia University (New York University since 2008). P. Davoli of the Università del Salento (Italy) has been the archaeological field director since 2004, with the author of this volume being the deputy field director (field director since 2022).[30]

The Columbia/NYU project was the first attempt at a systematic survey and excavation of the site of Amheida. It was (and is still) guided by a set of research questions that include economic growth and decline in Roman Dakhla, urbanism in Graeco-Roman Egypt, and oasite cultural history through an examination of the archaeological and documentary evidence.[31] The fact that a long historical period, ranging from the Old Kingdom to late antiquity, is archaeologically attested at Amheida makes the site an ideal case study to investigate these questions in a diachronic, long-term perspective.

The site of Amheida, definitively identified as ancient Trimithis, was known to scholars well before the Columbia team first arrived in Dakhla.[32] It had been visited by several explorers since the early nineteenth century; among them were A. Edmondstone, B. Drovetti, who noticed one of the Roman mud-brick pyramids; J. G. Wilkinson, who referred to the site with the modern name of Lémhada; and G. Rohlfs together with his scientific team.[33] In 1908, H. E. Winlock journeyed to Dakhla Oasis and visited Amheida, which he mentioned in his diary published in 1936.[34] A. Fakhry, who was the first archaeologist to conduct systematic investigation of sites in Dakhla in the late 1960s and early 1970s, went to Amheida in 1963.[35] In 1979, the Dakhleh Oasis Project (DOP) included the site in its comprehensive survey of

---

29. See the DOP website: http://dakhlehoasisproject.com.

30. For a full list of all team members since the 2004 season, see https://isaw.nyu.edu/research/amheida/directory/directory-2004. In 2013, the University of Reading began investigations in Area 1 at the northeast end of the site, under the direction of A. L. Boozer. This affiliated project is now sponsored by the City University of New York.

31. As outlined by Bagnall and Kaper (2015, 10).

32. There was still uncertainty, until the late 1980s, with respect to the identification of the site, as remarked in Bagnall and Kaper 2015, 1. Excavations at Ismant el-Kharab provided a conclusive identification of this site with the Greek toponym of Kellis, thus settling the debate on its possible identification with the modern site of Amheida: cf., for example, Wagner 1987, 190–92.

33. This summary was first put together by O. E. Kaper: see Bagnall and Kaper 2015, 89. Cf. also Edmondstone 1822, 49; Drovetti 1821, 103; Wilkinson 1843, II 363; Rohlfs 1875, 129.

34. Winlock 1936, 25, n. 19.

35. Osing 1982, 38.

the oasis and carried out test excavations.[36] It was during these investigations that the domed reception room of a fourth-century house, and its painted decoration, were discovered and partially exposed, in addition to pottery kilns at the northeast edge of the site (Area 1) and some tombs in the southern necropolis.[37]

The archaeological site was divided into eleven areas, four of which were archaeologically investigated from 2004 to 2015.[38] In addition to area excavations, a series of surveys were carried out.[39] In 2001–2002, a team from the Museum of London conducted a topographical survey of the site, which was continued, from 2005 onwards, by two Italian teams.[40] A geophysical survey was led in selected areas of Amheida by T. N. Smekalova and S. Smekalov, of the Physical Institute of Saint Petersburg State University, in 2005–2006.[41] Two ceramological surveys were conducted in 2013 and 2014.[42] In 2015, a small team headed by S. McFadden carried out a broad survey of painted plaster that was visible above ground throughout the site.[43] Additionally, a group of specialists led a geoarchaeological survey at Amheida during the 2011 and 2013 seasons.[44]

1.4. Topography of the Site and Main Excavated Features

The site of Amheida lies in the western half of Dakhla Oasis, a few kilometers to the southwest of the medieval Islamic village of El-Qasr (fig. 1.3). Amheida was a large settlement and attested as a *polis* (or city) in fourth-century documents found in Dakhla.[45] Surface survey showed pottery from all periods from the Old Kingdom (2686–2181 BCE) to the late Roman period,

---

36. Two numbers were assigned by the DOP to Amheida, i.e., 33/390-L9-1 for the site and 33/390-K9-4 for the necropolis at the south end of it: cf. Mills 1980, 269–72. The results of the DOP survey, carried out from 1977 to 1987, were published in Churcher and Mills 1999.

37. On the kilns, see Hope 1980, 307–11; Hope 1993, 123–27.

38. Davoli 2019, 46–80; Caputo 2020, fig. 2. For a list of yearly reports, see https://isaw.nyu.edu/research/amheida/reports. After 2015, fieldwork was temporarily halted at Amheida, as well as in the rest of the Western Desert. A study season was carried out on previously excavated finds in March 2022 and excavations at the site resumed in January 2023.

39. Davoli 2019, 48–51.

40. From firms Akra Iapygia (Lecce) in 2005–2006 and Ar/S Archeosistemi (Reggio Emilia), from 2007 until 2013. L. Davighi has been updating the site plan since 2015. For the yearly reports, see https://isaw.nyu.edu/research/amheida/reports.

41. Cf. https://isaw.nyu.edu/research/amheida/inc/pdf/geophysical_survey_2005-pdf and https://isaw.nyu.edu/research/amheida/inc/pdf/geophysical_survey_2006-pdf.

42. The 2013 team consisted of P. Ballet, J. Marchand, and C. Caputo. In 2014, the survey was carried out by P. Ballet and I. Soto Marín. For a report of the 2013 survey, see Caputo 2014, 163–77.

43. Other members of the team were D. Dzierzbicka, B. Norton, E. Ricchi, and A. Sucato. For a summary, see the 2015 excavation report at: https://isaw.nyu.edu/research/amheida/inc/pdf/report2015-pdf.

44. Bravard et al. 2016, 305–24; see also Davoli 2019, 48–53.

45. *P.Kell.* I G. 49.1–2; see Worp 1995; Bagnall and Tallet 2019, 101; Bagnall and Ruffini 2004. Cf. also Wagner 1987, 190–92, who emphasizes the importance of Amheida/Trimithis in comparison with other centers of the Great Oasis; however, the settlement is thought by Wagner to have always maintained the status of a village.

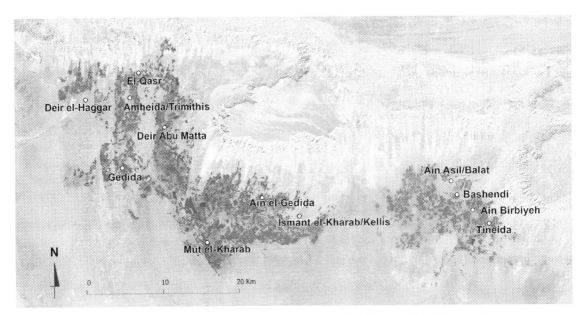

Fig. 1.3: Map of Dakhla Oasis (source: Google Earth; elaborated by B. Bazzani).

but it is yet unknown if the settlement was continuously inhabited or how big it was during each occupation phase.[46] Following its abandonment, which occurred between the end of the fourth and the early fifth century, the site was never reoccupied.[47] Luckily, looting has been limited to only a few areas; thus, most of the settlement has escaped significant damage, which is not, unfortunately, something that can be said for many other sites in the region.

Today, the archaeological remains spread over an area measuring about 2.5 km from north to south and 1.5 km from east to west. (fig. 1.4). Notwithstanding the harsh natural environment, the existence, as well as the large size, of the settlement depended on a secure and abundant supply of water, which is attested by numerous springs and wells that still dot the archaeological area.[48] The ancient city was likely much bigger than the area occupied by the archaeological remains, as attested by the constant reappearing of previously hidden features due to wind activity.[49] The Roman period settlement, which represents by and large the visible face of the site nowadays, was oriented north-south and was open, lacking any evidence for defensive walls.[50] The irregular ground was characterized by the presence of soft and cemented dunes and mounds of clay. At the center was a large hill, on top of which the main temple once

---

46. Davoli 2015b, 64; Davoli 2019, 52. Sand dunes accumulating in the proximity of the site, particularly along its western edge, as well as wind erosion, make it particularly challenging to develop a clearer picture of the original extent of the ancient settlement.

47. On the possible reasons for the abandonment of oasis sites such as Amheida, see n. 23 above.

48. Davoli 2019, 52.

49. Davoli 2015d, 21.

50. The third-century city, whose existence is archaeologically attested, is less well-known than its fourth-century phase: cf. Davoli 2015b, 65.

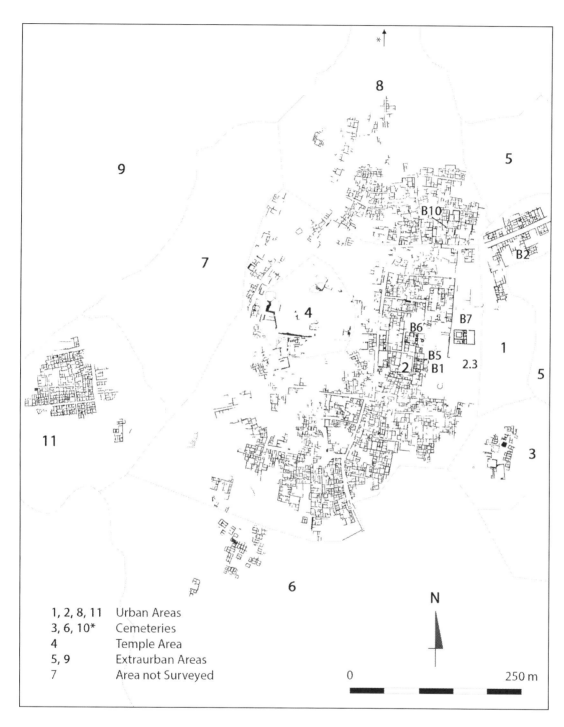

Fig. 1.4: Site plan of Amheida (2023).

Fig. 1.5: Remains of the *temenos* on the temple's hill (Area 4).

stood (fig. 1.5);[51] this hill was surrounded by smaller mounds separated by lower flat areas in between.[52] The plan of the city shows, in some areas, an attempt to follow an orthogonal orientation. However, the development of the site also followed, in many instances, the natural shape of the ground, resulting in a less than regular grid.[53] A dense network of streets and alleys, at times very narrow, creates the impression of an irregular spatial arrangement.[54] A main street runs from north to south, but it consists of two segments not perfectly in line with each other and can hardly be interpreted as a monumental thoroughfare.[55]

51. Davoli and Kaper 2006; Davoli and Kaper 2015. On the evidence for the earliest occupation phases on the temple hill, see Davoli 2015c. The temple area was enclosed by a wall of irregular perimeter, of which one segment, about 5 m in height, is still extant: see Davoli 2015b, 64. Although several blocks were unearthed, no longer *in situ*, in the temple area, many more were removed following the abandonment of the site and reused in buildings dated to the Ottoman period (1250–1571) in the nearby village of El-Qasr: see Davoli and Kaper 2015, 105. The existence, on the hill, of an animal necropolis, likely dating to the Late Period, is discussed in Davoli 2015e.

52. Davoli 2015d, 18.

53. Davoli 2011, 83–84.

54. See Davoli 2019, 54–61; 74–76 for a detailed presentation and analysis of the street network investigated at Amheida/Trimithis. On the labyrinthine layout of settlements built in arid environments (such as Amheida), see Davoli 2023.

55. Davoli 2015d, 18; Davoli 2015b, 68.

Fig. 1.6: View of the necropolis at the south end of Amheida.

The main construction material was sun-dried mudbrick, with baked bricks also employed in some buildings. Other materials that are largely absent from the archaeological record, but that must have been used in some quantity, include stone and wood.[56]

Amheida is surrounded on its south side by cemeteries, which extend 1.5 km in length and include numerous well-preserved mud-brick chapels of the Roman period (fig. 1.6).[57] Another group of tombs was in the proximity of a mud-brick pyramid located at the southeast end of the settlement (fig. 1.7). This large structure (preserved up to 8 m in height) was built on the highest mound of the cemetery and thus must have been a major landmark of the local built environment also in antiquity.[58]

That Amheida was a wealthy and sophisticated city, which had not only largely adopted the Greek language, but had also embraced Graeco-Roman culture and lifestyle, is attested by a wide range of archaeological and documentary evidence. One of the most striking discoveries was an impressive Roman-style public bath complex (*thermae*, labeled B6) built in the middle of the residential area of Trimithis (fig. 1.8).[59]

---

56. These building materials were likely subject to reuse, more than mudbricks, following the abandonment of the site.

57. The cemeteries have been surveyed but have yet to be fully investigated. One large tomb, in the shape of a tower, still stands to a considerable height to the north of the site; it was restored by the mission's architect N. Warner (2012, 368–71).

58. Kaper 2015; Davoli 2019, 61–62. On the restoration of the pyramid, see Warner 2012, 366–68. Another mud-brick pyramid can be seen at the south end of the main necropolis, also standing on a mound that must have emphasized its visibility also in antiquity.

59. Davoli 2015a; Davoli 2017; Davoli 2019, 63–65. The baths were built during at least three major construction episodes, as well as a couple of restoration phases, spanning from the third to the late fourth centuries: Davoli 2017, 194–95. The north area of the baths, where this room is located, seems to have been abandoned before completion, for reasons that are yet unknown. Evidence for the abandonment includes the discovery of some 20,500 stone and pottery *tesserae* that were stored, with others still to be cut, inside one of the rooms; work on the baths was abruptly halted before the mosaic was made. On the mosaic *tesserae*, cf. Nuovo and Prell 2020.

Fig. 1.7: View of the Roman pyramid (following restoration) at the southeast end of the site.

Industrial areas with workshops and kilns were surveyed at the northeast and southeast ends of the site.[60] The central area of Trimithis is occupied by numerous houses, often of a roughly square plan but with evidence of later additions. Although not fully excavated, several of them appear to have been opulent buildings, with painted decoration in Classical style and, in some instances, features in molded stucco.[61] To the southeast of the Roman baths is a house (B1) that effectively and beautifully showcases the affinity that at least some of the inhabitants of ancient Trimithis had with Graeco-Roman literary and artistic tropes. The house, which was fully excavated, lies in a centrally located and seemingly wealthy quarter (fig. 1.9).[62]

60. Hope 1980, 307–11; Davoli 2015b, 75; Davoli 2019, 69–70.
61. Large rectangular spaces, defined by two thick pillars in the middle, were surveyed in numerous houses and were preliminarily identified as banquet halls: see Davoli 2019, 69.
62. Davoli 2022 is the final archaeological report of the excavations carried out in building 1. The publication of the small finds from this house is forthcoming.

Fig. 1.8: View of the baths of Amheida (B6), showing the pillared hall (in the background) and a round pool (in the foreground).

Documentary evidence found inside the house revealed that the owner was Serenos, a member of the local *boule* (or city council) in the first half of the fourth century.[63] The house is known particularly for its painted walls, which were first unearthed in 1979.[64] Three rooms (11, 13, and 14) were decorated with geometric designs painted in vivid colors; room 1, which originally had a domed roof and was likely used to welcome and entertain guests, was adorned with figural vignettes, representing well-known scenes inspired by Classical literature, painted above geometric panels (fig. 1.10).[65]

Another striking find at the site was a room, adjacent to the northwest corner of Serenos's house, that was incorporated, in its latest stage, into the house and served as a storage space.

---

63. The several phases of Serenos's house was dated, based on archaeological and documentary evidence, to between 330–340 and about 365 CE: Davoli and Bagnall 2015, 86–87. On the ceramic evidence from the excavation of the house, see Caputo 2020.

64. McFadden 2014; McFadden 2015; McFadden 2019.

65. McFadden 2015, 193. Following excavation and documentation, the house of Serenos was completely backfilled due to its very fragile condition. In order to allow local communities, as well as visitors, to experience the wonderful decoration of Serenos's house in its architectural context, a reconstruction of the house was built at the edge of the site (Warner 2012, 373–78). Inside it, the team's archaeological artist D. Schultz and her colleagues recreated the painted decoration of all rooms as recorded during the excavations: see Schulz 2011; Schulz 2015.

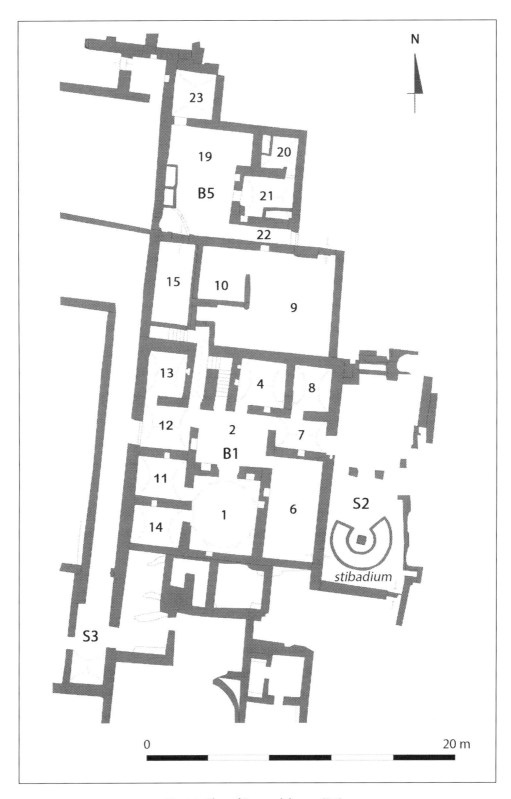

Fig. 1.9: Plan of Serenos's house (B1).

Fig. 1.10: Detail of a painted scene on the east wall of room 1 inside Serenos's house, showing the personification of the *polis* of Trimithis/Amheida (at the far left) and, to her right, a procession of Olympian deities witnessing the adultery of Aphrodite and Ares.

However, at an earlier time it was clearly part of another building, almost certainly a school (B5), which once consisted of at least three rooms.[66] The identification of this space as a schoolroom was based on the discovery of several Greek rhetorical exercises painted on its walls. These exercises were written in red ink and included lectional signs, likely added as teaching aides for students (fig. 1.11).[67]

Another house (B2) was excavated by the Amheida project in the northeast quarter of the city (fig. 1.12).[68] It was found, in poor condition, in an industrial area with remains of pottery workshops, which were built reusing earlier structures. The house is dated to the middle/second half of the third century and is of a similar plan to Serenos's house, but more modest (it has no domed reception room). It is clear that the two dwellings belonged to individuals of different socio-economic status.

66. Cribiore and Davoli 2013, 1–5; Cribiore 2015.
67. Cribiore, Davoli, and Ratzan 2008.
68. Boozer 2015.

Fig. 1.11: Rhetorical exercises in a schoolroom (B5) at Amheida.

Fig. 1.12: Aerial view of house B2 at Amheida.

A third house (B10), located in Area 8.1 in the northern sector of the site, was chosen as a target of excavation in 2015. Investigation of this domestic residence, of a very large size and bearing abundant evidence of painted—as well as gypsum-molded—decoration, was resumed in 2023 and is ongoing. The house was preliminarily dated to the a third-fourth century CE, but more excavations, as well as in-depth analysis of the finds collected thus far, are necessary in order to reconstruct and more precisely date the construction and occupation history of this house.[69]

1.5. Methodology of Excavation, Documentation, and Conservation

The excavations carried out between 2012 and 2013 and then in 2023 in the sector of the church (Area 2.3) followed the system that P. Davoli of the Università del Salento (Lecce, Italy) established and adopted, in her capacity as Archaeological Field Director, at Amheida from 2004 until 2022.[70] This method of stratigraphical excavation was based on the standards developed by A. Carandini, E. C. Harris, and the Museum of London.[71]

R. S. Bagnall held, as the director of the Amheida project, the scientific leadership and the responsibility for the organization and management of each excavation and study season.[72] The author was in charge of the excavations in Area 2.3. In that role, he established excavation goals and strategies in agreement with the project director and the field director (for the 2012–2013 seasons). He also led the team excavating the church and managed the data processing on site and at the excavation house.

A group of archaeologists supervised the digging in different areas (rooms or smaller quadrants inside the church), assisted by students and in collaboration with specialists, such as ceramicists and physical anthropologists, who were also active on site. Workmen hired from local communities were assigned to each area and carried out excavations following the established scientific standards, under the supervision of the archaeologists. The latter were also responsible for the documentation of the excavated sectors to which they had been assigned, helped by assistant supervisors.

Area 2.3 was first surveyed and mapped by the topographers and included in the general site plan (Fig. 1.4). Following the standards adopted at Amheida, the sector of the church was subdivided into a grid of squares measuring 10 by 10 m. This grid was visible on the AutoCAD map but was not physically laid out in the field, due to the location of the church at the top of a mound with relatively steep sides. The survey had revealed the outline of several walls of the church complex before excavation started;[73] therefore, it was decided that the best way to approach the investigation of the area was to excavate by room rather than by square.

---

69. Bagnall et al. 2017 contains a discussion of the archaeological context and the materials (chiefly ceramic vessels and wine tags) from the 2015 excavation season in house B10.
70. Davoli created a site manual for the Amheida project, to which regular updates are added each year. For a recent summary of the methods of excavation and documentation adopted at Amheida, see Davoli 2022, 29–34.
71. Spence 1994; Harris 1989; Carandini 2000.
72. In 2022, the leadership of the Amheida Project passed to D. M. Ratzan.
73. A few walls, especially in room 7 (see Sec. 4.4 below), stood at a considerable height above modern-day ground level; thus, their existence was already known before the surface clearance and survey of the area were carried out.

The stratigraphic method adopted at Amheida is built on a basic distinction between Deposition Stratigraphic Units (DSUs) and Feature Stratigraphic Units (FSUs). DSUs are three-dimensional units that are the result of natural or artificial deposition, for example layers of soil or windblown sand, collapse episodes, and fillings of domestic middens, hearths, or burial pits. These types of units have edges that are either natural or arbitrary, based on the extent of their excavation (which can be full or partial, as in the case of test trenches). FSUs consist, instead, of architectural features such as walls, floors, staircases, and vaults. They also include "negative" features, that is to say, units that resulted from the removal (in antiquity) of DSUs, for example in the case of foundation trenches or pits.

All DSUs and FSUs that were identified and excavated were assigned numbers and documented using pre-printed forms. These were created following common standards and included fields for elevations, measurements, spatial and chronological relationships, and detail description. All units were photographed; several DSUs, in particular artificial units, and all FSUs were drawn by hand in the field and later retraced digitally in AutoCAD.[74]

In advance of the beginning of excavations in Area 2.3, a survey of the whole sector was carried out with a total station and a digital plan was generated from the data that were gathered, downloaded, and then elaborated in AutoCAD.[75] The plan was regularly updated during the two seasons by the topographers of the Amheida team and the archaeologists. Additionally, photogrammetric images of several architectural features, mostly walls, burials, and remains of vaults, were taken during the excavations and processed, with the goal of acquiring precise and scalable plates; this also had the benefit of saving a considerable amount of time and resources.[76]

Plans (at 1:50 scale) were drawn each day, on millimeter paper, of the excavated areas and then digitized. These drawings included information such as the number and extent of the DSUs and FSUs under investigation, their elevations (as well the day height, all taken with a total station or an optical level), and the location (and elevations) of the small finds and samples. For some of the features that necessitated a higher level of detail, drawings at 1:20 scale were made. In addition to the graphic documentation, archaeologists took detailed field notes on standard forms, recording all excavation data and any relevant information.

The ceramic objects that were found, in complete or almost complete condition, were photographed in their original context and given field numbers. They were then brought to the ceramics laboratory at the excavation house, where they were cleaned, conserved, re-photographed, drawn, and fully documented. All pottery sherds, which were uncovered in large quantity in Area 2.3 at Amheida, were placed in plastic bags or buckets, again according to their

---

74. In the Amheida documentation, DSU numbers are generally surrounded by circles, while FSU numbers are within squares. The Harris matrices created for the stratigraphy of each room follow, instead, the standards set in the Harris Matrix Composer software (https://harrismatrixcomposer.com/#/), i.e., squares for deposition units and circles for feature units. In order to avoid confusion, all numbers in the matrices also include labels "DSU" or "FSU" (depending on the nature of each unit).

75. Davoli 2022, 25–28.

76. The software employed to process the photogrammetric images from the excavation of the church complex are Photometric and Meridiana. The photogrammetry was complemented by hand drawing, especially in the case of profiles and sections of walls that were at an angle, thus not allowing standard photogrammetric documentation.

archaeological contexts (either DSU or FSU). The ceramicists carried out a preliminary sorting of the sherds on site, performing a quantitative analysis of the different forms and fabrics.[77] Following a gross quantification of the ceramics from each unit, the sherds were generally returned to a dump on the site, except for those with a diagnostic value (for example, fragments of bases, rims, handles, etc.). These were drawn and photographed, with the aim of creating a comprehensive digital catalogue of the most representative forms and fabrics found.[78]

Forty-three Greek ostraka were retrieved in 2012 and 2013 among the pottery sherds that were collected during the excavation of the church complex, largely in foundation contexts.[79] They were allocated field numbers and photographed *in situ*;[80] afterwards, they were cleaned and photographed in the lab and their content translated and analyzed. In 2016, R. Ast and R. S. Bagnall published the ostraka from the church (from the 2012–2013 seasons) as part of volume II of ostraka from Amheida/Trimithis.[81]

Forty-six coins, many of which are poorly preserved or completely illegible, were found during the excavation of the church complex in 2012–2013, with twenty-one more specimens found in 2023.[82] Before collecting them, they were given field numbers and photographed *in situ*.[83] Conservators did a preliminary cleaning of all specimens, which were also photographed; however, for many years it was not possible to obtain accurate visual documentation for several coins that needed more in-depth cleaning.[84] Irrespectively of their condition, a small finds form was generated for each coin by the registrar, who entered their preserved weight, diameter, and thickness. D. M. Ratzan carried out the study of the available numismatic evidence and compiled a catalogue.[85]

In addition to ceramics and coins, several small objects were gathered during the excavations of the church complex in 2012–2013 and 2023. They belong to different categories, such as textiles, glass, bone, metal, and terracotta objects, fragments of opaque glass bracelets, and beads. Following excavation, the soil and sand from all depositional units were sieved, to ensure that all small finds (especially those of a small size) from each stratum would be

---

77. The Amheida project developed an SUQ (Stratigraphic Unit Quantification) form and adopted it for the quantitative analysis of the ceramic sherds. The same form was also used for the processing of other categories of small finds, for example plaster and charcoal.

78. This catalogue, authored by Clementina Caputo, will be included in the companion volume to this report (forthcoming).

79. Ten additional ostraka (whose publication is forthcoming) were found in 2023.

80. When writing was recognized on the sherds before they were collected.

81. Ast and Bagnall 2016.

82. In addition, six coins were retrieved on surface during an inspection to the site in 2017.

83. This was not the case for coins that were detected while sieving, thus no longer in their archaeological context. In March 2022, permission was granted to access the coins, which were kept in the magazine of the SCA inspectorate in Dakhla. All specimens were cleaned by Mahmoud Samir. For a brief report of the 2022 season, see https://isaw.nyu.edu/research/amheida/amheida-field-report-2022

84. Thorough cleaning and conservation of all coins, as well as their study and documentation, took place in 2023.

85. To be published in the companion volume to this report (forthcoming). Preliminary data are provided in this volume; the absence of a precise dating (or a broader chronological range) for coins in the text means that the specimens' condition did not allow for their identification and/or dating.

gathered and documented.⁸⁶ Small finds were preliminarily conserved *in situ* before they were collected, based on their condition upon discovery; then they were placed in buckets labeled with the corresponding stratigraphic units. Objects that were deemed of particular significance, such as coins and ostraka, were assigned field numbers. Photographs were taken of these finds in their archaeological context and each item was then placed in a separate tagged bag. Specialists cleaned and processed all small finds, and the photographer took pictures of each object with a scale. Special finds were catalogued, with a record created for each of them.⁸⁷

All fragments of painted plaster from the collapsed ceiling of the church were laid out on wooden trays, except for a few larger patches that were left *in situ* and eventually removed in 2023. The trays were labeled with the depositional units in which the fragments were found. Some units, especially those that covered large areas and included thousands of pieces of plaster, were additionally divided into quadrants, which were also marked on the trays. The aim was to facilitate the reconstruction of the ceiling's decorative patterns, by providing more specific information on each fragment's location at the time of discovery. D. Schulz led the phase of collection and preliminary conservation of the fragments, with the help of local conservator Bahaa Gomaa.⁸⁸

The human remains retrieved from four tombs (1–4) inside the church in 2012–2013 were analyzed by physical anthropologists T. L. Dupras and L. Williams, who provided information on the gender, age range, pathologies, and possible causes of death of the individuals who were buried in these tombs.⁸⁹ The bodies are currently kept in separate wooden boxes at the blockhouse on site, but they will be reburied following the completion of all analyses. In 2023, thirteen additional tombs were investigated in Area 2.3, i.e., tomb 5 (in room 6 to the south of the church, already identified in 2013); tombs 6–9 in room 2 (north crypt); tombs 10–16 in room 3 (central crypt); and tomb 17, in the area of the church facing the entrance into the now-disappeared apse. The bodies that had been laid in these burials were exhumed and preliminarily investigated by P. G. Sheldrick.

Following an established procedure, the small finds from Area 2.3 were registered by representatives of Dakhla's Coptic and Islamic Inspectorate of the Supreme Council of Antiquities (SCA). All objects are currently in SCA storage facilities in the oasis, generally accessible by permit.

Archaeologists collected numerous animal bones, organic materials such as fruit pits, wood, and charcoal, soot from the inside of pots, and also soil samples (including ash and

---

86. The surface layer, heavily contaminated and, as a consequence, without diagnostic value, was not sieved.

87. Due to the particular political and social conditions that followed the 2013 excavation season at the church, it was not possible to access the small finds for several years. Thankfully, several objects could be accessed and cleaned in 2022, following permission by the Egyptian Ministry of Tourism and Antiquities, and in 2023, with the reopening of the excavations at Amheida. Any remaining limitations in the study of each category of small finds, as well as of ceramics and coins, are stated in the introductions to the catalogues that are forthcoming (they will be published in the companion volume to this report).

88. For more detailed information on the remains of the painted ceiling, see Aravecchia 2020b; see also Ch. 6.

89. The results were first published in Aravecchia et al. 2015. The article will be re-published, with new data and conclusions from the 2023 season, in the companion volume to this report (forthcoming).

sand with organic inclusions) for zooarchaeological and archaeobotanical analysis.[90] The aim behind collecting these samples was to gather data that could shed light on diet and patterns of food consumption at Amheida and, more specifically, in the area of the church, both during its occupation history and after its abandonment.

Regarding the conservation of the archaeological evidence, the remains of the church complex in Area 2.3 were found in very poor condition, as will be discussed more in detail in Chapters 3 and 4. Walls in the east half of the complex are currently standing only a few centimeters above the ancient floor level, while the western half of the church has largely disappeared due to erosion and/or human intervention, leaving only its foundations *in situ*. As just mentioned above, only one room (no. 7), located to the south of the church, still has walls that are preserved to almost 2.5 m, in apparent defiance of the obliteration of most of the surrounding built environment.

The poor state of preservation of the church made its conservation a particularly pressing matter, during and immediately following excavations. The materials that were used in the construction of the complex consist largely of sun-dried mudbricks for foundations, walls, and colonnades; compacted clay for floors; mud and gypsum for plastering walls and ceilings; and wood for some architectural elements of doorways. The removal of windblown sand, which protected such fragile materials for centuries, suddenly exposed them to the dangers of physical, chemical, and biological deterioration, caused by harsh environmental conditions (such as sunlight, strong winds, sandstorms, movement of sand dunes, and salinization).[91]

Conservators developed new approaches and techniques, as well as testing new chemicals, in order to protect fragile architectural materials and painted decoration. However, the difficulty in accessing supplies—as well as the varying and often extreme conditions to which archaeological remains are subject in the field—make it hard to assess and set conservation standards and methods that can be applied under diverse circumstances. Due to the specific conservation issues faced during the investigation of Area 2.3, which is particularly exposed to the harsh natural elements, backfill was opted as the best conservation solution after excavation and documentation of the archaeological remains were completed;[92] the rationale for this choice was that backfill recreates the original conditions and protects from environmental and anthropogenic damage.[93] Considering that most of the church had already collapsed, been demolished, or deteriorated by the time of its discovery, particular attention was given to those features below ground that were more at risk of collapse or damage;[94] in particular,

---

90. Standardized forms were filled with basic information for each sample. The study of these materials and soil samples is yet to be performed; its results will be published in the companion volume to this report (forthcoming).

91. Zielinski 1999, 185.

92. Additional conservation work is planned for the church in future seasons, with the capping of the existing walls to protect them from further deterioration. The approach to conservation that was adopted for the church of Amheida followed the standards implemented by P. Davoli for the other buildings investigated at the site: see Warner 2012. I am indebted to architect N. Warner for sharing with me his vast expertise in the conservation of mud-brick architecture, especially at the time when I was involved in the excavations at the fourth-century hamlet of 'Ain el-Gedida (also in Dakhla). Overall, the methods adopted at Amheida reflect the choices made by archaeologists and conservators at other sites in Dakhla: see Schijns 2003.

93. On the conservation of mud-brick architecture at the site of Karanis, see Barnard et al. 2016.

94. As a consequence of prolonged exposure to the elements.

the funerary crypts (rooms 2–4) below the now vanished sanctuary were selected for complete backfill because of their relatively well-preserved, although incomplete, vaulted roofs, which were deemed in danger of collapsing after the removal of the rooms' fill. Additional areas that were completely backfilled, in order to prevent collapses, include test trenches 1 and 2, dug along the north aisle and at the west entrance into room 1, and rooms 11 and 13 to the south of the church, possibly part of the foundations of a staircase leading to the roof or an upper floor.[95] During the latest excavation season in 2023, test trench 4, excavated to the east of the now-disappeared apse, was also partially backfilled.

The numerous fragments of painted ceiling that were found in the stratigraphy of room 1 were collected and preserved by the conservators.[96] A few large patches were documented but left *in situ*, due to their very fragile condition, in the southeast corner of the nave. They were first covered with a layer of textile and then hidden below clean sand, which was kept in place by a row of mudbricks around the edges.[97]

Three seasons of excavation at the church of Amheida generated a considerable amount of data, consisting of forms and notes, plans, sections, drawings, and photographs. The documentation in hard format was left at the excavation house in Egypt. Nevertheless, the goal was to allow all specialists involved in the project easy access to all data following the end of fieldwork. Moreover, it was deemed necessary to organize the information in a way that would not only make it easily available, but also enable searches and comparisons. Therefore, all data were entered into a computer database that was developed by B. Bazzani for the Amheida project. The digital forms faithfully replicated those on paper; different team members entered and cross-checked the data and also digitized all plans and sections in AutoCAD, which were complemented by photogrammetric images. To reduce the risk of a loss of information, as well as errors in the data-entering process, all the documentation on paper was digitized and stored in the database, including all lists, day-notes, drawings, and forms. Each scanned form was linked with its matching digital version, with the aim of facilitating cross-checking. All photographic documentation was also added to the database and linked to the digital forms associated with each specific image.

As a result of the process described above, the Amheida team developed a database that allows for access to the entire body of field documentation, as well as cross-reference searches according to diverse parameters. For example, archaeological data can be searched by year, area, room, unit, etc., making the process of retrieving information easier and more effective. To further facilitate access to the documentation, by the members of the Amheida team as well as the general public, the database was made available on-line and open access and is regularly updated.[98] Crucially, the online database is a key resource that complements the information presented in this volume, and thus should be considered an integral part of it.

---

95. For a plan of the church complex, see fig. 3.2.
96. See esp. Sec. 6.2 below.
97. These larger fragments were eventually removed in 2023.
98. www.amheida.com. In January 2024, Mohamed Osman Abdollah began working on a geodatabase for the entire site of Amheida.

Chapter 2

Early Christianity in the Great Oasis

2.1. Archaeological Evidence from Dakhla[1]

Building 7 at Amheida is one of an increasingly large number of churches that have been discovered in Dakhla in recent decades.[2] These buildings dotted the natural and built landscape of the oasis, attesting to the fact that communities that openly identified themselves as Christian were well established, already by the early fourth century, even in this remote region of Egypt's Western Desert. The picture that has emerged from such investigations is one of a society that had embraced Christianity on a large scale and wished to showcase its religious affiliation through the erection, at times in prime locations, of distinctively Christian buildings. Significantly, the evidence of this process is not confined to the oasis's larger settlements, which likely had closer interaction with the main centers of the Nile Valley and, ultimately, the Delta in the exchange of both material goods and new ideas and religious beliefs. Indeed, even the inhabitants of the smallest and most isolated settlements in Dakhla adopted Christianity at the same time as their fellow town and city dwellers, as is suggested, for example, by the evidence from the small *epoikion* (farmstead) of ʿAin el-Gedida.[3] They also equally and actively participated in the process of Christianization of the oasis's physical environment, building churches that were, among other things, visual symbols of their Christian affiliation.

Written sources on Egyptian Christianity exist from the late second century in the form of literary papyri; specifically for the Great Oasis (which included both Dakhla and Kharga), primary sources are available only from the late third–early fourth century onwards.[4] Considering that the earliest archaeological evidence can also be dated to the early fourth century, the

---

1. This section builds upon, and expands, Aravecchia 2018, 7–20.
2. For a recent summary of the archaeological evidence, see Bowen 2019.
3. See Aravecchia 2021.
4. On the origins of Egyptian Christianity, cf., among others, Pearson 1986; Pearson 2007; Bowman 1996, 190–202; Wipszycka 1996; Davis 2004; Choat 2012; for an introduction to the archaeological evidence, see Brooks Hedstrom 2019. On the earliest documentary evidence for the spread of Christianity in the Great Oasis, see, most recently, Choat 2020; cf. also Gardner 2022 on the rise of Christianity at Kellis. On early Christianity in Kharga, cf. Ghica 2012.

picture of Christianity in the Western Desert is far from clear for the first three centuries of the common era.[5]

I have remarked elsewhere how our knowledge of Christianity in Dakhla was, until a few decades ago, significantly poorer when compared to the rich body of evidence from the nearby Kharga Oasis.[6] This had been previously explained by the remote location of Dakhla in relation to the Nile Valley and its military posts, which might have led to the abandonment of many oasite settlements by the late Roman period, possibly as a result of invasions by neighboring nomadic tribes.[7] In fact, evidence of early Christian places of cult, monasteries, and cemeteries is remarkably abundant in Kharga.[8] Nevertheless, the balance has been redressed in recent years, with numerous churches being identified and investigated in the Dakhla Oasis. A particular impetus was given by the establishment of the Dakhleh Oasis Project (DOP), established in 1978.[9] A decade-long survey carried out by the DOP recorded phases of occupation datable to ca. 300–700 CE, chiefly based on ceramic evidence, at over one hundred locations in the oasis, including inhabited settlements, caves, and cemeteries.[10] Following the survey, archaeological excavations were carried out by an Australian mission, under the direction of C. A. Hope, at the site of Kellis (modern Ismant el-Kharab). These investigations revealed a considerable body of evidence for fourth-century Christian architecture and burial customs in Dakhla. These finds were complemented in recent years by more data gathered at several other sites in the region, painting a significantly richer picture of the flourishing of early Christianity in the oasis.

In order to contextualize the church at Amheida with what is known about fourth-century Christianity in Dakhla, a brief discussion of the available archaeological evidence from the oasis is provided below.[11]

2.1.1. The Churches of Dakhla

A fourth-century church complex was investigated in the mid-2000s at the small hamlet of ʿAin el-Gedida, located roughly in the middle of Dakhla Oasis and in close proximity to the village

---

5. For a summary of the archaeological evidence, see Bowen 2010 and Bowen 2019.

6. Aravecchia 2018, 7.

7. Winlock 1936, 60–61.

8. See Vivian 2008, 117–72 for an overview of the main archaeological sites in Kharga. A brief introduction to early Christian sites and monuments in Kharga, with relative bibliography, is available below (cf. Sec. 2.3).

9. Cf. Sec. 1.2, esp. pp. 7–8.

10. Churcher and Mills 1999, 263–64. One must acknowledge, however, that it is not possible to establish, just on chronological grounds, a Christian affiliation for the individuals who lived (and/or were buried) at these sites in late antiquity. As mentioned earlier, documentary and archaeological sources point to the fact that Christianity was well established in Egypt already in the fourth century; it is equally known, though, that different ethnic, cultural, and religious groups (including Manichaeism and different forms of Christianity) are attested in the region at that time. On Manichaeism in Dakhla (with a particular focus on Kellis) and Egypt, see, among others, Gardner 2020, 95–105; Teigen 2021; Brand 2022. There is also evidence that some Egyptian temples were still operating in the third and even the early fourth century: see Bagnall 1993, 261–68.

11. Evidence pointing to the existence of a Christian community at Mothis/Mut el-Kharab, the old capital of Dakhla, is briefly discussed in Bowen 2017; however, the precise location of a church (or churches) at the site has not yet been discovered. Therefore, the site has not been included in the following section.

of Kellis (fig. 1.3).[12] The construction of the complex is dated to the early fourth century, on the basis of numismatic, ceramic, and inscriptional evidence. The church was built in the middle of one of the five mounds that made up the settlement and was surrounded by a network of streets and passageways as well as other structures; these included a small-scale industrial space with evidence of several bread ovens and a mud-brick temple that had been converted, in its latest occupation phase, into a ceramic workshop.[13]

The church complex consists of six rooms (figs. 2.1–2).[14] The church itself (room B5) is of a simple basilica type, with one nave and a semicircular apse placed at the east end, to the south of which was a small L shaped *pastophorion*. The church still shows the remains of a barrel-vaulted roof and mud-brick *mastabas* ("benches" in Arabic, the regular word for such features in the mud-brick architecture of the region) along the north, west, and south walls. The church opened to the north onto a large rectangular hall (A46, which must have been used as a gathering hall of some kind) through two openings placed along its north wall, consisting of a doorway at the west end and a large passageway in the middle.[15] Sometime during the fourth century, and for reasons that are still unknown, the central passageway was completely sealed with mudbricks, perhaps as part of a broader reconfiguration that affected especially the northwest sector of the complex.[16] The complex at ʿAin el-Gedida shares several typological similarities with other early Christian churches in Egypt and, in particular, with the so-called "Small East Church" of Kellis, one of three churches excavated at Kellis, fairly close to ʿAin el-Gedida (fig. 2.3).[17]

---

12. Archaeological excavations at ʿAin el-Gedida were first conducted, in 1993–1995, by an Egyptian mission of the local Coptic and Islamic inspectorate: see Bayumi 1998, 55–62. A Columbia University (now New York University) mission resumed excavations in 2006. Work at ʿAin el-Gedida was part of the broader Amheida project. Excavations at ʿAin el-Gedida lasted until 2008 under the author's field direction, with two study seasons following in 2009–2010: see Aravecchia 2018 for the final archaeological report.

13. Aravecchia 2018, 211–68. On the likely identification of ʿAin el-Gedida as an *epoikion*, i.e., a small rural settlement depending on a larger village (Kellis?) and associated with the management of a land estate, see Aravecchia 2018, 275–81; cf. also Aravecchia 2021.

14. For a comprehensive presentation and discussion of the church see Aravecchia 2018, 81–142; 187–210. See also Aravecchia 2012.

15. On the possible use(s) of gathering hall A46, for example as a space for women or catechumens and/or a refectory, see Aravecchia 2022. Low mud-brick benches were found in room A46, built against the north and east walls and along the easternmost section of the south wall. Four niches pierced the walls of this hall.

16. The sealing partially obliterated a stepped mud-brick podium that was built against the east side of the opening and was likely used in antiquity by a priest (or another member of the clergy) for the reading of Scriptures and preaching.

17. See Bowen 2003a. For an in-depth comparison of the two churches, see Aravecchia 2018, 200–5 and Aravecchia 2022. A survey, carried out by the DOP in 1981–82, exposed three churches at Kellis, one situated at the west edge of the site and the others located at the south end of the excavated area (Knudstad and Frey 1999, 189, 201, 205). Following the survey, they were excavated, between 1993 and 2001, by G. E. Bowen, member of an Australian mission directed by C. A. Hope (Bowen 2002; Bowen 2003a; most recently, Bowen 2022b). The archaeological evidence, chiefly ceramics and coins, points to the first half of the fourth century as the dating for all three churches at Kellis. This chronology shows how the fourth century was unquestionably a period of dramatic growth and flourishing of Christianity in the oasis (Bowen 2002, 81–84; Bowen 2019, 378). A volume on the three churches (Bowen 2023) was published after this book was completed.

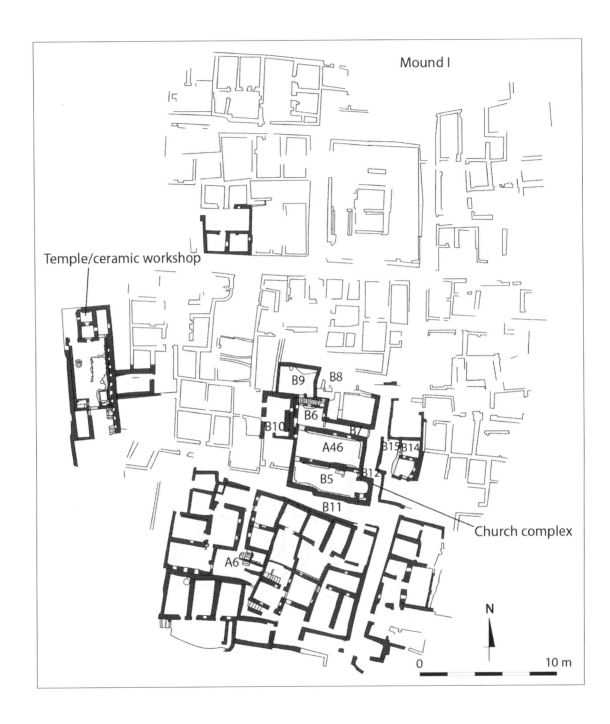

Fig. 2.1: Plan of buildings on mound I at ʿAin el-Gedida (tracing by K. DeMondo).

Fig. 2.2: Aerial view (to northeast) of the church complex of ʿAin el-Gedida (photograph by B. Bazzani).

The Small East Church and the church at ʿAin el-Gedida were both in use in the first half of the fourth century CE.[18] They also share similar dimensions, the same construction materials and techniques, and, most importantly, an almost identical layout. Their excavation also provided abundant evidence that the two churches were created by readapting older structures, whose original functions remain, in both cases, unknown.[19] The parallels between the churches testify to the popularity of artistic forms and idioms in Christian architecture over large regions of the Mediterranean, including geographically remote areas like the oases of Egypt's Western Desert.[20]

The Small East Church at Kellis is located at the southeast edge of a large, multi-roomed complex, whose original extent is unknown (fig. 2.3). The other place of Christian cult that was found within this area is the so-called "Large East Church," located against the southeast enclosure wall of this complex.[21] The Large East Church is of a basilica shape, with a central nave flanked by two side aisles that are defined by two rows of six columns each, as well as a "west return aisle" (a common feature of Christian architecture in Egypt, particularly attested

---

18. On the basis of numismatic evidence: for the Small East Church, see Bowen 2003, 164.
19. Bowen 2003a, 162–64.
20. Aravecchia 2018, 208–10.
21. Bowen 2002.

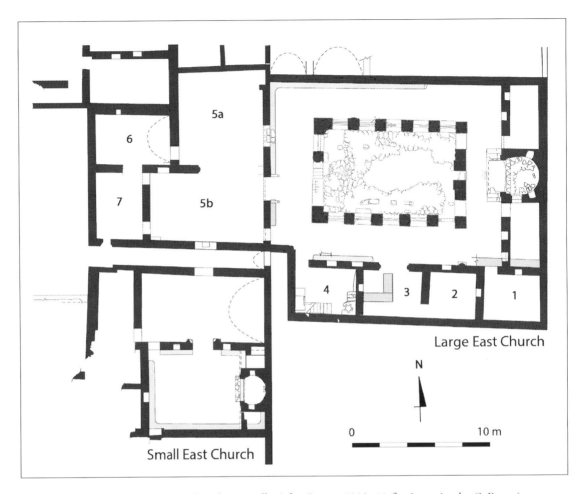

Fig. 2.3: Plan of the East Churches at Kellis (after Bowen 2002, 66, fig. 2; tracing by C. Fosen).

in Upper Egypt)[22] along the west wall of the church. An east transverse aisle, consisting of four columns, joins the north and south colonnades at their east ends, completing an ambulatory that runs along the four walls of the church. Two engaged pilasters frame a semicircular apse in the middle of the church's east wall, while along the south wall are four rooms that likely served utilitarian functions.[23] Overall, the Large East Church at Kellis is the basilica that offers the closest parallels to the church at Amheida among all the churches identified in Dakhla thus far.[24]

---

22. On the west return aisle in Upper Egyptian churches, see Grossmann 2007, 104–7.
23. One of the rooms contained evidence of a staircase and a bread oven. Bowen (2002, 71) associated the ovens with the baking of bread to be used in the Eucharistic liturgy.
24. For a detailed discussion of the parallels between the Large East Church at Kellis and the church at Amheida, see Sec. 7.6.

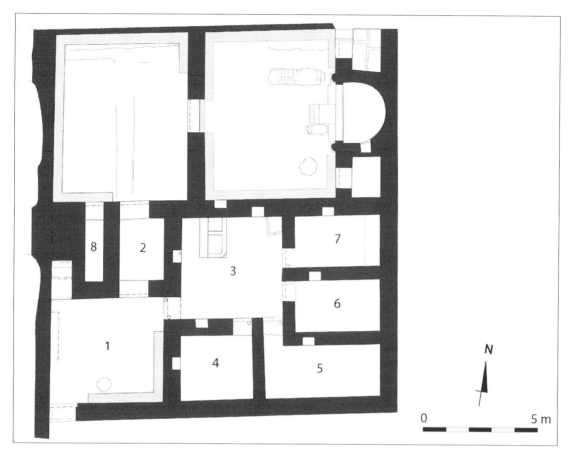

Fig. 2.4: Plan of the West Church at Kellis (after Bowen 2002, 76, fig. 8; tracing by C. Fosen).

The third church that was found at Kellis is the West Church, lying within a cemetery situated at the west end of the site (fig. 2.4).[25] The building is divided into two spaces, one to the west, possibly serving as a narthex, and another to the east (the nave), connected with the former via a central passageway. Low mud-brick benches run along the walls of both rooms. A semicircular apse, with a raised floor, is built at the east end of the church. It is framed by engaged columns and was once accessible from the west via a stepped platform. To the north and south of the apse are two rectangular service rooms that open directly into the nave. Based on the setting of the complex, as well as the fact that burials were found both inside and adjacent to the church, it is likely that the complex was used in the context of funerary rites and memorials.[26]

25. Bowen et al. 1993, 23–25. See also Bowen 2002, 75–81 and Bowen 2019, 371–72. According to Bowen (2002, 83), numismatic evidence suggests that the church was built after the mid-fourth century and was abandoned in the 390s.

26. Bowen 2002, 78–81; Bowen 2019, 371–73, 376, fig. 10; Hope 2003, 244–52; Molto et al. 2003, 347, 349; Hope and McKenzie 1999. Cf. also Sec. 5.5.

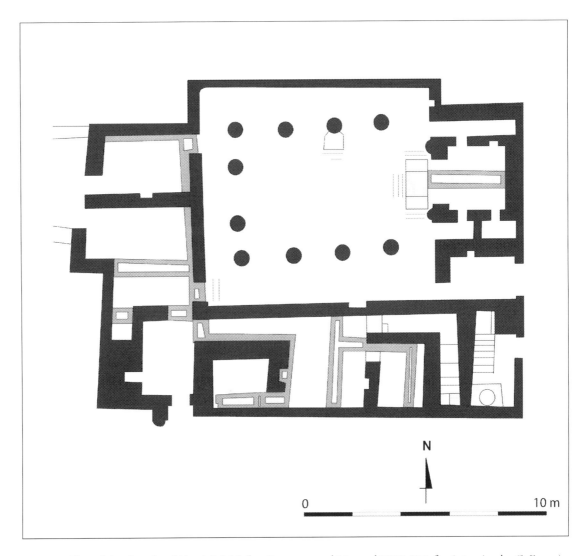

Fig. 2.5: Plan of the church at ʿAin el-Sabil (after Bayoumy and Masoud 2019, 356, fig. 3; tracing by C. Fosen).

Recent excavations carried out at the site of ʿAin el-Sabil, located about 2 km southwest of Kellis, revealed evidence of a well-preserved church that was built above pre-existing features and within a densely built environment (fig. 2.5).[27] The church was built following a basilica plan consisting of a central nave and two side aisles, as well as a west return aisle. A rectangular apse, framed by two semi-columns and with a raised floor, lies at the east end of the nave and is flanked by rectangular service rooms on its north and south sides. The apse was originally accessed by an unusual combination of a rectangular platform, with lateral steps along the

---

27. Bayoumy and Masoud 2019, 358. Several rooms were investigated along the west and south sides of the church; an aerial view of the site, as well as a recent visit to ʿAin el-Sabil in January 2024, confirmed the existence of several spaces immediately to the north and east (cf. Bayoumy and Masoud 2019, 355, pl. 2).

north and south sides, and a four-stepped *bema* protruding frontally onto the nave.[28] A set of rooms to the west and south of the church of ʿAin el-Sabil seem to have been functionally associated with it, including a kitchen where the bread for the Eucharistic liturgy might have (perhaps) been made.[29]

The church of ʿAin el-Sabil shares strong typological similarities with the church at Amheida and also the Large East Church at Kellis, both of which are dated to the fourth century.[30] The close proximity of ʿAin el-Sabil to Kellis, their apparently similar chronologies, and the documentary evidence[31] retrieved at ʿAin el-Sabil suggest that ties existed between the two settlements. ʿAin el-Sabil may indeed have been a rural center economically and administratively dependent on the larger village of Kellis, as was likely the case for the settlement of ʿAin el-Gedida.[32]

A church whose existence was known before the beginning of the DOP's survey is located at Deir Abu Matta, about 6 km southeast of Amheida, in the west half of Dakhla Oasis (fig. 1.3).[33] The remains consist of a large basilica, recorded by H. E. Winlock in 1908 as one of the few Christian sites known in Dakhla at the time.[34] There are also structures to the north, west, and southwest of the church, as well as Christian burials at the site (fig. 2.6).[35] The church itself is a rectangular building oriented east-west. The interior has suffered heavy damage, while the exterior walls are remarkably well preserved in some sections. On the basis of a reconstruction by P. Grossmann, the basilica was divided into a central nave and two side aisles by two rows of seven columns, with two additional columns forming a west return aisle.[36] Traces of a mud-brick bench can be seen along the north section of the west wall; another bench, no longer visible, would have been placed against the south wall. Evidence was detected of one narrow access, possibly a secondary entrance, near the west end of the north wall; the main doorway, not yet identified, may have been located in the middle of the basilica's west wall.[37] The sanctuary at the east end of the building consists of a triconch, accessed via an entrance framed by two engaged pillars, and two L-shaped *pastophoria*, located to the north and south of the triconch. Architectural features that predate the construction of the basilica

---

28. Bowen (2019, 371) emphasizes the uniqueness of this arrangement. Cf. also Sec. 7.2 below.
29. Bayoumy and Masoud 2019, 358, based on parallels from the Large East Church at Kellis: cf. Bowen 2002, 71.
30. The Large East Church at Kellis seems to have been built a few decades earlier than the church at Amheida; the former is dated to the early part of the fourth century, while the latter seems to have been erected in the mid- to-second half of the fourth century: see Sec. 7.4. The foundation of the church of ʿAin el-Sabil was also dated to the second half of the fourth century, on the basis of numismatic evidence: see Bayoumy and Masoud 2019, 358. Additionally, a few ostraka, which were discovered within a building adjoining the church, have been dated by R. S. Bagnall and R. Ast to the mid-fourth century, which may represent the last phase of use of the building: Bayoumy and Masoud 2019, 353–56; see also Ast and Bagnall 2016.
31. Masoud, Ast, and Bagnall 2021.
32. Bowen 2019, 371. On ʿAin el-Gedida and Kellis, cf. Aravecchia 2018, 283–84.
33. DOP number 32/405-A7-1: see Mills 1981, 185, pl. XI.; cf. also Churcher and Mills 1999, 264.
34. Winlock 1936, 24, pls. 12–13.
35. On the more recent fieldwork at Deir Abu Matta, see Bowen 2008; Bowen 2009; Bowen 2012b; Bowen 2019, 373. On the burials, see Bowen 2019, 377–78; Bowen and Dupras forthcoming. Cf. also Sec. 5.5 below.
36. Grossmann 2002a, plan 180. The little evidence that remains of the colonnades lies in the west half of the church; therefore, it is unknown if the church originally had an east return aisle.
37. Bowen 2008, 11.

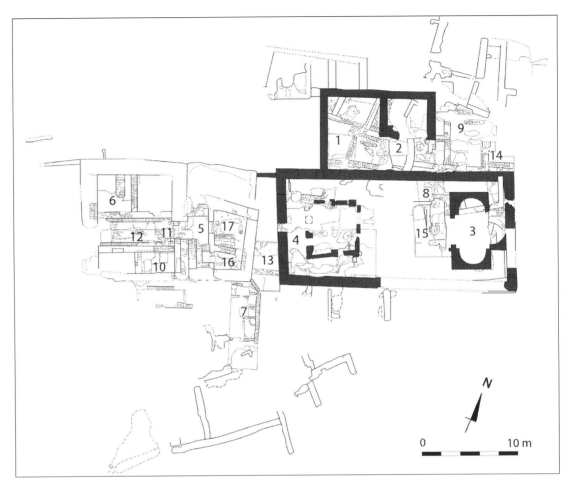

Fig. 2.6: Plan of the church (and adjacent structures) at Deir Abu Matta
(after Bowen 2012b, 430, fig. 1; tracing by C. Fosen).

were found to the north of the church and underneath it to the east.[38] Bowen also investigated a large, tower-looking building west of the church, in addition to other structures. Some of these features may be earlier than the church, while others were possibly built at the same time. Additionally, evidence was found of later alterations, following the abandonment of the church. This evidence includes burial pits that were dug inside the basilica following its abandonment.[39]

Some of the structures near the church of Deir Abu Matta may have been built as part of a small-scale monastic establishment,[40] whose existence in late antiquity is hinted at

---

38. Bowen 2012b, 448–49.
39. Bowen 2019, 377.
40. Bowen 2008, 8. The tower-like structure was identified as a monastic keep: see Mills 1981, 165; Grossmann 1991c.

by the modern Arabic toponym.⁴¹ Nevertheless, no evidence has yet been found to establish conclusively the monastic nature of the settlement.⁴²

Recent excavations at the site revealed coins, ceramics, and a few ostraka that were all dated to the fourth–sixth century CE, with negligible evidence that could be assigned to earlier or later centuries.⁴³ Based on the available data, the construction of the church was recently assigned to the fifth century, which is significantly earlier than the previously established chronology.⁴⁴

In 1980, the DOP survey recorded the remains of a church at Deir el-Malak, a site located 2 km northwest of the village of Masara, in the middle of Dakhla.⁴⁵ The church consists of a rectangular mud-brick building, internally divided into nine square areas by four cruciform pillars centrally placed (fig. 2.7). The church was originally covered with a dome over each of the nine areas.⁴⁶ Three semicircular apses were built against the east wall and formed the sanctuary;⁴⁷ two additional conches were added in the middle of the west and south walls; these apses protruded beyond the edges of the rectangular outline of the church, thus visually emphasizing its cruciform shape.⁴⁸ An annex was identified to the south of the church; it consists of a narrow entrance of an irregular shape that opens (to the east) onto a square room, once covered by a domed roof and ending with a semicircular apse at its east end. It is likely that this south annex was built shortly after the completion of the church and was functionally associated with it.⁴⁹ The chronology of the church of Deir el-Malak has yet to be established beyond doubt, due to the lack of sufficient dating material. Nevertheless, the little evidence that

---

41. Vivian (2008, 199) mentions that the site is also known as Deir al-Saba Banat ('Monastery of the Seven Virgins').

42. Bowen 2012b, 449. The author seems more open to a monastic identification in a later publication (Bowen 2019, 373).

43. Bowen 2012b, 449. About three decades earlier, the DOP team had found fifth-century coins and ceramics datable from the fifth to the seventh century at Deir Abu Matta: see Mills 1981, 185.

44. Bowen 2019, 373. Grossmann (1991b) believed that the church was built in the late sixth century; in a later publication (Grossmann 2002a, 566), the period immediately before the Arab conquest is mentioned in relation to the basilica's construction.

45. Mills 1981, 184–85; pl. X. The site was labeled as 31/405-M6-1; cf. also Churcher and Mills 1999, 263. No comprehensive excavations were carried out at the time, except for a brief testing involving a limited area within the sanctuary. An Australian team, directed by C. A. Hope and G. E. Bowen, visited the site in 2015 and recently published new information: see Bowen and Hope 2019a.

46. The domed roof, which may have been higher above the central space (Mills 1981, 184; Grossmann 1991d) is no longer preserved; however, evidence of springing, as well as squinching in several corners, is still visible: see Bowen and Hope 2019a, 419.

47. A *haikal* screen must have separated the sanctuary from the rest of the church: see Bowen and Hope 2019a, 419.

48. A fourth apse is not marked in the original plan of the church but appears in the reconstructed version by Grossmann (cf. Grossmann 1991d; more details were added in Grossmann 2002a, pl. 181). Bowen and Hope (2019a, 422) disagree and believe that that was the location of the original entrance, in line with the apse along the south wall of the church. No conclusive evidence is available, however, since no excavation or test trenching has been carried out in the north half of the church. On the possible location of the entrance along the north wall, cf. also Mills 1981, 184.

49. Mills 1981, 184. Grossmann (1991c, 822) labeled this space as a "chapel"; cf. also Bowen and Hope 2019, 422. Evidence of subsequent alterations was found in the southwest corner of the church and near the entrance of the south annex, pointing to later phases of use of the building: see Mills 1981, 185; Bowen and Hope 2019a, 422.

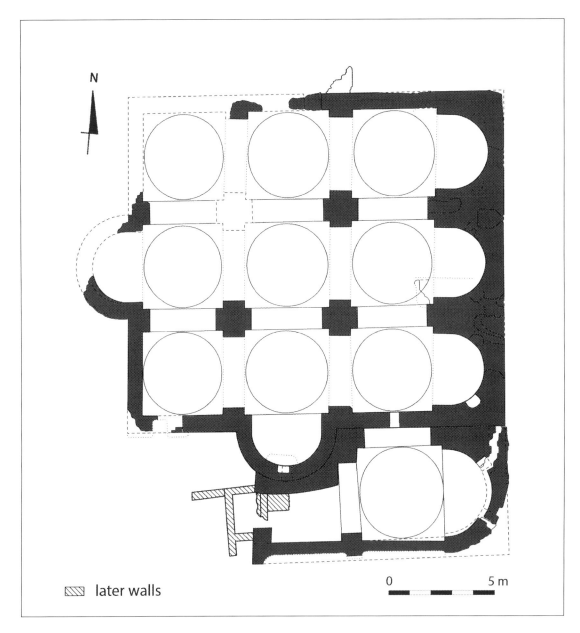

Fig. 2.7: Plan of the church of Deir el-Molouk (after Mills 1981, pl. X; tracing by K. DeMondo).

was gathered in 1980, as well as that from the more recent survey, suggests a significantly later date for its construction than that of any other churches known in Dakhla.[50]

50. A sixth-century dating was proposed in Schijns 1999, 7. Typological parallels were drawn by Grossmann (1991c, 822) with sixteenth-century churches around Akhmim. A possible sixteenth-century dating (extending into the seventeenth century) is reaffirmed in Grossmann 2002a, 567. The discrepancy between the above-mentioned chronology offered by Grossman and that proposed by Schijns is remarked upon by Bowen and Hope (2019).

2.1.2. Christian Cemeteries in Dakhla

In the first three centuries of the common era, exclusively Christian cemeteries are not attested anywhere in the East or West Mediterranean, apart from very few exceptions.[51] With regard to Egypt, there is documentary and archaeological evidence suggesting that Christians and non-Christians buried their dead in the same cemeteries during the third and fourth centuries.[52] However, at some point there was the development of self-consciously Christian cemeteries separate from non-Christian ones, even at the same site.

In recent decades, a growing body of evidence has become available on early Christian cemeteries in Dakhla. While the large necropolis at the south end of ancient Trimithis has yet to be excavated, the investigation of cemeteries at Kellis, Deir Abu Matta, and near El-Muzawwaqa has provided valuable information on Christian burial customs in the oasis.[53]

At Kellis, two cemeteries that were used by Christians are the so-called "Kellis 2" and the cemetery associated with the West Church, located at the west edge of the ancient settlement.[54] The "Kellis 2" cemetery is the larger of the two. It is situated to the east of the village and may have hosted up to 4,000 tombs.[55] Most of the graves that were systematically investigated since 1992 (over 770) consisted of simple burials dug into the clay ground, often marked by architectural features such as one-course mud-brick superstructures or *mastabas*; no grave stelae were found.[56] Remains of a few funerary chapels were discovered at the site, containing multiple burials.[57] The bodies of the deceased were simply laid at the bottom of the pits, wrapped in linen shrouds;[58] their orientation was uniformly to the west, with their heads facing east. Also following the standards of Christian inhumations was the paucity, or frequently complete lack, of funerary goods that accompanied the dead.[59] Bioarchaeological investigations revealed that both male and female individuals were buried at this cemetery and that they consisted not only of young and old adults, but also included infants and children, as well as fetuses.[60] Radiocarbon analysis points to a chronology for the use of the cemetery that ranges

---

51. Volp 2002, 106; Grossmann 2014, 94.
52. Johnson 1997; Bowen 2003b, with relevant bibliography.
53. The evidence from Dakhla has been most recently summarized by Bowen (2019, 375–77). Additional cemeteries were surveyed by the DOP team and identified as Christian in the west half of Dakhla: see Mills 1980, 273–75; Mills 1981, 182–90; Mills 1982, 97–101.
54. For a recent summary of the evidence on Christian burials at Kellis, see Bowen 2022a. On pre-Christian funerary customs at the same site, cf. Hope, McKenzie, and Nuzzolo 2022.
55. Based on an estimate by J. E. Molto (2002, 241).
56. Bowen 2019, 375. The absence of grave stelae is in striking contrast with their abundance at other Christian cemeteries, as attested, for example, at Saqqara: see Lloyd 1979.
57. Birrell 1999, 39, fig. 3; 40; the possibility was raised that these mausolea might have contained family clusters: see, most recently, Dupras et al. 2016, 288.
58. Birrell 1999, 41. Coffins were found in very few instances: see Bowen 2019, 375.
59. Bowen 2019, 375; Birrell 1999, 41.
60. Molto 2002, 243; Bowen 2003b, 178; Bowen 2012a; Dupras et al. 2016, 290–99.

from 100 to 450 CE, therefore allowing that at least some of the burials may have predated the spread of Christianity.⁶¹

Another, smaller cemetery that was in use at Kellis during the fourth century, and undoubtedly identified as Christian, was investigated at the west edge of the site. Within the cemetery, which was surrounded by a mud-brick wall that also enclosed the West Church, archaeologists excavated two monumental stone tombs (labeled West Tombs 1 and 2), as well as nine graves, placed in three clusters to the east of the church.⁶² It has been hypothesized that the eleven bodies found in an underground space below West Tomb 1 (adjacent to West Tomb 2) may have belonged to the same family, perhaps an important one at Kellis.⁶³

A cemetery of about 45 graves, in close proximity to a small village, was identified in 1979 by the DOP survey at El-Muzawwaqa, to the southwest of El-Qasr in the west half of Dakhla.⁶⁴ One tomb was opened and investigated at that time. The cemetery was the object of another survey and test excavation by an Australian mission in 2007, revealing both intact and disturbed burials dug into the bedrock, as well as pits that were never used for interment.⁶⁵ The bodies that were found in the intact graves were oriented east-west and did not contain funerary goods. Pending more extensive investigations, the dating of the cemetery was established to the fourth–fifth centuries, based on numismatic and ceramic evidence that was retrieved on site during the 1979 survey.⁶⁶

Additional Christian burials were identified at Deir Abu Matta, to the southeast of Amheida/Trimithis, at the time of the first DOP survey in 1979–1980,⁶⁷ with additional graves being found and excavated in more recent years.⁶⁸ The tombs are scattered in the area to the north and northwest of the church and in a set of rooms to the west of the basilica. More burials, most of which had been disturbed, were discovered within the church itself; especially intriguing is the fact that they seem to postdate the abandonment of the site, which took place, based on ceramic evidence, between the late sixth and the early seventh century.⁶⁹

The evidence from Dakhla adds to what is known from other Christian cemeteries investigated in Egypt. The best known of these is the necropolis of El-Bagawat, in the Kharga Oasis.⁷⁰ Another cemetery was excavated and published in Saqqara, near the Sacred Animal

---

61. Molto 2002, 243; Stewart, Molto and Reimer 2003, 376; Dupras et al. 2016, 286–88. The early end of the chronological range, and therefore the use of the cemetery before Christianity took hold at Kellis, has been challenged by Bowen (2003b, 168).

62. Hope and McKenzie 1999; Hope 2003, 241–46; 252; Bowen 2003b, 175–77; Bowen 2019, 376, fig. 10; 377. The area of the cemetery surrounded by the wall was of a trapezoidal shape; it measured 40.5 m east-west and to a maximum of 22.5 m north-south.

63. Bowen 2019, 377. Additional burials, identified as Christian, were found in a Kellis tomb (North Tomb 1), which, because of its decoration, must have originally been used by non-Christian villagers: see Hope 2003, 247–64; Bowen 2003b, 177–78; Bowen 2019, 377.

64. The village and the cemetery were classified as "Christian period sites" and labeled 33/390-I7-1 and 33/390-I7-2 respectively: see Mills 1979, 182.

65. Bowen 2008, 11–13, figs. 3–4.

66. Bowen 2008, 11; Bowen 2010, 19.

67. Mills 1981, 185.

68. Bowen 2012b.

69. Bowen 2019, 377.

70. For an essential bibliography, see Sec. 2.3, n. 100.

necropolis.⁷¹ In recent decades, fieldwork was carried out at more cemeteries identified as Christian, such as the "West Cemetery" at El-Deir and a necropolis at Dush, both in Kharga, and another at Fag el-Gamus, in the Fayyum.⁷²

Common patterns can be identified in funerary customs of the Christian period in Egypt, based on the data gathered in Dakhla and at the other cemeteries mentioned above.⁷³ These include: bodies wrapped in shrouds (or clothes) and lying supine at the bottom of a pit, with their head to the west (facing east);⁷⁴ comparatively few instances of coffins being used; minimal treatment of bodies; general paucity, or total lack, of funerary goods associated with the human remains;⁷⁵ burial pits dug into the ground, sometimes sealed with simple mud-brick structures. Generally, this evidence is consistent among Christian cemeteries excavated in the *chora* (countryside), thus pointing to the widespread adoption of very similar customs throughout Egypt, including the more remote region of the Western Desert.

2.2. Documentary Evidence from Amheida

The archaeological evidence for Christianity in Dakhla, as presented above, makes it abundantly clear that large segments of the local population had embraced Christianity by the early fourth century. The fact that purpose-built churches in a basilica style were built at that time, as attested, for example, at Kellis, also points to a well-established Christian presence in the oasis. Therefore, it does not seem unreasonable to assume that Christianity began spreading in the region even before then, also on the basis of third-century evidence for Christianity in nearby Kharga.⁷⁶

While the body of archaeological data on fourth-century Christianity in Dakhla (as well as in Kharga) is substantial, the picture offered by the contemporary papyrological sources

---

71. Publications include Lloyd 1979; Martin 1974; Martin 1981, esp. 69–87; Jeffreys and Strouhal 1980.

72. On the Christian cemetery at El-Deir, see Dunand, Coudert and Letellier-Willemin 2008; Coudert 2012; Dunand, Heim, and Lichtenberg 2012; Dunand 2019; Letellier-Willemin 2019. Cf. also Dunand and Letellier-Willemin 2019, 246–51. On the Christian cemetery at Dush, located about 800 m from the traditional necropolis, see Dunand et al. 2005, 4–6. See now Dunand et al. 2023 (which was published after this book was completed). On Fag el-Gamus, see, most recently, Pierce and Jensen 2020, including Ch. 15 for a full list of publications. This list is not exhaustive, as more Christian cemeteries are known from other Egyptian sites, e.g., Bawit, Antinoopolis, and Lycopolis.

73. Bowen 2019, 375. See also, most recently, Muhlestein and Fairbairn 2020 on the general features of Christian burials excavated at Fag el-Gamus.

74. On the east-west orientation of the bodies, and its possible significance, see Sec. 5.5, esp. pp. 339–40.

75. This is not always the case; there is evidence of grave goods, including beads, vessels, and jewelry, found in Christian cemeteries, e.g., in West Tomb 1 at Kellis; see Hope and McKenzie 1999, 56. Other examples of Christian burials containing funerary goods are attested at Kharga (in the necropolis of El-Bagawat; see Hauser 1932, 44–49 and, more recently, Kajitani 2006, particularly on textiles) and in the Fayyum (at Fag el-Gamus; see Muhlestein and Fairbairn 2020, 124–26; see also Muhlestein, Christensen, and Fairbairn 2020 about the intriguing discovery of "punched" vessels in some graves and Smith, Muhlestein, and Christensen 2020 on textiles and jewelry).

76. Choat 2020, 80–82.

is certainly less rich, but not entirely lacking.[77] In this regard, M. Choat provided insightful comments on documentary sources about the spread of Christianity at Kellis. In particular, he maintains that there is no solid ground to argue for a third-century dating of such evidence and that, even considering the documentary sources datable to the early fourth century, it is archaeology that, overall, provides a clearer picture of the flourishing of Christianity in Egypt's Western Desert.[78]

With regard to Amheida/Trimithis, excavations at the site revealed the rich and intriguing picture of an urbanized and sophisticated society, which had widely adopted not just the Greek language, but also Graeco-Roman literary and artistic tropes, as well as Classical educational models, customs, and habits. Thus, it was a society that was, and must have felt, very much connected with the wider Mediterranean world of late antiquity, notwithstanding the geographical remoteness of Dakhla. What seemed rather puzzling by the early 2010s, however, was that even after a few years of extensive investigations at the site, no archaeological evidence had yet been detected of churches or any other sort of Christian places of cult at Amheida. Indeed, the paucity, or rather complete lack, of such evidence, contrasted with the fact that, as is amply discussed above in Chapter 1, Trimithis was a large and important city of the oasis in the late Roman period. It was this baffling situation that gave the Amheida team the impetus to investigate Area 2.3 at the site, leading to the discovery of the fourth-century church.[79]

It should be remarked, however, that some documentary evidence was already available at the time of the discovery of the church, pointing to the existence of a Christian community at Amheida in the fourth century. This is not especially surprising, considering the evidence, both archaeological and documentary, that was collected at other contemporary sites in the oasis. R. S. Bagnall and R. Cribiore recently published this material, which, albeit not particularly abundant, significantly adds to our knowledge on early Christianity at Amheida.[80] This evidence comes primarily from the area where a temple once stood. It consists largely of ostraka with titles of members of the clergy (*presbyteroi*, i.e., priests, and deacons) and several names that can be unequivocally understood as Christian, such as Paulos and Timotheos.[81] To these, one can also add biblical names like Moses and Jonah.[82] One ostrakon (*O.Trim.* 2.819), found on the temple hill and dated to the fourth century, is a list of names that are both traditionally Christian and non-Christian; what is of particular interest is the use, at the beginning of the first

---

77. Choat 2020, 82.

78. Onomastic evidence may allow for the possibility—not yet proven beyond doubt—that individuals with typically Christian names may have lived at Kellis already in the late third century: see Choat 2020, 83–85, commenting on Bowen 2003b, 173–74.

79. Cf. Sec. 3.1.

80. Bagnall and Cribiore 2012; Bagnall and Cribiore 2015.

81. Bagnall and Cribiore 2015, 131. Five ostraka were found that contain the title of deacon, while two include that of priest: see Bagnall and Cribiore 2012, 409. On onomastics as evidence for the Christianization of Egypt, see Bagnall 1982; Bagnall 1993, 280–81; Choat 2006, 51–56; Blumell 2012, 237–79; and Choat 2020, 83. Based on Bagnall's approach, Bowen (2003b, 173–74) looked at onomastic evidence from Kellis, estimating the existence of a Christian community at the village from the mid-third century.

82. On the adoption of biblical names by early Christians, see Bagnall 1982, 110.

Fig. 2.8: Block from the temple area at Amheida, bearing a Greek inscription with a dedication to Ammon (infrared photograph by B. Bazzani).

line, of the term ὁ πατήρ (father), which Bagnall and Cribiore associate with an ecclesiastical or monastic environment.[83]

The most remarkable piece of evidence is a dipinto found on a limestone block, which was originally part of a cavetto cornice and was found in the area of the temple (4.1) in 2005 (fig. 2.8).[84] In the middle of this stone element someone wrote a Greek verse, which reads (in English): "Great Ammon is the pilot of the life of men."[85] As pointed out by Bagnall and Cribiore, this verse is a fitting representation of the syncretism, so widely attested in Egypt, that combines Greek literary traditions and Egyptian religious beliefs.[86] What is especially significant is that above this line someone added a few words. In particular, it seems that above the name Ammon, this person wrote *ete pnoute*, which is Coptic for "who is the Lord." Bagnall and Cribiore convincingly argue that this was subsequently added as a gloss, to suggest that it was the Christian God, and not Ammon, who was the true pilot of life.[87]

---

83. See Bagnall and Cribiore 2012, 411; Bagnall and Cribiore 2015, 135; cf. also Ast and Bagnall 2016, 256–57. An ostrakon from Kellis (*O.Kellis* 120) also contains the word πατήρ, in this case following a proper name, but, as the editor pointed out, it is unknown how the term should be understood: see Worp 2004, 110.

84. Inv. 3053.

85. ἀνθρώπων βιότοιο κυβερνήτης μέγας Ἄμμων

86. Bagnall and Cribiore 2015, 131.

87. Bagnall and Cribiore 2015, 133.

An additional piece of evidence consists of a graffito on a stone bearing the name of Horigenes, son of Ioannes. Horigenes is not, *per se*, a Christian name: indeed, it derives from the Egyptian god Horus. However, it was the name of a well-known Christian theologian from Alexandria. Ioannes, on the other hand, is certainly related to a Christian environment.[88]

In sum, these textual sources paint the picture of an active Christian presence at Amheida by the third quarter of the fourth century, which fully supports, in chronological terms, the information gathered during the excavation of the church in Area 2.3.

2.3. Early Christian Sites and Monuments in Kharga

A wealth of archaeological evidence on early Christianity is available from Kharga Oasis, located to the east of Dakhla and sharing strong ties with it in antiquity (fig. 2.9).[89] The remarkably rich heritage of Christian monuments in Kharga points to the existence of flourishing Christian communities in the oasis well before the Arab conquest.[90] Churches, monasteries, and cemeteries surveyed and/or excavated in Kharga unequivocally speak to the profound impact that Christian art and architecture had on the environment of that oasis.

The most important administrative center of Kharga in antiquity was Hibis, which was also the capital of the Great Oasis.[91] Hibis is located in the northern half of the oasis, at the crossroads of caravan routes that once connected the Nile Valley with numerous settlements of Egypt's Western Desert, including Dakhla, and beyond.[92] Not much is known, in terms of archaeological evidence, about the city in antiquity.[93] The best preserved remains at Hibis are those of a temple, dedicated to Amun-Ra, which was constructed in the Late Period and underwent additions in the Persian, Ptolemaic, and Roman periods.[94] Following the abandonment of the temple, a church was erected in the fourth century against the northeast corner of the complex, within its *temenos* wall (fig. 2.10). The church incorporated still-standing walls of the temple, with additional features being added that were largely built with reused materials.[95]

---

88. Bagnall and Cribiore 2015, 131.

89. For an introduction to Kharga, see Vivian 2008, 117–72. Bagnall and Tallet 2019 is a study of the two oases in antiquity; cf. especially Ch. 5 on the administrative history of the region, attesting to the links between Dakhla and Kharga. See now also Dunand and Lichtenberg 2024 (published after the completion of this book).

90. See Bagnall and Rathbone 2004, 249–61 for a summary of the archaeological evidence on Kharga in the Graeco-Roman and late antique periods.

91. See Bagnall and Tallet 2019, esp. 83–100.

92. Winlock 1941, 1–2; Vivian 2008, 118, 128–29; Paprocki 2019, 218–33, 240–50, 257–63; Ikram 2019.

93. Lythgoe 1908b, 208.

94. The temple was excavated by a team of the Metropolitan Museum of Art in the early 20th century and comprehensively reinvestigated in the 1980s by E. Cruz-Uribe; see Winlock 1941; Cruz-Uribe 1986; 1987.

95. For a brief description of the church, see Winlock 1941, 45–47, pl. LII. Cf. also, more recently, Ghica 2012, 195–97.

Chapter 2: Early Christianity in the Great Oasis

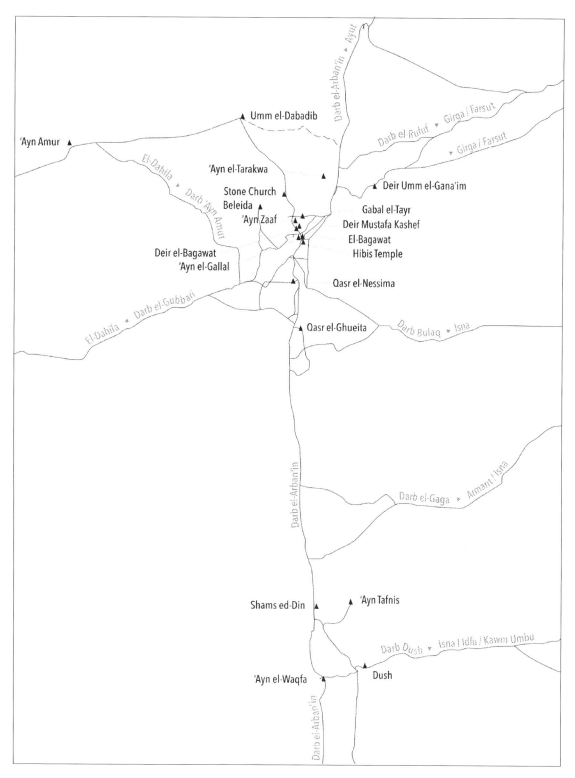

Fig. 2.9: Map of Kharga Oasis showing the location of early Christian sites (after Ghica 2012, 196, fig. 1; tracing by C. Fosen).

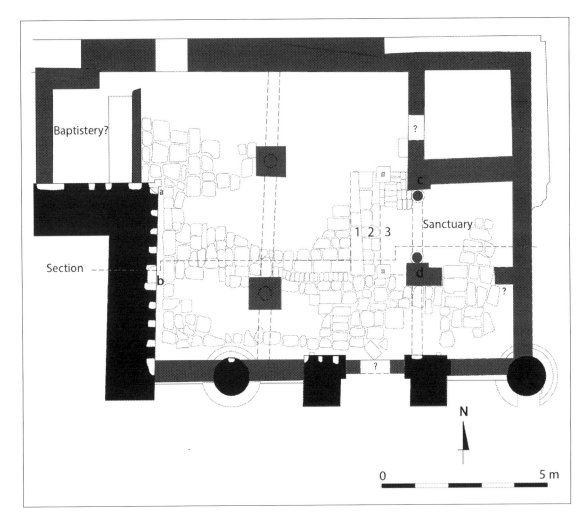

Fig. 2.10: Plan of the church in the temple of Hibis, Kharga Oasis (after Winlock 1941, pl. LII; tracing by C. Fosen).

The church was oriented east-west and had a tripartite sanctuary at its east end, with a rectangular apse flanked by two small square rooms.[96]

To the northeast of the Hibis temple is the site of ʿAin el-Turba, where Egypt's Supreme Council of Antiquities discovered in 2007 the remains, still unpublished, of a small mud-brick church (fig. 2.11). The building is oriented east-west and divided into a central nave and two side aisles by means of two colonnades, with low mud-brick *mastabas* lining the internal walls.[97] The colonnades ended, at their east ends, with engaged pillars framing a semicircular apse, in front of which were also two columns. The apse is flanked by two service rooms to the north and south; facing the sanctuary, at the east end of the nave, is a raised rectangular platform. The

---

96. The rectangular apse is attested in other fourth-century churches at Shams el-Din and Dush (in Kharga), as well as in the church of ʿAin el-Sabil and, likely, the church at Amheida (in Dakhla).

97. Ghica 2012, 197–99; Warner 2018a, 482, fig. 411/D.

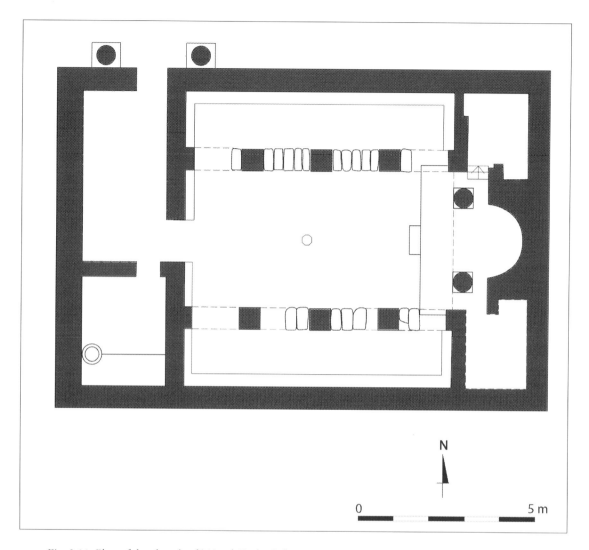

Fig. 2.11: Plan of the church of ʿAin el-Turba (after Warner 2018a, 484, fig. 412; tracing by C. Fosen).

only entrance into the church (built in the middle of the west wall) connected the basilica with a narthex that opened, in turn, to the north via a monumental doorway framed by columns.[98] Worthy of note is the octagonal stone base lying in the middle of the nave, interpreted by V. Ghica as part of an altar and alternatively by Warner as possibly the base of a lectern.[99]

Surely the best-known site from the Christian period in Kharga, and the one with the most dramatic visual impact over the oasis landscape, is the large cemetery of El-Bagawat (fig.

98. Warner 2018a, 485.
99. Warner 2018a, 490–91; Ghica 2012, 199.

Fig. 2.12: The Christian necropolis at El-Bagawat (photograph by author).

2.12).[100] The necropolis is in close proximity to Hibis and served as the burial ground for its inhabitants during late antiquity. The cemetery includes about 300 mausolea, including small tombs with one funerary chamber up to very complex, multi-room structures with finely ornamented chapels.[101] Additionally, numerous pit graves, dug into the ground and sealed with simple mud-brick superstructures marking their location, were found scattered among the mausolea.[102] This may suggest that the area was used for the interment of individuals of different social status and economic means. Based chiefly on numismatic evidence, the earliest phase of the cemetery was dated to the early fourth century.[103] No buildings were found at El-Bagawat that can be indisputably identified as churches.[104] A large rectangular building (no. 180) located in the middle of the cemetery was identified, in past scholarship, as a church, based on its monumentality, east-west orientation, and tripartite layout that is suggestive of a basilica

---

100. The necropolis was investigated by a mission of the Metropolitan Museum of Art at the beginning of the twentieth century and only partially published; see Lythgoe 1908a, 85–86; Lythgoe 1908b; Hauser 1932. For a more comprehensive discussion of the cemetery, see Fakhry 1951 and, more recently, Cipriano 2008 and Hadji-Minaglou 2020. Cf. also Zibawi 2003; 2005 (on the painted decoration of the funerary chapels).

101. Fakhry (1951) recorded 263 mausolea; in more recent years, a team of the IFAO identified 36 additional structures: cf. Ghica 2012, 192, n24.

102. Lythgoe 1908b, 203, 208, fig. 7. See also Cipriano 2008, 55–65.

103. Bowen 2010, 20, after Wilkinson 1928, 36. G. Cipriano (2008, 85–124) divided the history of the site into three phases, lasting from the fourth century (or possibly the end of the third) to the end of the fifth or beginning of the sixth century. See also Bowen 2010, 23, n. 38; Warner 2018a, 481. Although El-Bagawat was no longer in use as a cemetery after the early sixth century, there is epigraphical evidence suggesting that the site was still visited, for devotional purposes, until the seventh century: see Cipriano 2008, 125–30.

104. Some funerary chapels, such as nos. 24–25 (which belong to a monumental complex also including mausolea 23 and 26–29), as well as chapels 9, 66, and 90, were interpreted by Grossmann (1991b, 326) not merely as spaces used for funerary rituals, but also ones that served as standard churches. Apart from apparent typological similarities, the evidence is not conclusive on this matter; in general, these chapels are rather to be seen as structures associated with funerary practices in the context of family mausolea (Cipriano 2008, 49, 71–73).

Fig. 2.13: View (to northeast) of building 180 at El-Bagawat (photograph by author).

(fig. 2.13).¹⁰⁵ The edifice, inside of which no burials were found, was surrounded by a portico and contained mud-brick sigmoid benches, or *stibadia*, which were likely used for funerary meals in memory of the deceased.¹⁰⁶ The proximity of building 180 to many individual graves in the northern part of the necropolis allows for a suggestive hypothesis, i.e., that it might have been used for commemoration rituals by families whose deceased relatives were buried in simple tombs not associated with private or family mausolea.¹⁰⁷

The settlements of Deir Mustafa Kashef and of ʿAin Zaaf East, located to the northwest of the necropolis of El-Bagawat, offer significant evidence attesting to the efflorescence of Christian communities, in particular ascetic ones, in Kharga during the fourth and fifth centuries.¹⁰⁸ The monastic complex, and pilgrimage site, at Deir Mustafa Kashef lies on the side

---

105. This interpretation was first advanced after the partial exploration carried out by an American mission in 1930–1931: see Hauser 1932, 40. See also the discussion in Cipriano 2008, 74–83, esp. n. 152 on earlier interpretations of the building; 91–95 on its possible dating.

106. On the lack of burials inside the building, see Hauser 1932, 40.

107. Cipriano 2008, 79. As mentioned by the author, the condition of these burials does not allow us to know if they had once been paired with tables for offerings.

108. Müller-Wiener 1963; Vivian 2008, 141; Bagnall and Rathbone 2004, 253–54.

of a hill. It is surrounded by high and thick walls, clearly defensive in nature,[109] and comprises a church and numerous rooms, organized on different levels. Another complex, sometimes referred to as Deir el-Bagawat, is visible in the plain further west (fig. 2.14). It includes a church with a single nave that is (quite unusually) oriented north-south, broadside to the apse, with mud-brick benches lining its four walls.[110]

The remains discovered at ʿAin Zaaf East, located one kilometer to the north of Deir Mustafa Kashef, at the foot of a hill dotted with tombs, seemingly belonged to a monastery as well (fig. 2.15). A church was found in the northwestern corner of the excavated area, revealing different phases of construction and alterations. The original basilica consisted of a nave and side aisles, separated by means of two rows of columns and placed laterally to the semicircular apse at the east end of the church. At a later time, the east aisle was turned into a *khurus* (a room separating the sanctuary from the rest of the church) with three passages.[111] In a subsequent phase, the *khurus* and the apse seem to have been separated from the rest of the church and used as a chapel.[112]

Remains of a settlement, whose size and nature are yet to be determined, were investigated to the west of ʿAin Zaaf East.[113] The rather well-preserved ruins of a church lie in the southeast corner of this area (named ʿAin Zaaf West). The church is oriented east-west and consists of a nave without side aisles; a semi-circular apse is placed on axis with the nave at its east end (fig. 2.16).[114] The only entrance, located along the north wall, once connected the church with an adjoining anteroom. Noteworthy is also that the apse was built inside the room, against the east wall and not protruding onto the exterior.[115]

The wealth of data on early Christian monasticism in the region of Hibis and El-Bagawat was further enriched by the discovery of two monastic sites at ʿAin el-Gallal (North and South),

---

109. Ghica 2012, 200.

110. The complex was excavated by Egypt's Supreme Council of Antiquities. According to Ghica (2012, 204), the church showcases features suggestive of a monastic use of the building, which may have doubled as a gathering hall for monks.

111. Around the end of the seventh/beginning of the eighth century according to Ghica (2012, 222).

112. Ghica 2012, 222. The sites of ʿAin Zaaf East (and West, discussed below) were excavated by Egypt's Supreme Council of Antiquities; the results await publication.

113. Ghica 2012, 224–27.

114. Although the internal space of the church is not partitioned by colonnades, a partially preserved column lies in the middle of the nave in its west half: see Ghica 2012, 225, fig. 12, 227. Warner (2018a, 485, fig. 414, 490) compared the features with the stone base in the middle of the church at ʿAin el-Turba possibly associated with a lectern.

115. Warner 2018a, 485, fig. 414. The construction of the apse inside the room reflects the kind of alterations that were carried out in the early fourth-century Small East Church at Kellis, in Dakhla Oasis: see Bowen 2003a. According to Ghica (2012, 227), the apse of the church at ʿAin Zaaf West was originally rectangular and the partition wall separating the sanctuary from the nave was contemporary with it, therefore predating the construction of the semicircular apse.

Fig. 2.14: View (to south) of the monastic complex of Deir Mustafa Kashef (left) in relation to Deir el-Bagawat (right) (photograph by author).

Fig. 2.15: View (to southeast) of the church and monastic complex of ʿAin Zaaf East (photograph by author).

located about 1.5 km to the south of Deir el-Bagawat (fig. 2.17).[116] A church was identified in each sector. The one at ʿAin el-Gallal North is oriented east-west, but the nave (without

---

116. Ghica 2012, 206–10. The site was investigated by a team of Egypt's Supreme Council of Antiquities in the mid-1990s and in the early 2000s. According to Ghica (2012, 206; 210), the two areas investigated at ʿAin el-Gallal North and South are sectors of the same monastic complex, whose foundation may be traced back to the fourth-fifth centuries. They may have served different functions, with the north area perhaps used as a *xenodocheion* (a space to host pilgrims) and the south sector housing the monks.

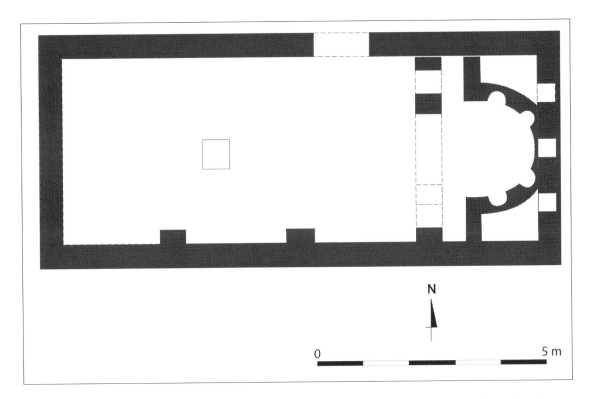

Fig. 2.16: Plan of the church of 'Ain Zaaf West (after Warner 2018a, 485, fig. 414; tracing by C. Fosen).

side aisles), originally vaulted, is not on axis with the east apse; rather, it is placed broadside to it.[117] The apse is flanked, to the north and south, by two rectangular *pastophoria*, which open directly onto the nave. The church was once accessible via two doorways placed in the southwest and northwest corners; the latter opened, in turn, onto an anteroom or narthex.[118] The church in the south sector is also oriented east-west and has a common tripartite layout, with a nave and two side aisles created by two colonnades and a semicircular apse at its east end.[119] The area of the sanctuary is separated from the nave by mud-brick *cancelli* (screens) and its entrance is framed by two small columns.[120] Access to the church was from the south, where a doorway led onto a narthex that ended with a semicircular apse against its north side.[121]

117. As in the church of 'Ain Zaaf East and at Deir el-Bagawat: cf. Warner 2018a, 483–84.
118. Ghica 2012, 208, n87. Another remarkable feature that was discovered at 'Ain el-Gallal North is a circular baptistery, free-standing rather than being sunk into the ground. An intriguing question is for whom this baptistery was intended in a monastic environment: cf. Ghica 2012, 208–9.
119. Puzzlingly, the south colonnade is made of square pillars, while the north one consists of round columns, except for piers at its east and west ends: see Warner 2018a, 485–86. The westernmost piers of both colonnades are engaged against the west wall of the church.
120. Square engaged pillars also framed the north and south ends of the conch, creating, together with the small columns, monumental openings onto spaces to the north and south: cf. Warner 2018a, 484, fig. 412.
121. As remarked by Warner (2018a, 485), the narthex is a widely attested feature in early Egyptian churches, although it is less common in the known examples from the Western Desert.

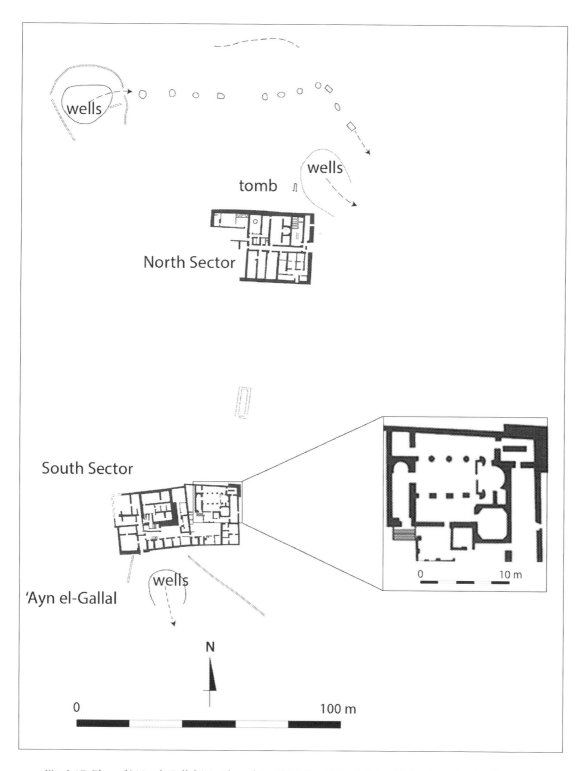

Fig. 2.17: Plan of ʿAin el-Gallal (North and South) (after Ghica 2012, 207, fig. 6; tracing by C. Fosen).

The north aisle opened onto small rooms at both its east and west ends; the south aisle led (to the east) onto a narrow *pastophorion*, accessible also from the apse, and a squarish, domed room against the southeast corner of the room.

A previously unknown church was identified and surveyed in 2011 at the north edge of Wadi Bagawat.[122] The church is oriented east-west and is of a small size. It comprises one nave, with no side aisles, and ends with a tripartite sanctuary built against the east wall. The sanctuary consists of a centrally placed elliptical apse, pierced by two niches and flanked, to the north and south, by rectangular *pastophoria* that open directly onto the nave. The church, which had a flat roof and was originally accessed via a doorway in the southwest corner, still shows evidence of windows along its walls.[123] The building was labeled the "Stone Church" because it is, quite remarkably, the only known church in the region to have been built of limestone rubble instead of the usual mudbrick.[124]

Additional evidence of early Christian architecture in the north part of the oasis was found at the sites of Umm el-Dabadib and 'Ain el-Tarakwa, surveyed in 2003–2004 by the North Kharga Oasis Survey (NKOS).[125] At Umm el-Dabadib the unexcavated remains of a fourth-century church are visible at the east end of a fortified settlement, clustered around a late Roman fort.[126] The church, as reconstructed by N. Warner (and, before him, by D. Arnold, who visited the site in 1978), is oriented east-west and is divided into a central nave and two side aisles of unequal width (fig. 2.18a).[127] The apse at the east end of the church was rounded and decorated with niches and engaged pilasters. It was accessed from the nave by means of a raised rectangular step and was framed by two square pillars.[128] These were in line with the north and south colonnades and were built against two columns, which were architecturally framed by two round walls flanking the apse.[129] To the north of the latter was a service room, accessible directly from the north aisle.[130]

The ancient settlement of 'Ain el-Tarakwa, located to the southeast of Umm el-Dabadib, hosts the remains of a mud-brick church, possibly dated to the fourth century, that was built

---

122. For a plan, see Warner 2018a, fig. 415.
123. Warner 2018a, 485; 488–89.
124. Warner 2018a, 481.
125. The survey was carried out, from 2001 to 2007, under the directorship of C. Rossi and S. Ikram. For a comprehensive presentation of the results of the survey, see, most recently, Rossi and Ikram 2018.
126. Rossi and Ikram 2018, 225–51. The village was abandoned towards the end of the fourth century, but a Christian monastic presence is attested during the fifth century, possibly at the site and certainly in its proximity. According to Rossi and Ikram (2002, 144b), the Roman fort at Umm el-Dabadib, as well as others in the region, may have been reused as monasteries in late antiquity. On a nearby cave dwelling, perhaps used as a Christian hermitage, see Rossi and Ikram 2006, 292–93, 300–1; Rossi and Ikram 2018, 268–71.
127. Warner 2018c. An additional column located between the western ends of the colonnades once formed a return aisle: Warner 2018a, 486; Warner 2018c, 239.
128. Screens separating the nave from the sanctuary may have been built between these pilasters: see Warner 2018a, 490.
129. It seems that the pilasters belong to a later construction episode than the round columns framing the apse: see Warner 2018c, 240.
130. The north aisle also opened onto a small rectangular room at its west end. It is not known if another *pastophorion* was symmetrically placed to the south of the apse.

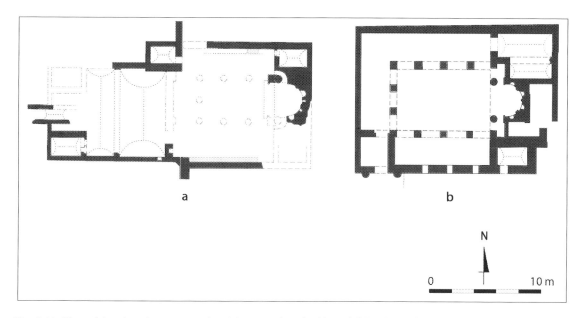

Fig. 2.18: Plan of the churches surveyed at (a) Umm el-Dabadib and (b) at ʿAin el-Tarakwa (after Warner 2018a, 484, fig. 412; tracing by C. Fosen).

inside the enclosure of a temple and blocked its *dromos* (fig. 2.18b).[131] The church, which shares strong similarities with that at Umm el-Dabadib,[132] is oriented east-west and has a basilica plan with a central nave separated from two side aisles by means of two colonnades. Two pillars, placed between the western ends of the two colonnades, form a west return aisle. The latter runs across the north aisle and the nave, but not the south aisle. The southwest corner of the church is occupied by a small square room that must have functioned as a vestibule; indeed, it was through this space that one would have accessed the church in antiquity. A rounded apse lies at the east end of the building. It is pierced by four niches with round tops, alternating with two engaged pilasters and an embedded column. The entrance of the apse was once monumentally framed by two columns, placed next to L-shaped spaces that might have led to *pastophoria* to the north and south.[133] There is evidence to suggest that the church was covered by a flat roof, perhaps higher above the central nave where it may have been furnished with a clerestory.[134]

Archaeological evidence for early Christianity also exists in the southern half of Kharga Oasis, albeit less abundant than in the northern half. Excavations conducted by a French mission of the Institut français d'archéologie orientale at the town of Dush (ancient Kysis) revealed traces of Christian presence at the site.[135] The extensive remains of the temple of Isis and Serapis

---

131. Warner 2018a, 483. On the dating of the church, see also Ghica 2012, 213.
132. Warner 2018c, 347; Warner 2018a.
133. Warner 2018c, 346; not visible in the plan. As remarked by Warner, excavation is needed to clarify the spatial relationship of the rooms to the north and south of the apse.
134. Warner 2018c, 346. Windows were also detected piercing the south wall of the church: see Warner 2018a, 488.
135. Bonnet 2004, 75–86.

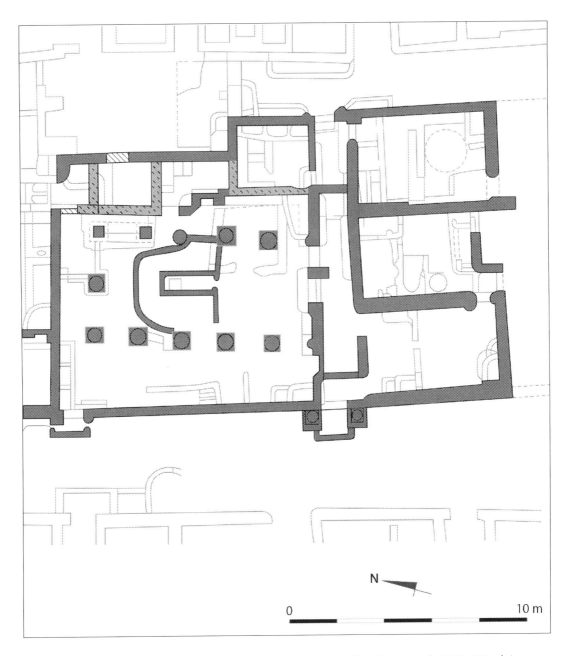

Fig. 2.19: Plan of the church of Dush (after Bonnet 2004, 83, fig. 68d; tracing by K. DeMondo).

show traces of alterations, carried out in antiquity, that are possibly associated with a refunctionalization of the temple as a church. A church was also found to the east of the temple; it seems to have been erected, during the fourth century, within preexisting structures (fig. 2.19). The northwest–southeast orientation, slightly slanted in comparison with the street running along the west side, may have been dictated by the existence of a staircase at the northeast corner.[136] The church was originally divided into a nave and two side aisles by two rows of columns; it had a return aisle along the northwest side and ended, at the opposite end, in a long, rectangular room that was interpreted as a choir.[137] This space was accessible from the nave via a monumental double-doorway flanked by two engaged columns. The choir was possibly vaulted and contained mud-brick benches;[138] an opening near its southwest corner connected this room with an annex and, through it, the exterior.[139]

A few kilometers to the northwest of Dush, French archaeologists discovered the remains of a fourth-century basilica at Shams el-Din (figs. 2.20–21).[140] Notwithstanding a different orientation, the church is typologically close to that found at Dush.[141] Indeed, it shows similar proportions and the same partition into central nave and side aisles, plus the west return aisle.[142] The sanctuary of the church at Shams el-Din consists of a rectangular apse framed by two engaged columns. The apse opens onto the nave via a platform, with steps built along its west side, and is flanked by two *pastophoria* to the north and south.[143]

Similarities were established between the church of Shams el-Din and another one found by the IFAO at Qasr el-Nessima, south of modern-day Kharga town.[144] This church, oriented east-west and of relatively small dimensions (9.5 by 7 m), is located at the south end of the village. The apse is circular (not rectangular, as in the church of Shams el-Din) and is slightly shifted southward, rather than being centrally placed along the east side of the church. It is framed by engaged pillars and separated from the rest of the church by means of two *cancelli*. A late fourth/early fifth century date was suggested for the foundation of this church.[145]

---

136. Bonnet 2004, 78.
137. Bonnet 2004, 78.
138. Mud-brick benches also lined up the interior walls of the main room.
139. A smaller opening, located at the northwest corner and opening onto the west aisle, was possibly used by the congregation. Additional rooms to the east and southeast of the church must have belonged to the same ecclesiastical complex, although their exact function is unknown.
140. Sauneron 1976, 410–11; Wagner 1987, 182–83; Bonnet 2004, 84, figs. 69–72; Vivian 2005, 84. An article on recent excavations at the church of Shams el-Din (Ghica et al. 2023) was published after this book was completed.
141. Bonnet 2004, 81. The church of Shams el-Din follows the common east-west orientation.
142. Like many other Christian places of cult, the church of Shams el-Din once opened onto a set of interconnected rooms, in addition to an exterior courtyard with benches and graffiti.
143. Based on the available plan, it seems that, at least in the latest phase of the building's life, only the south room opened onto both the apse and the nave.
144. Wagner 1991; Ghica 2012, 217–21.
145. Ghica 2012, 219.

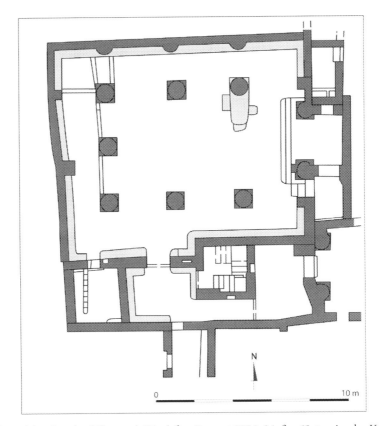

Fig. 2.20: Plan of the church of Shams el-Din (after Bonnet 2004, 84, fig. 69; tracing by K. DeMondo).

Fig. 2.21: View (to east) of the church of Shams el-Din (photograph by author).

Chapter 3

Area 2.3: The Church

3.1. The Excavation of Building 7

In 2012 archaeological investigation was carried out in Area 2.3, located toward the east end of the surveyed remains of Amheida, roughly half-way between the north and south edges (fig. 1.4).[1] Although archaeological evidence of buildings is lacking in Area 5 (to the east of Area 2), it is not possible to know for certain if the current eastern border of the site roughly corresponds to that of the fourth-century *polis*. Magnetometric surveys were conducted along the east boundary of the site during the 2005 and 2006 seasons by T. N. Smekalova and S. Smekalov.[2] Unfortunately, the results did not provide significant information on the built environment in this area, due to the minimal differences in magnetic properties between mudbricks and sand.[3] Nevertheless, an archaeological survey revealed a considerable number of ceramic fragments lying on the surface to the east of the church.[4] The presence of ceramic fragments, which had likely been used as chinking sherds or had been left behind when the site was abandoned, points to the likely existence of houses or other types of buildings in this area, which largely disappeared subsequently due to wind erosion and/or human intervention.[5] However, full-scale excavations are needed to prove this hypothesis beyond doubt.

Excavation focused on the top of a mound that grants an unobstructed view (likely also in antiquity) over extensive portions of the ancient city. The main goal was to investigate a large building (designated building 7/B7) that had been mapped a few years earlier during a topographical survey of Amheida.[6] At that time, numerous features were documented that, on the basis of comparative evidence from other sites in Dakhla and Kharga, pointed to a preliminary

---

1. For an introduction to the excavation of the church, see Aravecchia 2015a.
2. The reports of the magnetometric and electrical conductivity surveys are available online via NYU's Faculty Digital Archive at http://hdl.handle.net/2451/71598 (2005) and http://hdl.handle.net/2451/71599 (2006)
3. Davoli 2019, 49.
4. As shown in Davoli 2019, 48 (fig. 4.2).
5. On surface potsherds surveyed at Amheida, see Davoli 2019, 51.
6. The survey, which was carried out by Fabio Congedo and Valentino De Santis, is available online at http://hdl.handle.net/2451/71600.

Fig. 3.1: Aerial view (to southwest) of the church before excavation began.

identification of this space as a church. In fact, most architectural features of building 7 were already visible—although heavily eroded—at present-day ground level before excavation was undertaken (fig. 3.1).

Building 7 consists of a rectangular room (room 1) that once opened onto a set of three roughly square spaces (14–16)[7] to the east and an annex (rooms 5–12) to the south and southeast (fig. 3.2). A large rectangular space lies to the east of rooms 14–16; it remains unexcavated and its relationship with the rest of building 7 is unknown.[8] Most features of the complex, especially in its west half, suffered from severe wind erosion and/or destruction. Only one cluster of partially collapsed walls (later designated as room 7) was standing at some height above the ground, to the south of a large rectangular space that was labeled as room 1.[9]

7. Numbers 14–16 were artificially assigned to three spaces (now completely or almost disappeared) at the east end of building 7 and likely serving as an apse (room 15) and two side rooms or *pastophoria* (rooms 14 and 16). Rooms 2–4 are the underground crypts below rooms 14–16 respectively.

8. On the three spaces to the east of room 1, see Sec. 3.5 and Ch. 5. For a discussion of the south annex (rooms 5–12), as well as of the large room (courtyard?) at the east end of building 7, see Ch. 4.

9. The existence of buildings that stand at a considerable height in apparent isolation, seemingly defying easy explanation, considering the destruction caused by men and/or natural elements, can be witnessed throughout the site. This phenomenon is quite baffling and the reasons behind it are still being discussed. On the present (and constantly changing) condition of the archaeological remains at the site, in relation to the region's natural landscape, see Davoli 2015. On environmental deflation at Amheida, from the Pharaonic to the Roman period, see Bravard et al. 2016. On the common occurrences of sand accumulation and deflation in Dakhla, cf. also McDonald et al. 2001.

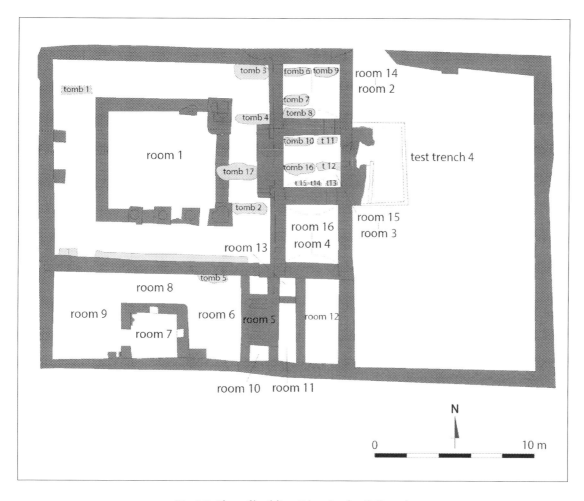

Fig. 3.2: Plan of building 7 (tracing by C. Fosen).

3.2. Room 1

Features

Room 1 measures ca. 12 m north-south by 13.65 m east-west) (figs. 3.3–4). It is poorly preserved, especially on its west side, where only the foundations of the west external wall (F14) and of the west colonnade foundation wall (F8) are extant (fig. 3.5). Features above floor level survive only in the east half of the room, to a height no greater than roughly 0.75 m in the southeast corner (F13).

Fig. 3.3: Aerial view (to northeast) of the church at the end of the 2012 season.

F15 is the north wall of room 1. It is best preserved at its east end and slopes down westwards.[10] Looking at the preserved top of the wall, it seems that its north face, which is yet to be investigated, was hacked out near the wall's east end, where it is abutted by wall F1.[11] The latter runs north-south and separates room 1 from rooms 14–16 (and 2–4 below them) to the east (fig. 3.6). It is preserved to its maximum height at its southern end, while it is in very poor condition towards its northern end (fig. 3.7).[12] A ledge juts out 8 cm from the west face of wall F1, at an elevation of 140.175 m.[13] Above the ledge are up to eight preserved courses of mudbricks in English bond. A coating of white gypsum plaster is still visible, mostly in the part between the south end of the stepped platform (F19, see below) and an opening located toward the south end of the wall.

---

10. Upper elevation: 140.690 m; lower elevation: 140.100 m (both elevations taken at the east end of the wall). For more elevations (taken within test trench 2), as well as a detailed description of the wall's south face, see Sec. 3.3.2 below. The south face was also exposed, at its east end, within the north crypt (room 2): see Sec. 5.2 below.

11. Upper elevation: 141.280 m; lower elevation: 139.425 m (a lower elevation was recorded in burial pit F31 of tomb 3: see Sec. 3.4 below).

12. Portions of the wall's west face, below floor level, were exposed in burial cuts F31 and F33 (in tombs 3 and 4); see Sec. 3.4. The north part of the wall's east face, at the level of its foundations, was investigated in room 2: see Sec. 5.2 below.

13. The ledge is at the same elevation as mortar aggregations on north wall F15, as well as a ledge on the north face of wall F9 and a recess in the east face of F14 (west wall of the church).

Chapter 3: Area 2.3: The Church

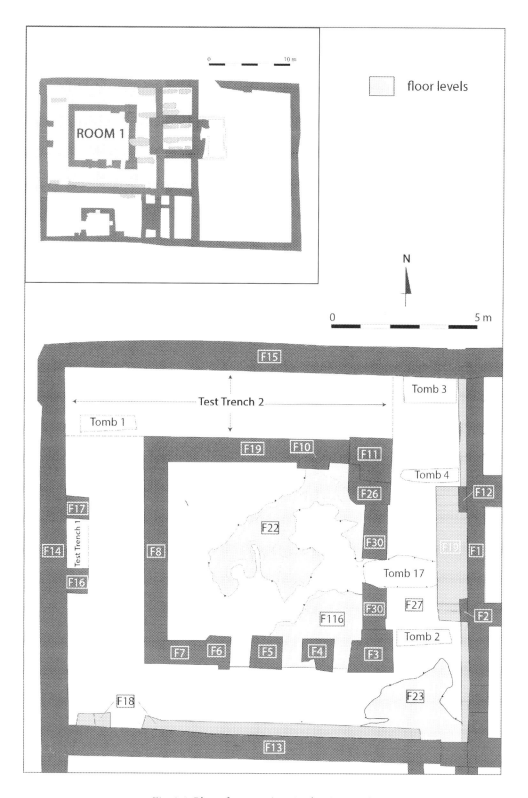

Fig. 3.4: Plan of room 1 (tracing by C. Fosen)

Fig. 3.5: View of the southwest corner of room 1, with walls exposed at foundation level.

This doorway measures 88 cm north-south by 65 cm east-west; it has a mud-brick threshold and indentations on its short sides, where a wooden beam or stone slab may have been placed in antiquity (fig. 3.8). The passage once connected room 1 with a now-missing space (the south *pastophorion*), designated room 16. Although no firm evidence is available, it is very likely that a symmetrically placed doorway originally opened from room 1 onto the no longer extant space (room 14) above room 2.

A low rectangular *bema* (platform; F19)[14] abuts wall F1 in its central part and appears to have allowed access onto the entrance of the apse (room 15) (figs. 3.9–10). F19 lies on the east-west axis of the room, at the opposite end of the doorway within west wall F14. It measures 4.26 m north-south by 1.06 m east-west and is ca. 50 cm high. The platform was accessible from the north and the south by means of two flights of steps, consisting of two steps each (figs. 3.11a–b). The *bema* was originally covered in white plaster; at a later date, perhaps when a mud floor was laid in the area of the east aisle, it received a coating of brown mud plaster, which completely concealed the earlier gypsum layer.[15] What is remarkable about the platform, in terms of its design, is the absence of steps along its west side. The existence of lateral steps is rather

---

14. Upper elevation: 141.190 m; lower elevation: 140.690 m.
15. The mud plaster largely decayed, currently exposing the layer of white gypsum plaster throughout most of the platform.

Fig. 3.6: View (to south) of the preserved top of F1 (east wall of room 1).

unusual in early Egyptian churches, since most *bemata* were accessed frontally.[16] Two examples of similar platforms are in the Large East Church at Kellis and in the recently discovered church of ʿAin el-Sabil, both located in Dakhla Oasis.[17]

To the north and south ends of platform F19 are two rectangular mud-brick bases (F12[18] and F2[19] respectively) (figs. 3.4; 3.12–13). One of them (F2) still retains scanty evidence of the lowest course of an engaged semi-column, 52 cm in diameter, abutting east wall F1.[20]

16. Grossmann 2002b, 155.
17. For a detailed discussion of these parallels, see Sec. 7.6 below.
18. Upper elevation: 141.050 m; lower elevation: 140.830 m.
19. Upper elevation: 141.260 m; lower elevation: 140.860 m.
20. This course consists of two wedge-shaped, iron-rich mudbricks. Most likely, another engaged semi-column was placed above F12 at the north end of the platform.

Fig. 3.7: View (to east) of the south half of wall F1.

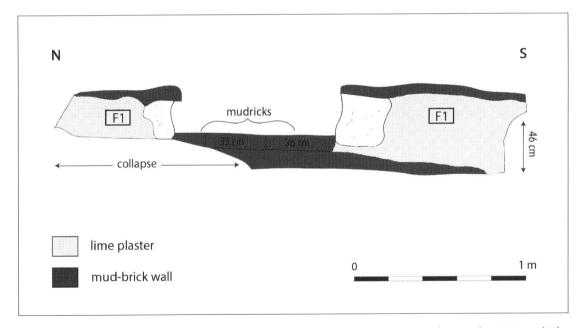

Fig. 3.8: Profile of the doorway, set in wall F1, opening from room 1 into room 16 (drawing by D. Dzierzbicka; tracing by C. Fosen).

Fig. 3.9: View (to southeast) of platform F19.

Fig. 3.10: View (to east) of platform F19.

Fig. 3.11: View of the north (a) and south (b) sets of steps in platform F19.

These features, which were originally covered (like the rest of the walls) with white gypsum plaster, originally framed a large opening, 1.90 m wide, which was accessible from room 1 via platform F19. The latter, as well as the remains of the two semi-columns, provide unequivocal evidence that this space was once architecturally linked with a room built at the east end of the church, in line with its central axis. This space (room 15), now largely vanished, was most likely the site of the apse, which was flanked by two side-chambers (rooms 14 and 16) presumably used as *pastophoria*.

The south boundary of the church is formed by wall F13,[21] made of mudbricks laid out in English bond and with small potsherds, as well as small pieces of iron-rich bricks, used in its construction to fill gaps. F13 runs east-west and separates rooms 1 and 4 from the south annex (fig. 3.14). It is best preserved in its east half and slopes down westwards, where no courses above the ancient floor level of the church are extant. The slanted profile of F13 closely follows that of parallel wall F15 (the north boundary of room 1) and was likely the result of wind erosion.

---

21. Upper elevation: 141.530 m; lower elevation (in room 1): 140.230 m.

Fig. 3.12: View (from above) of remains of rectangular base (F12).

Fig. 3.13: View (to south) of remains of rectangular base and semi-column (F2).

Fig. 3.14: View (to southwest) of room 1's south wall (F13) and mud-brick *mastaba* (F18).

Fig. 3.15: View (to south) of the east half of south wall F13 and *mastaba* F18.

The original coating of mud plaster and, above it, white gypsum plaster is still visible in the part of the wall standing above its foundations. At the east end of F13 are the remains of a doorway, with a well-preserved mud-brick threshold, which opens onto room 5 to the south (figs. 3.15–16). Two cavities, of irregular shape and different sizes, are visible immediately above

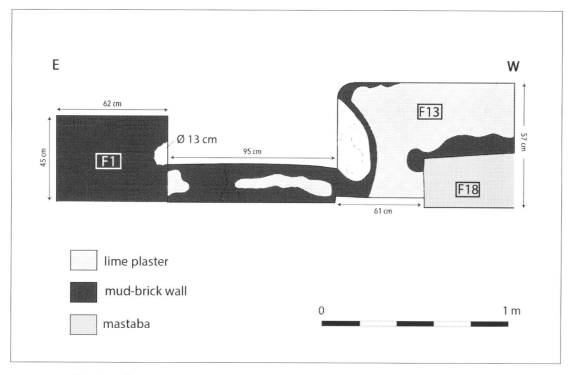

Fig. 3.16: Profile of the doorway, set in wall F13, connecting room 1 with the south annex (drawing by D. Dzierzbicka; tracing by C. Fosen).

the threshold, hacked into the east and west jambs. They likely resulted from the removal of a wooden or stone feature belonging to the doorway.[22] This passage once allowed access (via staircase F35) to a now-missing upper floor (or roof) and, via the lower landing of the staircase, to the rest of the south annex (rooms 6–12).

A mud-brick *mastaba* for the congregation was found running for more than 11.7 m along the inner face of the south wall F13 (F18; see fig. 3.14).[23] The current remains extend from 1.65 m to the west of wall F2 to 2.36 m to the east of wall F14. At that point, there is a gap, ca. 1.05 m wide, where the *mastaba* is not preserved. A smaller portion of the bench, about 1.17 m long, is extant further west, ending 25 cm from the southeast corner of room 1 (fig. 3.17). In this portion, the mud plaster has completely eroded, exposing seven mudbricks laid as headers on edge; these most likely belonged to the bottom course of the *mastaba*.[24] F18 is better preserved at its east end, while it follows the downward slope of wall F13, likely caused by wind erosion, as one moves west. The vertical surface of the bench is still partially coated in mud plaster and,

---

22. For dimensions and additional information about the doorway, see Sec. 4.2 below.
23. Upper elevation: 141.050 m; lower elevation: 140.260 m.
24. The mudbricks measure on average 36 by 17 by 8 cm, reflecting the most commonly attested size of mudbricks at Amheida (as it can be verified on the Amheida excavations' database: see www.amheida.com).

Fig. 3.17: Remains of *mastaba* F18, abutting wall F13, near the southwest corner of room 1 (view to south).

on top of it, a thin layer of white gypsum plaster.[25] Numerous inclusions, consisting of small pottery sherds and lime spots, were found within the remains of the bench; both the mud plaster and the mudbricks are also rich in organic material.

The poor state of preservation of the north wall of room 1 (F15) did not allow for the preservation of any mud-brick bench along that feature. It is nonetheless possible—in fact, probable—that a *mastaba* ran also along F15. It is also conceivable that benches existed against the east face of F14 (the west wall of the church), symmetrically placed to the sides of the central entrance. Unfortunately, no evidence is available, as F14 is preserved only in its foundation courses, due to extreme erosion and/or destruction in the west half of room 1.

North wall F15 is bonded, at its west end, with F14,[26] a north-south running wall that forms the western boundary of the church (fig. 3.18). No courses of F14 are preserved above the church's original floor level; all visible remains, particularly eroded in their southern half,

---

25. Hard sand encrustations are widespread on both the surface and the north face of the *mastaba*, particularly towards its east end.

26. Upper elevation: 140.310 m; lower elevation: 140.100 m (taken in the middle of the wall's east face before the excavation of test trench 1).

Fig. 3.18: View (to south) of the church's west wall (F14).

belong to the foundations of the wall, which was built in an irregular English bond. The west face of F14 remains unexcavated, while the central part of the east side was exposed in test trench 1.[27] The cleaning of the wall revealed a Greek ostrakon (*O.Trim.* 2.653), a well tag datable to ca. 275–350;[28] it is possible that the ostrakon had been embedded in the wall or that it adhered to it after it had been dumped as part of a foundation fill.

27. See Sec. 3.3.1 below.
28. Ast and Bagnall 2016, 196.

Fig. 3.19: Aerial view (to east) of room 1; the dotted line follows the foundation walls of the colonnades.

The main entrance into room 1 was most probably located along west wall F14. Against the latter's east face, roughly in the middle, are two square mud-brick bases (F16–17), which define a space placed at the west end of room 1's main axis (fig. 3.18). A test trench, excavated in the area of the doorway, revealed that the two square bases have very deep foundations. Thus, it is likely that these features once supported heavy architectural elements, framing a monumental doorway.[29] Furthermore, evidence of a narrow pathway, aligned with room 1's west doorway and main axis, was exposed to the west of the church, thanks to topographical work carried out at Amheida in 2012.[30]

Room 1 was divided into a central nave and side aisles by two rows of mud-brick columns (figs. 3.4 and 3.19). The north and south colonnades ran east-west, and their foundation walls were bonded at their east and west ends with north-south oriented foundation walls, which formed a rectangular stylobate. F9[31] is the north foundation wall, separating the north aisle from the central nave of the church (fig. 3.20). It measures 8.6 m in length and was built in

---

29. For a thorough discussion of test trench 1, see Sec. 3.3.1 below.
30. As discussed below (Sec. 7.5), this passageway may have in fact served to connect building 7 with the residential and public areas of Amheida, located to the west of Area 2.3. It would, therefore, underscore the function of the west doorway as the main entrance into the church complex.
31. Upper elevation: 140.770 m; lower elevation (at the west end of the wall, before the excavation of test trench 1): 138.130 m.

Fig. 3.20: View (to southwest) of F9, the foundation wall of the church's north colonnade.

English bond.[32] The wall, which is severely eroded especially in its western half, once supported up to five columns. Of these, evidence of only two (F10 and F11) remains. F10[33] consists of the south half of a square base and of the lowest course of a column (ca. 60 cm in diameter), which would have been the second one from the east end of the colonnade (fig. 3.21). The column consists of two whole and one fragmentary iron-rich, mud-brick wedges; the remains of the base (which measures 106 cm east-west) include two whole rectangular bricks, as well as a smaller, wedge-shaped one. White gypsum plaster is still visible on the south face of the column base, in line with the treatment of the columns of the south colonnade. F11[34] is positioned 85 cm to the east of F10; it comprises the remains of a heart-shaped pillar and a square base (ca. 1.45 m in length) forming a corner at the east end of the north colonnade (fig. 3.22).[35] The pillar was once formed by a roughly square post and two half-columns abutting its west and south sides. The engaged columns were about 60 cm in diameter and made of iron-rich wedge bricks.[36]

---

32. For a through discussion of F9's north face, see Sec. 3.3.2 below.
33. Upper elevation: 140.890 m; lower elevation: 140.750 m; max. preserved height: 14 cm.
34. Upper elevation: 141.050 m; lower elevation: 140.750 m; max. preserved height: 30 cm.
35. The base has a square recess in its southwest corner, where it adjoins F26. Its north edge seems to jut to the north of foundation wall F9 by roughly a brick's header.
36. On the origin and function of the heart-shaped pillar in ancient architecture, see Dell'Acqua 2013.

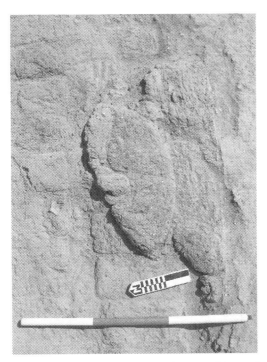 

Fig. 3.21: F10, a fragmentary column and base of the north colonnade.

Fig. 3.22: Remains of heart-shaped pillar and square base (F11) at the east end of the north colonnade.

The mud-brick foundations of an indistinct L-shaped feature (F26)[37] were found abutting the west and south side of pillar F11 (fig. 3.23). F26 measures 107 cm along its west side and 145 cm along its south side and is preserved to a maximum height of 15 cm. The remains are in poor condition, but the mortar lines between F26 and F11 are easily discernable; traces of white gypsum plaster along all sides can also be seen. F26 consists of a course of bricks set on edge, oriented east-west lengthwise, in its west half and of two rows of bricks (also set on edge, but oriented north-south lengthwise) in its east half. Although the archaeological evidence is quite scanty, the location of this feature suggests, chiefly on the basis of comparative analysis, a possible identification of this architectural element as a pulpit.[38]

Walls F9 and F7 are joined at their west ends by F8,[39] a foundation wall made of mudbricks laid out in irregular English bond (fig. 3.24). F8 runs north-south and measures 7.56 m in length. It is likely—although not attested archaeologically—that columns once stood on this foundation wall, forming a west return aisle that created an ambulatory along the inner perimeter of room 1.[40]

37. Upper elevation: 141.000 m; lower elevation: 140.850 m.
38. A particularly close structure, in terms of shape as well as location (at the east end of the north colonnade), is the pulpit at the church of Shams el-Din, located in Kharga Oasis (for a plan, see Bonnet 2004, 84, fig. 69. For an in-depth discussion of this, as well as other parallels, cf. Sec. 7.6 below).
39. Upper elevation: 141.710 m; lower elevation: 140.200 m; max. preserved height: 30 cm.
40. The west return aisle was a typical feature of churches particularly in Upper Egypt: see Grossmann 2002, 18–19. Cf. also Sec. 7.6 below for parallels.

Fig. 3.23: Remains of F26, likely a pulpit.

Fig. 3.24: View (to northeast) of foundation wall F8, forming the church's west return aisle.

Fig. 3.25: View (to west) of foundation wall F30.

The east foundation wall of the inner colonnade is F30 (fig. 3.25).[41] The wall, which runs north-south, is largely hidden below floor F22; thus, the bonding of its bricks and its relationship with pillars F3 and F11, as well as the remains of platform F26, are unknown. The part of F30 that was detected at floor level stretches from F26 to F3; it measures 7.74 m in length and up to 10 cm in height. This portion is in fact split into two segments by an east-west cut, which may belong to an unexcavated burial situated in front of the church's sanctuary.[42] It is not known if additional columns, in addition to pillars F11 and F3 and structure F26, originally stood along wall F30 in the proximity of the sanctuary. F30 may have defined an east return aisle, thus completing a four-side ambulatory running around the central nave of the church.

Wall F7[43] outlines the south edge of the inner colonnaded area (fig. 3.26). It runs east-west for a length of 6.35 m and is bonded with wall F8 at its west end, while the relationship with wall F30 at its east end has not been verified. F7 is poorly preserved and slopes down westwards due to erosion. It consists of up to seven visible courses of mudbricks laid out in irregular English bond. A vertical crack runs along the south face of the wall at a distance of 3.98 m from its west end. Further damage occurred to the upper edge of F7 below the southwest corner of column base F4. The remains of floor F22 conceal the top of wall F7 in the intercolumnar space between the preserved columns' bases (F3–6). The latter were built directly on top of F7, but their south edges seem to have partially rested on foundation fill and the floor of the south aisle (fig. 3.27).[44]

41. Upper elevation: 140.910 m; lower elevation: 140.740 m (in the cut between the two segments of the wall).
42. The cut is 135 cm from the north face of pillar F3 and 184 cm from the south face of platform F26.
43. Upper elevation: 140.730 m; lower elevation: 140.240 m.
44. This was likely the case also in the north colonnade, as attested below the north edge of F11's base.

Fig. 3.26: View (to northeast) of F7, the foundation wall of the church's south colonnade.

Fig. 3.27: View (to north) of remains of square bases and columns F4–F5 along the south colonnade.

F3,[45] preserved to the max. height of 49 cm, is the heavily degraded heart-shaped pillar, enclosed by a rectangular base, that forms a corner at the east end of the south colonnade (built on wall F7) (figs. 3.28–29). It is symmetrical with the other heart-shaped pillar (F11) that once stood at the east end of the north colonnade. The base of F3 measures about 1.5 m along its east and south side and is 22 cm high. A square recess is in the northwest corner, forming the southeast corner of the central nave. The east edge of the base once lay on the floor of the east aisle rather than on solid foundations, causing the formation of vertical cracks. Iron-rich bricks, shaped as wedges, were used in the construction of the two semi-columns, engaged against the north and west sides of the central square pillar. Wedge-shaped bricks were also used, together with regular mudbricks, in the construction of the base. The area where the semi-columns join the base is decorated by a rounded band about 5-cm thick, of which only scanty remains are visible. Both the pillar and its base were once fully coated in mud plaster, with a thin layer of white gypsum plaster over it.

About 60 cm to the west of the heart-shaped pillar is F4,[46] which consists of the severely eroded remains of a column, with a diameter of 61 cm, surrounded by a square base measuring 1.06 m in length (fig. 3.30). F4 was built with wedge-shaped iron-rich bricks as well as regular mudbricks, bonded by mud mortar with small chinking sherds. Traces of the original coatings of mud and white gypsum plaster are visible along the sides of the base. Similar measurements, construction materials, and state of preservation are shared by the two remaining columns (among those that are at least partially preserved) found to the west of F4, i.e., F5[47] and F6[48] (figs. 3.31–32).

Patches of the church's floor levels are preserved only in the eastern half of room 1, while all features in the western half are preserved at foundation level (figs. 3.33–34). The earliest floor that was detected in the northeast corner of room 1 is F21,[49] a compact layer of lime mortar containing a moderate quantity of ceramic sherds and a higher number of small pebbles (fig. 3.35). F21 was subsequently concealed by F20,[50] a floor layer of brown mud plaster with inclusions consisting of plaster fragments and lime spots (fig. 3.36). A bronze coin (inv. 15855), minted in Alexandria ca. 351–361 under Constantius II, was found embedded within this floor, which extends into the east aisle (in the area of the sanctuary) and predates the cutting of burial pits F31 and F33 (of tombs 3 and 4).

In the south aisle there is no evidence of a lime floor similar to F21. Large patches of a mud mortar floor (F27)[51] were exposed in the eastern half of the aisle, extending into the east aisle (fig. 3.37).

---

45. Upper elevation: 141.250 m; lower elevation: 140.810 m.

46. Upper elevation: 141.040 m; lower elevation: 140.830 m.

47. Upper elevation: 140.950 m; lower elevation: 140.840 m; max. preserved height (of column plus base): 17 cm.

48. Upper elevation: 140.840 m; lower elevation: 148.820 m. F6 is only minimally preserved, due to heavy erosion that affected the west half of building 7.

49. Upper elevation: 140.770 m; lower elevation: 140.730 m; average thickness: 2 cm. Parts of this floor were removed during the excavation of test trench 2 in the north aisle.

50. Upper elevation: 140.830 m; lower elevation: 140.760 m; max. thickness: 7 cm. All dimensions were taken in the portion of F20 that was removed within test trench 2.

51. Upper elevation: 140.760 m; the lower elevation is unknown, as the floor was not removed.

Chapter 3: Area 2.3: The Church

Fig. 3.28: Remains of heart-shaped pillar and square base (F3) at the east end of the south colonnade.

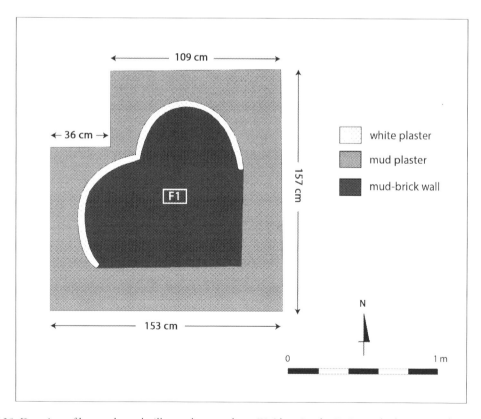

Fig. 3.29: Drawing of heart-shaped pillar and square base F3 (drawing by D. Dzierzbicka; tracing by C. Fosen).

Fig. 3.30: View (from above) of column+base F4.

Fig. 3.31: View (from above) of column+base F5.

Fig. 3.32: View (from above) of column+base F6.

Fig. 3.33: Aerial view (to east) of room 1, showing the remains of floor levels in its eastern half.

A Roman bronze coin (inv. 15818, a *maiorina* dated to 351–361) was collected during the investigation of this floor, which was cut by burial pit F24 (tomb 2) and was later covered by another floor level (F23).[52] The latter postdates the sealing of tomb 4, as it lies above the mud-brick superstructure (F32) of the burial pit. Patches of floor F23 were exposed also in the north half of the east aisle. A few ceramic sherds, none of them diagnostic, were found embedded in this floor level; the only small find from F23 to be inventoried (15856) was a complete bronze coin, a *Spes Reipublicae* issue dated to 355–361.

The largest patch of floor that was exposed in room 1 is F22, which consists of several layers of mud plaster.[53] The floor covers the central part of the nave, delimited by the foundations of the colonnade (F7–9 and F30) (figs. 3.34; 3.38–40). F22, whose preserved surface is very uneven, is completely missing in the westernmost part of this central area. On the basis of the available archaeological evidence, it seems that the floor of the central nave was about 10 cm higher than any of the upper floor levels in the north, east, and south aisles (and presumably also in the west return aisle, although no remains of floors were found there).

---

52. Upper elevation: 140.790 m; lower elevation: 140.680 m; max. thickness: 9 cm.
53. Upper elevation (in the northeast corner): 140.900 m; lower elevation (in the southeast corner): 140.710 m; average thickness: 7 cm.

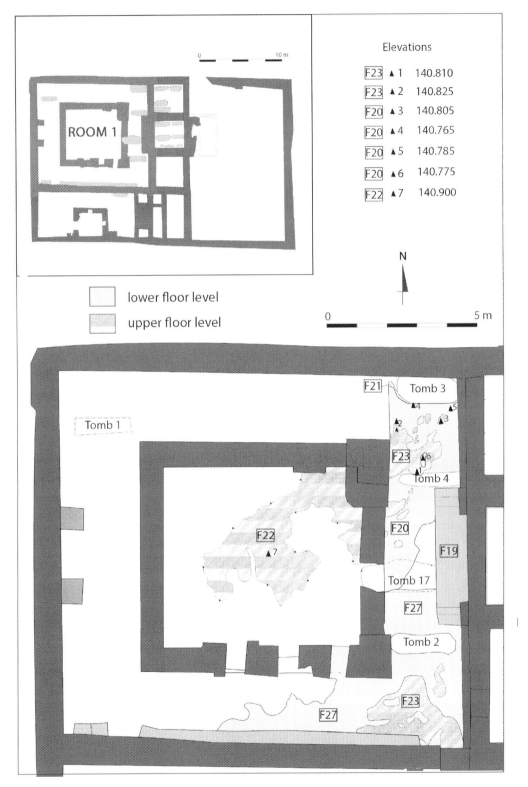

Fig. 3.34: Outline of floor levels in the central nave and in the east half of room 1 (tracing by C. Fosen).

Fig. 3.35: View (to west) of remains of floor F21 in the northeast corner of room 1.

Fig. 3.36: View (to south) of remains of floor F20 in the northeast area of room 1.

Fig. 3.37: View (to west) of patches of floors F23 and F27 in the southeast corner of room 1.

Fig. 3.38: View (to northeast) of remains of floor F22 in the nave of room 1.

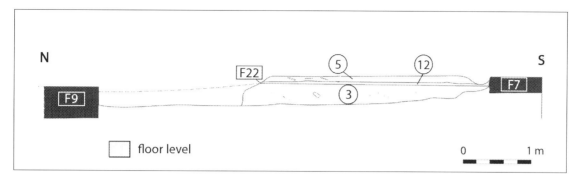

Fig. 3.39: N–S profile (looking east) of the stratigraphy of room 1 in the area of the nave (showing the extent of floor F22) (drawing by D. Dzierzbicka; tracing by C. Fosen).

Floor F22 was identified in 2012. In 2023 additional excavations were carried out in the eastern half of the nave and the east return aisle of room 1; the goal was to define the extent of the preserved portions of F22, as well as to detect any additional burials in the area facing the sanctuary.[54] Within the nave, only F22 had been revealed in 2012. However, more recent excavations of a portion of the collapsed ceiling (DSU5), which had been previously left *in situ* in the southeast quadrant of the nave, revealed a later mud floor level (F116).[55] This surface slightly slopes from southeast to northwest and was laid directly onto floor F22, probably as part of the latter's restoration. Indeed, the preserved floor was especially damaged in this area of the nave; in part, it had been completely removed where a big irregular cut (F115)[56] was detected in 2023. This cut affected especially the portion of the floor immediately to the west of colonnades' foundation F30, as well as the area to the north of columns F5 and F6 in the southern part of the nave. The nature of the pit is unclear; it may have resulted from the removal in antiquity of the most deteriorated parts of the floor, during a phase of restoration that preceded the abandonment of the church in the late fourth century. Alternatively, it may have been dug during robbery excavations in a post-abandonment phase of the building, or perhaps even resulted from natural erosion, due to prolonged exposure to natural elements following the collapse of the church's ceiling and walls.[57]

---

54. The investigation led to the discover of tomb 17 immediately to the west of F19, i.e., the stepped platform leading into the now-missing apse (room 15).
55. Upper elevation: 140.910 m; unexcavated.
56. Upper elevation: 140.810 m; lower elevation: 140.700 m; average thickness of excavated part: 5–7 cm.
57. The very irregular nature of the edges of the cut seemingly supports this last hypothesis.

Fig. 3.40: Mosaic of photogrammetric images of the church at Amheida, following the 2023 excavations (elaboration by L. Davighi; additional tracing by S. Alfarano).

Stratigraphy and finds (fig. 3.41)
Surface and subsurface accumulation layers

The deposits investigated inside room 1 consisted of original, intentionally deposited foundation fills,[58] as well as destruction and accumulation layers. The excavation of the church began with the removal of a surface layer (DSU1) throughout the church.[59] This was extended to rooms 14–16 (above rooms 2–4) to the east of room 1, in order to elucidate their outline and determine their relationship to the main body of the church.[60]

DSU1[61] consisted of windblown sand with a high concentration of pottery sherds[62] and several other inclusions; among these were pebbles, cobbles, mud-brick debris, glass sherds[63] and slag, fragments of faience,[64] bronze, and iron, dross, charcoal, pieces of shells, a fragment of a jar stopper made of gypsum,[65] and many animal bones, including part of a horn. The density of potsherds and other inclusions within this unit diminished a few cm below the surface. Remnants of white gypsum plaster (likely from the walls of room 1) and an exceptionally large quantity of fragments of painted plaster (from a decorated flat ceiling, now collapsed) were found throughout room 1, with a higher concentration in its central and east areas.[66]

---

58. Discussed in Sec. 3.3 below.

59. An additional unit (DSU0) was created to include objects that were retrieved during the cleaning of previously excavated features of building 7. These small finds include eleven Roman bronze coins, either complete or fragmentary: inv. 15854, dated to 351–361; inv. 16239, illegible; inv. 17017, assigned to the first–second centuries; inv. 17035, dated to 351–361; inv. 17097, dated to 335–341; inv. 16969, possibly a *centenionalis* and struck under Julianus in 361–363; inv. 16970, illegible; inv. 16971, broadly dated to the fourth century; inv. 16972–16973, assigned to the second half of the fourth century–beginning of the fifth; inv. 16974, dated to the fourth century. Inv. 16969–16974 were found during a visit to the site in 2017, lying on the ground near the stepped platform that led into the apse; it is likely that these specimens were once embedded in the compacted clay floor of the east return aisle and the east half of the nave, which partially disintegrated in time. DSU0 also includes three ostraka, one of which (inv. 16209) was found in room 6 and is mentioned in Sec. 4.3 below. The other two ostraka, both tags, were gathered within room 1; one (O.Trim. 2.649) is dated to 293/4 or 315/6, while the other (O.Trim. 2.730) is possibly dated to 287/8. See Ast and Bagnall 2016, 195 (O.Trim. 2.649) and 223 (O.Trim. 2.730).

60. The subsurface sand in these rooms was assigned DSU numbers 15–17: see Secs. 3.5 and 5.2 below.

61. Upper elevation: 141.300 m; lower elevation: 140.430 m; average thickness: 12 cm.

62. Among them were a flat base of a bowl (inv. 30039) and an incomplete mold for glass or faience vessels in the shape of a bunch of grapes (inv. 30092).

63. A few of the sherds were diagnostic and thus inventoried: a rim fragment from a plate of light yellow transparent glass (inv. 14558); four rim fragments of bowls (inv. 14585 and 15653, of yellow transparent glass; inv. 14586, of green transparent glass; inv. 15654, of colorless glass); and a rim fragment from a plate or large bowl of colorless glass (inv. 15655).

64. Including one diagnostic fragment of a collared bowl's rim with turquoise glaze, type T12.4 (Nenna and Seif el-Din 2000, 311, fig. 12). This type of faience vessel is fairly common in first- to middle-second century CE contexts in Egypt and imitates contemporary *terra sigillata* fine tableware forms. Faience vessels were progressively replaced by glass vessels during the third century CE (see Cervi 2015, 341–42, with previous references). As this fragment was recovered in a surface layer, its context is not reliable from a stratigraphic point of view.

65. In addition to an almost complete gypsum stopper (inv. 14570), which was inventoried as a small find from this deposit.

66. All fragments of painted plaster from DSU1 were collected on trays based on their location and inventoried as following: inv. 15691 (from the eastern half of the central nave); inv. 15692 (from the western half of the nave); inv. 15694 (from the northwest corner of room 1); inv. 15695 (from the west return aisle); inv. 15696 (from the east end of the north aisle); inv. 15697 (from the area above a collapse in the southeast corner of room 1); and inv. 15698 (from the southwest corner of the south aisle).

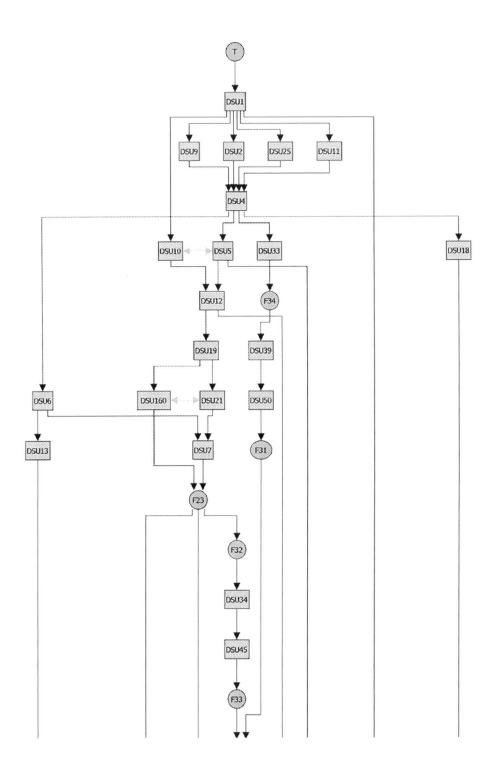

Fig. 3.41a: Harris Matrix of room 1.

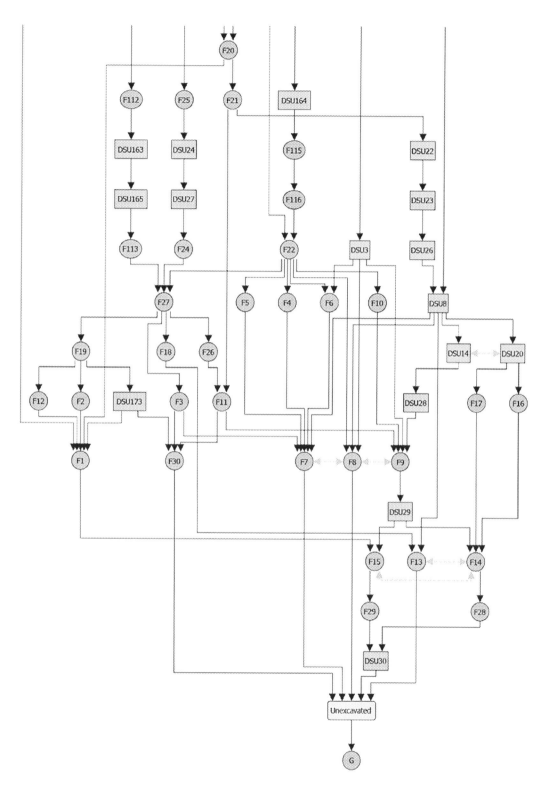

Fig. 3.41b: Harris Matrix of room 1.

Additional small finds, belonging to different categories, were retrieved in large numbers. Among these were: five Roman bronze coins (inv. 14566–14568, 15624, and 15772, all illegible); a fragment of a stone slab, possibly belonging to a column's base (inv. 14530); an amulet of worked amber/orange carnelian in the shape of a stylized scarab (inv. 14553);[67] one fragment of a bracelet made of black opaque glass (inv. 14569);[68] a complete bronze ring, plain and undecorated and thus unlikely to have been used as jewelry (inv. 14571); one fragment of molded gypsum plaster, probably a decorative element in the shape of a palmette (inv. 14573);[69] and a spherical bead made of blue transparent glass (inv. 15625). The removal of DSU1 revealed also four Greek ostraka: *O.Trim.* 2.475 (an account, dated to the second half of the fourth century); *O.Trim.* 2.488 (a tag, also dated to the second half of the fourth century); *O.Trim.* 2.489 (another tag, dated to 345/6); and *O.Trim.* 2.571 (of uncertain nature and assigned to the second half of the fourth century).[70] Unfortunately, these ostraka are of limited value for dating purposes, due to their location within a highly unreliable deposit.

The architectural features and the intentional deposits that remained *in situ* in the north and south aisles, as well as in the west return aisle, of the church were covered with a subsurface accumulation layer of yellow-beige sand (DSU4).[71] Baked bricks, sun-dried iron-rich mudbricks, and vault bricks were dispersed throughout the unit, which was most likely disturbed by intensive pitting following the abandonment of building 7.

---

67. The prothorax and the suture of the elytra are outlined only by incised lines, while the underside is plain. It has a central circular hole, pierced through the y axis. Typologically, this roughly corresponds to Tufnell type I (Tufnell 1984, 32–37). In the scarab from Amheida, the prothorax is indicated by two disjointed parallels line, instead of a single continuous segment. The surface of the scarab appears worn by weather agents and because of the presence of the hole through the y axis, it was probably incorporated into a finger ring or it was used as a pendant for a necklace or for earrings. Moreover, as the underside is plain, it can be interpreted as a protective amulet rather than as an administrative seal.

68. Glass bracelets (also known as bangles in the scientific literature) are cheap personal adornments, common in late antique contexts especially in the eastern Mediterranean. They are dated from the third century CE onwards and their production continued without interruptions during the Byzantine and into the early Islamic period with no substantial variations (Spaer 1988, 51–52). In the church, seven bracelets were recovered, three of which from room 1. The bracelets can be plain or decorated, monochrome or with colorful decoration; those from room 1 are all plain and monochrome and can be identified as Spaer A.2a (Spaer 1988, 54) or Cosyns D1 (Cosyns 2011, 86, table 30, 90–91). The only decorated bracelet (monochrome) is inv. 16060 from room 7 (see below) and is identified as Spaer B2a, B2b and B3aB2d (Spaer 1988, 55–56; fig. 3a, 3b, 5a4) or Cosyns D2 (Cosyns 2011, 86, fig. 53), with bulging inner section. The diameter of the bracelets from the church at Amheida is between 5 and 7 cm and, consequently, they were likely worn by both adult women and little young girls. Usually, the color of this typology of bracelets was intentionally dark thanks to the addition of ferric oxide (Fe_2O_3 and FeO) during the manufacturing process, as demonstrated by the study of P. Cosyns (Cosyns 2004, 15). Most likely, the color was just a "general vogue favoring the black color" (Spaer 1988, 52) or—instead—it had a specific meaning which, unfortunately, remains obscure.

69. Parallels of similarly-rendered palmettes were found at Amheida: one (inv. 50) was retrieved in room 1 of building 1 (the so-called "House of Serenos," dated to the fourth century) and another (inv. 16960) in room 7 of building 10, a large house, dated to the third-fourth century, currently being excavated in the north sector of the city.

70. Ast and Bagnall 2016, 125 (*O.Trim.* 2.475); 130 (*O.Trim.* 2.488–89); and 163 (*O.Trim.* 2.571). Another ostrakon (*O.Trim.* 2.727, a tag dated to ca. 275–350) was retrieved in DSU31 (=DSU1) during the 2013 excavation season (see Ast and Bagnall 2016, 222).

71. Upper elevation: 140.740 m; lower elevation: 139.870 m; max. thickness (measured in the west return aisle): 28 cm.

Disarticulated human remains, most likely from a disturbed burial, were found in the north aisle.[72]

A piece of column base F4 was recovered in the south aisle towards the bottom of DSU4, suggesting that a pit had been dug in this area in antiquity, although no traces of it were detected in the sandy matrix. The removal of this unit in the north aisle revealed large fragments of lime mortar, possibly from a destroyed portion of floor F21. Several pieces of plaster, both white and painted, were found throughout DSU4. They were consistent with those from other units (particularly DSU5 and DSU10) and they also seem to have originated from the collapse of walls, columns, and the decorated ceiling of the church.[73] DSU4 was mixed with many other inclusions; among them were pottery sherds,[74] mud-brick debris, a few pebbles and cobbles, glass slag and sherds,[75] limited fragments of faience, wood, bronze,[76] dross, shells, animal hair, and traces of charcoal and ash, as well as fruit pits and a very large number of animal bones. The range and quantity of the inclusions suggest that DSU4 may have been contaminated with material previously dumped to fill the church's foundations. Activities that took place in the area after the abandonment of building 7, such as the digging of pits and/or the partial reuse of structures (archaeologically witnessed in the south annex of the complex), may have contributed to a highly disturbed stratigraphy, in addition to natural erosion. Several other small finds were retrieved during the excavation of DSU4, including a fragment of molded gypsum plaster (inv. 14505, possibly part of the hair of a statue); a small patch of textile, with traces of white, blue, and yellow fibers (inv. 14523);[77] one Ptolemaic coin (inv. 15522, dated to 114–40 BCE); two Roman bronze coins (inv. 14576, possibly minted under Constantius II and dated to 351–361; and inv. 14605, a *nummus centenionalis* of Constantius II, minted in Antioch in 347–348); two globular beads (inv. 14602, made of green opaque glass, and 14603, of blue transparent glass); and an incomplete hair pin of worked bone (inv. 15609).

DSU4 also contained ten Greek ostraka: *O.Trim.* 2.578 (an account, dated to ca. 275–350); *O.Trim.* 2.635, 636, 642, 666, and 667 (well tags, dated to 285/6, 295/6 or 317/8, 286/7, 284/5, 291/2 respectively);[78] *O.Trim.* 2.732 (a tag, dated to 285/6?); *O.Trim.* 2.741 (a memo, broadly dated to 275–350); *O.Trim.* 2.743 and 745 (an order and a letter respectively, both

---

72. The human remains (FN63) were wrapped in textile.
73. Several trays and bags were filled with fragments from this unit, e.g., inv. 15699 and 15709–15710 (from the south aisle and the southwest corner of room 1); 15702 and 15706 (from the west return aisle); 15729 and 15748–15749 (from the north aisle and the northwest corner of the church).
74. A couple of pieces were inventoried because of their diagnostic value: inv. 15540 and 15646 (two complete round-cut sherds, used as plugs for stoppers). Two fragments of lamps were also included: inv. 14633 (the front part of a terracotta discus lamp) and 15520 (part of the handle of a double molded lamp).
75. Ten inventory numbers were assigned to diagnostic sherds of colorless, light green, and yellow transparent glass: inv. 14580 (one fragment of a plate's base); 14581, 14617, 14620, and 15580 (fragments of bowls' rims); 14606 (part of the rim, neck, and handle of a jug); 15778 (one fragment of a jug's rim); 14616 and 14619 (from the rims of beakers); 15678 (one fragment of a beaker's base).
76. Including three interconnected rings of a small bronze chain (inv. 14638), possibly part of a suspension chain.
77. For a parallel from the site of 'Ain el-Gedida (also in Dakhla), see Dzierzbicka 2018, 542, fig. 1, and 543 (cat. no. 4/inv. 21).
78. Dates are tentative for *O.Trim.* 2.635, 642, 666, and 667.

dated to ca. 275–350).⁷⁹ These ostraka offer valuable data in themselves but cannot be used to establish a firm dating for this deposition, due to its highly disturbed matrix.

The subsurface sand was arbitrarily distinguished as DSU11⁸⁰ in a doorway placed in east wall F1, which led from room 1 into what was probably the south *pastophorion* (room 16). The unit filled the space where a stone or wooden element (now missing) would have rested on top of the mud-brick threshold. The only inclusions within the yellow sand were fragments of white gypsum plaster (likely from the collapse of the surrounding features) and a few animal bones, which were found near the lower interface of the unit.

The removal of DSU11 revealed a layer of mud-brick debris lying directly on the threshold between rooms 1 and 4, at a relatively low depth below surface. This unit, which was labeled DSU13,⁸¹ was very compact and did not offer clues as to the type of collapse from which it originated. A few pottery sherds, fragments of white gypsum plaster, and two Roman bronze coins (inv. 15508–15509, the latter being a *nummus centenionalis* struck under Constantius II in 347–348) were also retrieved during the excavation of this deposit.

Collapse of external walls

The original floor of the church was largely missing in the north and west return aisles, or lying—where extant—beneath a very thin surface layer of accumulated sand (DSU1); therefore, no significant collapse or destruction layers were identified in this heavily disturbed and eroded area of room 1. Three small collapses (DSU2, DSU4, and DSU6) were identified and investigated in the better-preserved south aisle. DSU2⁸² was a wall and ceiling collapse resting below surface layer DSU1 in the southeast corner of room 1 (fig. 3.42). It consisted of large mud-brick fragments and mud-brick debris. Numerous fragments of white plaster, as well as fewer fragments of painted plaster, were found embedded in the collapse, together with traces of palm ribs and rib impressions on large lumps of mud. Among the inclusions of DSU2 were also pottery sherds, a few pieces of wood and bronze, glass sherds, and animal bones. One small find was collected within this unit: a fragment of a bracelet made of black opaque glass (inv. 14556).⁸³

Below DSU2, and separated from it by subsurface sand DSU4, was another collapse layer (DSU6),⁸⁴ which was scattered in the southeast corner of room 1 and also rested above the threshold of the doorway into room 5 (fig. 3.43). The unit consisted of complete and fragmentary mudbricks, mud-brick debris, a few pottery sherds, and a sizable amount of white plaster.

---

79. Ast and Bagnall 2016, 168 (*O.Trim.* 2.578); 189–90 (*O.Trim.* 2.635); 190 (*O.Trim.* 2.636); 192 (*O.Trim.* 2.642); 201 (*O.Trim.* 2.666); 201–2 (*O.Trim.* 2.667); 224 (*O.Trim.* 2.732); 227 (*O.Trim.* 2.741); 228 (*O.Trim.* 2.743); 229 (*O.Trim.* 2.745).
80. Upper elevation: 141.150 m; lower elevation: 141.070 m; max. thickness: 8 cm.
81. Upper elevation: 141.070 m; lower elevation: 140.970 m; max. thickness: 10 cm.
82. Upper elevation: 141.570 m; lower elevation: 141.290 m; max. thickness: 28 cm.
83. Spaer A.2a (Spaer 1988, 54) or Cosyns D1 (Cosyns 20011, 86, table 30; 90–91).
84. Upper elevation: 141.110 m; lower elevation: 140.750 m; max. thickness: 19 cm.

Fig. 3.42: View (to northeast) of collapse DSU2 in room 1.

Fig. 3.43: View (to south) of collapse DSU6 in room 1.

Fig. 3.44: Large fragment of plaster from DSU6 (likely from a doorway).

A few pieces were fairly large, including one that had finished edges forming right angles; it is possible that it was originally part of a doorway, either the one opening from room 1 onto the south annex or the other leading from room 1 into the south *pastophorion* (room 16) (fig. 3.44). Fragments of painted plaster from the church's collapsed ceiling were found as well; some of them were still attached to mud plaster bearing palm rib impressions.[85] Among other inclusions of DSU6 were animal bones and a negligible quantity of glass, faience, dross, and charcoal.

The two floor levels (F23 and F27) that were identified in the east half of the south aisle were covered with a compact layer of mud-brick debris, forming a thin concretion (fig. 3.45). The unit, which was removed as DSU7,[86] contained several white plaster fragments, a few pottery sherds, and animal bones. One illegible bronze Roman coin (inv. 15774) was also retrieved during the excavation of this layer.

The only other unit consisting of wall collapse that was excavated within room 1 was DSU9[87] (fig. 3.46). This was a small subsurface unit of mudbricks, presumably from south wall F13, which collapsed as one episode and still showed their original bond.[88] DSU9 rested partly on top of the *mastaba* (F18) lying against the north face of F13 and, partly, on the accumulated sand of DSU4 in the middle part of the south aisle. The collapse measured only 7 cm in thickness; likely, it would have once been wider, but it suffered from severe erosion along with the standing part of wall F13.

85. The painted plaster was documented as inv. 15713 and 15722.
86. Upper elevation: 140.820 m; lower elevation: 140.700 m; average thickness: 3 cm.
87. Upper elevation: 140.900 m; lower elevation: 140.830 m; approximate thickness: 7 cm.
88. In addition to this small section of the wall, the unit comprised mud-brick debris, a few pottery sherds, and a small quantity of dross.

Fig. 3.45: View (to west) of DSU7 in the south aisle (after partial removal).

Although no other wall collapses were documented in room 1, a preliminary survey of Area 2.3 (where building 7 is located) revealed that the north wall of the church had fallen northwards, while the west wall had likely collapsed to the west of room 1.[89] As for the other features of the church, including walls, columns, and most benches, it is possible that their fallen remains either disappeared because of wind erosion or were dismantled for reuse, or both.

89. Both areas have yet to be excavated.

Fig. 3.46: View (from above) of wall collapse DSU9 in the south aisle.

Stratigraphy inside the nave: Collapse of the ceiling and fragments from the east wall

The floor (F22)[90] of the central area of the church, delimited by the colonnade's foundations (F7–9 and F30) was covered with a thin layer of brownish-yellow sand (DSU12).[91] This unit contained a large number of fragments of painted plaster,[92] most likely from ceiling collapse episodes (DSU5 and DSU10) lying above this deposit as well as on another collapse (DSU19) that occurred, prior to the deposition of DSU12, in the area of the sanctuary. Other inclusions were ceramic fragments,[93] a couple of glass sherds, and animal bones. The removal of the unit also revealed a small patch of white, blue, and purple textile (inv. 14518), a fragment of carved wood with traces of green/turquoise painting (inv. 15847, possibly part of a piece of furniture), and an incomplete cylindrical object made of worked bone (inv. 15848, likely used as a handle or tool).

90. Recent archaeological investigation, carried out in 2023 in the east half of the central nave, revealed a coin (inv. 17065, dated to 347–348 CE) on the upper interface of floor F22. However, due to its unreliable archaeological context, the specimen has no diagnostic value.

91. Upper elevation: 141.070 m; lower elevation: 140.840 m; average thickness: 8 cm.

92. The fragments from this sand deposit were inventoried as 15760–15762, 15764–15765, and 15767.

93. Two diagnostic sherds were assigned inventory numbers, i.e., 30080 (the fragmented shoulder of a storage jar) and 30095 (the neck and shoulder of a big storage jar).

Fig. 3.47: Fragments of painted plaster, from the collapsed ceiling of room 1, retrieved in DSU5.

DSU12 seems to have accumulated when the church was no longer in use, but its ceiling was still intact for the most part. Subsequently, the unit was buried, in the central part of room 1, beneath a thin layer of ceiling collapse (DSU5)[94] (fig. 3.47). This stratum contained numerous patches, and an even larger number of small fragments, of painted plaster.[95] Some were attached to mud plaster, which still bore the impressions of palm ribs from the original flat ceiling. The investigation of DSU5 revealed also a few whole mudbricks and numerous mudbrick fragments, as well as pottery sherds, pieces of wood and charcoal, a few glass sherds, dross, and animal bones. An incomplete Greek ostrakon (*O.Trim.* 2.643) was also retrieved; it was a well tag, possibly dated to 285/6 and perhaps reused as a chinking sherd.[96]

The floor of the east aisle, adjacent to the apse and *pastophoria*, was also covered with thin sand layers. They were excavated as two units, i.e., an extension of DSU12 (discussed above) and the underlying DSU21.[97] The latter consisted of brownish-yellow sand and a few inclusions, such as ceramic and glass sherds, dross, one piece of faience, animal bones, and

---

94. Upper elevation: 141.160 m; lower elevation: 140.840 m; max. thickness: 17 cm.
95. All bags and trays with fragments of painted plaster were cataloged as inv. 15701, 15703–15705, 15707–15708, 15711–15712, 15714, 15716–15721, and 15725 (plus FN57 and FN64).
96. Ast and Bagnall 2016, 192–93.
97. Upper elevation: 140.890 m; lower elevation: 140.790 m; max. thickness: 9 cm. These data refer to DSU21.

small plaster fragments. The only small finds from this unit that were inventoried were a couple of Roman bronze coins (inv. 15773, broadly assigned to the fourth century, and inv. 15817, possibly identified as a fraction of a *centenionalis* and dated to 383–403). Between DSU12 and DSU21 was a small ceiling collapse (DSU19)[98] that abutted stepped platform F19 in front of the apse as well as east wall F1. The unit contained numerous patches and fragments of painted plaster embedded in the debris.[99] Most of them were still attached to remains of mud plaster, which still bore the imprints of palm ribs used in the construction of the ceiling (fig. 6.4).

A sizable layer of ceiling and wall collapse, including a few scattered column bricks, lay above DSU12 in the east aisle. This unit (labeled DSU10)[100] was very similar, both in elevation and inclusions, to DSU5 in the central nave and was likely part of the same episode. However, the two contexts were distinguished because DSU10 lay outside the central colonnaded area and contained scattered mudbricks from collapsed walls and columns.[101] The excavation of DSU10 revealed a wide range of inclusions, such as fragments of white gypsum plaster (likely from walls and columns),[102] numerous pottery sherds,[103] fragments of glass vessels, animal bones and hair, one fragment of a shell, and negligible quantities of bronze and dross. Among the inventoried small finds were four fragments of white, red, and blue-green textile (inv. 14517), a globular bead of blue transparent glass (inv. 15565), and an incomplete illustrated ostrakon, possibly representing a bird on a perch (inv. 15851) (fig. 3.48). Several large pieces, as well as small fragments, of painted plaster from the collapsed ceiling were also retrieved from this stratum.[104] The impressions of palm ribs were still visible in the mud plaster behind many of the fragments. The location of the collapse suggests that the painted plaster, which decorated the underside of the roof above the nave, extended over the area facing the sanctuary in the east aisle.

The large pit located in the eastern part of the central nave was filled by DSU164,[105] a unit of windblown sand mixed with several pottery fragments and moderate amounts of straw and charcoal. Two objects were retrieved during the partial excavation of this fill, i.e., a complete coin (inv. 17066, a *centenionalis* dated to 355–363) and a Greek ostrakon (inv. 17063) with no date in the text (and broadly assigned to the late third/mid-fourth century).

---

98. Upper elevation: 140.960 m; lower elevation: 140.850 m; average thickness: 10 cm.

99. The remains of painted plaster were assigned the following inventory numbers: 15759, 15763, 15766, 15769, and 15839.

100. Upper elevation: 141.260 m; lower elevation: 140.850 m; max. thickness: 37 cm.

101. The columns' bricks are wedge-shaped; they have an average radius of 17 cm and are 4 to 7 cm thick depending on the degree of erosion. These dimensions fit those of the wedge bricks still *in situ* within the colonnade.

102. One fragment of white plaster (FN82) bore Greek inscriptions: their publication by D. M. Ratzan (in the companion volume to this archaeological report) is forthcoming.

103. Including a diagnostic piece (inv. 30082) consisting of the base and body of a juglet.

104. All remains of painted plaster found within DSU10 were inventoried as 15731, 15733–15740, 15742–15747, 15750–15751, 15753–15758 (plus FN67).

105. Upper elevation: 141.850 m; lower elevation: 140.670 m; average thickness: 11 cm. The DSU was not fully excavated.

Fig. 3.48: Illustrated ostrakon (inv. 15851) from DSU10 in room 1.

3.3. The Foundations of Room 1

Severe erosion and human destruction combined to bring about the almost total disappearance of several mud-brick features of the church above floor level, especially in the western half of room 1. As a result, only foundation courses of its west wall (F14), as well as the wall connecting the north and south colonnades at their west ends (F8), were preserved. Parts of the foundations were exposed also in the western half of the church's north and south walls (F15 and F13 respectively) and in the western half of the north and south colonnades (F9 and F7).

Two test trenches (1 and 2, discussed below) were opened in the western half of the church. Both trenches (in particular test trench 2) revealed that the church had impressively deep foundations, which reached 3 m below ancient floor level in the northwest corner of room 1. As mentioned below in Sec. 3.3.2., the foundations of the church's exterior walls were built within trenches that cut through a mud-brick leveling layer.[106] Although it has not yet been determined if this deposit lay on top of bedrock or other depositional units (and/or the remains of earlier buildings), the foundations of the church testify to the considerable effort that was put into the construction of a sizeable and monumental building. The discovery in 2013 and 2023 of the underground funerary crypts (rooms 2–4) below the sanctuary (rooms 14–16) provided a possible explanation for the significantly deep foundations of building 7

---

106. At least in the northwest sector of building 7.

Fig. 3.49: View (from above) of test trench 1 after excavation.

3.3.1. Test Trench 1

Test trench 1 was opened along the east face of F14 (the west wall of room 1) and was framed, to the north and south, by square mud-brick foundations (F16 and F17) of what may have been (engaged) pillars or columns, framing a monumental west entrance into the church (figs. 3.4; 3.49). The excavated area was roughly rectangular in shape and measured 165 cm north-south by 75 cm east-west. The bottom of the foundations of both F16 and F17 was reached at 138.780 m, while west wall F14 had deeper foundations.

Features

As mentioned above, F16[107] is the south square foundation of the west entrance (figs. 3.50–51). It measures 78 cm north-south by 72 cm east-west and is preserved to a depth of 160 cm. It is located about 4.35 m to the north of the southwest corner of room 1 and abuts the east face

---

107. Upper elevation: 140.320 m; lower elevation: 138.780 m.

CHAPTER 3: AREA 2.3: THE CHURCH   101

of west wall F14. The exposed foundations consist of fifteen complete courses of mudbricks in irregular English bond, in addition to heavily weathered remains (4 cm thick) of an uppermost course. The first three (complete) courses from the top protrude northward by less than a cm compared to the lower courses. The lowest four courses are more regular and consist of alternating stretchers and headers on edge. The top of F16 shows an arrangement of four headers bound, to the north and south, by two stretchers oriented east-west (fig. 3.52).

About 165 cm to the north of F16 is the second square foundation (F17)[108] investigated in test trench 1 (figs. 3.53–54). F16 measures 72 cm north-south by 73 cm east-west (78 cm in its lowest course) and its preserved height is about 160 cm. Sixteen courses of mudbricks, not including a heavily eroded top layer, form the preserved foundations: the top four are stretchers and below is a more regular English-bond pattern of headers and stretchers. The four bottom courses are arranged as in the case of F16, i.e., with stretchers alternating with headers on edge. The top also reveals the same pattern, i.e., four headers between two east-west oriented stretchers, along both the north and south sides (fig. 3.55).

The part of west wall F14[109] (east face), which was cleared in test trench 1, shows twenty-one courses of mudbricks, including a very poorly preserved top layer, laid out in English bond (fig. 3.56).

As mentioned above, the two square foundations likely supported pillars or columns, possibly engaged with wall F14 against its east face. Both F16 and F17 seem to have been load-bearing, as the bottom course of their foundations was found at the considerable depth of ca. 160 cm below modern-day ground level. The space they flanked may have been the location of the main entrance into the church.[110]

Stratigraphy and finds (fig. 3.41)

The excavation of test trench 1 revealed a series of three depositional units, the latest of which was DSU18 (fig. 3.57).[111] It lay immediately below DSU4, a subsurface layer that extended in the north, west, and south areas of room 1.[112] Likely, DSU18 was not part of the original foundation fill of the west return aisle, but resulted from the collapse of features of the now-disappeared west entrance (including upper courses of F16–17) or, possibly, of upper sections of west fall F14. The matrix of the unit consisted of mudbricks and mud-brick fragments, with a high concentration of brick fragments made of red iron-rich clay in the north half of the trench. A concentration of hardened mud plaster, with fragmentary mudbricks embedded in it, was found in the southwest corner of the trench, against F14 and F16. DSU18 was mixed with moderate quantities of organic material and charcoal. Its excavation also revealed some pottery sherds, as well as a complete circular lid made from the base of a cooking pot (inv. 15824).

---

108. Upper elevation: 140.350 m; lower elevation: 138.760 m.
109. Upper elevation: 140.260 m; lower elevation: 140.100 m (elevations taken within test trench 1). For a general description of wall F14, see Sec. 3.2 above.
110. See Sec. 7.5 below. For a secondary entrance into the complex, via the south annex, see Sec. 4.1.
111. Upper elevation: 140.340 m; lower elevation: 140.090 m; max. thickness: 25 cm.
112. For a detailed discussion of this unit, see Sec. 3.2 above.

Fig. 3.50: View of north face of F16.

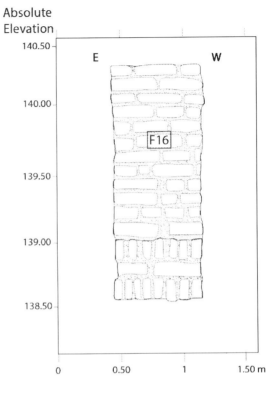

Fig. 3.51: Drawing of north profile of F16 (drawing by D. Dzierzbicka; tracing by C. Fosen).

Fig. 3.52: View of top of F16 (foundation of pillar or column).

Fig. 3.53: View of south face of F17 (foundation of pillar or column).

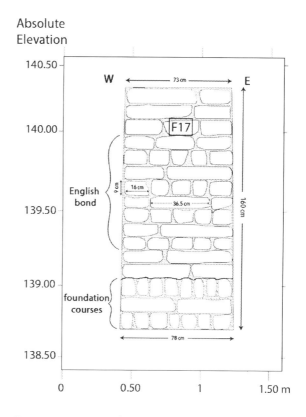

Fig. 3.54: Drawing of south profile of F17 (drawing by D. Dzierzbicka; tracing by C. Fosen).

Fig. 3.55: View of top of F17 (foundation of pillar or column).

Fig. 3.56: View of wall F14's east face inside test trench 1.

Fig. 3.57: View (from above) of DSU18.

Fig. 3.58: View (from above) of DSU8.

Below DSU18 lay DSU8,[113] a context of mud-brick debris and sand encrustations, mixed with grayish-brown sand and a wide range of inclusions, such as small quantities of potsherds, pebbles, ash, dross, wood, and a few animal bones (fig. 3.58). The unit, which seems to have been part of the original foundation fill of building 7, extended into the north and south aisles and in the west return aisle, but was removed solely in test trenches 1 and 2.

The removal of DSU8 in test trench 1 revealed a very thick deposit (DSU20)[114] of clean, yellow sand with few inclusions, consisting of ceramic sherds, four glass fragments, some animal bones, and a very moderate quantity of charcoal and wood. The only small find was a fragment of a bracelet made of black opaque glass (inv. 15601).[115] DSU20 was excavated down to the lowest courses of column or pillar foundations F16–17 (fig. 3.59). Almost certainly it had been deposited in this area following the construction of the west doorway's foundations; but it is also clear that it extended beyond the east edge of the test trench. Most likely, it was part of the original fill of the trenches that had been dug for the foundations of the church's external and colonnade walls.

---

113. Upper elevation: 140.200 m; lower elevation: 140.020 m; max. thickness: 18 cm (elevations and measures taken within test trench 1).
114. Upper elevation: 140.010 m; lower elevation: 138.470 m; max. thickness: ca. 150 cm.
115. Spaer A.2a (Spaer1988, 54) or Cosyns D1 (Cosyns 2011, 86, table 30; 90–91).

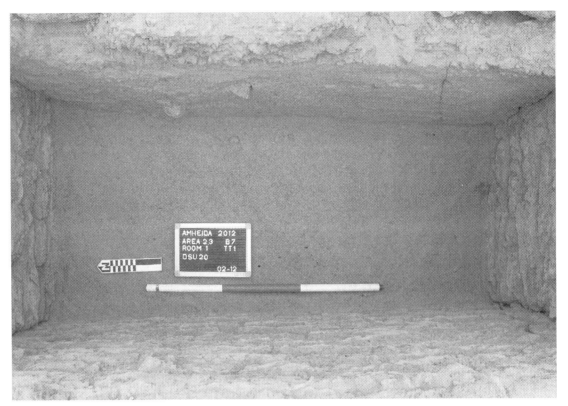

Fig. 3.59: View (from above) of DSU20 (at foundation level of F16–17).

3.3.2. Test Trench 2

Features

Test trench 2 was excavated in the north aisle of the church, with the aim of investigating and reconstructing—albeit tentatively—the building technique of the foundations of building 7 (discussed below). The trench is rectangular in shape and measures about 2.2 m north-south by 11.1 m east-west. It extends from the east end of colonnade foundation F9 to west wall F14 (figs. 3.4; 3.60–61). F15, the north wall of room 1, binds the trench to the north. During excavations, the lowest foundation courses of F9 and F14 were reached at 138.130 m and 137.440 m, respectively.

The east face of wall F14[116] shows, within test trench 2, thirty-two courses of mudbricks in English bond (fig. 3.62). The three upper courses (of those preserved) protrude slightly from the wall at an elevation of 140.040 m. A ledge is still visible at an elevation of 138.430 m, protruding from the east face by 16 cm. In the northwest corner of room 1, formed by walls F14–15, the original coating of mud plaster is well preserved.

---

116. Upper elevation (in test trench 2): 140.200 m. On F14, see also Sec. 3.2 above.

Fig. 3.60: Aerial view (to southeast) of building 7; the arrows indicate the east and west edges of test trench 2.

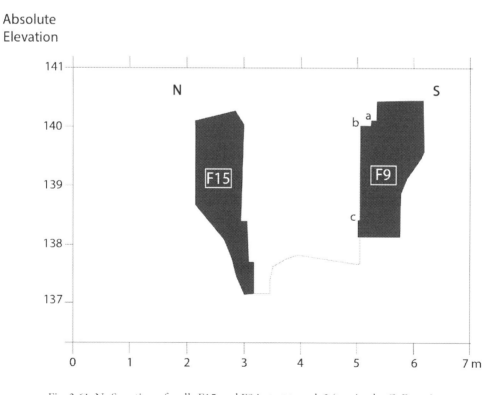

Fig. 3.61: N–S section of walls F15 and F9 in test trench 2 (tracing by C. Fosen).

Fig. 3.62: View of east face of wall F14 in test trench 2.

A big lump of mortar was found against this corner, lying above the lower ledge (fig. 3.63).[117] The lowest courses of wall F14 had been laid within foundation trench F28,[118] cut into mudbrick dump layer DSU30 (fig. 3.64). F28 was investigated only in test trench 2; the exposed part measures 196 cm north-south and 24 cm east-west.

The profile of wall F15,[119] revealed in test trench 1, shows an English-bond construction technique, although sand encrustations obscure many of the mudbricks' edges and mortar lines, especially in the ten courses from the preserved top (fig. 3.65). The wall is cracked 4.38 m from its east edge (fig. 3.66).[120] At an elevation of 140.170 m there are aggregations of mud mortar that are approximately at the same level as a ledge on the north face of F9 (foundation wall of the north colonnade) and a recess in the east face of west F14.

---

117. Upper elevation of the lump of mortar: 138.530 m.
118. Upper elevation 137.920 m; lower elevation: 137.440 m; max. depth: 48 cm.
119. Upper elevation: 140.520 m; lower elevation: 136.680 m (elevations taken within test trench 2). For additional details about wall F15, see Sec. 3.2 above.
120. A wall collapse surveyed to the north of building 7 most likely originated from this wall.

Fig. 3.63: View of northwest corner of room 1, with lump of mortar above ledge of walls F14–15.

Fig. 3.64: View (from above) of foundation trench F28.

Fig. 3.65: View of south face of wall F15 in test trench 2 (west part).

At an elevation of 138.380 m, a ledge protrudes from its south face by ca. 12 cm. The ledge is covered by a layer of sand less than 10 cm thick, smeared over with a cap of mortar. Another ledge, protruding by ca. 6 cm, is visible at the lower elevation of 137.650 m. The wall has very deep foundations, but the bottom course was not reached during the excavation of test trench 2. The foundation trench (F29),[121] however, was identified and partially investigated along the west end of the wall, for a length of about 100 cm (east-west) and an average width of 36 cm (north-south) (fig. 3.67). F29 cuts mud-brick debris layer DSU30 and has very irregular shape and edges. It joins foundation trench F28 of wall F14 in the northwest corner of room 1.

Test trench 2 is partially bounded, along the south edge, by the foundation wall of the church's north colonnade (F9)[122] (fig. 3.68). The wall, which was exposed to the lowest foundation course, consists of 27 preserved courses of mudbricks laid out in English bond.

---

121. Upper elevation 137.870 m; lower elevation: 137.190 m; max. excavated depth: 50 cm.
122. Upper elevation (within test trench 2): 140.460 m. See Sec. 3.2 above for further measurements and details about this wall.

Fig. 3.66: View of south face of wall F15 in test trench 2 (central part).

Fig. 3.67: View (from above) of foundation trench F29.

Fig. 3.68: View of north face of wall F9 in test trench 2.

It shows a vertical crack almost at its center.[123] At the elevation of 140.160 m, a foundation footing protrudes about 16 cm from the wall's north face, roughly at the same elevation where an accumulation of mud plaster was smeared along the south face of wall F15 (fig. 3.59, letter a).[124] The mud-brick courses above the level of the ledge are oriented slightly differently from those below it, presumably in an effort to reorient wall F9, so that it ran parallel to the north wall (F15) of room 1. Another ledge, protruding by a further 16 cm, was found at the elevation of 138.420 m (fig. 3.59, letter c). It is located at the same elevation of the upper bricks of the footing of west wall F14 and the footing of wall F9 (bonded with F8).

Stratigraphy and finds (fig. 3.40)

The excavation of test trench 2 began after surface layer DSU1, as well as subsurface deposit DSU4, had been removed from the north aisle, revealing floors F20–21 in the east half of the

---

123. Towards the east end of the excavated sector.
124. The protrusion indicated as (b) in the same plate is, in fact, part of the same ledge marked as (a). It looks different in the section because of the lack of mudbricks in some parts of the ledge at its lower level.

aisle.¹²⁵ In that area, a series of leveling layers was detected below floor F21, i.e., DSU22, DSU23, DSU26, and DSU8 (the earliest of the sequence; figs. 3.69–70).¹²⁶ DSU22 was the preparation layer of F21. It consisted of brown compacted mud with few inclusions, consisting of numerous potsherds, five glass fragments, lime spots, and three small pieces of wood. Two ash pockets were found within the unit. One (30 x 40 cm in size) was mixed with organic materials including burnt date pits; a second (measuring 34 by 40 cm) contained burnt animal bones. A small, pitched lid of a keg (inv. 30084) was found during the excavation of this unit, which lay above a yellowish-brown and gray deposit of sand and ash (DSU23).¹²⁷ The unit contained a very large quantity of ceramic sherds, plaster fragments, glass sherds, one fragment of faience, numerous animal bones, and moderate amounts of mud-brick fragments and pebbles. A series of ash and charcoal lenses, including two of a larger size (14 by 18 cm and 16 by 13 cm) than the others, were documented within the layer. The excavation of DSU23, which seems to have originated from a domestic dump (before its reuse as a foundation fill), revealed a remarkably large number of small finds: two clusters of textile fragments (inv. 14515, consisting of five fragments, and inv. 14519, comprising four small pieces); an almost complete stopper made of unfired clay (inv. 15826); one fragment of a zoomorphic figurine of fired clay, representing the rear of a quadruped animal (inv. 15834); one small piece of painted plaster on a thick layer of mud, with reed impressions on the back (from the church's collapsed ceiling; inv. 15840). Moreover, seven Greek ostraka were retrieved, i.e., *O.Trim.* 2.644–46 (well tags, dated to 286/7?, 294/5 or 316/7, and 296/7 or 318/9 respectively); *O.Trim.* 2.579 (a list, dated to ca. 275–350); and *O.Trim.* 2.723 and 734 (tags, dated to ca. 275–350 and 296/7 or 318/9, respectively).¹²⁸

Below DSU23 was another layer of dumped material (DSU26),¹²⁹ consisting of yellowish-brown sand mixed with a variety of inclusions: among them were an abundant quantity of ash and charcoal, mud-brick debris, pottery sherds, a few pebbles, glass sherds, many animal bones, and remains of down feathers. A few small finds were found associated with this unit: a small fragment of gypsum plaster, possibly part of an architectural decoration in the shape of an Ionic or Corinthian capital (inv. 14481);¹³⁰ a group of thirteen small fragments of textile (inv. 14510); two straps of leather tied into a knot, possibly part of footwear (inv. 14516); and two Greek ostraka, i.e., *O.Trim.* 2.580 (an account, dated to ca. 275–350) and 2.735 (a tag, also dated to ca. 275–350).¹³¹

The excavation of DSU23 revealed DSU8,¹³² the context of sand, ash, mud-brick debris, and sand concretions that was identified in the north, south, and west return aisle of room 1.

---

125. Both DSU1 and DSU4 are discussed in Sec. 3.2 above.
126. Upper elevation 140.770 m; lower elevation: 140.640 m; average thickness: 5 cm.
127. Upper elevation 140.480 m; lower elevation: 140.100 m; average thickness: 20 cm.
128. Ast and Bagnall 2016, 193–94 (*O.Trim.* 2.644–46); 169 (*O.Trim.* 2.579); 221 (*O.Trim.* 2.723); 224 (*O.Trim.* 2.734). An additional ostrakon (inv. 15671), with one line of (likely) decoration, was found in DSU23.
129. Upper elevation 140.530 m; lower elevation: 140.170 m; max. thickness: 18 cm.
130. Similar plaster volutes were found during the excavation of room 7 in building 10 (inv. 16964, 16965, and 16967).
131. Ast and Bagnall 2016, 169–70 (*O.Trim.* 2.580); 225 (*O.Trim.* 2.735).
132. This deposit is discussed in greater detail in Sec. 3.2 above.

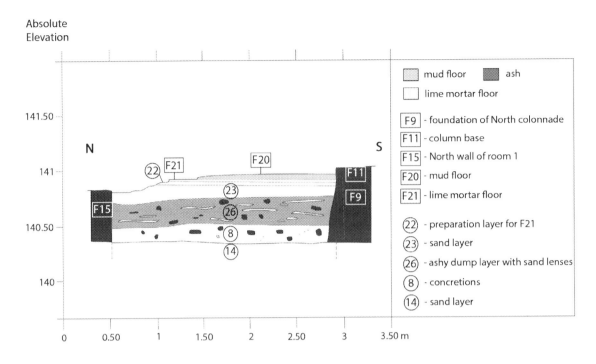

Fig. 3.69: East profile of test trench 1 (drawing by D. Dzierzbicka; tracing by C. Fosen).

Fig. 3.70: View of east profile of test trench 1.

Fig. 3.71: View (to east) of stratigraphy in test trench 2.

With the exception of the eastern half of test trench 1, where the floor levels were still extant (albeit in poor conditions), DSU8 was found directly below subsurface DSU4 elsewhere, due to heavy wind erosion.

DSU8 lay above a foundation fill deposit (DSU14)[133] of yellow sand (fig. 3.71). The layer contained pottery sherds, mud-brick fragments loosely dispersed throughout the sand, as well as white plaster and very few fragments of painted plaster (inv. 15732), which appear to be unrelated to those from the ceiling collapse of DSU5 and DSU10. Among other inclusions were numerous animal bones (some burnt), dross, charcoal, a couple of pieces of faience, glass sherds (including part of a lipped rim of a bowl, inv. 15672, and a fragment from the footring of a flask or a jug, inv. 14504), textile pieces (inv. 14520, consisting of one large fragment and two small pieces, and 14521, comprising several fragments made of white, red, purple, and blue threads), and a few small pieces of wood. Other small finds were retrieved during the excavation of this context: a complete round-cut sherd, made from the footring base of a cooking pot (inv. 15686); a small bowl with a complete profile (inv. 30086); two beads (one of transparent glass,

133. Upper elevation: 140.100 m; lower elevation: 138.730 m; average thickness: 140 cm.

inv. 15566, and the other of gold-in-glass, segmented and oblate, inv. 15822; and one Greek ostrakon, i.e., *O. Trim.* 2.733 (a tag, dated to 287/8?).[134]

Below DSU14 was another layer (DSU28)[135] that belonged to the foundation fill of walls in room 1's north aisle. It consisted of yellow sand deposited in neatly horizontal strata. It was considered as a separate unit from foundation fill DSU14 due to the presence of a darker horizontal line between the two units. The line was particularly noticeable in the south profile of the test trench cut across the west aisle. The lower interface of DSU14 is consistent with the elevations of ledges on F14 and F15 (room 1's west and north walls respectively), as well as F9 (foundation wall of north colonnade). The sand of the unit was mixed with moderate quantities of fragmentary mudbricks and baked bricks, potsherds, charcoal, dross, glass sherds, white plaster fragments, and some animal bones. One fragment of a gypsum stopper was the only small find (inv. 14522) recovered from this layer, which was fully removed only in the western section of test trench 2 (for a length of 2.66 m from west wall F14). Further excavation in this area revealed DSU29,[136] another layer of yellow sand resting immediately below the level of ledges in walls F14, F15, and F9. The unit, which showed patches of hardened sand on its surface, belonged to a series of intentional sand fills within the foundations of room 1's outer walls. It had been deposited prior to the building of the foundations of the colonnade (i.e., walls F7, F8, F9, and F30). The sand of this deposit had few inclusions, consisting of pottery sherds, fragments of plaster, and animal bones.

DSU29 filled foundation trenches F28–29, which had been dug for the construction of west wall F14 and north wall F15, respectively.[137] It also lay above DSU30,[138] a flat and compact mud-brick debris layer consisting of large fragments of mudbricks, clay, and sand (figs. 3.67; 3.72–73). It was undoubtedly an intentional deposit, prepared before the construction of the church began with the digging of foundation trenches F28–29, which cut DSU30. It is unknown if this deposit, which was exposed only in the west part of test trench 2 and was not removed, extended throughout the area of room 1 underneath its foundations.[139]

Discussion

The building of the foundations for the external walls, as well as the colonnade, of the church took place in several stages, marked by the deposition of leveling layers within the construction area. During the first phase, a flat and very compact layer of broken mudbricks was laid out. The full extent of this layer (DSU30), which was exposed in the west part of test trench 2, is still unknown. In particular, it remains to be determined whether it covered the entire surface beneath room 1, and if—and how far—it extended to the other rooms of building 7. Further investigations are also needed to know how thick this context is and if it was laid on top of *gebel* (geological surface), accumulation layers, or on other intentional deposits.

---

134. Ast and Bagnall 2016, 224.
135. Upper elevation: 138.970 m; lower elevation: 138.290 m; average thickness: 50 cm.
136. Upper elevation: 138.380 m; lower elevation: 137.570 m; max. thickness: 60 cm.
137. See pp. 108–12 above.
138. Upper elevation: 137.920 m; lower elevation: unexcavated.
139. The area of DSU30 that was exposed in test trench 2 measured ca. 190 cm north-south by 260 cm east-west.

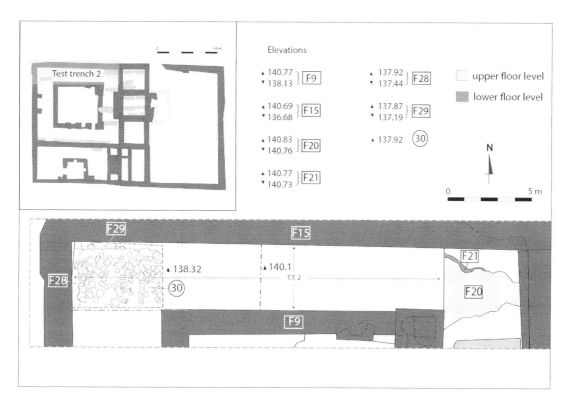

Fig. 3.72: Plan of test trench 2 at the end of the 2012 season (drawing by D. Dzierzbicka; tracing by C. Fosen).

Fig. 3.73: View (to east) of DSU30 in test trench 2.

Foundation trenches for the external walls of room 1 were cut into DSU30. They were relatively shallow, with an average width of less than 0.5 m within test trench 2. The first courses of the church's walls were then laid inside them, up to an elevation of ca. 138.400 m. This square mud-brick casement was subsequently filled with a leveling layer of clean yellow sand (DSU29), with some large pottery fragments scattered through it. Following this step, the foot of the bonded foundations of the central colonnade was laid, as could be observed in test trench 2 with regard to walls F8–9. The construction of the walls (both the external and colonnade foundations) continued, but a slight change in the width of the external walls occurred at this point: the inner faces of F14 (west wall) and F15 (north wall) receded from the face of the lower courses by 16 and 12 cm respectively, forming horizontal ledges. The church builders used the top of leveling layer DSU29 as a walking surface during this construction phase.[140] This interface was marked by coatings of mud mortar smeared along the surrounding walls, over a surface of up to ca. 20 cm from the walls into the trench. The purpose of these mortar layers is unknown. They did not have any structural function, as they rested on a cushion of sand in DSU29, about 10 cm above the mudbricks that formed the ledges at the elevation of ca. 138.400 m. Nevertheless, they appear to be intentional: the relatively regular size and pattern of these coatings suggest that they did not result from an accidental accumulation of mortar dripping from the walls during their construction.[141] It is possible that these mortar layers were applied as guidelines to build the upper courses of the walls or to prevent the sand of the foundation fill from obstructing the area of construction. Some patches of compacted sand and lumps of mortar were also found scattered throughout the top of DSU29.

After the mortar coatings were added, construction proceeded with the laying of approximately twenty more courses of the foundation walls. The space between them was subsequently filled with sand DSU28 and then DSU14. The surface of the latter may have then been used as another walking surface for additional construction work. During this phase the foundation walls of the colonnade, as well as the external walls, were built to their original, full height. At the same time, the upper surface of unit DSU14 seems to have become significantly more compact, with the appearance of concretions (DSU8) in the western halves of the north and south aisles, as well as throughout the west aisle.

The construction of building 7 continued with the laying of compact layers for the floor. A well-preserved sequence of these leveling units was exposed, below floor F21, in the east section of test trench 2. From bottom to top, the following contexts had been laid out: DSU8, DSU26, DSU23, and DSU22 (right below F21). It seems that the latter three units had been laid out earlier than any of the floor levels exposed throughout room 1.[142] In the western half of the room, these leveling layers disappeared completely, due to heavy erosion and/or human activity. All that remained were thin lenses of ash, as well as potsherds (including some ostraca), and a large quantity of fragmentary mudbricks and baked bricks; they were found in the interface between DSU8 and DSU4. As discussed above, the latter was a subsurface layer that

---

140. The top of the sand in DSU29 slightly abutted the first course of the upper sections of the walls.
141. The walls themselves still show very few traces of excess mortar.
142. An ashy layer, similar to DSU26, was noticed in the burial cut (F24) of tomb 2 in the east aisle.

Fig. 3.74: View (to south) of DSU3 in the northwest corner of the central nave (after partial excavation).

covered both the features (including walls, floors, and a *mastaba*), and the extant stratigraphy of foundation fills in the west, south, and north aisles of room 1.[143]

In the western part of the nave, where floor F22 is no longer preserved, a yellowish-beige sand layer (DSU3)[144] was distinguished (fig. 3.74). It abuts walls F7, F8, and F9, and fills the space between the colonnade foundations, below the original floor level of the nave. Only the upper part of this foundation fill was excavated as a subsurface sand level, heavily contaminated by DSU1. The sand in DSU3 had relatively few inclusions, consisting of mud-brick debris, potsherds, animal bones, and small glass fragments. Two small finds were registered while excavating this unit: a diagnostic sherd from a glass plate (inv. 14608) and a group of fragments of painted plaster (inv. 15700) from the collapsed ceiling of the church.

In addition to the sectors of building 7's foundations that were investigated in test trenches 1–2,[145] the excavation of tombs 3 and 4, in the northeast area of room 1, brought to light the west face of east wall F1 below the room's floor level. As mentioned above, a ledge,

---

143. Cf. Sec. 3.2 above.
144. Upper elevation: 140.720 m; lower elevation: 140.280 m; average thickness of excavated part: 21 cm.
145. A third test trench was excavated in room 13 of the south annex: see Sec. 4.8.1 below.

about 8 cm wide, was discovered at an elevation of 140.150 m, which corresponded to that of mortar accumulations on north wall F15 (140.170 m), of a small protrusion on west wall F14 (140.040 m), and of a ledge on wall F9, the foundation wall of the north colonnade (140.160 m).[146]

3.4. Tombs 1–4 and 17 in Room 1

In 2012–2013 four tombs (1–4) were identified and excavated within room 1. The human remains retrieved in all four burials were analyzed by physical anthropologists T. Dupras and L. Williams.[147] In 2023 an additional grave (tomb 17) was found inside the same room; preliminary analysis on the body that was exhumed was carried out by P. G. Sheldrick.[148]

Tomb 1 was found, in a very poor state of preservation, in the northwest part of room 1 in 2012 (figs. 3.2; 3.75).[149] Heavy erosion caused the burial pit to completely disappear. Indeed, no superstructure, or the outline of the original pit, could be detected, but the human remains (FN127) were found still *in situ* within DSU14, a sand context that was part of the foundation fill of the church's walls in this sector.[150] In order to keep material associated with the burial as a discrete collection unit, the deposit immediately surrounding the human remains was excavated as a separate unit (DSU25).[151] It consisted of yellow-brownish sand and contained many fragments of human tissue, hair, and textile (the latter inventoried as 14514) and moderate quantities of charcoal, pottery sherds, plaster, and fragmentary mudbricks.

The body was that of an adult male (fig. 3.76). It rested in a supine position with the head to the west, facing east. The legs were stretched out and arranged close together. The right arm was bent at the elbow and the right palm, which lay near the left elbow, was clenched into a fist. The left arm was laid along the body, with the palm resting on the pelvic area. Although the context of the burial was heavily spoiled, the body was found in relatively good conditions. Remains of textile around the head, chest, and arms suggest that the body was wrapped in a shroud.

To the northeast of FN127, disarticulated human remains (FN63)[152] were found in subsurface layer DSU4, with no evidence of their original burial context. They consisted of bones of the lower legs, broken off at the knee and partially wrapped in textile. The body might have been originally interred in building 7; however, since its remains were found in an unreliable context below the modern-day surface, at a considerably higher elevation than

---

146. See Sec. 3.2 above.
147. Aravecchia et al. 2015, esp. 27–37.
148. Sheldrick 2023. The final report on the human remains from building 7, including the five bodies discovered in room 1, is forthcoming in the companion volume to this archaeological report.
149. During the excavation of test trench 1 in the north aisle of the church; see Sec. 3.2 above.
150. For a discussion of this depositional context, see Sec. 3.2 above.
151. Upper elevation: 139.980 m; lower elevation: 139.790 m. DSU25 was an arbitrary unit, which could not be distinguished from DSU14 in the archaeological record; it was not included in the Harris matrix of room 1.
152. Upper elevation: 140.110 m.

 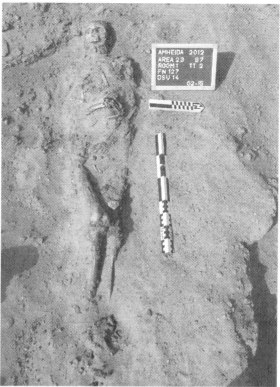

Fig. 3.75: View of excavation of tomb 1. Fig. 3.76: View (to west) of human remains (FN127) in tomb 1.

FN127, it is likely that the body had been brought to light by the erosion process that particularly affected the west part of room 1. Once the remains had been exposed, or were close to the surface, they might have attracted the attention of looters or animals, which dismembered them.

Tombs 2–4 are all located in the east return aisle of room 1 (figs. 3.4; 3.77). While tomb 3 lies in the northeast area of the church, near the entrance into room 14 (the room, now disappeared, above the funerary crypt excavated as room 2), tombs 2 and 4 were found in the proximity of the sanctuary (room 15), immediately to the south and north (respectively) of the stepped platform (F19) that once led into the apse. Tomb 2 was excavated during the same year, while tombs 3–4 were investigated in 2013.

Tomb 2 is rectangular in shape and is oriented east-west. The burial pit (F24)[153] measures 64 cm north-south by 220 cm east-west and is 121 cm deep.[154] It cuts through a lower floor level (F27) in the south part of the east return aisle, between a pillar base (F3) and room 1's east wall (F1) (figs. 3.4; 3.77). The burial, which was found intact, was covered with a mud-brick superstructure (F25),[155] which measured 57 cm north-south by 206 cm east-west and had an

---

153. Upper elevation: 140.680 m; lower elevation: 139.470 m.
154. Length and width of pit F24 were taken at the top.
155. Upper elevation: 140.860 m; lower elevation: 140.680 m.

Fig. 3.77: Aerial view (to southwest) of building 7, showing the location of tombs 2–4 along the north wall of room 1 (tomb 2 is shown backfilled).

average thickness of 12 cm (figs. 3.78–79). Remains of a subsequent floor (F23) were found on top of the superstructure, which consisted of whole and broken bricks. These were laid on bed in eleven rows against the south side of the pit, with more bricks filling the space left against the north edge of F24. The removal of the superstructure revealed a few pottery sherds and a bronze ring (inv. 14496, undecorated and probably not jewelry).

The fill of pit F24 was excavated as DSU24,[156] which was made of yellow-brownish loose sand mixed with scattered mud-brick fragments, lenses of ash and charcoal, animal bones, plaster, and glass fragments, two small pieces of bronze, and a large quantity of ceramic sherds. The inclusions found in this context suggest that DSU24 likely belonged to a refuse layer, originally used as foundation fill in the area of the east return aisle of room 1. Three Greek ostraka were retrieved during the excavation of this deposit inside tomb 2: *O.Trim.* 2.647 (a well tag, likely dated to 284/5) and *O.Trim.* 2.725–26 (two tags, the first dated to 275–350 and the second possibly to 285/6).[157]

The layer immediately surrounding the human remains was excavated as a separate unit, i.e., DSU27.[158] As the layer above it, this DSU consisted of yellow-brownish sand with many inclusions, such as pottery sherds, a few mud-brick fragments, two pieces of glass, fragments of human bones, moderate quantities of wood, charcoal, olive and date pits, and nine small pieces of textile (inv. 14507).

The deceased was a teenaged female. Her body (FN139) was laid supine but in an unusual S-shaped position (fig. 3.80). The head, facing east, was propped up against the west

---

156. Upper elevation: 140.690 m; lower elevation: 139.840 m.
157. Ast and Bagnall 2016, 194 (*O.Trim.* 2.647); 221–22 (*O.Trim.* 2.725–26).
158. Upper elevation: 139.840 m; lower elevation: 139.470 m.

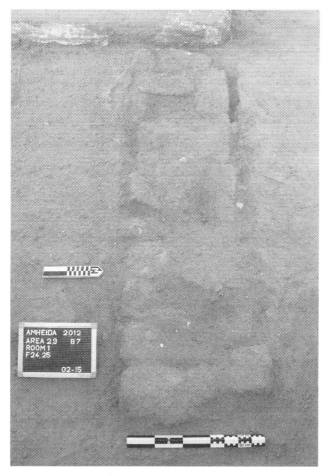

Fig. 3.78: View (to west) of burial pit F24 and superstructure F25 of tomb 2.

side of the burial pit, while the feet were pressed flat against the eastern edge. The legs were slightly bent, with the knees pointing south. Also, the spinal column was not straight. The arms were stretched out along and slightly above the body, with the palms resting flat on the pelvic area. The pelvis itself was at an angle, with the left hipbone higher than the right one. The reason for the awkward position of the body inside tomb 2 may be that the deceased was too tall to fit into the excavated burial pit, which became smaller as it became deeper. Therefore, the body had to be squeezed into the bottom of the shaft, since it could not be laid flat on its back.

Tomb 3 is a roughly rectangular burial, with a simple mud-brick superstructure, oriented east-west. It lies against the northeast corner of the north aisle, along the inner faces of north wall F15 and east wall F1 (figs. 3.4; 3.77). The burial pit (F31)[159] measures 90 cm north-south by 204 cm east-west and has a depth of 140 cm.[160] It cuts into floor levels F20 and F21 in the northeast corner of room 1.

159. Upper elevation: 140.770 m; lower elevation: 139.365 m.
160. Length and width of pit F31 were taken at the top.

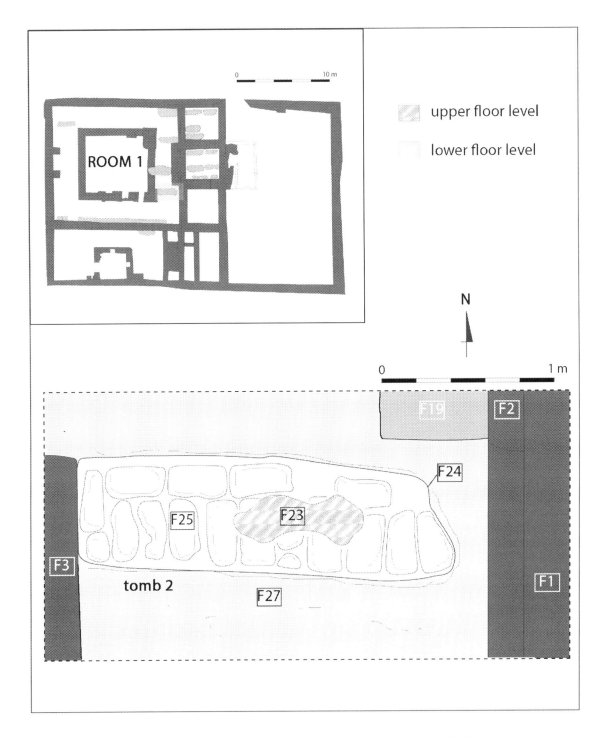

Fig. 3.79: Plan of tomb 2 in room 1 (drawing by D. Dzierzbicka; tracing by C. Fosen).

Fig. 3.80: View (to west) of human remains (FN139) in tomb 2.

Fig. 3.81: View (to west) of burial pit F31 and superstructure F34 (lower level) of tomb 3.

Tomb 3 was found intact. Its superstructure (F34)[161] measured 86 cm north-south by 196 cm east-west, with an average thickness of 13 cm (figs. 3.81–83). It consisted of two levels of bricks: the top layer was made of randomly scattered fragments of mudbricks, while the bottom layer had whole and broken bricks laid on bed across the burial pit in seven rows that occupied the eastern 1.5 m of the pit. The remaining space at the western end was filled, instead, with randomly placed broken bricks, as in the top layer.

Immediately above superstructure F34 was a thin layer (DSU33),[162] ca. 15 cm deep, of loose windblown sand, including mud-brick debris, a few potsherds, charcoal and plaster fragments, animal bones, and a small piece of glass. Below F34, and sealed by it, was the pit fill (DSU39)[163] of tomb 3. It consisted of a layer (ca. 100 cm deep) of sand mixed with a small amount of dumped material, such as mud-brick fragments, charcoal, painted plaster, and animal bones, as well as a relatively large quantity of pottery sherds.

161. Upper elevation: 140.615 m; lower elevation: 140.395 m.
162. Upper elevation: 140.685 m; lower elevation: 140.525 m.
163. Upper elevation: 140.395 m; lower elevation: 139.405 m.

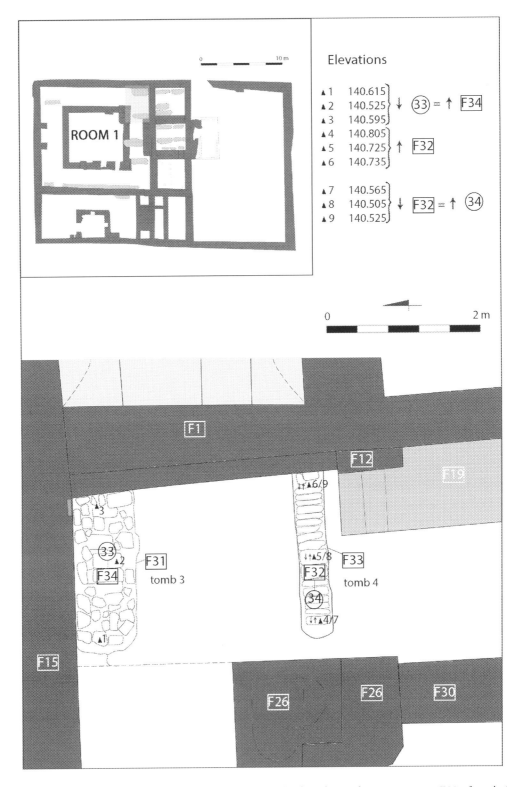

Fig. 3.82: Plan showing superstructure F34 (upper level) of tomb 3 and superstructure F32 of tomb 4 (drawing by D. Dzierzbicka; tracing by C. Fosen).

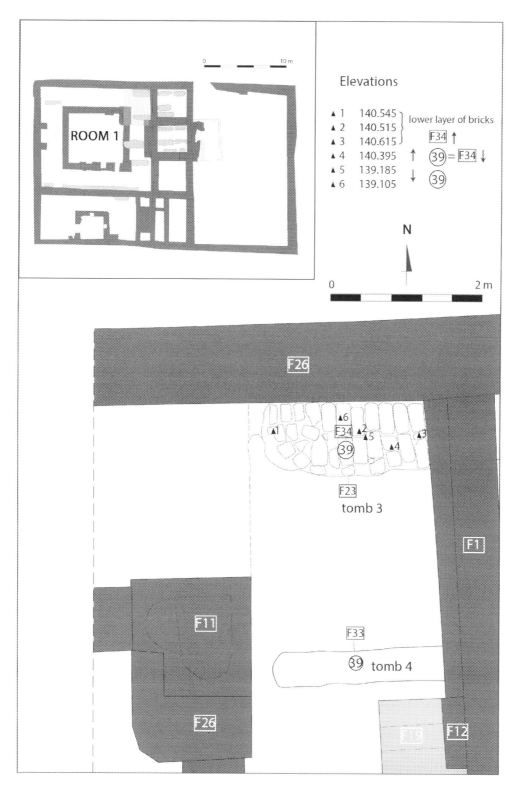

Fig. 3.83: Plan showing superstructure F34 (lower level) of tomb 3 (drawing by D. Dzierzbicka; tracing by C. Fosen).

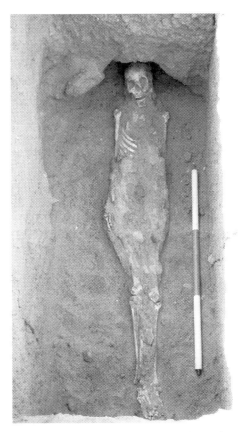

Fig. 3.84: View (to west) of human remains (FN12) in tomb 3.

A bronze coin (inv. 15932, illegible) was found in this context, together with four Greek ostraka: O.Trim. 2.637 (a well tag, dated possibly to 286/7)[164] and O.Trim. 2.728 (a tag, dated between 275 and 350),[165] as well as inv. 15904 and inv. 15933 (both likely decorative designs).

The part of the pit fill that was removed around the human remains was investigated as a separate context (DSU50),[166] ca. 15 cm deep. It consisted of sand with several organic inclusions: fragments of human tissue, textile bits (including inv. 15946), charcoal, small pieces of wood, animal bones, and seeds, as well as a few pottery sherds and plaster fragments.

The deceased (FN12) interred in tomb 3 was an adult female (fig. 3.84). Her body was laid supine, with her head facing east. Her arms lay along her body, with palms resting on the pelvic area. The body had been originally wrapped in a shroud, of which only a few fragments are extant in very poor condition. The top of the head lay in a cavity dug into the west side of the burial cut, near its bottom. It is possible that this was done in order to accommodate the body at the bottom of the pit, which may have been of an insufficient length to host the human remains.

164. Ast and Bagnall 2016, 190.
165. Ast and Bagnall 2016, 222.
166. Upper elevation: 139.475 m; lower elevation: 139.365 m.

Fig. 3.85: Aerial view (to south) of building 7 after surface clearance in 2012. The dotted rectangle comprises an area with loose mudbricks above tomb 3.

Tomb 3 presents unusual features compared to the other burials investigated within building 7. Its superstructure was placed relatively deep inside the burial pit. Furthermore, no traces of the upper floor were detected above the uncommonly wide burial cut. It cannot be ruled out that tomb 3 originally had two superstructures, i.e., a lower one (F34) inside the burial pit (F31) and a higher one (no longer extant) that rose slightly above the latest floor level of room 1. The idea of a superstructure rising above floor level is supported—or, at least, not ruled out—by the placement of the tomb in the corner of room 1, where such a platform would not have obstructed people's movement.[167] Loose mudbricks, which were found along room 1's north wall (F15), in the proximity of the northeast corner, may have been surviving elements of this structure. These mudbricks can be seen in aerial photographs that were taken after surface clearance in Area 2.3 (fig. 3.85).[168] Apart from the above-mentioned clues, the material evidence is, however, insufficient to advance this idea beyond reasonable speculation.

Tomb 4, of a rectangular shape, is located to the south of tomb 3 and to the north of platform F19 in the east return aisle (figs. 3.4; 3.77). The burial pit (F33),[169] which cuts the lower floor of room 1 (F20), measures 40 cm north-south by 212 cm east-west and has a depth

---

167. Burials with double superstructures are attested at the Kellis 2 cemetery: Bowen 2022a, 346, fig. 14.3d; 347.
168. The bricks were removed as part of DSU4 during the 2012 excavation season.
169. Upper elevation: 140.805 m; lower elevation: 139.805 m.

Fig. 3.86: View (to west) of burial pit F33 and superstructure F32 of tomb 4.

of 100 cm.[170] The pit, which was intact at the time of its discovery, was sealed with a mud-brick superstructure (F32),[171] which measured 40 cm north-south by 194 cm east-west and was 20 cm thick (fig. 3.86). The superstructure, which was partly concealed, roughly at its center, by a patch of the upper floor (F23) of room 1, consisted of 19 mudbricks. Sixteen of them were laid on edge across the burial pit. In the central part, three bricks were laid on bed, one at the bottom and two above it. The bricks were closely spaced, with some sand and potsherds in between. After the removal of F32, pit fill (DSU34)[172] was revealed. It consisted of loose yellow sand and contained pockets of ash with charcoal, as well as molded gypsum plaster and painted plaster. Among the inclusions were also moderate quantities of mud-brick fragments, pebbles, mortar, one glass fragment, 116 pottery sherds, two fragments of hair, one fragmentary pit, and two animal bones. Since the burial pit cuts through a garbage layer at its western end, it is possible that fill DSU34 belonged, before the digging of the tomb, to the same refuse unit.

170. Length and width of pit F33 were taken at the top.
171. Upper elevation: 140.725 m; lower elevation: 140.505 m.
172. Upper elevation: 140.565 m; lower elevation: 139.825 m; average thickness: 60 cm.

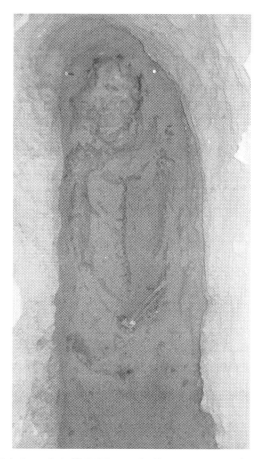

Fig. 3.87: Partial view of pit fill DSU45 and of human remains (FN13) in tomb 4.

The lowermost part of the pit fill was distinguished as DSU45,[173] in order to separate the soil surrounding the human remains in tomb 4 (fig. 3.87). The layer was made of yellow-brownish sand mixed with numerous pottery sherds, limited charcoal, animal bones, plaster, glass, and wood fragments, and one date pit. Fragments of textile and soft tissue, once part of the decayed human remains (inv. 15947) in tomb 4, were also found in DSU45.

The deceased was an adult male. His body was laid supine, with his head to the west (facing east). The right arm rested along the body, with the palm of his right hand on the pelvic area. The left arm had a stiff elbow joint, which resulted in the forearm projecting upwards. The body was wrapped in a shroud, now preserved only in fragments. After the deposition of the body, and before the backfilling of the pit, three bundles of myrtle, rosemary, and palm leaves, of which traces were found as part of FN4, had been placed on top of the body in the area of the arms, chest, and abdomen.[174]

173. Upper elevation: 140.005 m; lower elevation: 139.365 m; max. thickness: 47 cm.
174. Copious evidence exists for the use of myrtle and rosemary wreaths in Christian burials at Kellis: see Hope and McKenzie 1999, 56; Bowen 2019, 377. Cf. also Thanheiser 1999, 89.

Fig. 3.88: Aerial view (to east) of tomb 17 in room 1 (during excavation).

Tomb 17 was identified during the 2023 season at the east end of room 1, in a prominent position facing the apse of the church (now-disappeared room 15) (figs. 3.4; 3.88). The pit (F113)[175] was cut through lower floor F27 in the eastern aisle of room 1, between platform F19 to the east and colonnade foundation F30 (joining the foundations of the north and south colonnades at their east ends). The pit is rectangular in shape, measuring 100 cm north-south by 263 cm east-west. It reaches a maximum depth of 105 cm below the lower floor level, narrowing towards the bottom by ca. 50 cm. It cut DSU173[176] (a leveling sand layer) and, in part, the above-mentioned foundations of the colonnade F30. The pit was sealed with a

175. Upper elevation: 140.840 m; lower elevation: 139.890 m.
176. Upper elevation: 140.680 m; lower elevation: 138.890 m; max. thickness: 79 cm. DSU173 consisted of grayish-brown sand mixed with large quantities of pottery sherds and fragments of plaster, large amounts of ash, charcoal, slag, pebbles, and mud-brick debris. This layer was part of the foundation fill of the east aisle of room 1 and is very similar to DSU8, another foundation layer detected in test trenches 1 and 2 (cf. Secs. 3.3.1 and 3.3.2 below). These deposits were made of backfill material that likely came from the church's surroundings and especially from the area to the east of building 7, where evidence for industrial activity can still be detected above surface (C. Caputo, personal communication, January 2023).

mud-brick superstructure (F112)¹⁷⁷ (figs. 3.89–90). It measured 94 cm north-south by 234 cm east-west and consisted of complete and fragmentary mudbricks laid in two parallel rows near the southern and northern edges, with a more irregular layout in the middle. The superstructure was slightly shorter than the overall length of the cut, leaving the eastern portion of the burial pit unsealed.

The fill of tomb 17 was DSU163,¹⁷⁸ a layer of brownish-yellow sand with numerous inclusions, such as mud-bricks debris, pebbles, pottery sherds, ash, fragments of white plaster, straw, slag, animal bones, and charcoal.¹⁷⁹ Below the fill, at a depth of about 70 cm from the level of the church's walking surface, excavations exposed a trapezoid wooden coffin, complete although decayed due to termites' activity (inv. 17098) (fig. 3.91).¹⁸⁰ Although it was impossible to retrieve the coffin in its entirety, due to its very poor condition, its original shape and size (217 by 70 cm) could be discerned. It seems that, in order to fit the coffin inside the pit, the original cut was enlarged by ca. 20 cm to the east along its east edge, towards the bottom.

The coffin contained organic brown sand (DSU165)¹⁸¹ directly in contact with the complete skeleton (FN55) of an elderly man, about 50 to 65 years old and ca. 1.65 m tall, laid supine with his hands on the pelvic area, and wrapped in several layers of textiles (fig. 3.92).¹⁸² The preservation of the human remains was significantly better than in the case of the other bodies discovered inside the church and the underground crypts. This is likely due to the fact that many bones, particularly the skull, were encrusted with crystalline mineral deposits. The individual, who seems to have died of a severe sinus infection, was found with some dried organs, such as his brain, liver, lungs, and skin tissues. The prominent position of the burial immediately facing the apse, the use of a wooden coffin and of different layers of textiles to protect the body of the deceased lead to the assumption that the individual interred in tomb 17 was a prominent figure within the Christian community that worshipped in building 7 at Amheida.

As discussed above, most burials inside room 1, as well as tomb 5 located along the outer face of the south wall, were found intact. The only exception was tomb 1 in the northwest corner of the room, which was subject to heavy erosion and perhaps human disturbance. The burial pits were dug through earlier floor levels of the church and were then sealed with a simple mud-brick superstructure, with bricks laid out in an overall regular fashion.

---

177. Upper elevation: 140.690 m; lower elevation: 140.350 m; max. thickness: 10 cm.
178. Upper elevation: 140.600 m; lower elevation: 139.960 m; max. thickness: 39 cm.
179. The cut was likely backfilled reusing material from the excavation of the pit in leveling layer DSU173.
180. Wooden coffins are rarely found in Christian burials; out of hundreds of tombs in the K2 cemetery at Kellis, only one wooden coffin was identified, which was coated with a layer of gypsum plaster and still bearing traces of painted decoration: Bowen 2022a, 353. No traces of painting or gypsum plaster were detected in the heavily decayed coffin inside tomb 17. Very few wooden coffins were also found at El-Bagawat: cf. Hauser 1932, 48. No evidence of wooden coffins was found in the pre-Christian K1 cemetery at Kellis: Hope, McKenzie, and Nuzzolo 2022, 331.
181. Upper elevation: 140.160 m; lower elevation: 139.940 m; average thickness: 20 cm. The unit was mixed with moderate quantities of mud-brick debris and pottery fragments.
182. Sheldrick 2023, 16–17. A preliminary study of the textiles allowed the identification of at least three different types: the first one, probably linen, undecorated and with a fine-textured fabric, had been wrapped around the body of the deceased; the second layer was of a coarse-weave fabric, while the third (external) layer appeared to consist of a well-made fabric, with a fringe along the edges and an embroidered decoration in dark red parallel lines.

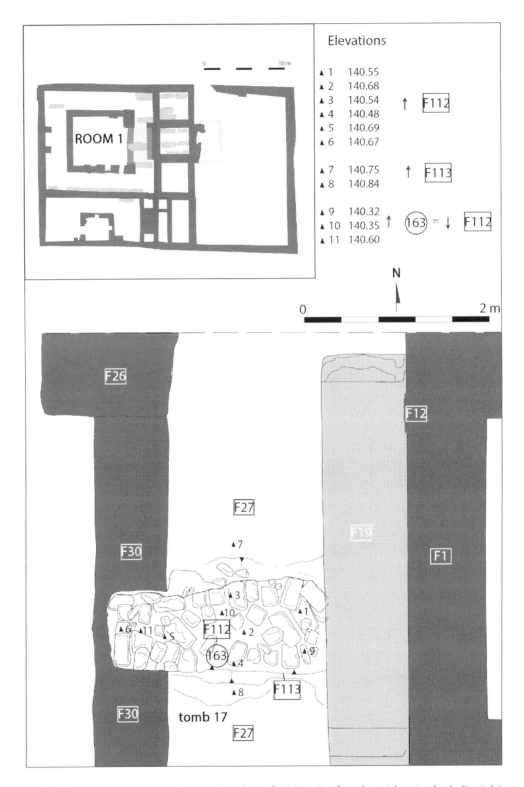

Fig. 3.89: Plan showing superstructure F112 and outline of pit (F113) of tomb 17 (drawing by L. Davighi; tracing by S. Alfarano).

Fig. 3.90: View (to west) of superstructure F112 and outline of pit (F113) of tomb 17.

Fig. 3.91: View (to east) of coffin (inv. 17098) inside tomb 17.

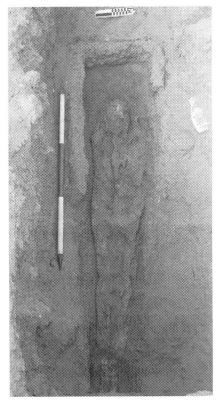

Fig. 3.92: View from above of human remains (FN55) in tomb 17.

The tombs that were investigated (tombs 1–4) were single interments and did not contain any funerary goods or objects revealing the religious affiliation of the deceased. The bodies were originally wrapped in shrouds, fragmentarily preserved in a few instances, and were laid supine, with their heads to the west (facing east). Their arms were placed along their bodies, with the palms resting, in most cases, on the pelvic area.[183] No evidence of intentional mummification was detected on any of the deceased individuals.[184]

All these features, including the east-west orientation and position of the bodies, the general lack of funerary goods, and the presence of simple mud-brick superstructures to seal the tombs, are widely attested in early Christian burials found in Dakhla, in particular at Kellis, Deir Abu Matta, and at a site northeast of the Roman cemetery of El-Muzawwaqa.[185]

183. The only exception was the body found in tomb 1. As mentioned above, the right arm of the deceased was bent at the elbow and the right palm, clenched into a fist, rested on top of the abdominal area.

184. This is not necessarily to be expected in the context of fourth-century Christian burials. In fact, there is evidence, both documentary and archaeological, that mummification was not abandoned with the spread of Christianity, but continued into the fourth century in the region of the Western Desert and elsewhere in Egypt: for a summary of some of the evidence, see Bowen 2003b, 169 and, more recently, Dunand 2019 and Dunand and Letellier-Willemin 2019, esp. 246–51.

185. Bowen 2003b (Kellis); Bowen 2008 (for the cemetery located to the northeast of El-Muzawwaqa, which is labeled as site 22/390-I7-2 in Mills 1979, 168); Bowen 2012a (Deir Abu Matta). For a summary of the evidence from Kellis, see also Bowen 2019.

They reflect funerary customs that were widespread, by the fourth century CE, in the context of Christian burials within, as well as beyond, Dakhla Oasis.[186]

3.5. Rooms 14–16

The sanctuary of the church at Amheida consists of three rooms aligned, from north to south, along the east wall of room 1. They were labeled rooms 14–16, respectively (figs. 3.2; 3.93–94). Together, they form a rectangle that measures 13.95 m north-south by 4.95 m east-west, separating room 1 from the large enclosure to the east of building 7. Upon inspection of the three rooms at present ground level, it was immediately clear that their features had almost completely disappeared, due perhaps to human intervention and/or natural causes, such as wind erosion. Originally, these spaces existed at roughly the same level as room 1, albeit at a slightly higher elevation. This was certainly the case for room 15, which was accessible from the church by means of a stepped platform (F19). Remains of engaged semi-columns (F2 and F12), located in front of this space, attest to the existence, in antiquity, of a monumental doorway leading into this room. A smaller doorway was also identified at the south end of wall F1, once providing access from the church onto room 16. Unfortunately, the near-total disappearance of features in room 14 did not allow to identify the passageway that must have led (based on the relatively standard layout of this type of basilicas) from the east aisle of room 1 into this space.

Room 15, located at the east end of the main axis of the church, in line with the west entrance into building 7, was identified as the area where the apse once stood. It was flanked by two service rooms or *pastophoria* (room 16 to the south and room 14 to the north). Below the apse and the two *pastophoria* were three underground crypts (rooms 2–4), excavated in 2013 and 2023.

Room 14 was investigated in 2013. What was visible at ground level, when excavations began, were in fact the upper parts of sub-structures once supporting the now-missing room above, also forming an underground crypt. These features included walls, a barrel-vaulted roof, and remains of a mud-brick platform laid out above the vaulted ceiling.[187] Due to the lack of archaeological evidence for the upper room, it was decided to keep the label of that missing space as room 14, while the underground crypt was named room 2.

---

186. Cf. Coudert 2012 and Dunand et al. 2008 and 2012 on a Christian cemetery located at El-Deir (Kharga Oasis). The burials showcase numerous similarities with those documented in Dakhla, although there are no remains in the examples from El-Deir of superstructures (Coudert 2012, 454). See Lythgoe 1908, 207–8 on early Christian interments at El-Bagawat (Kharga); Martin 1974, 20 and Jeffreys and Strouhal 1980 on Christian burials at Saqqara. On minimal discrepancies with the east-west orientation of the deceased, see Rahtz 1978. Cf. also the discussion in Sec. 5.5 (esp. pp. 339–41). The paucity, or absence, of funerary goods in early Christian burials is attested also in graves throughout the Eastern Mediterranean: see Fox and Tritsaroli 2019, 110.

187. The investigation of this space is discussed in detail in Sec. 5.2 below. The platform may have been built to flatten the area above the vault of the underground crypt (room 2), thus creating a solid, flat surface below the floor of the north *pastophorion* (room 14).

Fig. 3.93: Aerial view (to northeast) of the area of the sanctuary and *pastophoria* (before excavation of the crypts).

The excavation of rooms 15 and 16 took place in 2023. The heavily deteriorated condition of the features visible at ground level did not allow to gather a precise idea of these two spaces' original size (which, however, must have been about the same as that of the crypts underneath them, i.e., rooms 3 and 4, respectively). No remains of features were detected in relation to the apse (room 15).[188] Scanty evidence is available for room 16, namely the bottom courses of its west perimeter wall (F1) and the threshold of the doorway[189] that was built into this wall and opened onto room 1 (fig. 3.95).[190] The stratigraphy of room 16 consisted of just two units, i.e., DSU1 (surface windblown sand, highly unreliable) and DSU17,[191] consisting of subsurface yellow sand, mixed with some potsherds, mud-brick debris, and a few pebbles.

---

188. Not even of the platform on which the floor of the apse would have been set. It is also unknown whether the central apse once opened directly onto the side *pastophoria*.

189. Upper elevation: 141.120 m.

190. One remaining course of the south wall (F13) is still visible by the room's southwest corner. The north and east walls (F78 and F59, respectively) are preserved only below floor level; thus, they are included in the discussion of the south crypt (room 4) underneath room 16. The evidence also includes two stratigraphic units (DSU115 and DSU126) that were excavated inside the south crypt, but seemingly originated from the collapse of the north half of room 16's west wall (F1) into the space below.

191. Upper elevation: 141.050 m; lower elevation: 140.660 m; max. thickness: 40 cm.

Fig. 3.94: Photogrammetric mosaic of rooms 14–16 (above rooms 2–4 respectively).

Fig. 3.95: View (to west) of remains of room 16. Photograph taken during the first day of excavation of the underground crypt (room 4).

The unit lay above DSU111, which was assigned to the stratigraphy of room 4 below room 16.[192] A detailed presentation and discussion of the evidence for the three underground crypts (rooms 2–4) follows in Chapter 5.

---

192. See Sec. 5.4 below.

Chapter 4

Survey and Excavations to the South the Church

4.1. Introduction

The 2012 excavations inside the church focused on room 1, comprising the central nave and the side aisles. As mentioned in an earlier chapter, the area to the north and west of the church was left to be explored at a later date, while the sector to the east, including the apse (room 15) and the two service rooms (room 14 to the north and room 16 to the south), was the object of a surface survey during the same year.[1] Also, an exceptionally large space was identified to the east of building 7. It is rectangular in shape and measures 17.8 m north-south by 11.3 m east-west. It is delimited to the west by walls F59 and F76, which form the east boundary of building 7, and, to the north and south, by walls that seem to be the continuation of F15 and F40 respectively. Based on the overall layout of building 7, as observed at the floor level of the church, one may argue that this space became part of the church complex when the south annex was added. Nevertheless, in the absence of in-depth investigations, it is impossible to know if this was one large courtyard, perhaps used as a *kathesterion* (a space for visitors), such as the one adjoining the contemporary church of Shams el-Din in Kharga Oasis,[2] or if it was in fact partitioned into several rooms, whose preserved walls are currently obscured by sand. The survey revealed a break, almost 2 m wide, at the west end of the north wall, but it is unclear if this was the main entrance into the room or access to it was originally placed somewhere else. There are no sufficient archaeological data to determine if (and how) this space was connected—if at all—with the rest of building 7, either at the level of the church itself or of the underground crypts. Indeed, the tops of the four walls, which are the only features not hidden below the sand, dramatically slope down eastwards and are at an elevation lower than that of the church's floors.

---

1. The area of the sanctuary (including the crypts underneath the apse and the two *pastophoria*) was investigated in 2013 and 2023: see Sec. 3.5 above and Ch. 5 below.
2. See Wagner 1987, 182.

Again, only in-depth excavation of the area to the east of rooms 2–4 can provide answers in this regard.[3]

Excavation in the sector to the south of the church took place in 2013 and revealed a cluster of nine spaces (rooms 5–13), built along the south wall (F13) of room 1. They cover a rectangular area that measures ca. 6 m north-south by ca. 19.5 m east-west (figs. 4.1–3). This annex to the church is bounded to the south by wall F40. The latter was built, at least in the sections exposed along its north face, with mudbricks laid in English bond. However, the south face of this feature, which is preserved to a significant height above ground level in its middle section,[4] is severely eroded and shows a bond consisting mostly of headers (fig. 4.4). Although a single FSU number was assigned to the entire south boundary of the annex, it is possible that the wall consisted in fact of two or more separate segments, which were built in line with each other.[5] Further excavation is needed in the area to the south of F40, in order to expose the foundation courses throughout the wall's length and clarify their construction process.[6]

Both the east and west sector of the south annex (including rooms 9 and 11–13) were subject to severe wind erosion, with little surviving above floor level. Architectural features are significantly better preserved in the central area (rooms 5–8), where some walls are still standing over two meters in height.[7] Evidence for episodes of collapse, which include ceiling plaster with palm rib impressions as well as pieces of wood,[8] paired with the absence of any traces of vault bricks, suggests that these spaces had flat roofs.

Rooms 5–13 form a dense cluster of spaces, with access available from the north and the south. The main entrance into this sector of building 7 seems to have been located along the southern wall (F40). The threshold of a broad doorway (almost 2 m in width) is still visible in the southeast corner of room 6; it once led from the outside into room 6 and the rest of the complex. A second doorway, placed in the southeast corner of room 1, opened onto staircase 5 and, via its landing, onto room 6, a centrally located space within the south sector of building 7. An internal corridor (room 8), running along the north wall (F42) of room 7, connected room 6 with room 9 to the south. Room 7 was accessible from room 9 through a doorway in its west wall. A third, much narrower passageway (room 10), located in the southeast corner of room 6, opened onto space 11. Due to the very poor state of preservation of the features (well below the original floor level) in the southeast corner of building 7, it is not known how room 12 was accessed in antiquity, while room 13 (as discussed below) seems to have formed one space together with room 11 originally.

---

3. A test trench (4) was excavated to the east of room 3 in 2023, but the evidence that was retrieved did not allow to answer the questions above: cf. Sec. 5.3.2 below.

4. Elsewhere, only a few courses of mudbricks are visible above the wall's foundations.

5. One segment may have consisted of the south wall of rooms 6, 7, and 9; another may have run along rooms 11–12, at the east end of the annex; finally, a small segment may have been built between walls F36–37, at their south ends, within room 10. All this remains, however, purely hypothetical and in need of further investigation. Cf. the discussion of F40 in the separate sections below.

6. Only then separate feature numbers could be assigned.

7. F41 and F40 in rooms 6 and 7.

8. These destruction layers include: DSU36–37 and DSU54 in room 6; DSU80 and DSU82 in room 7; DSU38 in room 8; DSU46 and DSU57 in room 10.

Fig. 4.1: View (to southeast) of building 7's south annex (before excavation).

Fig. 4.2: Aerial view (to southwest) of excavated rooms to the south of the church.

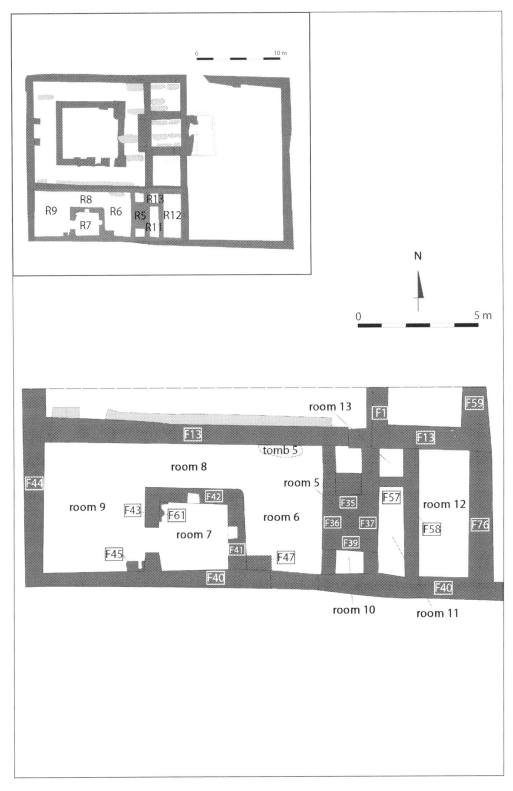

Fig. 4.3: Plan of rooms 5–13 (tracing by C. Fosen).

Fig. 4.4: View of south face of wall F40.

The spaces located to the south of room 1 do not belong to the same construction episode of the basilica church; however, the available evidence does not point to a significant hiatus between the two phases. Room 6 was undoubtedly associated, in terms of its function, with the church itself. Indeed, an east-west oriented burial (tomb 5) was found in this room along the south face of wall F13 (the south wall of the church). The burial pit (F56) was cut into the lower floor (F51) of the room and its mud-brick superstructure (F52) was partially covered by remains of the upper floor (F50), similarly to tombs 2 and 4, which were excavated inside room 1.

Furthermore, materials and techniques used in the construction of rooms 5–13 were consistent with those adopted in rooms 1–4 (the church with its crypts), as well as throughout the site. Their walls are coated with white gypsum plaster on top of mud plaster. As observed in the side aisles of the church, two floor levels of compacted clay were detected also in rooms 6 and 8–9.[9]

Rooms 6 and 8–10 formed an open and easily accessible area within the complex to the south of the church, with a main entry located along the south wall (F40) and no spaces separated by closed doorways. As for the passageway connecting room 6 with room 10 to the east, a mud-brick step was found at floor level, but there is no evidence suggesting the existence, in antiquity, of a wooden door. In contrast, the remnants of a door pivot, discovered in a hole within the threshold between rooms 5 and 6, suggest that these two spaces were once separated by a door. The existence of additional doorways would have allowed for some control of access to, and movement within, rooms 7 and 11–12. These spaces may have served more utilitarian functions than rooms 6 and 8–10, although this must remain conjecture, as sufficient archaeological evidence is lacking.

---

9. Patches of these walking surfaces were documented as lower floors F51 and F55 and upper floors F50 and F54.

Fig. 4.5: Aerial view (to south) of room 5.

4.2. Room 5

Features

Room 5 is a space occupied by the remains of a staircase and its lower landing (figs. 4.3; 4.5). It is rectangular and measures 4.16 m north-south by 2.40 m east-west, with walls preserved to a maximum height of 55 cm above floor level.[10] Room 5 opened onto the church via a doorway placed at the east end of room 1's south wall (F13). It allowed access from the church itself into room 6 and the whole south annex. The staircase, which once connected the ground floor of building 7 to its roof or second level (no longer extant) is very poorly preserved. The remains

10. From the top of the preserved substructure of the staircase to the ancient floor level (in the lower landing).

Fig. 4.6: View (to east) of wall F37 in room 5.

consist of a lower landing, which bears evidence of two floor levels (F38 and F46), and a flight of steps (F35) ascending towards the south. The stairs were supported by a rectangular mud-brick platform bonded with walls F36, F37, and F39, which formed the platform's west, east, and south sides.

F37 is the east wall of staircase F35 and forms also the east boundary of room 5 (fig. 4.6).[11] It is heavily eroded above floor level, with only six courses, laid in English bond, preserved at its north end (west face).[12] Within room 5 there is a rectangular recess[13] in the wall (measuring 102 cm north-south by 25–35 cm east-west) that extends from the threshold into room 1 to staircase F35. Its mud-plastered horizontal surface is 13 cm lower than the above-mentioned threshold and the plaster descends onto floor F38. The recess was created in order to maintain, within room 5, the same width of the doorway that opened from room 1 into room 5 itself. The latter also served as the point of access into room 6 (as well as the rest of the south annex) and to the staircase leading to the roof (or an upper floor) of the church complex. Therefore, this space was essential in allowing access to—and movement within—the different areas of building 7.

11. The east side of the wall is described in Sec. 4.8 below, which also includes elevations of the feature (see pp. 215–16 and n. 151).
12. No plaster is preserved on the vertical surface of this wall in room 5.
13. Upper elevation: 140.825 m; lower elevation: 148.695 m.

Fig. 4.7: View (to north) of wall F13 in room 5, with threshold into room 1.

The north side of room 5 is formed by a stretch of wall F13, which is preserved here to its highest level (fig. 4.7). Within this room, ten courses of the wall are visible, laid out in English bond, on its east face. No plaster is preserved; only a layer of sandy mortar can be seen, smeared over three courses of mudbricks, below the threshold that once connected rooms 1 and 5. The threshold measures 80 cm north-south by 95 cm east-west and is defined, against its south side facing room 5, by six baked bricks laid on bed (fig. 4.8).[14]

F13 is abutted by F36,[15] which is the wall separating rooms 5 and 6. Within room 5, F36 is bonded with staircase F35 for most of its length, except for the north end of the wall, which was once pierced by the doorway opening onto room 6 (fig. 4.9). The only extant feature is the threshold, which measures 110 cm north-south by 52 cm east-west.[16] It is formed by the three lowest courses of wall F13 visible above the ancient floor level of adjacent room 6. The threshold is covered with patches of mud plaster, which obscure the brick bond. At the north end of the

14. For a description of the north face of the threshold, see Sec. 3.2 above.
15. Elevations and a description of the west face of the wall are provided in Sec. 4.3 below.
16. Upper elevation: 149.585 m; lower elevation: 140.365 m.

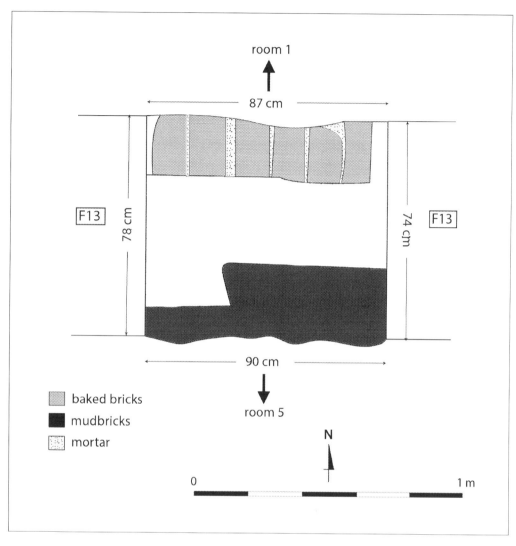

Fig. 4.8: Drawing of upper surface of doorway between rooms 1 and 5
(drawing by D. Dzierzbicka; tracing by C. Fosen).

feature, in the proximity of wall F13 an irregular pit is cut into the threshold.[17] Its investigation revealed traces of wood at the bottom. It is likely that they belonged to a wooden pivot of a door that once separated room 5 from the rest of the south annex. An additional hole is visible in north wall F13, at the level of the threshold and in line with its west end (fig. 4.10).[18] The cavity is surrounded by a wider recess,[19] where the face of the wall appears to have been hacked away. Possibly, the hole originally held another structural element of the wooden door between rooms 5 and 6.

17. Dimensions of the pit: 32 by 30 cm; depth: 8 cm.
18. Measurements of the hole in F13: 17 cm (hor.) by 12 cm (vert.), with a depth of 22 cm.
19. The recess measures 30 by 30 cm and is 10 cm deep.

Fig. 4.9: View (to east) of threshold between rooms 5 and 6.

Immediately to the south of the threshold is a cavity set within the bottom courses of F36's west face.[20] The irregular shape of this fissure, as well as its location at the level of the threshold, suggests that it may have been caused by the removal of a feature—perhaps a wooden plank—located above the threshold, or belonging to the now-missing doorway. A bronze coin (inv. 16047), dated to 351–361, was found embedded in wall F36, in the area of the threshold between rooms 5 and 6.

As mentioned above, room 5 is largely occupied by the remains of staircase F35,[21] consisting of a rectangular mud-brick substructure and three preserved steps near the lower landing (figs. 4.11–13). The substructure measures 3.04 m north-south by 2.36 m east-west and is preserved to a max. height of 55 cm.[22] The extant steps of the staircase are 110 cm wide and 30 cm deep;[23] they are made of mudbricks laid on two courses each, with wooden planks lining the outer edges. These planks, which were found in a poor state of preservation, were originally square in section, measuring 8 by 8 cm. On the third step from the bottom, the plank is inserted into a 6 cm recess within the east wall.[24]

20. The hole measures about 36 by 36 cm and its max. depth is 13 cm.
21. Upper elevation: 141.215 m; lower elevation: 140.665 m.
22. The width includes walls F36–37 (part of the substructure and flanking the steps of the staircase).
23. The second and third steps, which were fully exposed, measure 18 cm in height.
24. For an in-depth discussion of the staircase, including its hypothetical reconstruction, see Sec. 7.3 below.

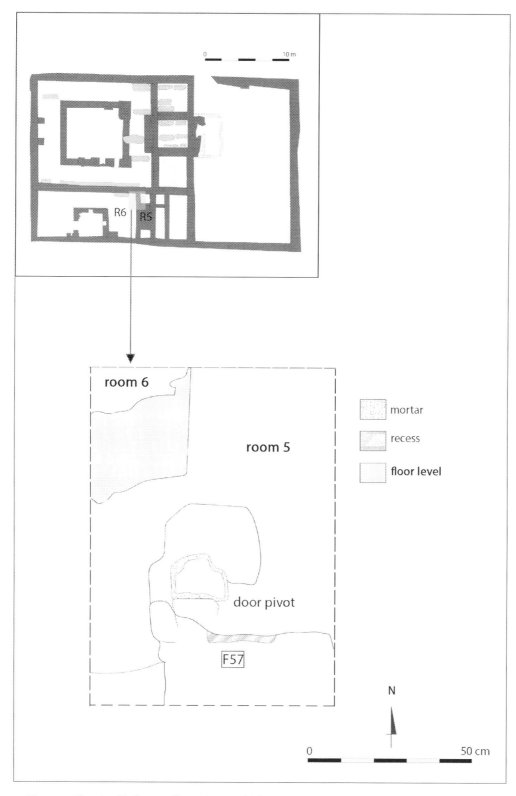

Fig. 4.10: Sketch of hole in wall F13 (room 5) (drawing by D. Dzierzbicka; tracing by C. Fosen).

Fig. 4.11: View (to south) of staircase F35 in room 5.

Two floor levels were found and documented inside room 5, more precisely in the area of the lower landing of staircase F35 (fig. 4.14). F38[25] is the later floor and its remains are visible in the eastern half of the landing. It is made of mud plaster, with hard sand incrustations (presumably not part of the original floor) covering the preserved surface in its entirety.[26] Mostly obscured by F38 is the lower mud plaster floor of room 5 (F46).[27] This is exposed along the threshold between rooms 5 and 6 and, in part, along wall F13. Its surface is uneven, with small pottery sherds, lime spots, and even a few fruit pits embedded in it.

25. Upper elevation: 140.695 m; lower elevation: 140.595 m; average thickness: 5 cm.
26. These concretions also covered the adjacent recess within wall F37.
27. Upper elevation: 140.595 m.

Chapter 4: Survey and Excavations to the South the Church

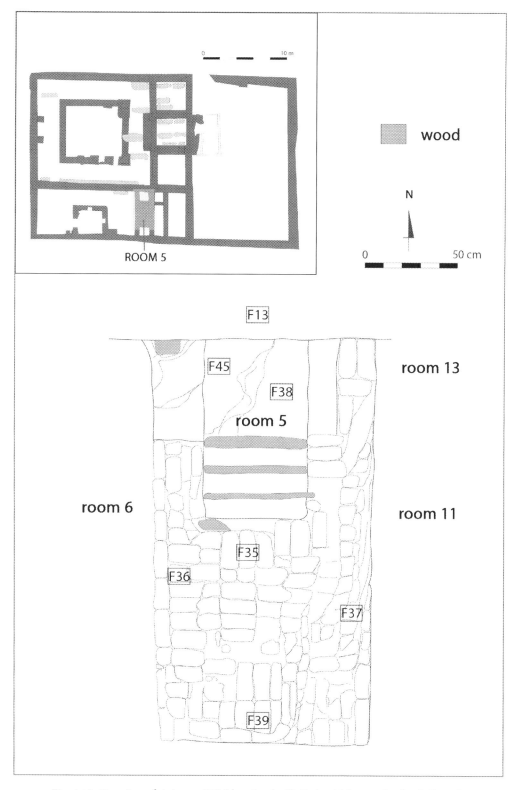

Fig. 4.12: Drawing of staircase F35 (drawing by D. Dzierzbicka; tracing by C. Fosen).

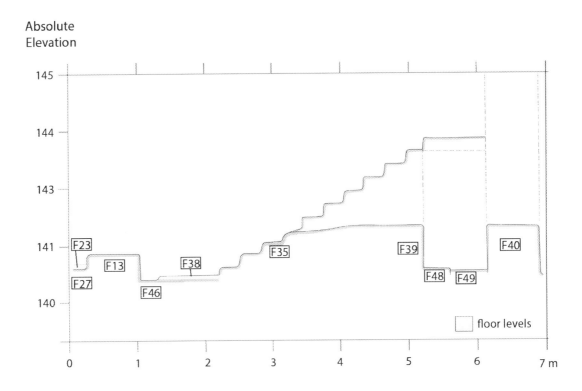

Fig. 4.13: N–S section of staircase F35 (looking E), reconstructed (drawing by D. Dzierzbicka; tracing by C. Fosen).

Stratigraphy and finds (fig. 4.15)

The remains of the staircase's mud-brick substructure were found exposed to the elements. The only stratigraphy extant inside room 5 was limited to the preserved steps of the staircase, as well as the lower landing. The removal of the surface layer of windblown sand (DSU31)[28] from this area led to the discovery of a wall-collapse unit (DSU35)[29] (fig. 4.16) The mudbricks were scattered in several patches, the largest of which lay in the doorway between rooms 5 and 6.

---

28. Upper elevation: 141.275 m; lower elevation: 141.025 m; average thickness: 5 cm (elevations taken in room 5). Numerous small finds were found in DSU31 before numbers could be assigned to the rooms of the south annex. These objects include: several diagnostic fragments of glass vessels (inv. 15859–15860, 15907, 15917–15921, 16036–16037, 16039–16044, 16058); a complete iron peg (inv. 15906); a fragmentary wooden peg (inv. 16074); a bracelet fragment made of black opaque glass (inv. 15923); two beads, one of white faience with turquoise glaze (inv. 16035) and the other of dark green glass (inv. 16056); an *aryballos*-shaped bead of glass (inv. 16045; similar to Arveiller-Dulong and Nenna 2011, 193, no. 248); one fragment of a terracotta figurine representing an animal, possibly a bird (although its interpretation is still disputed; inv. 16067); and one fragment from the upper valve of a circular ceramic lamp (inv. 16068). The discus of the lamp is decorated with a standing naked human figure, who is front facing. It is similar to inv. 11632, from house B2 at Amheida, depicting the "three Graces" (see Dixneuf 2015, 234–35, group 71a, no. 152). According to a parallel from Karanis (Shier 1970, 117, pl. 36 no 315) this type of lamp can be dated between the mid-first to the mid-second centuries CE. However, the poor state of preservation of the fragment from the church does not allow a secure identification of the scene depicted.

29. Upper elevation: 141.235 m; lower elevation: 140.095 m; average thickness: 13 cm.

Fig. 4.14: View (to east) of patches of floors F38 and F46 in room 5.

Another cluster extended above the threshold of wall F13, leading from room 1 into room 5. The unit included whole mudbricks, as well as mud-brick debris, lime spots, and a few potsherds. Based on the scatter pattern of the bricks, it is possible that the collapse came from the staircase in a northward direction. Both DSU31 and DSU35 rested above a layer of loose yellow sand (DSU41),[30] which was mixed with moderate quantities of mud-brick fragments, lime spots, ceramic sherds, animal bones, white plaster, wood fragments, and a few date pits. Some of these inclusions may belong to a domestic refuse context, dumped within room 5 before the collapse episode (DSU35) occurred.

30. Upper elevation: 141.035 m; lower elevation: 140.775 m; average thickness: 14 cm.

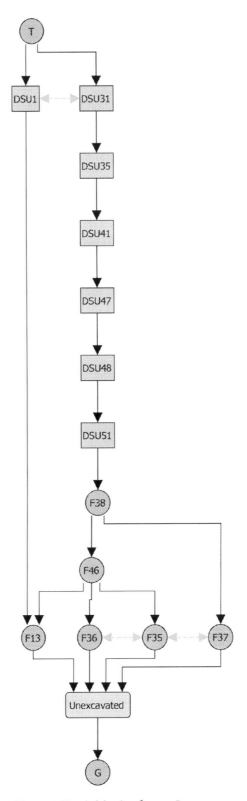

Fig. 4.15: Harris Matrix of room 5.

Fig. 4.16: View (to northwest) of DSU35 (wall collapse) in room 5.

Following the excavation of DSU41, a compact layer of mud-brick debris (DSU47),[31] including a few larger fragments of mudbricks and pottery sherds, was identified in the northwest corner of room 5, where it also covered the threshold of the doorway leading into room 6 (fig. 4.17). Below DSU47 (as well as below DSU41 in the rest of room 5's north area) was a layer (DSU48)[32] of clean and loose yellow sand, with small fragments of mudbricks scattered throughout it. Among the inclusions were also a few animal bones and wood fragments. The only small find retrieved during the excavation of the unit was a fragmentary iron nail (inv. 15941). DSU48 rested above the remains of the upper floor of room 5 (F38) and, in the northwest corner of the staircase's lower landing, a thin layer of loose brown sand (DSU51).[33] The fill, which contained a moderate quantity of potsherds and a few animal bones, abutted upper floor F38 and lay over lower floor F46, in the west part of the same room. It also covered the threshold (part of wall F36) opening onto room 6 and abutted the lowest step of staircase F35.

31. Upper elevation: 140.945 m; lower elevation: 140.745 m; average thickness: 20 cm.
32. Upper elevation: 140.745 m; lower elevation: 140.625 m; max. thickness: 12 cm.
33. Upper elevation: 140.625 m; lower elevation: 140.565 m; average thickness: 4 cm. It was equivalent to sand unit DSU53 excavated in room 6, immediately to the west of staircase F35.

Fig. 4.17: View (to south) of DSU47–48 in room 5.

4.3. Room 6

Features

Room 6 is a large rectangular room of the south annex (figs. 4.3; 4.18). It measures 5.76 m north-south by 3.40 m east-west, with walls preserved to a maximum height of 2.16 m above floor level (towards the south end of the west wall). Although most features of the room show signs of severe erosion, there is evidence in the archaeological record that this space was originally covered with a flat ceiling (discussed in the next section). Room 6 is bound by wall F36 to the east, F40 to the south, F41 to the west, and F13 (the south wall of the church) to the north. It opens onto several spaces via doorways along its east, south, and west sides. A wide opening within wall F40 provided the only direct access into the south annex from the outside.[34] Immediately north of wall F41, room 6 opens onto passageway 8 to the west; two

---

34. The only other entrance (that was identified) was from room 1 (the church) via the small doorway in room 5.

Fig. 4.18: Aerial view (to south) of room 6.

additional thresholds, placed at the south and north ends of east wall F36, once gave access to passageway 10 and room 5 (and from there to the church itself, as well as to an upper floor or roof via staircase F35), respectively. Room 6 was evidently the place with the highest degree of accessibility within building 7, and where the strongest form of control of access to the other spaces of the complex could be exercised.

F13,[35] which is the north wall of building 7's south annex, is best preserved in room 6, where it is abutted by the superstructure (F52) of tomb 5. Thirteen courses of mudbricks, laid in English bond, are extant above the latest floor level near the entrance into room 5, to a maximum height of 108 cm (fig. 4.19). Within room 6 large patches of grayish-brown mud plaster, as well as of superimposed white gypsum plaster, are visible near the east and west ends of F13's south face. Between rooms 5 and 6 the mud plaster ends abruptly in a straight vertical line, visible above the west edge of the threshold and reaching up to 68 cm on top of the threshold itself (fig. 4.7). This line may be related to the presence in antiquity of a doorway between the two rooms, as suggested by evidence discussed above.[36]

Wall F13 is abutted to the south by wall F36,[37] which forms room 6's east boundary and separates it from room 5 (fig. 4.20). At the north and south ends of F36 are two thresholds,

35. Upper elevation: 141.530 m; lower elevation (in room 6): 140.325 m.
36. See Sec. 4.2.
37. Upper elevation: 141.215 m; lower elevation: 140.335 m.

Fig. 4.19: View (to north) of wall F13 in room 6.

Fig. 4.20: View (to east) of wall F36 in room 6.

leading into rooms 5 and 10, respectively.[38] The wall is preserved to a maximum height of ca. 90 cm near the threshold into room 5. It becomes progressively shorter towards the south, likely because of natural erosion. The mudbricks seem to be laid out in English bond, although the west face of the wall is largely covered in mud plaster, which obscures the courses of bricks.

38. For a description of the threshold into room 5, see Sec. 4.2; concerning the doorway into room 10, see Sec. 4.7 below.

Fig. 4.21: View of wall F40 (north face), wall F41 (east face), and platform F47 in the southwest corner of room 6.

These are visible, for the most part, on the preserved top of the wall, where they have been exposed by erosion. Several patches of white plaster are preserved in the north part of F36, smeared on top of the mud plaster.

The south side of room 6 is formed by part of wall F40. Within this space, the wall was found in very poor condition; it is best preserved in the southwest corner of the room, where it dramatically slopes down eastwards (fig. 4.21). The south face, heavily eroded, reveals up to 12 courses of mudbricks laid out in English bond. The north face, in contrast, is still smeared with mud plaster and, over it, white gypsum plaster. Remains of a doorway, consisting of jambs and a threshold, are visible in the eastern sector of F40 within room 6 (fig. 4.22). The doorway, 197 cm wide, served as the only entrance into building 7 from the south. Some of the original mudbricks that formed the threshold were discovered in place, covered with mud plaster.[39] A patch of the upper floor (F50) of room 6 still lies on top of these bricks. An irregular row of mud-brick fragments, delimiting this doorway from the area further south, may have constituted a border for this floor; it may have thus been contemporary with it. Wooden beams, rectangular in section, were inserted into the east and west jambs of the doorway, immediately above the level of the threshold (fig. 4.23).[40] Traces of what may have been a wooden doorframe are still

39. Upper elevation of the threshold: 140.425 m.
40. East jamb's beam: 13 cm thick, 30 cm high. West jamb's beam: 13 cm thick, 20 cm high.

Fig. 4.22: View (to south) of threshold between room 6 and the (unexcavated) area south of building 7.

visible on top of each beam. The remains of two planks were found set against the south side of both the east and west jambs.[41] They both seem to have been lined with white stones embedded in white mortar.

The significant width of the threshold and the remains of the wooden elements inserted in the doorjambs, as well as a few heads of large bronze nails that were found in the vicinity, suggest that the passageway was originally closed with a double door.[42] Notwithstanding the dimensions of this opening, the latter may have still been secondary to the doorway that was originally located in the middle of the church's west wall (F14), which allowed direct access from the outside into the church proper.

F40 is abutted along its north face by a north-south wall (F41),[43] which separates room 6 from room 7 to the west (fig. 4.24). The wall is bonded at its north end with east-west wall F42 (the north wall of room 7) and forms a round corner with it. F41 is built of both red, iron-rich

---

41. Measurements (in cm) of the visible faces of the beams: 75 (length) by 20 (width) by 20 (height), against the south side of the east jamb; 57 (length) by 12–20 (height) (width not available), against the south side of the west jamb. A round hole, 10 cm in diameter and 20 cm deep, pierces the east beam in the middle.

42. On the south face of wall F40, an irregularly shaped recess is visible near the west doorjamb, at an elevation of 141.605 m. The recess measures 71 cm (max.) in length by 45 cm (max.) in height. It may have held a hinge or an element of the door's lock, since it is located at ca. 120 cm above the level of the lower floor of room 6.

43. Upper elevation: 142.245 m; lower elevation (in room 6): 140.315 m; max. preserved height: 216 cm.

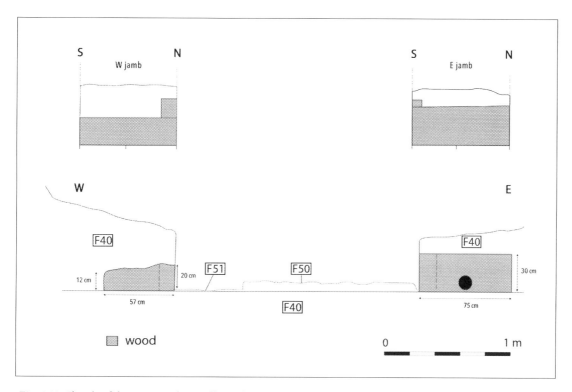

Fig. 4.23: Sketch of doorway within wall F40 (into room 6) (drawing by D. Dzierzbicka; tracing by C. Fosen).

mudbricks, as well as beige ones, laid in English bond with some irregularities. It is relatively well preserved up to a height of about 1 m; its east face is smeared with mud plaster and a few scattered patches of white gypsum plaster up to 94 cm above lower floor F51. The highest preserved courses of the wall are severely weathered down to about half of the wall's original thickness, revealing the back of a niche that was once set in the wall's west face.[44]

As mentioned above, two different floor levels (F50 and F51) are partially preserved within room 6 (figs. 4.25–26).[45] F50[46] is the upper mud plaster floor, preserved in uneven patches in room 6 and extending into room 8 to the west. It lies on a sandy preparation layer ca. 8 cm thick. Its surface is made of gray mud plaster, with fairly large potsherds and white plaster fragments embedded in it. Patches of the floor conceal the burial (tomb 5) located along the north wall (F13). Against south wall F40, the floor was also found on top of the bricks that constitute the threshold of the south doorway into room 6. The other floor level (F51)[47] was identified at a lower elevation, in the region where upper floor F50 was missing in room

---

44. The niche is described in Sec. 4.4 below.
45. The later cleaning of the preserved patches of the two floors revealed a Greek ostrakon (O.Trim. 2.503, a note for the delivery of date stones dated to ca. 350–370; Ast and Bagnall 2016, 136–37).
46. Upper elevation: 140.515 m; average thickness of the plaster: 2 cm. The floor was not excavated.
47. Upper elevation: 140.425 m; average thickness of the plaster: 3 cm. As in the case of the upper floor, F51 was left unexcavated.

Fig. 4.24: View (to west) of wall F41 in room 6.

6. F51 cuts through burial pit F56 and extends into passageway 8 to the west. It is made of light grayish-beige mud plaster with lime spots; its surface is weathered and in a poor state of preservation. A small find (inv. 16290) was retrieved embedded in this floor: a fragmentary wooden object, possibly a peg once used in a door's locking system.

A low rectangular platform (F47)[48] is built against the southwest corner of the room (figs. 4.21; 4.27–28). It measures 56 cm north-south by 104 cm east-west and is 15 cm high. This feature abuts the white-plastered surfaces of walls F40 and F41 and stands on top of the upper floor (F50) of room 6. The edges of the platform were laid using bricks and fragments of bricks on bed. Two of the bricks on the northern edge are baked; the others are sun-dried mudbricks. Inside, the space was filled with sand and mud-brick debris, while the top surface of the feature was smeared with mud plaster.

48. Upper elevation: 140.585 m; lower elevation: 140.465 m.

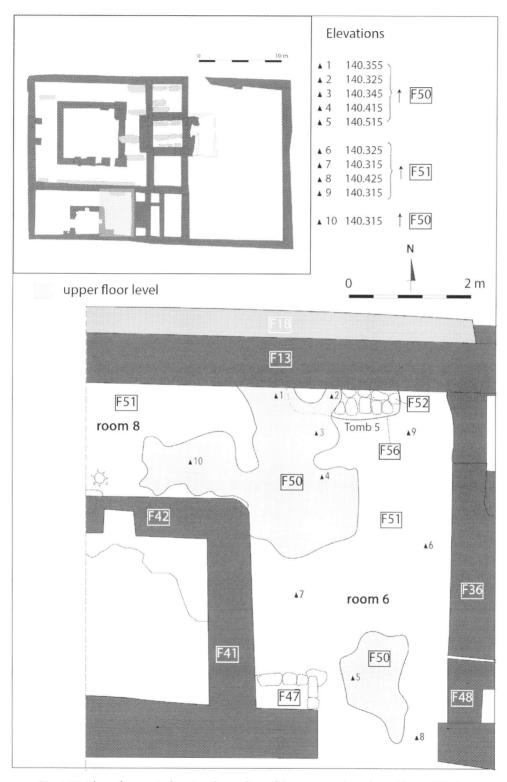

Fig. 4.25: Plan of room 6, showing the outline of the preserved patches of floors F50–51 (drawing by D. Dzierzbicka; tracing by C. Fosen).

Fig. 4.26: View (to southwest) of floors F50–51 in room 6.

Fig. 4.27: View (to south) of platform F47 in room 6.

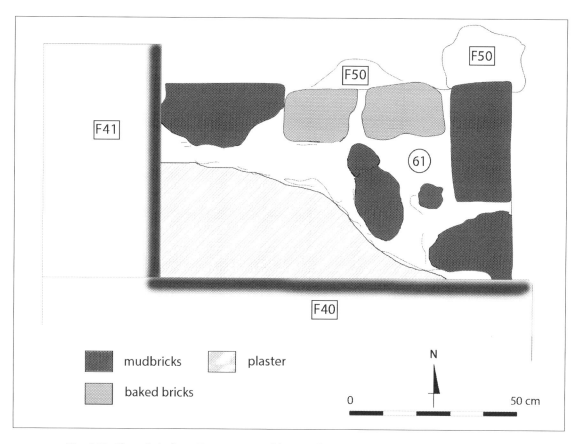

Fig. 4.28: Plan of platform F47 in room 6 (drawing by D. Dzierzbicka; tracing by C. Fosen).

Stratigraphy and finds (fig. 4.29)

The stratigraphy documented in room 6 largely consists of episodes of ceiling and wall collapse, as well as room fills down to occupation level. The foundations of walls were not investigated within this space.

An abundant amount of windblown sand (DSU31),[49] mixed with numerous inclusions such as potsherds, mud-brick debris, and pebbles, was removed from the entire surface of room 6 (fig. 4.30). A cluster of three (fragmentary) patches of mud and white plaster (DSU37)[50] from the collapse of the room's flat ceiling, was revealed in the northern half of this space, mixed with a limited amount of mud-brick fragments (fig. 4.31). Impressions of palm ribs marked one side of the patches, while a coating of white gypsum was still visible on the opposite side.

---

49. Upper elevation: 141.085 m; lower elevation: 140.725 m; average thickness: 30 cm (elevations taken in room 6).
50. Upper elevation: 141.015 m; lower elevation: 140.905 m; average thickness: 9 cm.

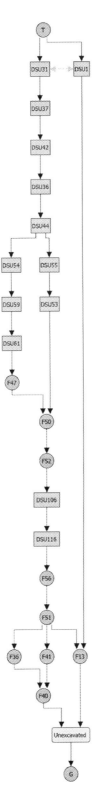

Fig. 4.29: Harris Matrix of room 6.

Fig. 4.30: View (to southwest) of room 6 before excavation.

Fig. 4.31: View (to southeast) of DSU36–37 in room 6.

The three collapse fragments measured between 7 and 12 cm in width and rested on loose yellow sand (DSU42),[51] which extended throughout most of the northern half of the room. Modest quantities of mud-brick debris, crumbled plaster, lime spots, and pottery sherds were scattered throughout this unit, which lay above DSU36.[52] This unit was a large mud-brick collapse, both of walls and of the room's original ceiling. It was exposed in the middle and in the north part of the room, extending between the east and west walls and roughly following an arc-shape.[53] The unit was very thick and contained large mud-brick fragments embedded in compact debris. Numerous complete mudbricks, some of which still bore traces of white gypsum plaster, were found within this layer, together with remains of the original flat ceiling, which displayed impressions of palm ribs on one side and white plaster on the other (like the fragments of DSU37). Among the other materials retrieved within the collapse were potsherds, a fragmentary shell, a piece of sandstone, a couple of animal bones, and a very large number (about one thousand) of fragments of wood, which likely belonged to the beams once supporting the roof.[54]

Following the removal of DSU36 in the north half of room 6, as well as surface layer DSU31 in the south half, a layer of yellow sand (DSU44)[55] was investigated, which stretched throughout this space. The room fill contained loose mud-brick debris, a few baked bricks, and a concentration of white gypsum plaster in the northwest corner of the room. Some of the fragments bore traces of gray, red, or black paint. Among the inclusions were pottery and glass sherds, lime spots, wood fragments, and animal bones. Several small finds were retrieved during the excavation of this context: a complete bronze coin (inv. 16007), dated to 318–383; fragments of iron tacks (inv. 16011, 16016–16017); two pieces of an iron plate, possibly a hinge for a door or furniture (inv. 16013); a fragment of an iron and bronze object (inv. 16015); a complete bronze plaque, rectangular in shape and with two iron nails preserved, one on each surface (inv. 16029);[56] a fragmentary iron plaque, roughly oval in shape (inv. 16226); and a fragment from a glass conical beaker/lamp (inv. 16018).[57]

DSU44 rested above three different archaeological contexts: DSU53–55. DSU54[58] consisted of a wall and ceiling collapse, located in the southwest quadrant of room 6. The unit contained several complete mudbricks (as well as one baked brick) and a very large amount of mud-brick debris, wood fragments (some bearing traces of white plaster and likely part of the now-missing flat roof), and small pieces of gypsum plaster. At the northern end of the unit, a concentration of charcoal and ash, as well as a few burnt potsherds and animal bones,

---

51. Upper elevation: 140.925 m; lower elevation: 140.535 m; max. thickness: 16 cm.
52. Upper elevation: 141.105 m; lower elevation: 140.835 m; average thickness: 27 cm.
53. In the middle of the room, it lay directly below surface layer DSU31.
54. Two larger fragments of beams were registered as FN10 and FN11.
55. Upper elevation: 140.785 m; lower elevation: 140.325 m; average thickness: 30 cm.
56. It was possibly used as a lock plate for a small box or furniture (like a cupboard or chest of drawers).
57. I 106C2 (Isings 1957, 129–130); AR 66.2 (Rütti 1991, 74), dated from the end of the third to the fourth century CE. This conical beaker/lamp is largely represented in fourth-century CE contexts in Egypt, and it is characterized by the presence of "coloured blobs" (Isings 1957, 128) made of opaque glass, generally blue. See also, for example, Kunina 1997, 336–39, nos. 421, 423, and 424.
58. Upper elevation: 140.625 m; lower elevation: 140.465 m; max. thickness: 16 cm.

was found—perhaps evidence of post-abandonment activities that took place within room 6. More traces of wood, charcoal, and ash were found, within the same area, in a yellow sand layer (DSU59)[59] below collapse unit DSU54. DSU59 also contained a few pottery sherds and a moderate amount of mud-brick debris. The unit extended above brick platform F47 in the southwest corner of the room and the remains of upper floor F50 and lower floor F51. Parts of the upper surface of platform F47, originally coated with mud plaster, are missing; in those areas, DSU59 rested above the fill of F47 (DSU61).[60] The latter was made of dumped material, such as grayish-brown mud-brick rubble in a brown sandy matrix. It also contained a couple of animal bones, numerous wood fragments, small pieces of gypsum plaster, and some glass fragments (including a diagnostic sherd from a bowl or plate of *millefiori* glass: inv. 16208).

As mentioned above, the removal of DSU44 revealed two additional contexts: DSU53 and DSU55. The latter[61] was a compact mud-brick collapse located in the central and north parts of room 6, but also extending westwards into room 8. The mudbricks were greatly deteriorated (possibly before collapse), with no complete bricks retrieved. The unit also contained white plaster fragments, one piece of red-painted plaster, lime spots, pottery sherds, one glass fragments, and a few animal bones. Below DSU55, as well as throughout most of room 6 below DSU44, was an occupation layer of brown sand (DSU53),[62] mixed with mud-brick fragments, pottery sherds, white gypsum plaster (some with traces of yellow or dark painting), one glass sherd, one bronze fragment, fruit pits, and animal bones. Three bronze coins (inv. 16008, a *nummus* minted under Constantine in 328–329; inv. 16026, assigned to the fourth century; and inv. 16027, illegible), as well as a bead of green opaque glass (inv. 16002), were retrieved during the excavation of this unit.[63]

4.3.1. Tomb 5 in Room 6

Tomb 5 is an east-west oriented burial that was found at the north end of room 6, along the south face of wall F13 (figs. 4.32–33).[64] The pit (F56),[65] of a rectangular shape and measuring 46 cm north-south by 181 cm east-west, cuts lower floor F51. When the grave was first identified, the cut was clearly discernible only along its east side, as well as in the east half of its south edge. The west and southwest sides, on the other hand, were covered and obscured by a patch of upper floor F50, which also concealed the west part of tomb 5's superstructure (F52).[66] The removal of floor F50 above the grave revealed that F52 consisted of two parallel rows of whole

---

59. Upper elevation: 140.595 m; lower elevation: 140.315 m; thickness in the east half of the unit: 15 cm.
60. Upper elevation: 140.575 m. The unit was not excavated.
61. Upper elevation: 140.535 m; lower elevation: 140.375 m; max. thickness: 16 cm.
62. Upper elevation: 140.585 m; lower elevation: 140.375 m; max. thickness: 16 cm.
63. DSU53 also spread into the southeast area of passageway 8, to the west of room 6 (see Sec. 4.5 below). A fourth coin (inv. 16025), a *maiorina* struck under Constantius II in 355–361, was found in the portion of DSU53 that extended into room 8.
64. Tomb 5 was identified in 2013 and fully investigated during the 2023 excavation season.
65. Upper elevation: 140.255 m; lower elevation: 138.99 m.
66. Upper elevation: 140.355 m; lower elevation: 140.060 m.

Fig. 4.32: View (to north) of tomb 5 in room 6.

and fragmentary mudbricks laid on bed; more precisely, almost all bricks in the south row were complete and laid next to each other as stretchers, while the north row, along wall F13, was made of more fragmentary bricks, laid as headers in a somewhat irregular fashion. Immediately below the superstructure lay the remains of what was probably a mat made of palm reeds (inv. 17011, measuring 163 cm north-south by 30 cm east-west) (fig. 4.34). Its function is unclear: it may have been used to provide support to the mud-brick superstructure laid on top of it, although this is unattested in the other burials from building 7.

The burial pit (F56) was filled by a unit (DSU106) of loose yellow sand, mixed with scattered pottery sherds and mud-brick debris.[67] A complete ostrakon (inv. 17015, a note for the delivery of 70 *matia* of date stones that was most likely dated to 350–370) was gathered within DSU106; the lower part of this unit, surrounding the human remains found in the pit, was documented as DSU116.[68] The unit consisted of sand like DSU106 and had several inclusions,

---

67. The ceramic sherds from this unit, as well as DSU116 below it, can be dated to the second half of the fourth century (C. Caputo, personal communication, January 2023).

68. Upper elevation: 139.690 m; lower elevation: 139.141 m.

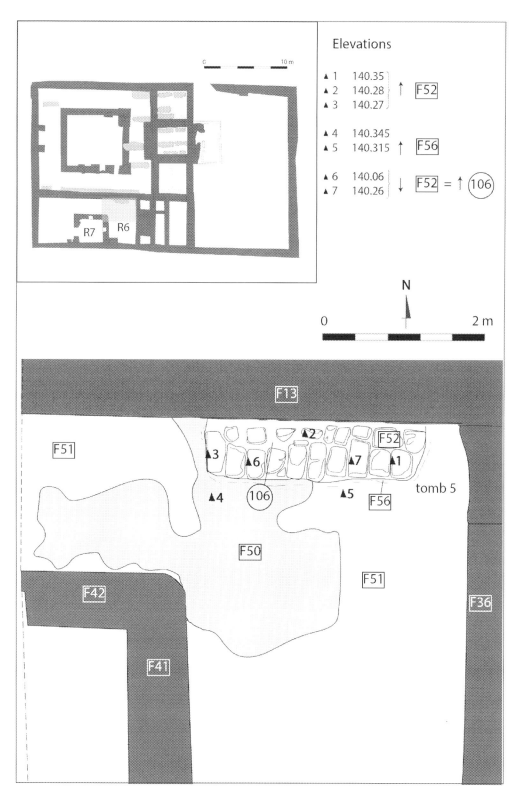

Fig. 4.33: Plan of tomb 5 in room 6 (drawing by D. Dzierzbicka; tracing by C. Fosen).

Fig. 4.34: Remains of palm-rib mat (inv. 17011) below the superstructure of tomb 5.

such as mud-brick fragments, charcoal, plaster fragments, pottery sherds, four fragments of glass, and a small quantity of wood. The presence of rubble material in the fill of tomb 5 (DSU106+DSU116) suggest that the pit was backfilled utilizing material from the excavation of the tomb in the foundation trench of wall F13.

Tomb 5 contained the complete skeleton (FN5) of a young woman of approximately 25 years of age at death (fig. 4.35).[69] She was laid supine at a depth of about 60 cm, facing east, with the hands flexed over the pubic area. Under the skull there was evidence of one layer of yellow, tightly woven textile which disintegrated to powder. Other than the ostrakon mentioned above, no other artifacts or aromatic vegetation were found near the body.

69. Sheldrick 2023, 2.

Fig. 4.35: Human remains (FN5) inside tomb 5.

4.4. Room 7

Features

Room 7 is a roughly square space, measuring 2.75 m north-south by 2.85 m east-west and with walls preserved to a maximum height of 2.42 m (south wall) above floor level. The room is located in the west half of the south annex, built against pre-existing wall F40 (figs. 4.3; 4.36). It was a relatively less accessible space than the surrounding rooms; indeed, anyone entering the annex via the main south doorway had to cross three spaces (rooms 6, 8, and 9) in order to access room 7; alternatively, four rooms had to be traversed (5–6 and 8–9) if approaching from the church (via the north doorway in room 5). Room 7 is the best-preserved space not only of the south annex, but also of the whole church complex. Its features were found in fairly good condition, with the south wall towering over the poorly preserved remains of the church and its adjacent spaces. Although the ceiling is now missing, some evidence was found in the archaeological record pointing to the existence in antiquity of a flat roof.

The function of room 7 is unknown; however, its restricted access compared to its neighboring spaces, as well as its entrance away from the main doorway into the south annex, suggest a possible use of this space as a storage room. Further evidence of such a function (discussed below) is the series of holes in walls F40–41 and F43, which may point to the existence in antiquity of wooden shelves in this space.

Fig. 4.36: Aerial view (to south) of room 7.

The north wall of room 7 (F42)[70] is preserved to a height of ca. 140 cm above floor level (figs. 4.37–38). Its south face is covered in gray mud plaster, rich in lime spots and organic particles. This treatment of wall F42, which can be noticed in all four vertical surfaces of room 7, contrasts with the finishing used in the surrounding spaces (rooms 6, 8, and 9), where walls were covered in white lime plaster on top of mud plaster. In the middle of wall F42, near its preserved top, are the remains of a plastered niche.[71] The lower half of a whitewash band, once framing the entire niche, is still visible.[72] Wall F42 is abutted by a two-burner stove at its west end (F61, discussed below); due to the use of this stove in antiquity, the first 12 cm of the wall plaster in that corner are completely blackened (all the way up to the preserved top). A 37-cm wide section at the north end of wall F43 (on its east face, which is completely covered with mud plaster and incrustations) is also blackened for the same reason (fig. 4.39). F43,[73] which is bonded with F42 and binds room 7 along its west side, is pierced by the doorway connecting this space with room 9.[74] A hole, 8 cm in diameter and located 103 cm above the lower floor, is

70. Upper elevation: 141.305 m; lower elevation: 139.935 m.
71. Width: 52 cm; depth: 43 cm; max. preserved height: 17 cm.
72. Length of the preserved band: 115 cm; max. preserved height: 52 cm.
73. Upper elevation: 141.575 m; lower elevation: 140.075 m.
74. The remains of the doorway are described in detail in Sec. 4.6 below.

Fig. 4.37: View (to north) of wall F42 in room 7.

visible at the south end of this wall.[75] This cavity may have been the emplacement for a wooden feature, perhaps part of a shelf that was likely set into the south wall of room 7.

North wall F42 is bonded, at its east end, with F41,[76] which forms the east boundary of room 7 (figs. 4.40–41). Gray mud plaster, rich in organic particles and lime spots, obscures most of the west face, although the upper part of the wall is severely eroded in its central section and completely missing at its north end. A niche with a rounded top pierces the central part of the wall.[77] The back of this niche is preserved only 14 cm from its floor; above it is a hole that was likely caused by extreme erosion and/or partial collapse of the wall's east face. Both the floor and sides of the niche are covered with well-preserved mud plaster, and it is likely that the rounded top, which is formed by a double course of headers, was plastered as well.

Below the bottom of the niche is a series of round, as well as elongated, holes, set at a height of 94–110 cm above the floor level along the whole length of the wall.[78] Additional holes[79] were found, at a height of 160 cm above floor level, in the south part of the wall, which is in better condition. It is possible—in fact, very likely—that more holes were set further north above the niche but disappeared due to severe damage of the wall in that area. As mentioned

---

75. Ca. 10 cm north of wall F40.
76. Lower elevation (in room 6): 140.315 m. For upper elevation and max. height of this feature, cf. n. 43 above.
77. The measurements of the niche are (in cm): 61 (height) by 55.5 (width) by 40 (depth).
78. These cavities range in size from 3.5 to 12 by 7 cm and are 5 to 12 cm deep.
79. These holes measure from 3.5–16 by 10 cm.

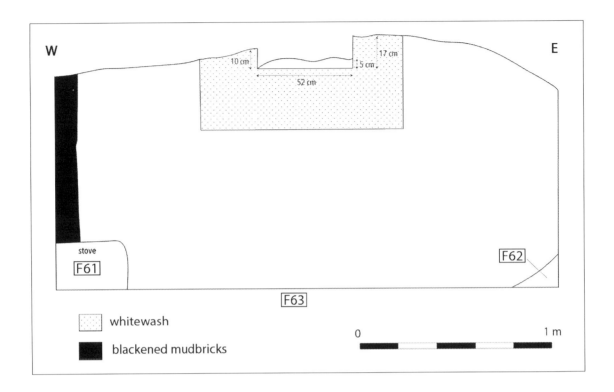

Fig. 4.38: Sketch of wall F42 (south face) (drawing by D. Dzierzbicka; tracing by C. Fosen).

above, one may reasonably argue that these cavities were created to fix a set of wooden shelves or pieces of furniture (now vanished) against wall F41.

The north, west, and east walls of room 7 were part of the same construction episode. The east and west walls (F41 and F43 respectively) abut preexisting wall F40,[80] which delimit this space along its south side (fig. 4.42). This wall forms the south boundary of the entire south annex of building 7; however, it is preserved to its maximum height (of almost 2.5 m) in room 7, while it is severely degraded in rooms 9, 6, and 10–12. Inside room 7, the north face of F40 is mostly obscured by mud plaster, which in turn is covered by incrustations. Only the uppermost courses of mudbricks (of both reddish and beige clay) are exposed, due to wind erosion, and reveal the wall's English bond. A series of holes can be seen in the wall at a height of 94–155 cm;[81] they likely fulfilled the same function that was argued earlier on for the cavities piercing walls F41 and F43.

---

80. Upper elevation: 142.500 m; lower elevation: 140.075 m (both elevations taken within room 7).
81. They range in size from 3.5 to 5 cm in diameter.

Fig. 4.39: View (to west) of wall F43 in room 7.

Fig. 4.40: View (to east) of wall F41 in room 7.

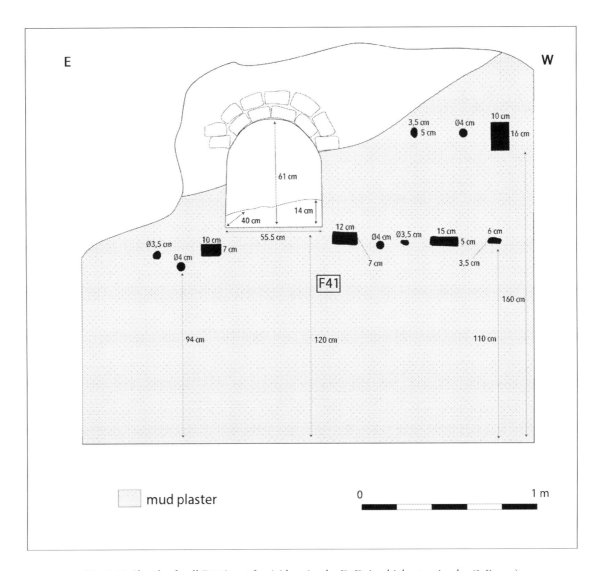

Fig. 4.41: Sketch of wall F41 (west face) (drawing by D. Dzierzbicka; tracing by C. Fosen).

Patches of two different floor levels (F62–63), both made of mud plaster, were identified in room 7. F62[82] is the upper floor, largely preserved in the area of the doorway and extending into the middle of room 7 (pl. 4.43). Smaller patches are visible in the northeast corner, below the east niche, and along south wall F40. The mud plaster contains inclusions of organic particles, fruit pits, charcoal, and potsherds. Burnt spots were also documented on the surface of this floor, likely related to the latest occupation phase of room 7. The lower floor of room 7

---

82. Upper elevation: 140.185 m; lower elevation: 139.935 m; average thickness: 10 cm. The existing patches of F62 (as well as those of F63) were not removed.

Fig. 4.42: View (to south) of wall F40 in room 7.

(F63)[83] is exposed in numerous places where upper floor F62 is missing. It is best preserved in the northeast corner, where its surface is relatively smooth and level. The visible inclusions consist of organic particles and potsherds.

As mentioned above, a two-burner stove is placed against the northwest corner of room 7 (F61)[84] (figs. 4.44–45). It is very similar in structure to stove F45, found in room 9, but is in a significantly worse state of preservation, with its south and east sides no longer extant.[85] The stove measures 87 cm north-south by 40 cm east-west and is preserved to a max. height of 21 cm. It consists of three bricks laid, on their long edges, along the walls in the corner, two along west wall F43 and one along north wall F42. One brick, laid on bed between the burners, is preserved in the middle of the feature. The north burner was likely open along its east side, while the south one was closed and formed a square that measured about 20 by 20 cm and had rounded corners. The whole stove is covered with mud plaster, which turned black inside the

---

83. Upper elevation: 140.155 m.
84. Upper elevation: 140.195 m.
85. For parallels, see n. 126 below.

Fig. 4.43: View (to east) of upper floor F62 in room 7.

burners. Further evidence for the use of this feature consists of a thin deposit of ash (DSU87) inside both burners. Unfortunately, it remains difficult to establish a relationship between this feature and the two floors of room 7, since no evidence for the latter was detected in the immediate vicinity of the stove. The available evidence suggests, however, that F61 was built at a late stage, following a period of abandonment that is also witnessed in room 9 at the west end of the south annex.

Stratigraphy and finds (fig. 4.46)

The relatively good condition of the walls of room 7, especially in its southern half, seemingly contributed to the higher degree of preservation of its internal stratigraphy, in comparison with that of the church or any other space of the south annex. A very modest and sparse accumulation of windblown sand (labeled DSU31, like the rest of the surface layer throughout the south annex) lay on top of an extensive wall collapse (DSU32),[86] which filled the entire room (fig. 4.47).

---

86. Upper elevation: 142.500 m; lower elevation: 140.875 m; max. thickness: 90 cm.

CHAPTER 4: SURVEY AND EXCAVATIONS TO THE SOUTH THE CHURCH

Fig. 4.44: View (to northwest) of stove F61 in room 7.

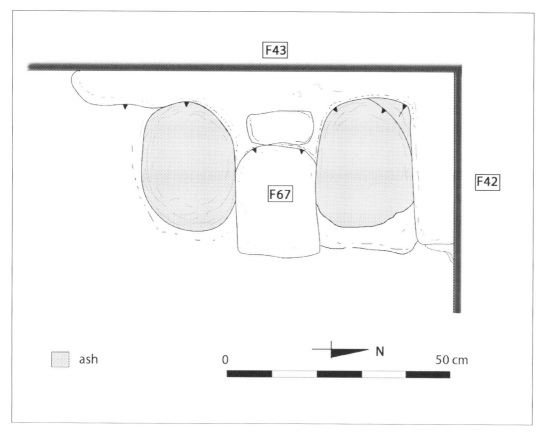

Fig. 4.45: Plan of stove F61 in room 7 (drawing by D. Dzierzbicka; tracing by C. Fosen).

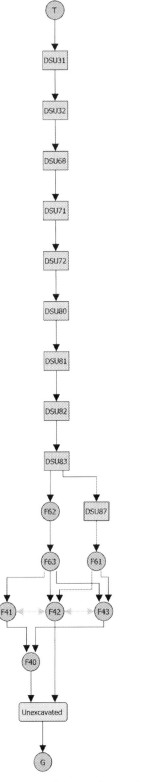

Fig. 4.46: Harris Matrix of room 7.

Fig. 4.47: View (to south) of collapse DSU32 in room 7.

The DSU consisted of large portions of mud-brick walls, with reddish, iron-rich bricks bonded with mud mortar and partly covered with mud plaster. Based on their location and distribution pattern, it seems that several of these pieces once belonged to the north wall (F42) of room 7. A very large amount of mud-brick debris was also part of this unit, within a sandy matrix that was mixed with cobbles, numerous potsherds, charcoal particles, faience and glass fragments, one small piece of bronze, and a few animal bones. Two Roman coins (inv. 16048, minted under Valens in 364–378, and 16059, illegible) were also retrieved while excavating DSU32.

The removal of the above-mentioned collapse revealed a yellow sand layer (DSU68)[87] that filled the entire room. The numerous pottery sherds, as well as mud-brick fragments, associated with this deposit most likely came from collapse units resting above and below it. Other inclusions of DSU68 consisted of animal bones, one piece of plaster (with traces of black paint), and a few fragments of wood. A Greek ostrakon (*O.Trim.* 2.729, a tag dated to 275–350)[88] and

---

[87]. Upper elevation: 141.625 m; lower elevation: 140.825 m; max. thickness: 35 cm.
[88]. Ast and Bagnall 2016, 222–23.

Fig. 4.48: View (to east) of collapse DSU80 in the doorway of room 7.

one fragment of a bracelet made of black opaque glass (inv. 16060)[89] were also found within this deposit.

As mentioned above, DSU68 rested above an earlier wall collapse episode (DSU71), which was split into two clusters: a large patch of wall,[90] with mudbricks still bonded together with mortar, leaned against south wall F40 (east half), while a layer of mud-brick debris and mud dust[91] was found sloping towards the northwest corner of room 7, near its entrance. A few pottery sherds and animal bones were found within DSU71, which lay on top of a natural deposit of windblown sand (DSU72).[92] The layer extended throughout room 7 and was found, in the areas not occupied by collapse DSU71, directly below room fill DSU68. Within the sand there were some potsherds, numerous date and olive pits, and one animal bone, as well as one fragment of light brown textile (inv. 16107).

The removal of DSU72 exposed two separate units: a collapse episode (DSU80) and a natural deposit of windblown sand (DSU81). DSU80[93] was found in the area of the threshold between rooms 7 and 9 and likely originated from the collapse of the upper part of the doorway (fig. 4.48). It contained whole mudbricks (of walls), mud-brick debris, and fragments of mud

---

89. Spaer B2d (Spaer 1988, 55; fig. 4) or Cosyns D2 (Cosyns 2011, 86, fig. 53), with bulging inner section.
90. Upper elevation: 141.845 m; lower elevation: 141.275 m; size: 60 cm north-south by 80 cm east-west.
91. Upper elevation: 141.395 m; lower elevation: 140.625 m; max. thickness: 47 cm.
92. Upper elevation: 141.275 m; lower elevation: 140.385 m; max. thickness: 88 cm.
93. Upper elevation: 140.845 m; lower elevation: 140.385 m; max. thickness: 43 cm.

and gypsum plaster, as well as pieces of wood and one date pit. The fragments of wood were largely decomposed, and it is unclear whether they were originally part of a wooden element from the ceiling or a door's lintel (or the actual door). However, a few of them were still attached to mud plaster, suggesting that they may have belonged, in fact, to a flat roof of mud and palm ribs. Eight joining fragments of a glass rim (inv. 16249), likely of a lamp, were gathered while removing the collapse.

Below DSU80, as well as sand fill DSU72, was the above-mentioned sand layer DSU81,[94] which extended throughout the room. This unit contained a few fragments of mud and white gypsum plaster, potsherds, one glass sherd, charcoal, small pieces of wood, animal bones, and numerous fruit pits. Additionally, two small finds were documented during the excavation of this stratum, i.e., a complete segmented bead, either of yellow glass or of gold-in-glass (inv. 16118),[95] and a fragmentary wooden object with traces of white plaster (inv. 16122), likely a decorative element from a screen or furniture item. The inclusions that were part of DSU81 suggest that the layer may have been mixed with materials associated with some phase of post-abandonment reoccupation of room 9. This is also testified to by the existence of the two-burner stove (F61) that was built, at a late stage in the construction history of this space, against the northwest corner.[96]

Following the removal of DSU81, a collapse layer (DSU82)[97] was exposed in the area of the doorway, sloping down eastwards and spreading onto the southwest quadrant of room 7 (fig. 4.49). The unit consisted of whole mudbricks, mud-brick debris, and mud plaster fragments, some of which were in the shape of a corner and likely came from the doorway. Numerous pieces of wood were also retrieved; a few of them were still attached to mud plaster. It is likely that most, if not all, of the wooden fragments within DSU82 originally belonged to some elements of the doorway, such as the lintel, one of the jambs, or the door itself. A flat stone—perhaps another element of the doorway or of a wall—was found within this collapse, in addition to a few potsherds.

The occupation level of room 7 (labelled DSU83)[98] was identified below collapse DSU82, in the southwest sector of the room, and sand layer DSU81 everywhere else. DSU83 was a thin deposit of fine, light brown sand resting on top of the two ancient floor levels (F62–63). The sand was more yellow and loose near the doorway, where the unit was covered by collapse DSU82, and rich in organic particles closer to the interface with the floors. Two isolated mudbricks were found in the southeast corner of the room. The fill was mixed with a wide range of inclusions, such as mud-brick debris, fragments of mud and gypsum plaster (some of which bearing traces of paint in different colors), potsherds, glass and bronze fragments, remains of white and painted plaster, pieces of wood, ash, and charcoal, as well as fruit pits and

---

94. Upper elevation: 140.455 m; lower elevation: 140.065 m; average thickness: 30 cm.
95. Segmented beads were usually molded along their length in grooved stone molds, with a single open valve. Such molds were discovered, for example, at Kom el-Dikka in Alexandria in a third-century CE context; in the same area, a sandwich gold-glass beadmaking place was also identified (Majcherek 2018, 46).
96. It is unlikely, however, that DSU81 was in phase with the stove, since it lay above it.
97. Upper elevation (in the threshold): 140.325 m; lower elevation: 140.185 m; average thickness: 10 cm.
98. Upper elevation: 140.285 m; lower elevation: 139.935 m; max. thickness (below collapse DSU82): 10 cm.

Fig. 4.49: View (to southwest) of DSU82 in room 7.

animal bones. Several of these materials were most likely related to the use of the stove for the preparation of food. Additionally, the investigation of DSU83 revealed three small finds, which consisted of two Roman coins (inv. 16210, illegible, and inv. 16217, datable to the first half of the fourth century CE) and one Greek ostrakon (*O.Trim.* 2.502, a memorandum for a delivery order dated to 275–350).[99]

The last deposition to be documented within room 7 was the fill of the two-burner stove (F61). The unit, labelled DSU87[100] (fig. 4.44), was made of ash and sand and contained a few potsherds, fragments of wood, one glass sherd, and one animal bone. The only small find retrieved within this unit was a bead of light blue glass (inv. 16228). Although likely contaminated, this unit resulted largely from cooking activities that took place on the stove.

---

99. Ast and Bagnall 2016, 136.
100. Upper elevation: 140.065 m; lower elevation: 139.925 m; max. thickness: 14 cm.

Fig. 4.50: Aerial view (to east) of room 8.

4.5. Room 8

Features

Room 8 is a rectangular space that measures 1.80 m north-south by 4.24 m east-west and has walls that are preserved to a maximum height of 1.37 m above floor level (east half of south wall). It originally functioned as a passageway between room 6 to the east and room 9 to the west (figs. 4.3; 4.50). The latter opened onto room 7 to the east and could be accessed only via corridor 8, which is defined by wall F13 to the north, shared with the church (fig. 4.51). Only the lowest four courses of mudbricks are exposed within the south face of the wall in room 8. The upper courses are covered by a thick layer of mud plaster, which is in turn coated with white gypsum plaster.[101] The south boundary of room 8 is formed by wall F42,[102] which is shared with room 7 (fig. 4.52). Due to severe erosion, the north face of the wall dramatically slopes down towards its west end, where it stands only up to four courses of mudbricks above floor level. The eastern half is better preserved and shows a round corner where it is bonded with wall F41.

---

101. The white plaster extends from 28 to 73 cm above the lower floor, while the mud plaster is visible from 17 to 73 cm above the lower floor.

102. Lower elevation: 140.425 m (above lower floor F51 in room 8). For the upper elevation of the wall, see Sec. 4.4 above.

Fig. 4.51: View (to north) of wall F13 in room 8.

Most of the north face of F42 is smeared with mud and white gypsum plaster, which obscure the bond of the wall;[103] the only exceptions are the mudbricks at the west end, as well as a small area at the east end, of F42, which show an irregular English bond.

No evidence for the existence of doorways was found along the north and south side of this space, which therefore granted a high degree of mobility and ease of access to the neighboring rooms. Notwithstanding the poor state of preservation of the features, evidence was found, in the stratigraphy of room 8, pointing to the existence in antiquity of a flat roof. However, it is not possible to rule out that the ceiling fragments originated from any of the adjacent spaces, particularly room 7.

The excavation of this passageway revealed substantial traces of different floor levels, which were in phase with floors detected in adjacent rooms 6 and/or 9 (fig. 4.53). The latest floor, of compact and hardened clay, was F50.[104] It was exposed, in uneven patches, along the

---

103. The white plaster, which is partly covered with mud incrustations, is preserved up to a height of 80 cm above the lower floor (F51) of the room. A burnt spot, 46 cm in length, is visible at the bottom of the wall, reaching up to 28 cm above lower floor level. It is likely the result of firing activities that took place in room 8 in antiquity (pre- or post-abandonment).

104. Upper elevation (taken in room 6): 140.515 m (preserved upper elevation in room 8: 140.315 m).

Fig. 4.52: View (to south) of wall F42 in room 8.

south wall of room 8 and, more extensively, within room 6.[105] It rested on the remains of an earlier mud floor (F51),[106] which was found in both rooms 6 and 8 (fig. 4.54).[107]

Isolated remains of a deteriorated mud floor (F54)[108] can be seen in the area where room 8 opens onto room 9 (fig. 4.55). The floor has several visible layers, with the uppermost one preserved against wall F42 in the southwest corner of room 8. It does not survive in the center and in the eastern half of the passageway, but extends about 80 cm westward into room 9. F54 lies above floor F51 but, due to the poor condition of all floor levels in this area, it is unclear if F50 and F54 were, in fact, different features or were laid out as part of the same floor. F54 is covered with incrustations, which obscure its upper surface. Where exposed, it is light gray in color and has coarse organic inclusions.

Stratigraphy and finds (fig. 4.56)

The stratigraphy of room 8 is not particularly complex. Unfortunately, this space, like most others inside building 7, was exposed to severe wind erosion and/or human action. Apart from south wall F42, shared with room 7, no contexts were found that can be linked with the collapse of either north wall F13 or a ceiling (if, in fact, there was one originally).

105. F50 is described in Sec. 4.3 above (see p. 163).
106. Upper elevation (taken in room 6): 140.425 m (preserved upper elevation in room 8: 140.315 m).
107. For a brief description of F51, see Sec. 4.3 above (see pp. 163–64).
108. Upper elevation (in room 8): 140.345 m.

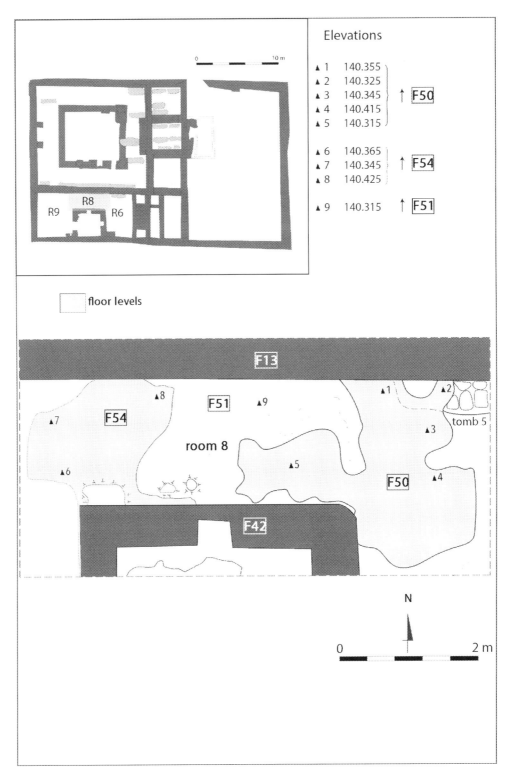

Fig. 4.53: Plan showing the preserved extent of floors F50, F51, and F54 in rooms 6 and 8–9 (drawing by D. Dzierzbicka; tracing by C. Fosen).

Fig. 4.54: View (to southeast) of floors F50–51 in room 8 (room 6 is in the background).

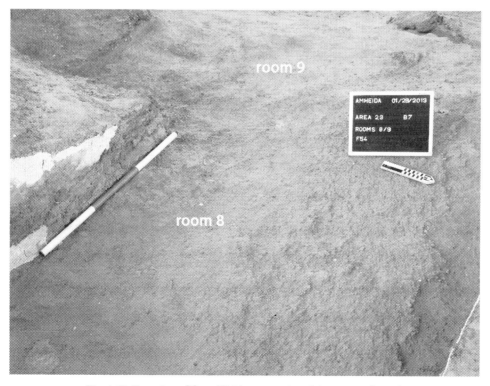

Fig. 4.55: Remains of floor F54 in rooms 8–9 (view to southwest).

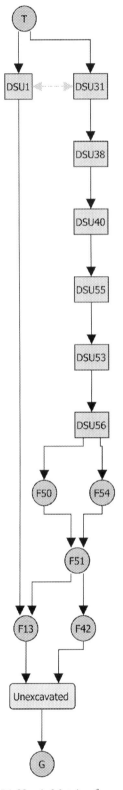

Fig. 4.56: Harris Matrix of room 8.

Fig. 4.57: View (to south) of collapse DSU38 in room 8.

The surface layer (DSU31),[109] consisting of windblown sand with several inclusions, extended throughout room 8, as well as the rest of the south annex. This unit equals DSU1, i.e., the surface layer that covered room 1, including wall F13 (the south wall of the church and the north wall of room 8). Below DSU31, evidence of a wall and ceiling collapse (DSU38)[110] was found throughout the central part of room 8 (fig. 4.57). The unit consisted of whole and incomplete mudbricks, as well as small fragments of the flat roof.[111] Numerous ceramic sherds were gathered and lime spots detected during the investigation of the unit. The collapse extended northwards up to wall F13, with bricks loosely scattered to the north and west of the unit. It is clear that this collapse was part of wall F42 to the south and took place after the final abandonment of the south annex in antiquity. As mentioned earlier, it is more difficult to say if the ceiling fragments found in this unit belonged to a flat roof once covering room 8 or room 7.

109. Upper elevation: 140.985 m; lower elevation: 140.725 m; max. thickness: 26 cm (along north wall F13; elevations taken in room 8).
110. Upper elevation: 141.275 m; lower elevation: 140.475 m; average thickness: 50 cm.
111. Some fragments still showed imprints of palm reeds on one side and white gypsum plaster, coating a smooth surface, on the inner ceiling.

Fig. 4.58: View (to west) of DSU38 in room 8.

A thick layer of brownish-yellow sand (DSU40)[112] was investigated below collapse DSU38, above and against the remains of wall F42 in the central part of room 8 (fig. 4.58).[113] The unit contained isolated fragmentary bricks, lime spots, some pottery sherds, wood fragments, a few animal bones, one piece of charcoal, and a very large quantity of mud plaster fragments, several of which still bore impressions of palm ribs on one side. One piece was particularly large (fig. 4.59): it measured 20 cm by 79 cm and still showed traces of white gypsum plaster attached to one of its sides. The discovery of the ceiling fragments below the collapse gives some support to the possible existence of a light flat ceiling covering the passageway (room 8) between rooms 6 and 9. Two small finds were registered during the excavation of this context, i.e., a fragment of a bronze ring with oval section (inv. 15930) and a small piece of iron (inv. 15942, possibly a nail shaft).

---

112. Upper elevation: 140.875 m; lower elevation: 140.295 m; average thickness: 30 cm.
113. In 2023, a coin (inv. 17048, dated to the second half of the fourth century CE) was found while cleaning the wall for photographic documentation.

Fig. 4.59: Large fragment of mud plaster with palm reed impression (and white plaster on the opposite side), found in room 8.

The removal of DSU38 revealed the occupation level (DSU56)[114] of room 8, consisting of a compact sand and mud-brick debris layer above floors F50, F51, and F54. The deposition unit was mixed with some pottery sherds, numerous fragments of white gypsum plaster, one small piece of wood, and two sherds of glass. In the southeast corner of the room, DSU55—and DSU53 immediately below it—lay between collapse DSU38 and occupation level DSU56. They were mostly found in adjacent room 6, but slightly extended into room 8.[115]

4.6. Room 9

Features

Room 9 is the westernmost space of the south annex (figs. 4.3; 4.60). It is rectangular in shape and measures about 5.10 m north-south by 4.35 m east-west, with walls preserved to a maximum height of 1.45 m above floor level (south half of east wall). This space was found in very poor condition; erosion and/or human destruction were particularly severe in its western half, where

---

114. Upper elevation: 140.475 m; lower elevation: 140.295 m; average thickness: 12 cm.
115. They were described in detail in Sec. 4.3 above (see p. 171). A mid-fourth-century coin (inv. 16025) was gathered in the part of DSU53 inside room 8.

Fig. 4.60: View (to southeast) of room 9 in the south annex.

the floor is missing and the walls are preserved only at foundation level. Corridor 8 allowed access into room 9, which in turn opened, through a doorway piercing the south end of its east wall, onto room 7. Due to the heavily damaged features in much of room 9, it is impossible to verify if any doorway once existed offering direct access to room 9 from the outside.

Room 9 is bounded to the north by the westernmost part of wall F13[116] (fig. 4.61). Eight courses of mudbricks are visible above the latest floor at the east end of the wall's south face. An additional eight courses were exposed at foundation level near the west end of F13. The mudbricks, most of which are iron-rich and reddish in color, were laid in English bond, then plastered over with mud and finally coated with white gypsum plaster. Inside room 9, the remains of the mud and gypsum coatings can be seen in the eastern half of the wall, continuing into room 8.

F13 is abutted to the south by wall F44,[117] which forms the west edge of room 9 (fig. 4.62). It is not preserved above foundation level, due to severe erosion of all features in this area. F44 is aligned with the west wall (F14) of room 1 (the church proper) and shares with it the same thickness (ca. 95 cm). A maximum of four courses of mudbricks, laid in English bond, was exposed on the east face of F44 within room 9. This feature is bonded, at its south end, with

116. Lower elevation (within room 9): 139.865 m.
117. Upper elevation: 140.195 m; lower elevation: 139.525 m.

Fig. 4.61: View (to north) of wall F13 in room 9.

Fig. 4.62: View (to west) of wall F44 in room 9.

wall F40,[118] which defines the southern boundary of this room (fig. 4.63). Within room 9, F40 is only extant above floor level in the southeast corner, where remains of the original coating of white gypsum plaster, on top of mud plaster, are still visible.[119]

118. Upper elevations: 140.525 m; lower elevation: 139.645 m (elevations taken in room 9).
119. For a length of 94 cm west of wall F43.

Fig. 4.63: View (to south) of wall F40 in room 9.

To the east, room 9 is bounded by wall F43,[120] which abuts wall F40 to the south and is shared also by room 7 (fig. 4.64). The upper courses of F43 suffered from erosion and are best preserved at their south end, where they abut wall F40. The mudbricks exposed on the west face are laid in English bond; however, several courses remain obscured by mud plaster, as well as white gypsum plaster towards the south end of the wall.[121] F43 is divided into two segments above floor level; in the middle are the remains of a doorway (1 m wide) that once allowed access from room 9 into room 7 (fig. 4.65). The threshold consists of a course of bricks of wall F43, plastered on their upper surface, and of a wooden beam (6 cm high and 13 cm wide) lying above it and inserted into the west face of the wall.[122] Along the south face of the doorway is a vertical groove (9 cm wide and 2 cm deep), probably associated with a now-missing jamb. A small rectangular hole is visible, within room 9, near the northern end of the threshold; it is unclear, however, if it can be functionally related to the doorway itself.

---

120. Upper elevation: 141.605 m; lower elevation: 140.275 m (both elevations taken at the north end of the wall inside room 9).

121. The white plaster is preserved to a height of 67 cm above ground level, and it is abutted by stove F45 (described below).

122. 24 and 30 cm of the beam are visible within the north and south portions of the wall, respectively.

Fig. 4.64: View (to east) of wall F43 in room 9.

Patches of two floor levels of mud plaster (F54–55) are extant only in the eastern half of the room (fig. 4.66). F54[123] is found near the opening at the northeast corner and extends into passageway 8.[124] Remains of an earlier floor (F55)[125] are also visible in the northeast quadrant of room 9, partly below F54. This lower floor consists of multiple layers, which can be easily discerned along the west edge of the preserved patch and seem to belong to the same phase.

A two-burner stove (F45) was found, in a relatively good state of preservation, against the southeast corner of room 9, where it abuts south wall F40 and east wall F43 (figs. 4.67–69).[126] It also abuts debris DSU64 and is abutted by plaster layer F53,[127] which rests on top of both DSU63–64. F53 slopes eastward from the middle of the room, then becomes slightly higher next to the doorway into room 7. The west edge of this surface is broken and very uneven due to erosion, which also affected underlying DSU64. A section of F53 was cut, from east to west,

123. Upper elevation (in room 8): 140.365 m.
124. See Sec. 4.5 above.
125. Upper elevation: 140.245 m; lower elevation: 140.105 m; max. thickness: 14 cm.
126. Similar stoves were found, for example, in the hermitages at Naqlun: see hermitage 87, room 12 (fifth century) in Godlewski 2010, 237, fig. 8; hermitage 25 (sixth–ninth centuries) in Godlewski 1990, 31–32, fig. 2; hermitage 44 (second half of the fifth century) in Godlewski 1998, 81–82; hermitage 85, room 10 (sixth century) in Godlewski 2008, 202, fig. 10.
127. Upper elevation: 140.375 m; lower elevation: 140.235 m; max. visible thickness: 2 cm.

Fig. 4.65: View (to east) of doorway between room 9 and room 7.

and its north part was removed. Only one potsherd and the complete base of a small bottle of greenish-yellow glass (inv. 16046) were retrieved. F53 seems to be contemporary with, and functionally related to, the stove, as it formed a pathway leading to it from passageway 8 to the north along wall F43. This evidence suggests that the stove was not built in phase with the room, but likely postdates its first episode of abandonment, when debris had already started accumulating within this space.

The stove is made of mudbricks and is covered with mud plaster rich in organic inclusions and with attached pieces of white plaster.[128] The western burner is a squarish hole (18 by 21 cm, with a max. depth of 27 cm), with rounded corners that are smoothed over with plaster. While the west burner is closed on all four sides, the east burner (18 cm wide) is open along the north side and its brick backing is higher than that of the western burner by 10 cm. A shallow pot stand (or impression), measuring 15 cm in diameter, is still visible between the two burners against south wall F40. The west burner is black on the inside but not above its edges, while the east burner also displays traces of burning on its backing, to a height of 29 cm above the bottom.

128. The layout of the bricks is almost completely obscured by the mud plaster.

Fig. 4.66: View (to northeast) of preserved patches of floors F54–55 in room 9.

Fig. 4.67: View of the southeast corner of room 9, with post-abandonment installations.

Fig. 4.68: View (to southeast) of stove F45 in room 9.

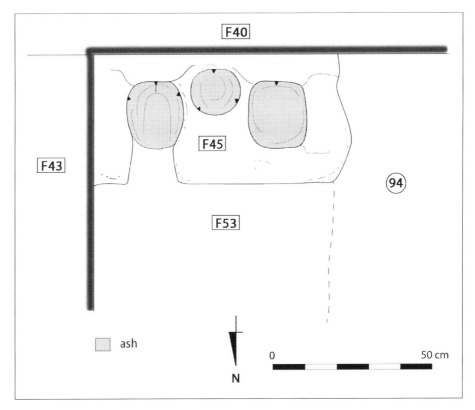

Fig. 4.69: Plan of stove F45 in room 9 (drawing by D. Dzierzbicka; tracing by C. Fosen).

CHAPTER 4: SURVEY AND EXCAVATIONS TO THE SOUTH THE CHURCH   205

Traces of ash and burnt particles adhere to the pot stand/impression in the middle. Remains of a thin deposit of ash (DSU88, described below) inside the burners are additional evidence of the stove's use before the final abandonment of room 9 in antiquity.

Stratigraphy and finds (fig. 4.70)

The archaeological contexts, including collapse episodes and room deposits, were better preserved in the eastern half of room 9, where clear evidence of post-abandonment reuse of this space was recorded. Walls and depositional units were almost completely missing, above floor level, in the western half of room 9, due to particularly severe erosion. In this area, walls were found only at foundation level and the original floor had disappeared, exposing its preparatory layers and the fills of the walls' foundation trenches.

Following the removal of surface layer DSU31[129] throughout room 9, two unreliable deposits of sand were revealed: DSU52 in the western half of the room, heavily eroded; and DSU43 in the better-preserved eastern half. DSU52[130] was a layer of sand fill lying above an area in which the floor did not survive. The sand was yellow and loose and contained a wide range of inclusions, such as potsherds, a few mud-brick fragments, lime spots, charcoal, and ash, glass fragments, pieces of white gypsum plaster (one with traces of red paint), wood, bronze, and iron fragments, as well as organic material (hair) and a few animal bones. A Greek ostrakon (O.Trim. 2.782),[131] dated to ca. 275–350, was also found during the excavation of this unit, whose inclusions were more numerous at the interface with DSU62[132] below. The latter was the preparatory layer for floor F55 and was exposed in the western half of room 9. DSU62 was a dump layer consisting of brownish-yellow sand, mixed with a large quantity of ceramic sherds, mud-brick fragments, lime spots, and pockets of ash and charcoal, as well as a few burnt seeds. An incomplete circular stopper of unfired clay (inv. 16038) was found while cleaning the surface of the unit, which was left unexcavated.

In the east half of room 9, DSU43[133] was a deposit of yellow sand, with a similar matrix to that of DSU31 that was removed above it; indeed, the sand was loose and mixed with a large quantity of inclusions, such as several potsherds, mud-brick debris, white plaster fragments (some of which bear traces of gray paint), lime spots, glass sherds, and a few animal bones. Below this unit was a large patch of plastered wall collapse (DSU58),[134] located towards the east end of the room. It lay within a compact brownish-yellow sandy matrix and included a sizeable piece of white plaster in the middle of the collapse. Several more fragments of white gypsum plaster were gathered, some still bearing traces of mud plaster and/or gray painting.

---

129. Upper elevation: 140.645 m; lower elevation: 140.045 m; average thickness: 26 cm (elevations taken in room 9).
130. Upper elevation: 140.135 m; lower elevation: 139.945 m; max. thickness (in the southwest corner of room 9): 19 cm.
131. Ast and Bagnall 2016, 241.
132. Upper elevation: 140.115 m.
133. Upper elevation: 140.495 m; lower elevation: 140.265 m; average thickness: 15 cm.
134. Upper elevation: 140.425 m; lower elevation: 140.265 m; average thickness: 16 cm.

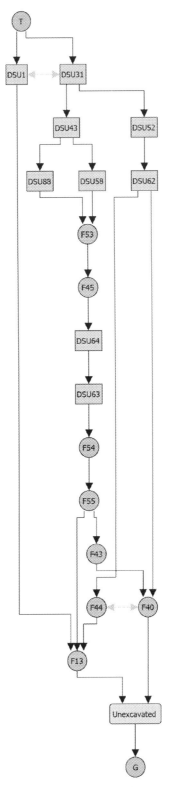

Fig. 4.70: Harris Matrix of room 9.

Among other inclusions found within this unit, and possibly the result of contamination due to its proximity to the surface, were a few mud-brick and wood fragments, small potsherds, and one animal bone. Immediately to the west of DSU58 lay a compact collapse layer (DSU64),[135] made of mud-brick detritus mixed with potsherds, lime spots, charcoal, a few wood fragments, and one animal bone (fig. 4.67). Some pieces of white gypsum plaster were also retrieved; two of them (inv. 16049) were painted yellow and the larger fragment bore inscribed motifs and one Greek letter (epsilon). The shape of DSU64, which sloped from west to east along room 9's east wall, was undoubtedly intentional, as it was covered almost completely by a layer of mud plaster (F53, discussed above) that followed the same outline. Both DSU64 and F53 were related to the construction of ceramic stove F45 in the southeast corner of room 9. As noted earlier, this took place during a phase of reuse of the south annex (or at least part of it), following the earlier abandonment of the area and the collapse of some of its features. The investigation of stove F45, as well as the plastered area in front of it (F53), revealed DSU88.[136] This unit consisted of a thin layer of ash and sand, mixed with charcoal, potsherds, and a few fragments of gypsum plaster. It filled the bottom of the east burner of the stove and extended to its immediate surroundings, as a byproduct of firing and cooking activities that took place in this room in antiquity.

Subsurface layer DSU43 rested not only above DSU58 and DSU64 (discussed above), but also on top of a thin brownish layer of loose sand (DSU63)[137] in the northeast quadrant of room 9. This fill, which was found at the occupation level above the remains of floors F54–55 and was partly concealed below F53, was mixed with mud-brick debris, potsherds, charcoal, and plaster fragments, a few of which had traces of yellow paint. Moderate quantities of mud dust, likely from decayed floors F54–55, were also found.

4.7. Room 10

Features

Room 10 is a narrow corridor located to the south of staircase 5. It once connected room 6 to the west and room 11 to the east (figs. 4.3; 4.71). The passageway is rectangular in shape and measures 1 m north-south by 2.35 m east-west, with walls preserved to a maximum height of 0.65 m above floor level (middle of north wall). It is delimited to the north by wall F39 and the south wall (F40) of the south annex. Two thresholds, which are extensions of walls F36–37, bind the room to the west and east, respectively.

---

135. Upper elevation: 140.405 m; lower elevation: 140.315 m; max. thickness (where removed): 9 cm. The unit was exposed on its east side and in parts of its upper surface, where the plaster was absent most likely because of erosion. Only a section at its north end was removed.

136. Upper elevation: 140.245 m; lower elevation: 140.155 m; max. thickness: 9 cm.

137. Upper elevation: 140.375 m; lower elevation: 140.225 m; max. thickness (in the excavated part): 8 cm. The unit was not completely removed.

Fig. 4.71: Aerial view (to northwest) of the church complex, showing the location of room 10.

F39[138] is the wall separating room 10 from staircase 5 to the north (fig. 4.72). It is part of the block of bonded walls of the staircase (also including flight of steps F35 and side walls F36–37) ascending southwards from room 5. Above floor level, the remains of wall F39 are covered with mud plaster (and so covering the bond) and a relatively well-preserved patch of white gypsum plaster. Below floor level, a broad foot (ca. 30 cm wide) protrudes from the wall's south face and is bonded with the two thresholds into room 10 along its west and east sides. The foot is still partially covered by upper floor F48 and is abutted by lower floor F49. Along its east end, where it meets wall F37, F39 is abutted by a wooden threshold element. The threshold that exists between rooms 10 and 11—and is seemingly part of wall F37—measures 75 cm north-south by 57 cm east-west.[139] Remains of what may have been a mud-brick jamb are still visible against the south side of the threshold.[140] An illegible Roman coin (inv. 16225) was found embedded in the thick layer of mud plaster that covers this threshold.

138. Upper elevation: 140.875 m; lower elevation: 140.445 m. The wall measures 2.35 m in length and is preserved to a max. height of 65 cm (middle of the wall); the width is unknown.
139. Upper elevation: 140.465 m.
140. The remains measure 16 cm north-south by 57 cm east-west.

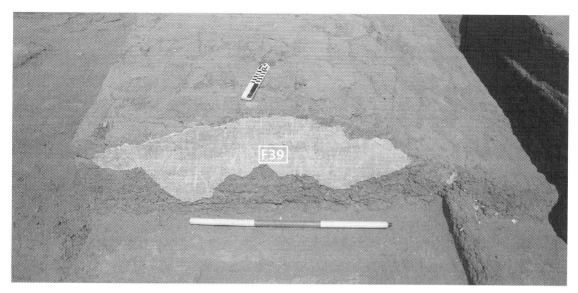

Fig. 4.72: View (to north) of wall F39 in room 10.

As discussed above, F40 is a long east-west oriented wall that form the south boundary of the church's south annex and, in particular, of rooms 6–7 and 9–12. Within room 10, the north-south oriented walls F36 and F37 seem to abut the west and east segments of F40 respectively, with the space between them (measuring ca. 120 cm in length) filled with a block of mudbricks (fig. 4.73).[141] This partition forms the central segment of the south wall of room 10. It is unknown, however, if this is a structurally separate feature or if it shares foundations with F36–37 (and/or with the east and west segments of wall F40). The north face of this segment is coated with mud plaster and white gypsum plaster, which is seen also on the north wall of room 10; the south face is covered only with mud plaster.

The west edge of corridor 10 is defined by a threshold that opens onto room 6 and measures about 1 m north-south by 50 cm east-west.[142] It is almost completely covered by the remains of F48,[143] which is the upper mud plaster floor of corridor 10 (fig. 4.74). The preserved floor patch, of a rough L-shape, also lies on top of the broad foot of north wall F39. It is made of a layer of sandy, light gray mud mortar with few organic inclusions and some potsherds. Its surface is largely covered with incrustations. The mud plaster that covers south wall F40 in this room seems to have dripped onto the surface of F48; it therefore seems to be later than this floor. In the northeast corner of room 10, F48 abuts north wall F39, as well as the wooden threshold of the doorway into room 11 to the east.

---

141. Upper elevation: 140.865 m; lower elevation: 140.475 m; max. visible height: 39 cm.
142. The threshold is a south extension of wall F36. Upper elevation (of floor F48 above threshold): 140.515 m.
143. Upper elevation: 140.535 m; the lower elevation is not available, as the floor was not removed; its visible thickness is 2 cm.

Fig. 4.73: View (to south) of wall F40 in room 10.

Fig. 4.74: View (to west) of floors F48–49 in room 10.

Chapter 4: Survey and Excavations to the South the Church   211

A lower floor level (F49)[144] was found in the southeast part of room 10 (fig. 4.74). It is rectangular in shape and is delimited by the threshold in wall F37 to the east and wall F40 to the south. It lies on a layer of sand and its surface is 2–3 cm lower than that of upper floor F48. F49 is made of fine light gray mud plaster with embedded potsherds. It is largely missing along wall F40. The relationship between the two floor levels is unclear. It is possible, however, that F49 was originally part of the higher floor F48 but subsequently collapsed to a lower elevation, due to the relatively soft preparation layer in the southeast sector of room 10. The cause may have been the pressure created by the two collapse layers (DSU46 and DSU57) that were excavated in this area of the corridor. Furthermore, the mud plaster applied on wall F40 descends only to the level of the upper floor; no traces of a plaster layer are visible on the wall at the elevation of lower floor F49.

Stratigraphy and finds (fig. 4.75)

The stratigraphy of room 10 consisted of a few wall and ceiling collapses and room fills. As all other spaces in the south annex, room 10 was filled with a highly contaminated surface layer of windblown sand (DSU31).[145] Two small finds were gathered from this DSU within room 10: a diagnostic rim fragment of a glass bowl (inv. 15936) and another fragment of a rim from a glass beaker (inv. 15943).

DSU31 rested on a mud-brick collapse context (DSU46)[146] that extended throughout most of the (limited) surface of corridor 10 (fig. 4.76). It consisted of mud-brick debris from a wall mixed with lime spots and pottery sherds. Small pieces of mud plaster from a collapsed ceiling were also found in this unit, about 3–7 mm thick and still bearing traces of gray painted plaster on one side. Numerous fragments of white gypsum plaster (5–7 mm thick) were retrieved from this unit as well; most likely, they originated from the walls of room 10, as suggested by the similarly treated wall surfaces still extant.

The removal of collapse DSU46 revealed a yellow sand layer (DSU 49)[147] covering the area of the entire room. The sand was loose and mixed with a few mud-brick fragments (perhaps from the collapse unit above), potsherds, lime spots, small pieces of wood, and one animal bone. Numerous pieces of white plaster were gathered as well, some of which on mud mortar and others on white gypsum mortar. A few fragments still showed traces of light gray and yellow painting.

DSU49 lay above the remains of upper floor F48 and, in the east part of the room, DSU57,[148] a wall and ceiling collapse layer (fig. 4.77). DSU57 consisted of mud-brick debris mixed with a moderate quantity of potsherds, wood fragments, two glass sherds, and lime spots.

---

144. Upper elevation: 140.515 m; thickness: 2 cm.
145. Upper elevation: 140.855 m; lower elevation: 140.675 m; average thickness: 5 cm (elevations taken in room 10).
146. Upper elevation: 140.675 m; lower elevation: 140.575 m; max. thickness: 10 cm.
147. Upper elevation: 140.655 m; lower elevation: 140.475 m; average thickness: 7 cm.
148. Upper elevation: 140.575 m; lower elevation: 140.465 m; max. thickness (east half of the unit): 7 cm.

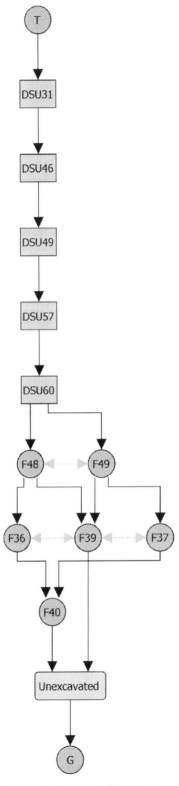

Fig. 4.75: Harris Matrix of room 10.

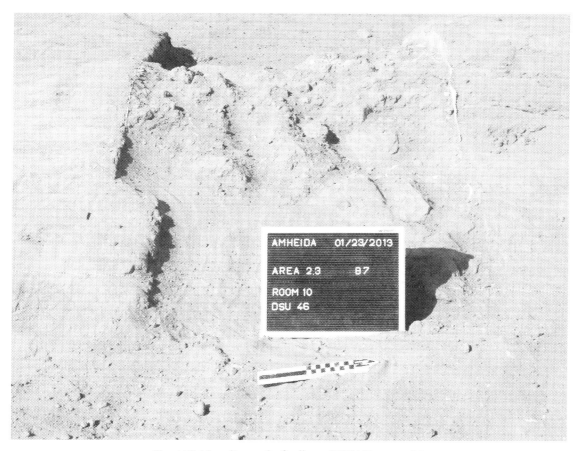

Fig. 4.76: View (to west) of collapse DSU46 in room 10.

The collapse included a very large number of fragments of white plaster, some of which were attached to either mud-brick debris (from the collapse of walls) or mud plaster still bearing impressions of palm ribs (likely from a collapsed ceiling).

DSU60[149] was the earliest deposit in corridor 10. It lay at the occupation level in the east half of the room, above lower floor F49 and, partially, upper floor F48. It was also found above the wooden threshold element placed in the east doorway of the passageway. The unit was made of clean sand, with relatively few inclusions such as mud-brick and plaster fragments, ceramic sherds, and lime spots.

---

149. Upper elevation: 140.535 m; lower elevation: 140.345 m (taken in a hole within lower floor F49); max. thickness: 12 cm.

Fig. 4.77: View (to west) of collapse DSU57 in room 10.

4.8. Rooms 11 and 13

Features

Rooms 11 and 13 are located near the east end of building 7's south annex, immediately to the south of room 16 (likely the church's south *pastophorion*) (figs. 4.3; 4.78–79). Room 11 is a rectangular space measuring 3.80 m north-south by 1.03 m east-west, with walls preserved to a maximum height of 0.75 m above floor level (wall F37 near the northwest corner of the room).

Fig. 4.78: Aerial view (to south) of rooms 5 and 11–13. The photograph shows rooms 11 and 13 after the removal of wall F57.

Its original function is unknown, but it is possible that the room was once utilized as a storage space, placed below a staircase located at an upper level. Room 13 may also have been located beneath the same hypothetical staircase, although there is evidence to suggest it would have not been used for storage purposes.[150] Room 13 is a roughly square space that measures 1.20 m north-south by 1 m east-west. Its walls are preserved to a maximum height of 0.83 m above floor level (north end of west wall F37). No traces of the original floors were detected in either room 11 or 13, whose remains seem to largely consist of foundation walls and fills.

The two rooms seem to have initially formed just one rectangular space, which measured about 5.1 m north-south and was parallel to rooms 5+10 to the west and 12 to the east. At some point, perhaps in relation to the construction of the above-mentioned upper staircase, a short east-west wall (F57) was built above part of the foundation fill, at the elevation of 139.805 m. This partition wall, abutting west wall F37 and east wall F58, divided the original space into two rooms. During the excavation of the test trench inside room 13, F57 was removed due to danger of collapse.

F37[151] is the west wall of both rooms 11 and 13, as well as the east wall of staircase F35 in room 5 (fig. 4.80). It abuts the south wall of the church (room 1) and is bonded with east-west wall F39 (north wall of room 10). It also seems to abut the south wall of building 7's south annex. The east threshold between rooms 10 and 11 was also built within this wall. F37 was erected in English bond, visible below floor level on its east face. In room 11, a maximum of twenty-

---

150. Cf. Sec. 7.3 below.
151. Upper elevation: 141.155 m; lower elevation: 139.065 m (within test trench in room 13); max. preserved height: 209 cm.

Fig. 4.79: View (to north) of room 11 and test trench 3 in room 13 (after the removal of wall F57).

four courses of mudbricks were exposed.[152] The part above the (now missing) floor level was covered with mud plaster, a patch of which is extant 110 cm to the north of the doorway into room 10. Potsherds and lime spots were found attached to the plaster.[153]

The east edge of both rooms 11 and 13 is defined by wall F58[154] (fig. 4.81). It was built with mudbricks laid out in English bond. A maximum of eight courses are preserved above the original floor (now lost). The foundation courses are concealed in room 11, but visible in room 13, where the entire height of the wall was exposed. The four lowest courses of F58 recede slightly (by 6 cm) from the west face of the wall, while a course juts out by 3 cm—still from the west face of F58—directly below floor level. In the northeast corner of room 13, the foot of F58 consists of stretchers on edge and stands on the fill of the foundation trench of wall F13.

152. In room 13, the wall is covered in concretions, which obscure the bond and make it impossible to detect any traces of plaster.
153. See Sec. 4.8.1 below for a discussion of the foundation courses of F37 (in rooms 11 and 13).
154. Upper elevation: 140.945 m; original lower elevation (north end of the wall): 139.025 m; max. height: 192 cm.

Fig. 4.80: View (to northwest) of wall F37 in rooms 11 and 13.

In the corner where F58 abuts F13 to the north, a patch of mortar (ca. 130 cm long and 50 cm high) spreads onto the eight uppermost courses of F58, as well as extending onto the surface of F13 (fig. 4.82).Further south, the west face of wall F58 is partially covered by a patch of coarse gray mud plaster, 2.5–5 cm thick and mixed with organic inclusions, small potsherds, and lime spots.[155]

Room 11 is bounded by wall F40[156] to the south (fig. 4.83) Within this space F40 was exposed to a maximum of 15 courses of mudbricks, laid in English bond and belonging to the foundations of the wall below floor level.

The north side of room 13 consists of wall F13,[157] which separates the church (room 1), including the south *pastophorion* (room 16), from the south annex of building 7 (fig. 4.84).

---

155. The plastered area measures 150 cm in length and 25 cm in height; it begins at 90 cm and ends at 240 cm from the south end of the wall.
156. Upper elevation: 140.335 m; lower elevation 139.085 m (both elevations taken in room 11).
157. Upper elevation 141.140 m; lower elevation: 137.375 m. Within room 13, the wall is abutted by F37 and F58.

Fig. 4.81: View (to north) of wall F58 in rooms 11 and 13.

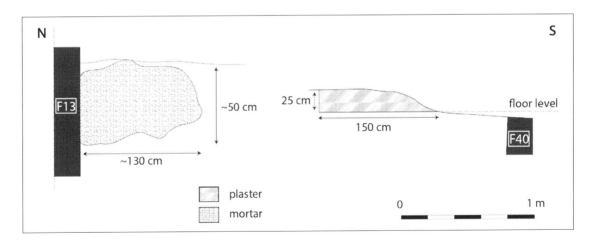

Fig. 4.82: Sketch of mortar and plaster areas on the west surface of wall F58 (drawing by D. Dzierzbicka; tracing by C. Fosen).

Fig. 4.83: View (to south) of wall F40 in room 11.

Forty-six courses of mudbricks, laid in English bond, were exposed in room 13. No plaster can be seen on this wall above the original ground level, besides traces of mortar smeared over the corner formed by F13 and F58.[158]

As noted above, F57[159] is a mud-brick partition wall that separated rooms 11 and 13 (figs. 4.85–88). It consisted of bricks laid in no particular bond, built on a layer of dumped material mixed with sand and some loose mudbricks and mud-brick debris. Its foot, which consisted of two and a half mudbricks, protruded by ca. 20 cm from its north face. The latter appeared more uniform and orderly than the south face, where the bricks do not form an even vertical surface and the top of the wall was 23 cm further to the south than the bottom course. On the north face, the lower courses were relatively horizontal, with mudbricks laid on bed. At the level of the upper ledge of west wall F37, the courses were more irregular, sloping from west to east. The mudbricks in the uppermost courses were stacked in no particular order, with the highest preserved course consisting of headers on edge.

---

158. For a discussion of the wall's foundations, visible in the test trench dug in room 13, see Sec. 4.8.1 below.
159. Upper elevation: 140.965 m; lower elevation: 139.805 m; max. height: 112 cm.

Fig. 4.84: View (to north) of wall F13 in room 13.

Fig. 4.85: View of the north face of wall F57 (in room 13).

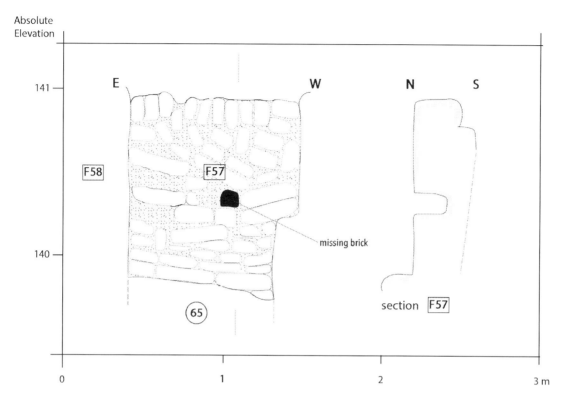

Fig. 4.86: Prospect of the north face of wall F57 (drawing by D. Dzierzbicka; tracing by C. Fosen).

In terms of its construction process, the wall seems to have been built from the north side, where the feature, which leaned southwards, was more uniform and showed better craftmanship. A cavity still visible in the upper ledge of wall F37, within room 13, may be associated with the building of wall F57. The purpose for the construction of the latter is obscure. Most likely, it did not have a structural function; rather, it may have been erected to block off the north part of the area defined by walls F23, F40, F37, and F58 (i.e., the surface of rooms 11+13) and keep the deposits accumulated in it from pouring southwards. The north face of the wall was abutted solely by windblown sand, while the deposits found to the south of F57 were substantially different. It is possible that at some point in antiquity the stratigraphic units accumulated in the north part of this space (i.e., room 13) were removed, to the depth of 139.805 m, for reasons that remain unknown. Subsequently, wall F57 was built and the space to the north was filled with sand.

Fig. 4.87: View of the south face of wall F57 in room 11.

Stratigraphy and finds (fig. 4.89)

A layer of windblown sand (DSU31),[160] mixed with numerous inclusions, was removed from the surface of room 11, as well as from that of room 13.[161] A compact mud-brick debris unit (DSU67)[162] was exposed at the south end of room 11. It may have originated from the collapse of features within this room, although it was mixed with materials more usually associated with a domestic dump. A few fragments of baked bricks were found in DSU67, which also contained some potsherds, wood and glass fragments, and numerous animal bones. One fragment of a jar stopper (inv. 16054) with a Greek label stamped on a jar stopper dated to ca. 275–350 (O.Trim. 2.731)[163] was retrieved during the excavation of this unit.

160. Upper elevation: 141.125 m; lower elevation: 140.475 m; average thickness: 15 cm (elevations taken in rooms 11 and 13).
161. For a discussion of the stratigraphy of room 13, see Sec. 4.8.1 below.
162. Upper elevation: 140.485 m; lower elevation: 140.315 m; max. thickness: 16 cm.
163. Ast and Bagnall 2016, 223, no. 731. As the impression of the vessel's rim, neck, and part of the shoulder are preserved, it is possible to argue that the mud stopper once sealed a jar with rounded rim and short neck, identified as type 511. Mud stoppers are a common seal for wine amphorae and wine jars, probably because they ensured a good transpiration of the wine and the release of gas eventually accumulated in the container (on this topic see, for example, Murray, Boulton, and Heron 2000, 594–95). Generally speaking, at Amheida mud stoppers are usually found in contexts dated until the first half of the fourth century CE, while they are less common in later contexts. As inv. 16054 was found in a wall collapse, it was probably re-used as inclusion in a mudbrick.

Fig. 4.88: View (from above) of the top of wall F57.

Underneath both surface layer DSU31 and DSU67 was a loose, yellow sand deposit (DSU66),[164] which extended throughout the room. This subsurface unit was mixed with dumped material, including a large number of animal bones (as well as two fragments of horns), small quantities of wood and charcoal, date pits, a few glass fragments, pottery sherds, and mud-brick debris. The small finds that were gathered within DSU66 consist of: a Roman bronze coin (inv. 16063), dated to the fourth century CE; a diagnostic rim fragment of a glass bowl (inv. 16061); one bead of transparent blue glass (inv. 16062); a circular stopper made of unfired clay (inv. 16070); and four textile fragments made of brown fibers (inv. 16106). A few mudbricks were found scattered in this unit, especially close to its interface with the unit below. The removal of DSU66 exposed a small and thin deposit of mud-brick debris (DSU74)[165] near the northwest corner of room 11, against the east face of wall F37 (fig. 4.90). In addition to small mud-brick fragments and mud dust, the layer contained a few pottery sherds, animal bones, and fruit pits.

---

164. Upper elevation: 140.785 m; lower elevation: 140.005 m; max. thickness (in the north half of room 11): 58 cm.
165. Upper elevation: 140.275 m; lower elevation: 140.125 m; average thickness: 15 cm.

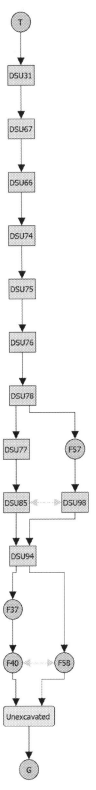

Fig. 4.89: Harris Matrix of room 11.

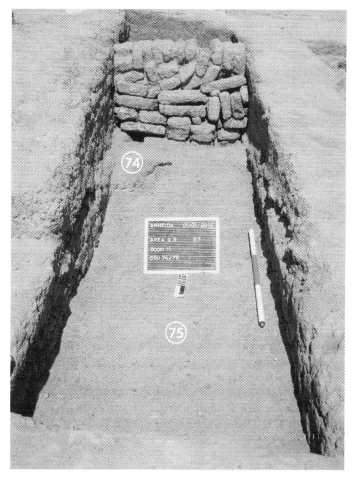

Fig. 4.90: View (to north) of DSU74 and DSU75 in room 11.

Below DSU74, as well as DSU66 in the rest of room 11, was another layer of yellow sand (DSU75)[166] (fig. 4.90). Among the inclusions were a few potsherds and modest quantities of cobbles, mud-brick fragments, plaster, glass, and a few animal bones. The only small find retrieved within this unit is a fragment of rounded rim from a glass jar (inv. 16117).

DSU75 rested above three different foundation fills, i.e., DSU76–78, all seemingly consisting of dumped material (fig. 4.91). DSU76[167] was a layer of brownish-gray sand excavated in the north half of room 11, as well as further south along west wall F37. In the north part of the room, it is substantially thicker than in other areas. The deposit contained thin lenses of yellow windblown sand and was mixed with mud dust, small mud-brick pieces, pottery sherds, one glass fragment, ash, charcoal, a few fruit pits, and animal bones. One rim fragment (inv. 16126), from a small cup made of faience, was found during the excavation of this unit.

166. Upper elevation: 140.345 m; lower elevation: 139.955 m; max. thickness: 25 cm.
167. Upper elevation: 140.095 m; lower elevation: 139.755 m; max. thickness (in the north half of the room): 45 cm.

Fig. 4.91: View (to north) of DSU76–78 in room 11.

DSU78[168] was a layer of yellow sand lying below DSU75–76 and extending throughout most of room 11, with the exception of the area along south wall F40. The unit was mixed with moderate quantities of ash and charcoal, glass sherds, a few wood and bronze fragments, and some animal bones. Most of the potsherds that were found in DSU78, together with some mud-brick debris and loose bricks, lay towards the bottom of the unit.[169] The only small find retrieved in this context was a glass rim fragment of a conical beaker/lamp (inv. 16124).[170]

168. Upper elevation: 139.935 m; lower elevation: 139.495 m; max. thickness: 45 cm (at the center of the room).
169. Near the interface with DSU77 (discussed below).
170. It has a sliced-off rim, very slightly bulging and vertical walls; it is colorless with a light green/yellowish tint. It seems to have wheel incisions, but they are difficult to discern due to the presence of white patina in places and due to numerous cracks. Based on a preliminary analysis, this beaker/lamp has parallels with form I 106a/b (Isings 1957, 126–27) and form AR 66 (Rütti 1991, 73–74). This typology, generally with an unworked rim, was very popular throughout the fourth century CE (Isings 1957, 127).

CHAPTER 4: SURVEY AND EXCAVATIONS TO THE SOUTH THE CHURCH   227

In the southern part of room 11, the excavation of DSU75 and DSU78 revealed a brown layer of mud-brick debris (DSU77)[171] that sloped from south to north (likely reflecting the dumping pattern of this foundation fill from the edge of south wall F40 into the room). All mud-brick fragments were of relatively small sizes, with no whole bricks found in this unit. DSU77 contained several inclusions such as animal bones, fruit pits, pottery sherds, and a few fragments of wood, glass, and bronze objects, in addition to one piece of white plaster on gypsum-rich mortar with traces of red paint. Four Roman coins (inv. 16186, a *Securitas Reipublicae* issue of Valens dated to 364–378; inv. 16187, a *maiorina* minted in 351–361; inv. 16188 and 16216, both dated from the second half of the fourth century to the first half of the fifth)[172] were found within this fill, together with one base fragment (inv. 16227) from a small bottle/*unguentarium* of light green glass.[173]

DSU76–78 rested above a very thick foundation fill (DSU85)[174] consisting of dumped material that spread throughout room 11 (fig. 4.92). It consisted of laminated strata of sand and ash and was very rich in inclusions such as charcoal, fragments of textile, wood, bronze, and dross, glass sherds, one peach pit, one shell, one piece of faience, animal bones, and very large quantities of potsherds and plaster fragments. The latter included several pieces of white plaster, on gypsum-rich mortar, carrying traces of red or yellowish paint. Several small finds were retrieved during the excavation of this fill: seven rim fragments of glass bowls (inv. 16219, 16222–16223, 16231–16234); one rim fragment, possibly from a glass lamp (inv. 16220); one fragment of a sliced-off rim of a beaker/lamp (inv. 16221);[175] one small piece of a rounded outflaring rim of a glass plate (inv. 16235); four joining fragments of a rim from a glass plate or large bowl (inv. 16236); an almost complete small ceramic bowl (inv. 30117); one fragment of an unfired clay stopper (inv. 16275);[176] a small piece of the upper valve of a frog lamp, decorated with palm branches (inv. 16238);[177] a complete globular bead of transparent green glass (inv. 16224). Four Greek ostraka were also found within this context: *O.Trim.* 2.532 (a delivery order, dated to 3 December 362); *O.Trim.* 2.650 (a well tag, dated to ca. 275–350); *O.Trim.* 2.652 (another well tag, dated to 294/5 or 316/7); and *O.Trim.* 2.736 (a tag, dated to 329/30 or 339/40).[178]

In the northern part of the room, DSU85 was equally difficult to distinguish from a thin, ashy layer (DSU76) and DSU78 lying immediately below it. It is possible that these three

---

171. Upper elevation: 140.015 m; lower elevation: 139.585 m; max. thickness: 30 cm (in the southwest corner of the room).

172. These late coins are intriguing, as they seem out of keeping with the dating of most of the other dumped material.

173. Based on a preliminary analysis, it was possible to establish a parallel with type I 82B1 (Isings 1957, 97) and type AR 135 (Rütti 1991, 119–20), dated to the end of the first–second century CE. The fragment was likely part of dumped material.

174. Upper elevation: 139.775 m; lower elevation: 139.055 m; max. thickness: 67 cm (in the northwest corner of the unit).

175. Similar to inv. 16124; it has wheel-incisions, a common characteristic for this fourth-century CE beaker/lamp.

176. Along the edge, a stamp, possibly in a rectangular field, is preserved; only two Greek letters are visible (perhaps Iota and Pi).

177. Similar to Bailey type Q 2153 EA (Bailey 1988, 261; pl. 49), dated from the third to the fourth century CE.

178. Ast and Bagnall 2016, 152 (*O.Trim.* 2.532); 195 (*O.Trim.* 2.650); 196 (*O.Trim.* 2.652); 225 (*O.Trim.* 2.736).

Fig. 4.92: View (to north) of DSU85 (= DSU98 below wall F57) in room 11.

units were in fact part of the same deposit of dumped material, consisting mainly of ash and sand. DSU85 is equal to DSU98 excavated below wall F57.

Below DSU85 lay a deposit of fine, compacted sand and ash (DSU94)[179] (fig. 4.93). The unit was exposed throughout room 11, except for a baulk that was created, in the north part of the space, to keep wall F57 from collapsing. DSU94 was not excavated but revealed, near its surface, patches of hardened sand and a moderate number of inclusions, such as pottery sherds and small fragments of mudbricks.

A different DSU number (98) was assigned to the unit below east-west wall F57, which separated room 11 from room 13 to the north (fig. 4.94). The unit was arbitrarily distinguished from the adjacent stratigraphic units DSU84–85, to which it was equal. DSU98 consisted of yellowish-brown sand mixed with ash, charcoal, and mud-brick debris. A few large fragments of mudbricks, as well as a complete one, were found in this context and were possibly related to the construction of wall F57 above it. Among the other inclusions were numerous pottery sherds, some pieces of white plaster (some of which still bore traces of red and yellow painting),

---

179. Upper elevation: 139.125 m; the unit was not excavated.

Fig. 4.93: View (to north) of DSU94.

dross and wood fragments, a few glass sherds, and animal bones. Additionally, two small finds were registered while investigating this fill: a glass fragment of a footring (possibly of a plate; inv. 16251); and an almost complete circular stopper with a rectangular stamp made of mud plaster (inv. 16241).[180]

4.8.1. Test Trench 3 in Room 13

A test trench (labeled test trench 3) was excavated throughout room 13, in order to expose the foundations of north wall F13, west wall F37, and east wall F58 in this room (figs. 4.95–96).

180. Three Greek letters are discernible, i.e., ΧΙΗ (or ΗΙΧ).

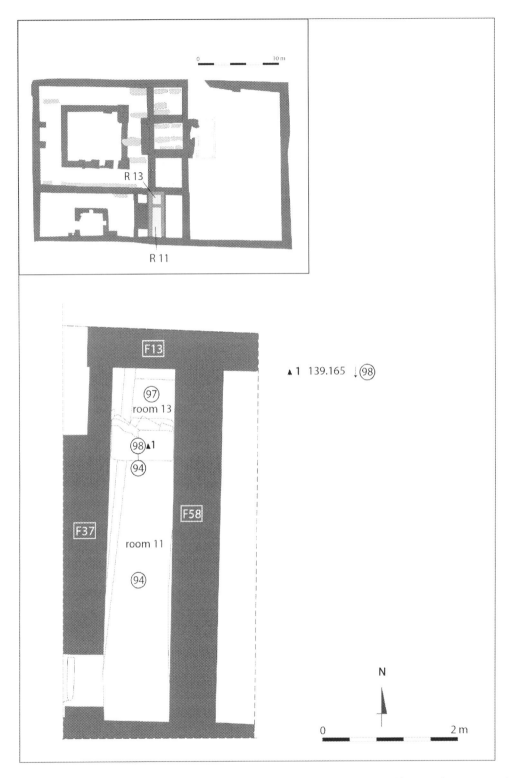

Fig. 4.94: Plan of rooms 11 and 13, showing the extent of DSU94 and DSU97–98 (drawing by D. Dzierzbicka; tracing by C. Fosen).

Fig. 4.95: View from above of room 13 after excavation.

The removal of surface layer DSU31 (discussed above) revealed DSU65,[181] a unit of loose windblown sand that was possibly part of the foundation fill inside room 13. It contained very few inclusions, consisting of fragments of wood, plaster, animal bones, few pebbles, and pottery sherds. Following the excavation of DSU65, a thick layer of yellowish-brown sand (DSU84)[182] was exposed. It was part of the foundation fill for walls F37 and F58 and lay below the bottom bricks supporting partition wall F57. DSU84 was mixed with several small mud-brick fragments and abundant mud dust. Many ceramic sherds were also found, as well as a few animal bones, one glass sherd, two pits, and a small quantity of wood, charcoal, and plaster. The matrix of this context suggests that DSU84 originated from a domestic dump before it was used to fill the foundation trenches of the east and west walls of room 13. Underneath this context was DSU86,[183] a hard and compact deposit of very fine, loamy sand, beige-gray in color. It is at the level of this deposit that the orientation of F58 (east wall of room 13) changed slightly, with the lower courses of bricks shifted by ca. 5 cm eastwards. DSU86 was mixed with ash and moderate quantities of ceramics and one animal bone. One badly weathered fragment of shoulder and body of a lamp (inv. 16302) was retrieved during the excavation of this context.

181. Upper elevation: 140.845 m; lower elevation: 139.575 m; max. thickness: 127 cm (along the north wall).
182. Upper elevation: 139.695 m; lower elevation: 139.155 m; max. thickness: 54 cm (in the south half of the room).
183. Upper elevation: 139.165 m; lower elevation: 139.075 m; max. thickness: 9 cm.

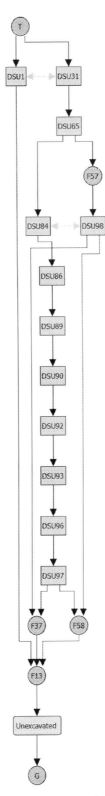

Fig. 4.96: Harris Matrix of room 13.

CHAPTER 4: SURVEY AND EXCAVATIONS TO THE SOUTH THE CHURCH   233

The stratigraphy below DSU86 revealed a series of additional foundation fills: DSU89–90, DSU92–93, and DSU96–97, all of which seem to have consisted (like DSU84 and DSU86 above) of discarded material from domestic dumps. Immediately below DSU86 was DSU89,[184] a deposit of yellow sand with some ceramic inclusions, as well as two animal bones and one plaster fragment. This unit rested above DSU90,[185] a deposit of grayish-brown sand mixed with abundant quantities of mud-brick debris, pottery sherds, and animal bones, in addition to some small pieces of plaster, a glass sherd, and four wood fragments. DSU90 lay above a context of scattered mudbricks (DSU92),[186] identified in two deposits along the foundations of walls F37 and F58. The bricks may have formed the lowest stratum of DSU90 and were at the bottom of the foundation trenches dug for F37 and F58. Their removal revealed numerous mud-brick and ceramic fragments, as well as lime spots, wood, and charcoal inclusions. Below this unit, as well as DSU90 in the remaining part of room 13, was DSU93,[187] a layer of yellow sand mixed with several potsherds, pieces of white plaster, and a few animal bones. Several small fragments of mudbricks were scattered throughout the unit at the interface with the underlying unit (DSU96). The latter[188] was a layer of very compact mortar-like sand, with few inclusions consisting of ash and small ceramic sherds. The unit formed a fairly levelled surface, ca. 3 cm thick, over more than half of the area of the test trench; it did not extend to the southeast corner or along wall F58 (fig. 4.97). A ledge, jutting out of the south face of north wall F13, was found directly below DSU96.[189] Further investigation underneath this unit, as well as below DSU93 (in the southeast sector of the test trench), revealed a layer of yellow sand (DSU97; fig. 4.97)[190] mixed with several pottery sherds, charcoal parts, fragments of white plaster, gypsum mortar, and a few animal bones. The unit extended throughout the area of the test trench and abutted the bottom courses of north wall F13.

The removal of the archaeological contexts in the test trench inside room 13, as well as the excavation of room 12, revealed that both west wall F37 and east wall F58 had ledges protruding from their east faces at elevations of 140.325 m and 140.260 m respectively (immediately below the floor levels inside rooms 11 and 12).[191] The bottom courses of the two walls were reached at elevations of 139.065 m (F37) and 139.025 m (F58). The lower courses of mudbricks below the ledges had a slightly different orientation than that of the upper courses, which were shifted by a few degrees to the northwest, although the walls remained parallel. The reason for the change in orientation is obscure, but it is unlikely that the lower courses of both F37 and F58 belonged to different, i.e., earlier, walls. It seems that the foundations of the two walls were built parallel to one another as part of the same construction phase. When floor level was reached, the orientation of the upper courses was slightly adjusted, in order to make

184. Upper elevation: 139.075 m; lower elevation: 138.955 m; max. thickness: 12 cm.
185. Upper elevation: 138.955 m; lower elevation: 138.705 m; max. thickness: 25 cm.
186. Upper elevation: 138.785 m; lower elevation: 138.695 m; max. thickness: 9 cm.
187. Upper elevation: 139.615 m; lower elevation: 138.495 m; max. thickness: 112 cm.
188. Upper elevation: 138.495 m; lower elevation: 138.315 m; max. thickness: 18 cm.
189. See immediately below for a discussion of the ledge in wall F13.
190. Upper elevation: 138.415 m; lower elevation: 137.405 m; max. thickness: 110 cm.
191. An additional, lower ledge was found towards the foundation level of wall F37. It protruded from the east face by 20 cm, at an elevation of 139.385 m.

Fig. 4.97: View (from above) of DSU96–97 in test trench 3 inside room 13.

both walls perpendicular to F13 (the south wall of rooms 1 and 4). As seen above, similar alterations seem to have been carried out during the construction of wall F9 in the north aisle of the church.

The above-mentioned ledge on wall F13 was found at 138.295 m, jutting out by 12 cm from its south face (figs. 4.98/a and 4.99). The sixth course below this ledge is in line with the face above the ledge itself (fig. 4.98/b). The four courses below recede to the north by a further 5 cm (fig. 4.98/c). The lowest visible course, made with mudbricks laid on bed, recedes by an additional 8 cm (fig. 4.98/d). Therefore, the lowest 11 courses of F13 constitute a broad foot that filled the wall's slightly V-shaped foundation trench.

A vertical crack runs through the foundation courses of F13, from the ledge up to an elevation of 140.025 m. At that level, a wooden beam, 8 cm thick, is inserted horizontally into the wall, in place of one course of bricks. Its east and west ends are not visible, but the beam seems to predate the building of walls F37 and F58, at least to their full height. Certainly, it does not extend further east than F58's east face, since there are no traces of it on the profile of F13 exposed in room 12. The beam, as well as six courses of bricks below it, are smeared with a layer of mortar, which corresponds, in color and composition, to the mortar used in the construction of walls F37 and F58. It is possible that, while digging the foundation trenches for these two walls, the crack was discovered in the foundations of F13 by the builders of the south annex; a wooden beam was then inserted into the wall, in order to prevent further damage.

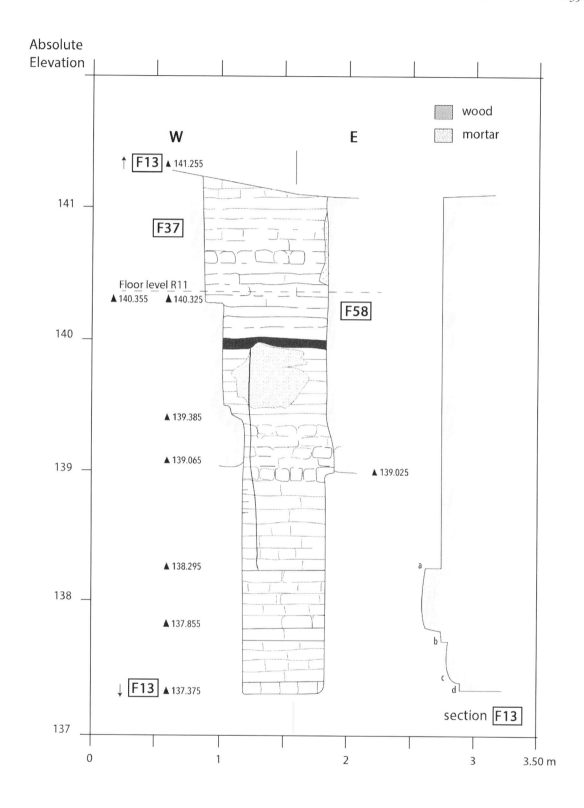

Fig. 4.98: Prospect of south face of wall F13 in room 13 (drawing by D. Dzierzbicka; tracing by C. Fosen).

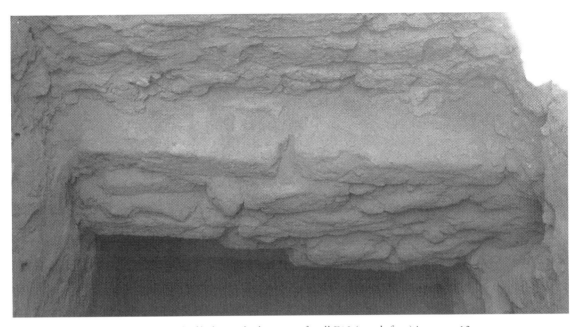

Fig. 4.99: Detail of ledge at the bottom of wall F13 (south face) in room 13.

Subsequently, the crack and the beam were smeared with mortar that had been prepared for the construction of F37 and F58.

The bottom of the foundation courses of wall F13 was reached at 137.375 m. This elevation proved to be consistent with that of wall F14 (west wall of room 1, which is bonded with F13), exposed in test trench 2 in 2012. The bottom course of F14 was found at the elevation of 137.440 m.

East and west walls F58 and F37 proved to have significantly shallower foundations than north wall F13, which was part of the external casing of rooms 1–4. This discovery provided further evidence pointing to a different—perhaps slightly later—construction phase for the south annex than that of the church.[192]

4.9. Room 12

Features

Room 12 is a rectangular space located at the east end of the south annex (figs. 4.3; 4.78). It has a rectangular shape and measures 5.35 m north-south by 2.25 m east-west. Its extant walls are preserved to a maximum height of 0.50 m above the ancient floor level (in the northwest

---

192. That said, there is no indication, based on the available ceramic, numismatic, and papyrological evidence (ostraka), that the construction of the south annex occurred at a significantly later time.

Fig. 4.100: View (to north) of upper surface of wall F40 in room 12.

corner). All features in this room suffered from severe erosion and, in the case of the floor, extensive damage caused, most likely by human intervention.

Both the west and east walls of the room (F58 and F76 respectively) are bonded with south wall F40 and abut wall F13 to the north. F58, F76, and F40 were thus built as part of the same construction episode, which followed the construction of F13 (the south wall of both room 1/the church and room 16/the south *pastophorion*). It is unclear what kind of roof covered room 12, although there is some evidence pointing to the existence in antiquity of a flat roof involving wooden elements. It is also uncertain as to how one accessed this space in antiquity, as there are no extant remains of any entrance from the church itself or from outside building 7. It is likely that room 12 was entered via room 11 to the west, possibly through a doorway located at the south end of wall F58.

South wall F40[193] is not extant above floor level in room 12 and only its upper surface was partially exposed (fig. 4.100). Instead, west wall F58[194] was cleared for a total height of ca. 125 cm, 50 cm of which above the ancient floor level of the room (fig. 4.101). Coarse gray mud plaster with lime spots, small pebbles, potsherds, and organic particles covers the upper courses throughout its length. In the northern half of the wall, where the floor is not preserved, a ledge juts out of the east face immediately below floor level, at an elevation of 140.255 m. The ledge is not aligned with the upper courses of the wall: it protrudes by 21 cm at the north end of F58 and by only 6 cm about 2 m to the south. In the northwest corner of room 12, remnants of wood are preserved above the ledge adhering to the face of the wall (fig. 4.102/a).[195]

193. Upper elevation: 140.265 m; lower elevation: 140.045 m (both elevations taken in room 12).
194. Upper elevation: 140.945 m; lower elevation (in room 12): 139.665 m.
195. They were found at the same elevation of a piece of wood set against wall F57, perpendicular to and abutting wall F58 in adjacent rooms 11 and 13.

Fig. 4.101: View of north half of wall F58 (east face) in room 12.

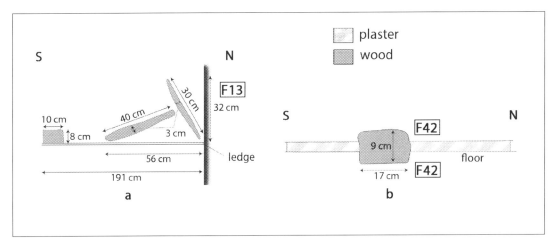

Fig. 4.102: Sketches (not to scale) of wooden elements above ledge of wall F58 (a) and of cavity inside the same wall (b) in room 12 (drawing by D. Dzierzbicka; tracing by C. Fosen).

Fig. 4.103: View of north half of wall F76 (west face) in room 12.

An additional piece was found on the ledge of F58 in room 12, about 190 cm from the north end of the wall and embedded in the plaster of the abutting floor.[196] About 155 cm from the south end of F58, a rectangular cavity (17 by 9 cm) pierces the east face of the wall at floor level (fig. 4.102/b). There is no trace of wall plaster in this area, which corresponds to a small hole found within the floor. Although the shape of the hole and the cavity in the wall are fairly regular, they need not have been intentional.

Excavations below floor level in room 12 revealed a further eight courses of wall F58.[197] They show numerous traces of ash and pieces of charcoal adhering to its surface, likely from dumped material that filled the foundations of the wall.[198]

Wall F76[199] runs north-south, parallel to F58, and forms the eastern boundary of room 12, as well as of the entire south annex of building 7 (fig. 4.103). Only the west face of the wall in room 12 was exposed. F76 is very poorly preserved above the ancient floor level. A total of ten courses, laid in English bond, are visible from the bottom of the excavated area near the northeast corner of the room. Just three courses are extant above the elevation of the floor; these show traces of a mud plaster coating, which extends from the top of the preserved wall to an elevation of 140.455 m.[200] Similarly to wall F58, charcoal fragments and ash, as well as lime

---

196. More fragments of wood were also found within room 12 above floor level, attached against wall F76 (see below).
197. About 220 cm to the south of the northwest corner of the room.
198. A similar situation was noticed with regard to the foundation courses of east wall F76 (see below).
199. Upper elevation: 140.585 m; lower elevation: 139.755 m; max. exposed height: 83 cm.
200. This elevation is consistent with the floor level of room 12. The plaster remains were found up to 150 cm south of the northeast corner of the room.

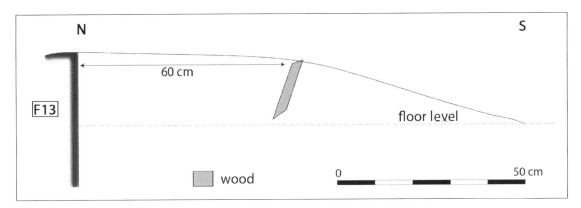

Fig. 4.104: Sketch of wooden elements against wall F76 (west face) in room 12 (drawing by D. Dzierzbicka; tracing by C. Fosen).

spots and small potsherds, are attached to the mortar of wall F76 below floor level, possibly from dump layers that served as foundation fills.[201]

A cluster of wood fragments (measuring 15 by 4.5 cm) was found attached to F76, above floor level, in the northeast corner of the room (fig. 4.104). It may have been part of dumped material, but its location above floor level, as well as other wood pieces found against west wall F58, suggest that all these fragments may have once belonged to a flat roof covering this space.

The north side of room 12 is defined by a portion, 113 cm long, of wall F13,[202] which also served as the south wall of the church (room 1) and of the south *pastophorion* (room 16) (fig. 4.105). The few courses of this wall that are preserved above floor level are obscured by an uneven layer of gray mud plaster, which descends to the elevation of 140.355 m and continues onto the west face of wall F76. Seven courses of mudbricks were exposed below the original floor; they were laid in English bond and still show traces of charcoal, ash, and potsherds, as noticed also in the case of abutting walls F58 and F76 below floor level.

The floor of room 12 (F60),[203] made of mud plaster, is largely missing. Only one patch is preserved abutting the east face of wall F58, in the south half of the room (fig. 4.106). A Roman coin (inv. 16212), a *centenionalis* minted in Alexandria under Constantius II or Julianus and dated to 355–363, was found embedded in the upper surface of the floor.

Stratigraphy and finds (fig. 4.107)

The stratigraphy of room 12 consisted of alternating layers of sand and of wall collapses that were removed down to floor level and, where the latter was missing (especially in the north half of the room), below the floor's preparation layer.

---

201. Additional evidence was detected against north wall F13 underneath floor level (see immediately below).
202. Upper elevation: 140.945 m; lower elevation: 139.725 m (both elevations taken in room 12).
203. Upper elevation: 140.275 m; average thickness: 3 cm. The extant patch, from which elevation and thickness were taken, was not removed.

Fig. 4.105: View (to north) of wall F13 in room 12.

The removal of a contaminated surface unit of windblown sand (DSU31)[204] revealed a context of loose mud-brick debris (DSU69),[205] which was scattered throughout most of the room. It contained a large amount of broken mudbricks and mud-brick detritus and was mixed with potsherds, wood fragments, charcoal, a couple of glass sherds, and a few animal bones. Two small finds were retrieved within this unit, a fragment of a rounded base, possibly belonging to a conical beaker/lamp (inv. 16057)[206] and two joining fragments of a bronze chain (inv. 16064), possibly used as a suspension chain (perhaps for a lamp?).

DSU69 lay on top of a yellow sand layer (DSU70)[207] that was also found, in irregular patches in the north and south halves of the room, directly below surface layer DSU31. The sand was mixed with a moderate quantity of ceramic sherds, glass, wood, plaster, and mud-brick fragments, as well as animal bones. The excavation of this unit revealed two small finds: a

---

204. Upper elevation: 140.815 m; lower elevation: 140.005 m; max. thickness: 13 cm, in the southeast corner of the room (elevations taken in room 12).

205. Upper elevation: 140.745 m; lower elevation: 140.125 m; max. thickness: 23 cm.

206. I 106D (Isings 1957, 130–31), dated to the fourth century CE. The base is very small (only 1.7 cm in diameter) and it most likely could not have stood upright. In fourth-century contexts a similar base can also be associated with toilet bottles/*unguentaria*.

207. Upper elevation: 140.515 m; lower elevation: 140.045 m.

Fig. 4.106: View (to south) of room 12 during excavations (the dashed line shows the extent of preserved floor F60).

Roman bronze coin (inv. 16071, illegible) and one fragment of an undefined glass base, with a slightly concave inner side, likely from a beaker/lamp (inv. 16120).[208]

Following the removal of DSU70, a brown layer of mud-brick debris and some sand (DSU73)[209] was exposed in the north part of room 12, where the original floor level was not preserved.[210] The unit broadly followed the outline of collapse unit DSU69, which was separated from it by sand layer DSU70. DSU73 was particularly hard and compact against west wall F58.[211]

208. Probably form I 106B (Isings 1957, 127), dated to the fourth century CE.
209. Upper elevation: 140.695 m; lower elevation: 139.645 m; max. thickness (excavated): 100 cm. The unit was not fully removed.
210. The unit, however, was also detected above remains of floor F60.
211. This was not a uniform context; it included areas that were richer in mud-brick debris and others that were sandier.

CHAPTER 4: SURVEY AND EXCAVATIONS TO THE SOUTH THE CHURCH 243

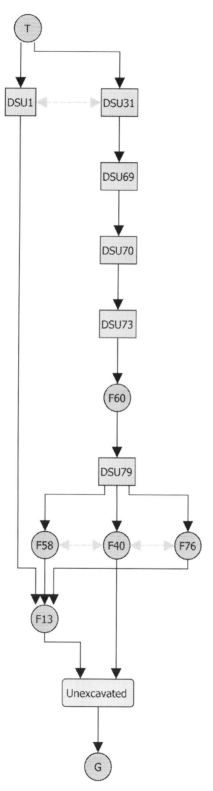

Fig. 4.107: Harris Matrix of room 12.

Some of the mudbricks may have originally belonged to this wall, but the overall matrix of the unit points to dumped material, which seems to have been deposited after the abandonment of the room.[212] DSU73 contained a few whole mudbricks, numerous brick fragments and pottery sherds, cobbles, animal bones, fruit pits, wood fragments, charcoal and ash, pieces of white gypsum plaster (some of which bearing traces of yellow or red paint), bronze fragments, and several glass sherds, as well as glass slag. A comparatively large number of small finds were retrieved during the excavation of this unit: five bronze coins (inv. 16099, a *nummus centenionalis* minted under Constantius II or Constans in 347–348; inv. 16101, a *maiorina* struck under Constantius II and dated to 351–361; inv. 16102, another *maiorina* minted under Constantius II in 352–355; inv. 16189, illegible; inv. 16288, a *maiorina* struck under Constantius II and dated to 351–361); one fragment of bronze nail with a rectangular head (inv. 16112);[213] a complete gypsum-plaster stopper (inv. 16113); one fragment of a bracelet made of black opaque glass (inv. 16114); four diagnostic sherds of glass vessels (inv. 16105 and 16109–16111);[214] an almost complete small ceramic plate, likely used as an incense burner (inv. 30104); and an almost complete medium-sized ceramic bowl (inv. 30105).

The last unit that was documented—although not removed—in room 12 was DSU79,[215] a preparation layer for floor F60. It was exposed in the southern and eastern parts of the room, where the floor and walls seem to have suffered particularly extensive erosion. The unit consisted of fine grayish sand, with an abundance of inclusions such as ash and charcoal parts, numerous pottery sherds, and fruit pits. A barely legible Roman bronze coin (inv. 16289, dated to the second half of the fourth century to the first half of the fifth) was found on the exposed surface of DSU79, at the interface with DSU70.

---

212. Since it lay, in part, above the original floor level and filled an area, in the north half of the room, where the floor was missing.

213. The almost complete fragment was also interpreted as a decorative tack, possibly for clothing.

214. Inv. 16105 is a fragment from the base of an *unguentarium*; inv. 16109 once belonged to the rim of a short-necked jar; inv. 16110 is a fragment of rounded lip fold-in, possibly of a bowl or a large beaker; inv. 16111 is part of the footring of a plate.

215. Upper elevation: 140.255 m (in the northeast corner of the unit).

Chapter 5

The Underground Funerary Crypts

5.1. The Excavation of Rooms 2–4

Archaeological investigations of the east sector of building 7, in the area under the now-disappeared sanctuary (rooms 14–16), led to one of the most exciting findings associated with the church of Amheida. In 2013 a funerary crypt, with three sealed burials, was discovered underneath room 14, in the northeast corner of building 7. It was in a remarkably good state of preservation, especially in comparison with the rest of building 7 (figs. 3.2; 5.1–2). Excavations at the church were resumed ten years later and revealed two additional underground crypts, one (room 3) located below the apse (room 15) and the other (room 4) lying beneath the south *pastophorion* (room 16).[1] The three underground spaces were interconnected via two doorways, which were aligned along the same north-south axis and pierced the north and south walls of the central crypt. Access to these underground spaces was only from the church above, through a square trapdoor built at floor level in the northwest corner of the south *pastophorion* (room 16). It is certain that the three crypts (i.e., rooms 2–4) were not created under the sanctuary of building 7 at a later stage. Indeed, the archaeological evidence shows beyond doubt that these underground spaces were planned and built as structurally integral parts of the church. A detailed discussion of the crypts' features and stratigraphy, as well as of the sealed burials that were found in two of the three rooms, follows below.

---

1 In addition to revealing a fourth burial (tomb 9) in room 2: see Sec. 5.2.1 below..

Fig. 5.1: Aerial view (to southwest) of building 7 during the 2023 excavation season, with the three crypts (room 2–4) in the foreground.

5.2. Room 2

Room 2, excavated in 2013,[2] is a rectangular and fairly spacious crypt, measuring 3.30 m north-south by 3.52 m east-west. The walls are almost completely preserved, to a maximum height of 2.52 m above floor level (at the west end of south wall F64) (figs. 5.2; 5.4). Room 2 was an underground space lying below now-missing room 14 (the north *pastophorion*). It was accessed via a doorway set into the eastern half of the south wall. This opening led into room 2 from the crypt (room 3, discussed in the following section) located below the apse of the church. The north crypt was not directly connected with the rest of the church at the upper level, and it was not directly accessible from the exterior of building 7.[3] Room 2 was used for the deposition of burials. Four intact tombs (6–9) were found, set into the foundation fill of the church, along the west wall and in the northeast corner of the crypt.[4]

---

2. The number was assigned to the crypt following investigation that revealed how the north *pastophorion* (originally labeled as room 2) had completely disappeared. The now-missing north *pastophorion* was then labeled room 14.
3. No evidence was found for direct access from the putative *kathesterion* to the east of building 7 into the area of the three crypts.
4. See Sec. 5.2.1 below. The central part of the room, as well as the area near the doorway along the south wall, were left empty, in contrast with room 3, where the space was entirely filled with graves.

Chapter 5: The Underground Funerary Crypts

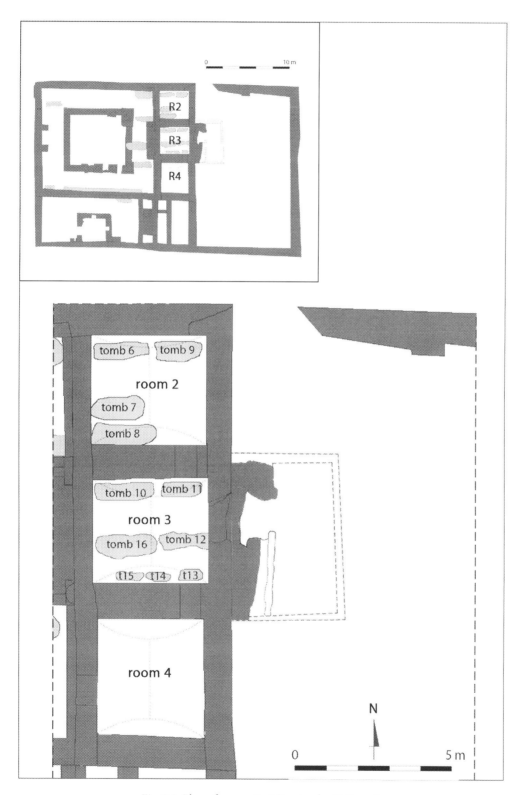

Fig. 5.2: Plan of rooms 2–4 (tracing by C. Fosen).

Fig. 5.3: 3D model of underground crypts (rooms 2–4) (elaborated by L. Davighi).

Fig. 5.4: Aerial view (to southwest) of room 2 (north crypt) before excavation.

Features

The room was originally covered by a barrel-vaulted ceiling, which was found intact in all but its central, highest parts. The vault, which is oriented north-south, is built of iron-rich mudbricks, measuring ca. 42 by 20 by 7.5 cm. These are laid on edge and lean slightly to the north.[5] White chinking stones, ca. 5 by 7 by 3 cm in size, are inserted vertically between the mudbricks, every other course, but potsherds were also used in the construction of the vault.[6] The latter is coated, on its inner face, with a thick layer of mud plaster, which extends to the four walls of the crypt. Along the top of north wall F15, the vault is supported by mudbricks laid on edge, slightly leaning eastwards and sitting on a ledge that juts out from the wall's south face. The preserved west and east portions of the vaulted roof are labeled as F65[7] and F66[8], respectively (figs. 5.5–6). A thick layer of plaster obscures the joint between F65 and west wall F1, as well as between F66 and east wall F59, making it impossible to identify the lower edge of the vault where it sprang from the wall.

The fill of the wedge created by walls F1 and F59 and the barrel vault was covered with a layer of mortar. A mud-brick platform was then laid, likely as a base for the floor of the north *pastophorion* (room 14) above it. The remains of this platform (F67 and F68) consist of a layer of bricks laid on edge below a layer of bricks laid on bed (figs. 5.3; 5.5). F67[9] lies above vault spring F65 and is preserved only in the southwest corner of the crypt's roof. It consists of mudbricks laid on edge and bonded with sandy mortar. This patch extends for 125 cm north-south and includes two rows of bricks against the southwest corner, laid perpendicularly to west wall F1.[10] The remainder of the preserved feature, to the north and to the east, consists of bricks laid parallel to the same wall. F68[11] rests on top of the fill of vault spring F66, along east wall F59. It is preserved in two severely eroded parts at the north and south ends of the ceiling, with a break in the middle (fig. 5.7). The north patch measures 134 cm north-south by 74 cm east-west. Two layers of mudbricks are visible; the bottom one consists of bricks laid on edge, parallel to wall F59 in two rows.[12] The upper course is made of bricks laid on bed and perpendicular to F59. The south patch of F68, 148 cm north-south by 70 cm east-west, displays the same construction technique, although only the layer of bricks on bed is visible.

---

5. The mudbricks' rings were set at an angle to prevent them from sliding down before the mortar had set. This method developed in areas where wood was scarce, as it allowed for building vaults without using a wooden centering structure. The mudbricks used in these vaults were typically thinner and lighter than those used for the construction of wall mudbricks. They often show grooves applied with fingers on the flat sides of the bricks before drying, as this likely helped to prevent slippage. In the case of the vaults in the crypts of building 7, the inclination of the mudbricks is minimal, pointing to a construction technique half-way between that utilizing some kind of scaffolding and that without the use of any supporting beams; that is to say, the custom of laying the mudbricks at an angle was maintained, but the vaulting was probably carried out using a centering structure. Cf. Husselman 1979, 50–56; Van Beek 1987, 96–103; Lancaster 2015, 39–48, n. 44.

6. The use of this method for bedding the mudbricks over the entire surface of the vault is also attested in room 4, particularly in the collapse of the vault (DSU120–121) that was found inside the crypt (see Sec. 5.4 below).

7. Upper elevation: 140.775 m (south end of preserved patch).

8. Upper elevation: 140.645 m (south end).

9. Upper elevation: 140.905 m.

10. Each row is 88 cm long.

11. Upper elevation: 140.595 m.

12. Ten of these bricks are exposed in the northeast corner of the room.

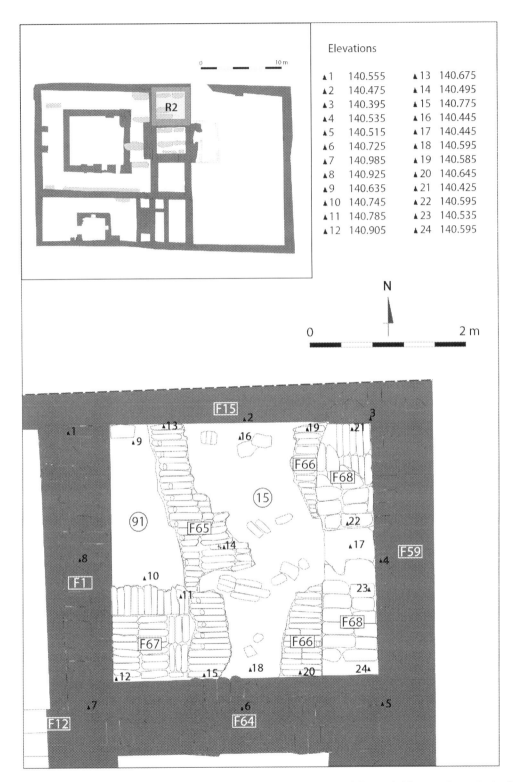

Fig. 5.5: Plan of room 2 before excavation, with features visible at the level of the vault (drawing by D. Dzierzbicka; tracing by C. Fosen).

Fig. 5.6: Remains of vaulted ceiling above room 2 (view to north).

Fig. 5.7: View (to southwest) of platform F68 above the vault of room 2.

Fig. 5.8: View (to north) of wall F15 inside room 2.

The north wall of the crypt is F15,[13] which also defines the entire northern boundary of building 7 (fig. 5.8). Within room 2, the south face of the wall is coated throughout with a thick layer of mud plaster, rich in organic particles, lime spots, and charcoal fragments and partially hidden by sand concretions. The wall is intact up to the height of 151 cm from floor level.[14] Above this area is a horizontal break that runs along the wall, with the uppermost part (measuring 61 cm in height and consisting of six courses of mudbricks) tilted towards the north. The plaster is partly missing in this sector of the wall and exposes mudbricks laid in English bond. At the bottom of F15, a ledge juts out by 5 cm, directly below the area where the plaster descends from the walls onto the floor's preparation layer.

F15 is abutted, at its west end, by wall F1. The latter runs north-south and forms the western boundary of rooms 14–16 (and underground rooms 2–4), separating them from the main body of the church. The east face of F1 was exposed within room 2 down to floor level, where it is abutted by tombs 6–8.[15] The wall is completely covered in mud plaster, which

13. Upper elevation: 140.555 m; lower elevation: 138.385 m; max. preserved height: 2.1 m.
14. Apart from a vertical crack ca. 45 cm east of wall F1.
15. Discussed below in Sec. 5.2.

Fig. 5.9: View (to west) of wall F1 inside room 2.

includes large organic particles, lime spots, and charcoal fragments, and is extensively hidden by concretions (fig. 5.9). The coating of plaster hinders the bond and, as mentioned above, makes it impossible to detect where the vault springs off the wall. The plaster descends onto the floor level at an elevation of 138.305 m, 8 cm below the level of the floor in the center of the room and forms a narrow channel along the wall.

At the opposite (east) end of room 2 is wall F59,[16] which was found in good condition (fig. 5.10). F59 binds rooms 14–16 along their east side but was investigated only in room 2. The wall is fully coated, on its exposed face, with the same thick layer of mud plaster, rich in organic inclusions and lime, that was detected on wall F1. The plaster hides the bond of F59, at the bottom of which is a ledge jutting out westwards by 5–8 cm. This ledge, which is visible where the floor is missing, is at a lower elevation (of about 6 cm) than that of wall F15's ledge. Also, the floor abutting F59 is 11 cm lower than in the center of the room and forms another shallow channel, which runs along the face of this wall.

16. Upper elevation: 140.515 m; lower elevation: 138.225 m; max. height: 231 cm.

Fig. 5.10: View (to east) of wall F59 inside room 2.

Wall 59 is abutted to the south by F64,[17] an east-west oriented wall that forms the south edge of room 2 and separates it from the space below room 15, i.e., room 3 (figs. 5.11–12). Like all the other walls of this crypt, F64 is completely covered with mud plaster. The west half of the wall is abutted by tomb 8, while a doorway is set at its east end, with a mud-brick threshold that is 18 cm higher than the room's floor. This feature allowed access into the north crypt from room 3, the crypt below the apse. The doorway is 174 cm high, 67 cm wide, 94 cm deep, and has a vaulted top. A recess, 70 cm high and 15 cm deep (on average) pierces the west side of the doorway.[18] Its irregularity, as well as the fact that no plaster is visible on its surface, suggests that it was accidentally damaged or intentionally hacked out to allow the passage of something large.[19]

17. Upper elevation: 140.985 m; lower elevation: 138.315 m.
18. Another recess, 9 cm high, 12 cm wide, and 3 cm deep, was found in the eastern jamb, about 120 cm above floor level.
19. Perhaps the coffin that was found in tomb 9. Due to the poor quality and fragility of the material of which it was made, the coffin must have been assembled and sealed *in situ* (see Sec. 5.2.1 below), probably in room 4 and then moved into room 2.

Fig. 5.11: View (to south) of wall F64 inside room 2.

A thick and uneven mud floor (F75),[20] with embedded potsherds and small stones, extends throughout room 2 (fig. 5.13). It was found in a relatively good state of preservation, with only the northeast corner missing.[21] The floor, which lies on sand and mud-brick debris, is cut by pits F69 (along the north wall of the room and encompassing pits F80 and F81 of tombs 6 and 9 respectively), F71 (tomb 7), and F73 (tomb 8). Along the walls of the crypt are plastered channels, about 20 cm wide, through which the plaster from the walls descended onto ledges along north wall F15 and east wall F59, as well as onto the preparation layer below floor level. These narrow channels are ca. 3–5 cm lower than the level of floor F75 in the middle of the room. Traces of fingerprints from the application of the mud are still visible on the surface of these channels. It is unknown why this narrow area along the four sides of the room was at

20. Upper elevation: 138.385 m; lower elevation: 138.335 m; thickness: 2–5 cm.
21. The area not covered by the floor measures about 95 by 95 cm. In 2013, it was yet unclear as to why F75 was missing in this area, considering the overall good condition of most features inside the crypt. Further excavation, resumed in 2023, led to the discovery of a tomb (labeled 9) that had been dug in this quadrant of the room. Although this finding provided an answer for the missing floor, it is still puzzling as to why a new floor patch was not smeared on top of the grave (which also lacked a mud-brick superstructure).

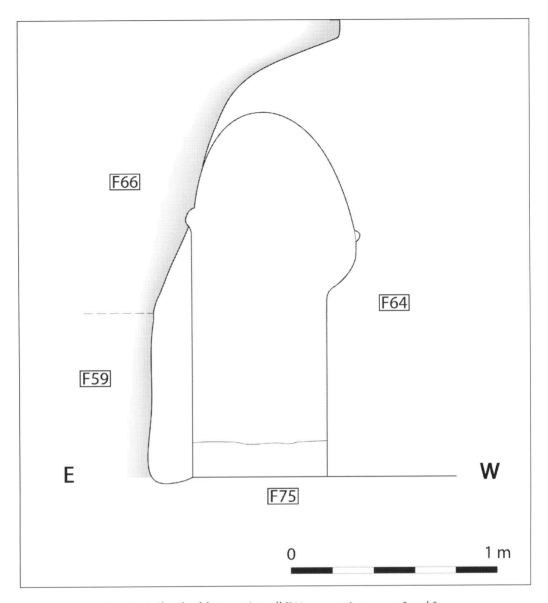

Fig. 5.12: Sketch of doorway in wall F64, connecting rooms 2 and 3
(drawing by D. Dzierzbicka; tracing by C. Fosen).

a lower elevation and the descending plaster of the walls was not covered, as one would have expected, by the mud plaster of the floor. Remains of an earlier floor level (F108+F111) were detected inside the crypt in 2023, cut by all four tombs placed inside the room (figs. 5.4; 5.14–15). This floor, consisting of several thin layers of compacted mud, with a few small potsherds and pebbles embedded, lay below a sand preparation layer for upper floor F75. It was cut by

Fig. 5.13: View from above (to south) of floor F75 and burials inside the north crypt (room 2).

tombs 6–8 along the west wall of the crypt, as well as two large cuts (F109[22] and F110[23]) in the middle of the room. Two patches of this early floor were identified, one (F108)[24] in the west of room 2 and the other (F111)[25] in the east half of the crypt. The cleaning of F111 revealed one fragment of an open faience vessel with a foot ring (inv. 17056), embedded in the floor near the doorway connecting the north and central crypts.

The digging of these burials partially cut through the foundation trenches of the room's perimeter walls. The north interface of burial cut F81 (in tomb 9) shows a mud-brick ledge[26] directly below the level where the plaster from the wall descended on the floor cut by pit F69 (fig. 5.16): This ledge juts out by 16 cm from the vertical surface of the wall (F15).[27] Within tomb

22. Upper elevation: 138.270 m.
23. Upper elevation: 138.270 m. Both F109 and F110 were documented, but not fully excavated.
24. Upper elevation: 138.270 m; the feature was left unexcavated.
25. Upper elevation: 138.260 m; this part of the floor was left unexcavated as well.
26. Upper elevation: 138.340 m.
27. This ledge is likely the same as that found in test trench 2 (in the north aisle of room 1) at the elevation of 138.380 m: cf. Sec. 3.3.2 above.

Fig. 5.14: Aerial view (to north) of room 2, showing the extent of the earlier floor level (F108+F111).

9, another ledge is visible at a lower elevation.[28] It protrudes by ca. 19 cm more and consists of a row of headers (in its uppermost course). The ledge seems to continue in the corner where north wall F15 is bonded with east wall F59.

The foundation of north wall F15 was also exposed in the burial pit of tomb 6 (F80), which partially cut through the inner face of F15. In the western portion of the wall, the lower ledge was cut by the burial pit. The ledge is still visible in the east interface of the cut for a height of two courses of mudbricks. Within tomb 6, the foundation wall continues for nine courses, arranged in alternating rows of headers and stretchers to the bottom of the burial pit.

Stratigraphy and finds (fig. 5.17)

The fill of room 2 consisted of windblown sand and collapse episodes of walls and vaults. The sand was arbitrarily divided into DSU15, DSU100, and DSU103, in order to establish a

---

28. Upper elevation: 137.700 m. This lower ledge was identified also in test trench 2, with an upper elevation of 137.650 m: cf. Sec. 3.3.2 above. The bottom of the foundation of the north wall was not reached; the excavation stopped at elevation 137.470 m.

CHAPTER 5: THE UNDERGROUND FUNERARY CRYPTS 259

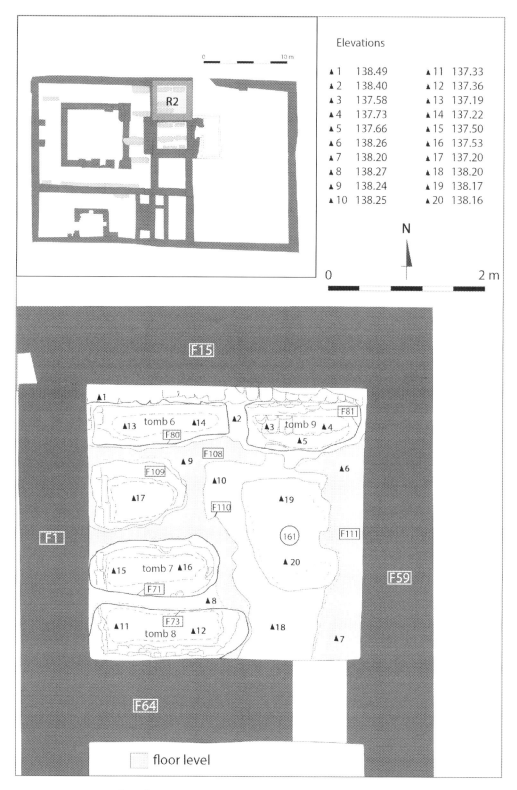

Fig. 5.15: Plan of room 2 at the end of the 2023 season (drawing by L. Davighi).

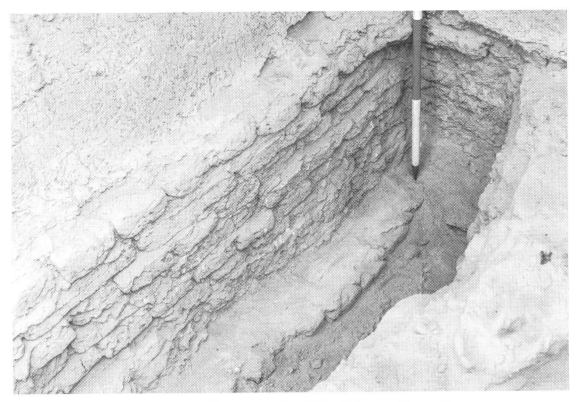

Fig. 5.16: View of foundations of wall F15 within tomb 9 (room 2).

chronological relationship of the sand deposits, found at different elevations, with the collapse units that rested within and were surrounded by them. Following the removal of a thin surface layer of windblown sand (DSU1), DSU 91 and DSU15 were revealed. The former[29] consisted of a compact layer of grayish-beige sandy mortar, which filled the spring of vault F65 above the west wall of the crypt. DSU15[30] was a thick subsurface unit that had naturally deposited into the room through the missing part of the vault, which ran from north to south in the middle of room 2. The stratum was made of windblown sand and scattered mudbricks, as well as mudbrick fragments (fig. 5.18). The bricks came from the partial collapse of both the walls and the vault of room 2. The unit was also mixed with pottery sherds, some pebbles, small pieces of white gypsum plaster (one of which bearing traces of red paint), negligible quantities of faience, glass, animal bones, and a few fruit pits.

DSU15 rested above two collapse episodes (DSU99 and DSU101) and a natural sand fill (DSU100) (fig. 5.19). DSU99[31] was a minor collapse that occurred in the central and east parts of the vault, sloping from west to east. It resulted from either the collapse of a wall (perhaps belonging to the now-missing north *pastophorion*) or part of adjacent platform F68, whose

---

29. Upper elevation: 140.745 m; the unit was left unexcavated.
30. Upper elevation: 140.860 m; lower elevation: 139.935 m; max. thickness: 95 cm.
31. Upper elevation: 140.815 m; lower elevation: 139.585 m; max. thickness: 60 cm.

mudbricks have the same dimensions as those identified in the collapse. A few pottery sherds were gathered during the excavation of the unit, which partially lay above DSU100.[32] This was a context of windblown sand that extended throughout room 2; it contained large and small pieces of mudbricks,[33] which may have belonged to walls once standing above the crypt or to the platform (F67+F68) built on top of the vault. DSU100 contained a few pottery sherds and fragments of white gypsum plaster (with traces of green and yellow paint). A complete iron nail (inv. 16250) was also found while excavating this unit.

A collapse episode of part of the vault (labelled as DSU102)[34] occurred before the formation of DSU100 in the southwest quadrant of the crypt, sloping from the northeast and accumulating against the southwest corner of the room (fig. 5.20). DSU102 contained both wall and vault mudbricks lying within a sandy matrix. Among the inclusions were numerous pottery sherds, as well as some animal bones, glass sherds, dross, wood fragments, charcoal, and small pieces of mortar and plaster, both white and painted. Four small finds were also gathered within this unit: a fragment of a bracelet made of black opaque glass (inv. 16270), two illegible Roman coins (inv. 16271–16272), and a Greek ostrakon (O.Trim. 2.572, dated to ca. 275–350).[35] It is likely that DSU102 originated from the south part of the vault, along south wall F64, and fell on top of pre-existing sand unit DSU103. The latter[36] extended throughout large part of the room (fig. 5.21); it sloped from north to south and, from the center of the room, towards the east and west, thus causing the accumulation of DSU102 (mentioned above) in the southwest corner of the room. The windblown sand of DSU103 likely poured into the crypt following the collapse of the north half of the vault. A small concentration of iron-rich mud-brick rubble was found towards the lower interface of the unit, in the middle and towards the south wall of the room. Additional mud-brick fragments were scattered throughout DSU103, which also contained potsherds, many wood fragments, animal bones, and small pieces of white and painted plaster (especially in the southeast part of the deposit); the latter likely originated from collapsed structures once standing above the crypt. An almost complete iron nail was the only small find (inv. 16274) retrieved during the excavation of this unit.

DSU103 rested on top of two collapse layers: DSU101 and DSU105. DSU101[37] was first discovered against the north wall (F15) of room 2 (fig. 5.18); from there, it sloped down southwards and extended throughout more than half of the crypt. The collapse consisted of mudbricks fallen from wall F15, but also contained parts of vault F65+F66.[38] Small lenses of sand were found between clusters of wall and vault collapse. DSU101 contained some loose mudbricks, but the majority had been crushed into small fragments. Among the inclusions were potsherds, pieces of white gypsum plaster (some with traces of orange and red painting), a few animal bones, one small wood fragment, and a couple of glass sherds.

32. Upper elevation: 139.935 m; lower elevation: 139.295 m; max. thickness: 65 cm.
33. One brick was made of white lime mortar, with coarse desert sand used as temper.
34. Upper elevation: 139.615 m; lower elevation: 138.655 m; max. thickness (in the southwest corner): 96 cm.
35. Ast and Bagnall 2016, 164.
36. Upper elevation: 139.345 m; lower elevation: 138.325 m; max. thickness: 100 cm.
37. Upper elevation: 140.005 m; lower elevation: 138.495 m; max. elevation (near north wall F15): 90 cm.
38. Two large fragments of the vault, measuring 215 by 45 by 20 cm and 64 by 45 by 20 cm, were found in this unit.

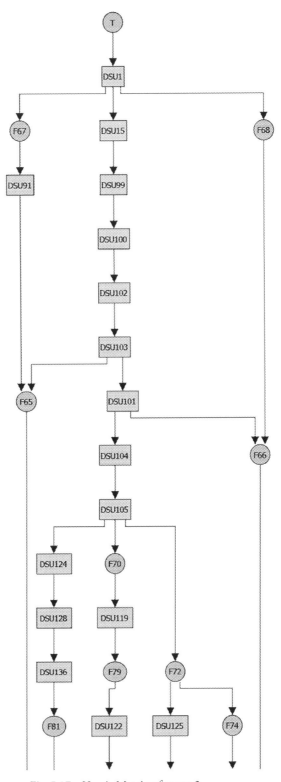

Fig. 5.17a: Harris Matrix of room 2.

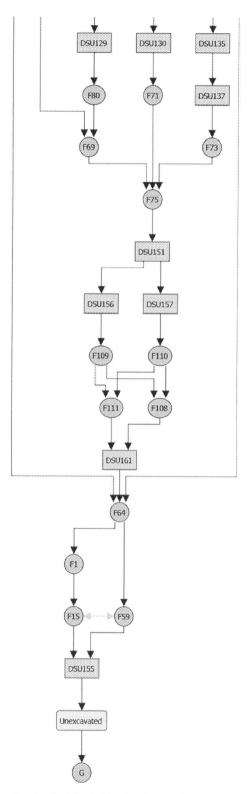

Fig. 5.17b: Harris Matrix of room 2.

Fig. 5.18: View (to southwest) of DSU15 below F65 (west portion of room 2's vault).

An illegible (but likely late fourth- or early fifth-century) complete Roman coin (inv. 16273) and a small fragment of another bronze coin were discovered while investigating this unit.

The removal of DSU101 exposed a layer of yellow sand (DSU104),[39] which was mixed with a few pottery sherds, fragments of slag, wood, and white gypsum plaster (with traces of black and red paint), charcoal, glass sherds, and animal bones. Both this context and DSU103 (discussed above) lay above DSU105,[40] which in turn lay directly above the floor of the crypt and was its earliest deposit, following the sealing of the latest burial. The unit consisted of brownish-yellow sand, mud-brick debris, and complete mudbricks scattered throughout the room. The debris was more copious and formed a thicker deposit in the north half of the crypt (fig. 5.22). Among the inclusions were pottery sherds, one piece of faience, fragments of mud and white gypsum plaster (some of which painted in orange, yellow, green, and black), small quantities of ash, charcoal, dross, wood, and a few animal bones. A complete cooking pot (inv. 30129), heavily blackened on its external surface, was found in the northeast corner of the crypt, to the east of tomb 6 (fig. 5.23).

39. Upper elevation: 139.225 m; lower elevation: 138.375 m; max. thickness: 62 cm.
40. Upper elevation: 138.655 m; lower elevation: 138.315 m; max. thickness (in the northern half of the room): 27 cm.

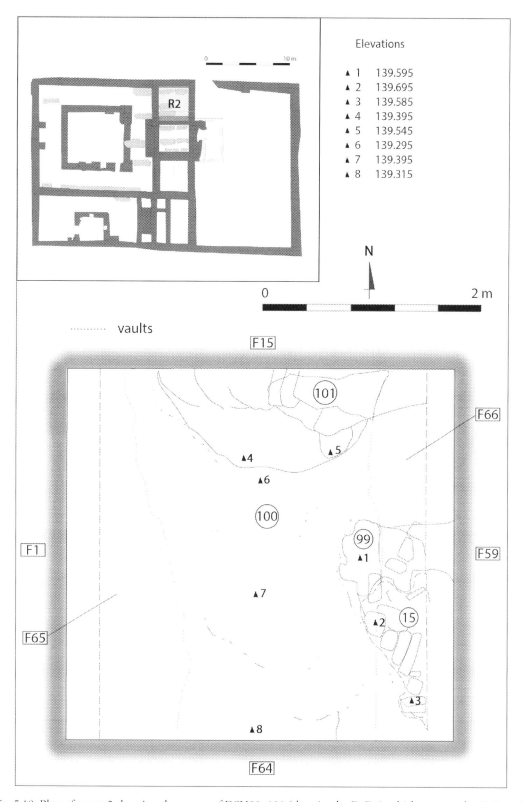

Fig. 5.19: Plan of room 2 showing the extent of DSU99–101 (drawing by D. Dzierzbicka; tracing by C. Fosen).

Fig. 5.20: View (to southwest) of collapse DSU102.

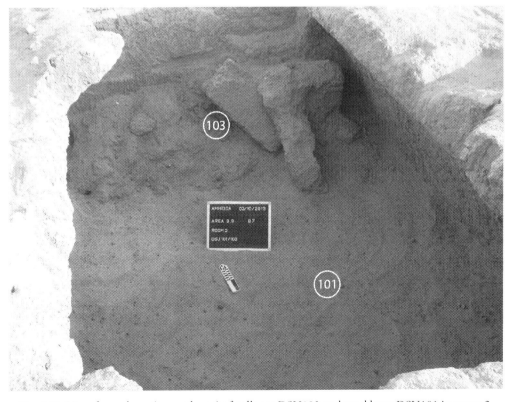

Fig. 5.21: View from above (to northeast) of collapse DSU103 and sand layer DSU101 in room 2.

Fig. 5.22: Detail of DSU105 in the northeast corner of room 2.

Fig. 5.23: View (to north) of cooking pot (inv. 30129) *in situ*.

It contained a black substance (collected for further analysis) mixed with remains of white mortar (found on the inner surface and on the bottom of the vessel), as well as a few fish bones and a non-diagnostic potsherd. Due to its location in the proximity of a sealed burial, it is possible that the pot had been placed and left inside the crypt as a funerary offering (or used during rituals connected with inhumation, the so-called *refrigerium*).[41] A concentration of plant remains (FN59), discovered above the mud-brick superstructure (F70) of tomb 6, may also be associated with a grave offering in memory of a deceased.[42]

In 2023 room 2 was emptied of the sand with which it had been backfilled at the end of the 2013 season. The excavation of the tombs in this crypt led to the removal of parts of upper floor F75, below which a layer of loose yellow sand (DSU151),[43] mixed with pottery fragments and moderate amounts of mud-brick debris and charcoal, was exposed. An ostrakon (inv. 17054), consisting of two lines of Greek (without date), was the only small find retrieved within this unit, which had likely been laid to level the ground surface and to provide some kind of preparation layer for the upper floor. DSU151 was documented only in parts of room 2, particularly in its northern half, while along the southern edge of the crypt the upper and lower floor levels lay directly on top of each other. Thus, the earlier floor (F108+F111) was exposed either below F75 or DSU151. This surface rested above DSU161,[44] a preparation layer consisting of brownish-yellow compacted sand, which had likely been used to level within the crypt the sloping ground of the hill on which the church was built.[45] Floor F108+F111 lay also on top of DSU155,[46] a foundation deposit consisting of compacted clean sand, with only minimal charcoal inclusions.

Overall, the objects discovered in the stratigraphy of room 2 can be divided into three categories: objects from collapsed walls and vaults; objects that fell into the crypt through the broken vault, but originally belonged to the *pastophorion* above (now missing); and, finally, objects originally connected with the crypt. The ostrakon (O.Trim. 2.572) and coins (inv. 16271–16273) that were found in collapses DSU101 and DSU102 can be assigned, with a fair degree of probability, to the first category, as they were likely to have been mixed in with the building material. The complete vessel (inv. 30129) and the cluster of plant remains (FN59) found in DSU105, as well as a long piece of wood (FN56)[47] from DSU103, were most likely associated with room 2. As mentioned above, the pot and, in particular, the organic remains may have been some kind of offering for the deceased placed in burial 6.

---

41. See Sec. 5.5 below, esp. p. 340.

42. A sample of the vegetal remains was collected for further analysis. For a discussion of the cooking vessel and the remains of plants found inside the north crypt, see Sec. 5.5 below.

43. Upper elevation: 138.420 m; lower elevation: 138.160 m; max. thickness: 27 cm.

44. Upper level: 138.180 m.

45. The same leveling layer was documented also in the eastern halves of the two other crypts (rooms 3–4), between the earliest floor level and foundation fill DSU155 (=DSU162 in room 4, while in room 3 the layer was documented in the section of tomb 12's pit, but not assigned a number).

46. Upper level: 137.590 m (measured in the burials' cuts). The same foundation deposit was identified also in rooms 3 and 4 (central crypt and south *pastophorion*, respectively).

47. It was originally speculated that the fragment of wood once belonged to a door element (perhaps a jamb), as its discovery near the crypt's doorway seemed to suggest. However, the analysis of the walls within the passageway does not seem to confirm this hypothesis. No evidence could be detected attesting to the existence of wooden jambs on this doorway (or on the very similar doorway leading from room 4 into room 3).

A small number of finds from different units can be tentatively assigned to the context of the now-lost north *pastophorion*. Fragments of white liquid mortar, with impressions of chisel marks, may point to the existence of a feature (or features) made of stone blocks once standing not in the crypt, which did not contain any stone elements, but in the service room above. Following the destruction, or dismantling, of this hypothetical feature (or features), the pieces of mortar were left behind and fell subsequently through the hole in the vault into room 2, together with windblown sand. It is possible that the numerous fragments of painted plaster retrieved inside the crypt, especially in DSU103, found their way in the same way as the pieces of liquid mortar. It cannot be established if the plaster fragments originally belonged to wall painted decoration or were, instead, part of an ornate ceiling. Since no evidence of painted wall plaster was found in building 7, it is more likely that the north *pastophorion* had a flat painted roof, as was the case for the nave of the church.

5.2.1. Tombs 6–9 in Room 2

In 2013, three roughly rectangular burials (tombs 6–8), oriented east-west, were uncovered in room 2 along its west wall (figs. 5.24–26).[48]

An additional tomb (9) was identified in 2023 in the northeast corner of room 2, where the two floor levels (F75 and F108+F111) were completely missing.

The burial pit of tomb 7 cuts through upper floor F75; its superstructure seems to extend over tomb 8 (in the southwest corner of the crypt), which seems to cut only through the earlier floor level (F108+F111).[49] Therefore, the available evidence points to the existence of two distinct burial phases. Considering that mud floors, such as those attested in room 2 and throughout building 7, deteriorated very easily, and also that patches of compacted mud were often smeared to level, restore, or replace the original floors, it is doubtful that the chronological interval between the two burial phases identified in the north crypt was very long.

Tomb 6 is located against the northwest corner of the north crypt, along wall F15 to the north and wall F1 to the west (figs. 5.24–25). The oval-shaped burial cut (F80)[50] measures 55 cm north-south by 182 cm east-west. F80 seems to have been dug within an earlier pit (F69), which extends (along the north wall) to the east edge of the crypt; F69 was possibly excavated to remove the floor of the crypt in preparation for the digging of pits associated with tombs 6 and 9.

Tomb 6 was covered with a superstructure (F70)[51] measuring 62 cm north-south by 180 cm east-west (fig. 5.27). F70 was built with mudbricks laid in two rows parallel to north

---

48. The superstructures of the tombs, which were found intact, were documented but, due to time limitations, they were not removed during the 2013 season.

49. The relationship of burial cuts F80 and F81 (of tombs 6 and 9, respectively) with the floor levels of room 2 is harder to establish, since both floors F75 and F108+F111 are missing in the area of the two tombs (following the digging of pit F69 along the north wall of the room, likely in preparation for the digging of pits F80 and F81).

50. Upper elevation: 138.400 m; lower elevation: 137.190 m.

51. Upper elevation: 138.395 m; lower elevation: 138.200 m; max. thickness: 29 cm. Plant remains, collected as FN59, were found on top of this superstructure.

Fig. 5.24: View (to west) of tombs 6–8, at the end of the 2013 season.

wall F15. The south row of bricks consists of eight whole and fragmentary bricks, followed by a mud-plastered area, ca. 40 cm in length from east to west, at the east end of the row. The bricks' arrangement along the north wall is more irregular and concealed in part by plaster. A cluster of debris, measuring about 34 by 30 cm and covered with mud plaster, was found at the east end of this row. F70 does not extend to the east end of the burial pit; while it is possible that the superstructure was intentionally shorter, matching the length of the superstructures of tombs 7 and 8 (F72 and F74 respectively),[52] it seems more plausible that the east end of F70 was damaged or removed when burial pit F81 (tomb 9) was dug in the northeast corner of the room.

The removal of the superstructure of tomb 6 exposed DSU119,[53] a unit of dark gray-yellow sand mixed with some potsherds, mud-brick debris, and moderate amounts of charcoal. DSU119 was laid to fill the uppermost part of the pit up to the level of the floor of the crypt.

---

52. A similar discrepancy in size between burial pit and superstructure was noticed in tomb 8 in the southwest corner of the crypt.
53. Upper elevation: 138.240 m; lower elevation: 138.070 m; max. thickness: 15 cm.

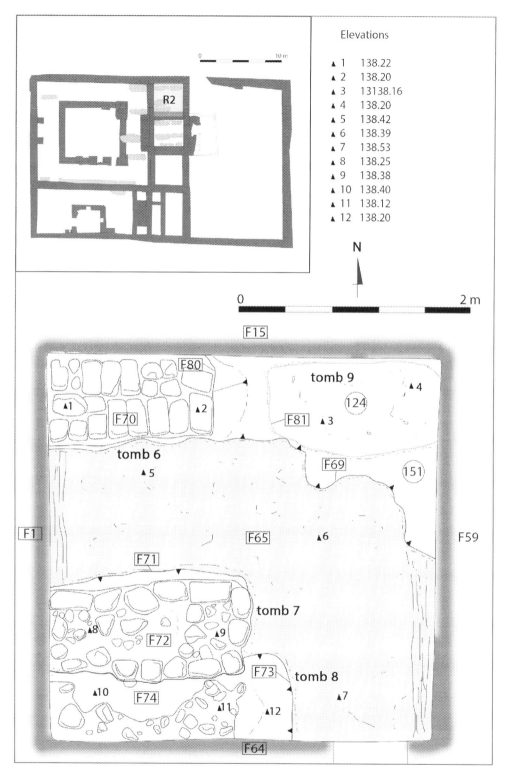

Fig. 5.25: Plan of tombs 6–9 in room 2 before excavation
(drawing by D. Dzierzbicka and S. Alfarano; tracing by C. Fosen).

Fig. 5.26: Hypothetical reconstruction of room 2 (view to southwest) (by C. Ullendorff).

Immediately below this fill was an earlier mud-brick covering (F79),[54] which consisted of a row of mudbricks laid (on bed) parallel to the north wall (fig. 5.28). F79 lay above pit fill DSU122,[55] made of dark yellow sand containing small amounts of pottery sherds, mud-brick debris, and charcoal.

The lowermost part of the fill was artificially distinguished as DSU129,[56] in order to separate the soil around the human remains. The unit had the same matrix as DSU122, except for the lack of charcoal parts and the presence of numerous fragments of textiles.

The presence of mud-brick debris and potsherds in the fill (DSU122+DSU129) of the burial suggests that the pit was backfilled with material originating from the excavation of the tomb in wall F15's foundation trench. The profile along the east edge of the pit shows how the upper and lower ledges of the wall were cut when the pit was created. The east interface of the pit also reveals how an additional 20 cm of soil were cut near the bottom of the grave, in order to fit the feet of the deceased.

Tomb 6 hosted the skeletal remains (FN23) of a middle-aged man, approximately 40–50 years of age at death (fig. 5.29).[57] He was laid supine at the depth of about 98 cm, facing east, with his hands placed against his upper thighs. The individual was about 1.69 m tall. The discovery of fragments of textile within the layer surrounding the bones (DSU129) indicates that the body had been wrapped in a shroud or buried with clothing.

54. Upper elevation: 138.070 m; lower elevation: 137.910 m; average thickness: 7.8 cm.
55. Upper elevation: 137.980 m; lower elevation: 137.330 m; max. thickness: 62 cm.
56. Upper elevation: 137.380 m; lower elevation: 137.190 m; max. thickness: 12 cm.
57. Sheldrick 2023, 4–6.

Fig. 5.27: View (to west) of tomb 6.

Tomb 7 is located in the southern half of room 2. As is the case for the two other tombs in the north crypt, the west short end of tomb 7 rests against west wall F1. The burial pit (F71),[58] ovoidal in shape and cutting through the room's upper floor (F75), measures 70 cm north-south by 160 cm east-west and is the shortest of the burial pits in room 2. It is also shorter than the tomb's superstructure (F72),[59] which measures 70 cm north-south by 172 cm east-west. F72 is not as neatly constructed as superstructure F70 in tomb 6 (figs. 5.24–25; 5.30). A clearly discernible outline was created using complete, or almost complete, mudbricks laid on bed above the later floor's level. The inner area was then packed with scattered clusters of mudbrick fragments, while a gap between the north edge of the burial cut and the north side of the superstructure was filled with sand. F70 partially overlapped on its south side the covering of tomb 8, thus revealing two different phases of burials within room 2.

---

58. Upper elevation: 138.365 m; lower elevation: 137.490 m.
59. Upper elevation: 138.415 m; lower elevation: 138.260 m; max. thickness: 13 cm.

Fig. 5.28: View (to north) of lower mud-brick covering (F79) inside tomb 6 (room 2).

Fig. 5.29: View of human remains (FN23) inside tomb 6 (room 2).

Fig. 5.30: View (to southwest) of tombs 7–8.

The pit of tomb 7 was filled with DSU125,[60] a layer of dark yellow sand mixed with mud-brick debris, scattered pottery fragments, and charcoal parts. The lowermost part of this fill was documented as a separate unit (DSU130),[61] in order to separate the soil immediately surrounding the human remains. Also, in the case of tomb 7, the discovery of mud-brick debris in the fill of the pit suggests that the cut was backfilled with material from the foundations of west wall F1, following the interment of the deceased.

The excavation of tomb 7 exposed a complete, well-preserved skeleton (FN24) of an adolescent (12–15 years old at death) laid supine, facing east, with the left hand placed against the left upper thigh and the right arm on the pelvic area (fig. 5.31).[62] The body was probably wrapped in a shroud, twelve fragments of which (inv. 17044) were found above the feet of the deceased in DSU130.[63] The skull preserved the hair gathered in braids, one of which was placed on the forehead. Although the sex in this juvenile individual could not be determined, the remains of the braided hair suggest that this individual was a young woman.

60. Upper elevation: 138.290 m; lower elevation: 137.700 m; max. thickness: 56 cm.
61. Upper elevation: 137.730 m; lower elevation: 137.500 m; max. thickness: 20 cm. This unit had the same matrix and inclusions as DSU125.
62. Sheldrick 2023, 6–7.
63. A preliminary study of the fragments revealed a plain tabby weave, with strings seemingly twisted in an S-direction.

Fig. 5.31: View (to west) of human remains (FN24) inside tomb 7 (room 2).

Tomb 8 is located in the southwest corner of room 2, immediately to the south of tomb 7. The burial pit (F73)[64] was dug along south wall F64 and west wall F1 and through lower floor F108. It measures 70 cm north-south by 212 cm east-west[65] and reaches a maximum depth of 98 cm. Tomb 8 was sealed by a poorly preserved superstructure (F74)[66] that measured 64 cm north-south by 176 cm east-west (figs. 5.24–25; 5.30). F74 consisted of fragmentary mudbricks, which formed an irregular perimeter along the north, west, and south sides of the burial cut and only partially covered the tomb fill. The east side of the superstructure was 42 cm shorter than the east edge of the burial pit, but in line with superstructure F72 above tomb 7. On the north side, the superstructure of tomb 8 was covered by that of tomb 7, thus pointing to two different burial phases within this crypt. However, the fact that the length of superstructure F74 (tomb 8) matches the length of the burial pit (F71) of adjacent tomb 7, rather than that of its own burial pit,[67] leaves the possibility open that F74 may be contemporary with superstructure F72 in tomb 7. Even if the burial pit of tomb 8 had been dug before the one in tomb 7, it is

---

64. Upper elevation: 138.315 m; lower elevation: 137.33 m. Foundation courses of F1 and F64 (west and south walls respectively) are visible along the western and southern sections of the pit.
65. Therefore, it is substantially longer than the adjacent burial pit (F71) of tomb 7, as well as the pit (F80) of tomb 6.
66. Upper elevation: 138.405 m.
67. As noted above, the same difference between the length of the burial pit and that of the superstructure of tomb 8 was noticed also in the case of tomb 6 in the northwest corner of the crypt.

Fig. 5.32: View (to west) of human remains (FN27) inside tomb 8 (room 2).

possible that its superstructure was later remodeled so that its length would match that of tomb 7. Notwithstanding the lack of conclusive evidence, it is worth remarking that an effort seems to have been made to build superstructures of matching dimensions above the tombs inside crypt 2, in spite of the differing sizes of the burial pits.

The rectangular cut of tomb 8 was filled by a layer of dark yellow sand (DSU135),[68] with inclusions consisting of mud-brick debris, small potsherds, and scattered charcoal fragments.[69] The lowermost part of this fill was distinguished as DSU137,[70] so that the soil close to the human remains could be documented separately.

At a depth of ca. 83 cm, excavations revealed a complete, well-preserved skeleton (FN27) of an adult female about 35–45 years old at death (fig. 5.32).[71] The body had been laid supine, facing east, with the hands flexed over the pubic brim. No artifacts or textile fragments were found associated with the body.

68. Upper elevation: 138.270 m; lower elevation: 137.450 m; average thickness: 80 cm.
69. As in the case of tombs 6 and 7, the matrix of the fill points to the reuse of material previously dug out from the foundations of walls F1 and F64 for the backfilling of the pit.
70. Upper elevation: 137.500 m; lower elevation: 137.330 m; max. thickness: 14 cm.
71. Sheldrick 2023, 7–10.

Fig. 5.33: View (from above) of burial cut F81 of tomb 9 (room 2).

Tomb 9 was found in 2023 against the southeast corner of room 2, abutting the north and east perimeter walls (F15 and F59, respectively) of the north crypt (fig. 5.25). The burial pit was not visible on the surface, due to the disappearance of the floor in this area; this had been caused by the excavation (in antiquity) of cut F69 along the north wall. Only investigations inside this cut allowed the identification of the grave.

The burial pit (F81)[72] is rectangular and measures 58 cm north-south by 140 cm east-west, reaching the maximum depth of 95 cm below floor level F75 (fig. 5.33). No mud-brick superstructure was detected above the pit; at floor level, a complete jar filled with fish bones (inv. 30129), probably related with the funeral rituals after the deposition, or in memory of, the deceased, was found at floor level above the tomb.[73]

The upper fill of tomb 9 (DSU124)[74] consisted of dark yellow sand mixed with mud-bricks debris, pottery fragments, and small pieces of charcoal. The removal of DSU124 revealed an oval-shaped coffin (inv. 17039), slightly tapering toward the lightly convex bottom (figs. 5.34–36).[75] It was covered by a flat lid (of which 37 fragments were found) and sealed (probably

---

72. Upper elevation: 138.450 m; lower elevation: 137.580 m.
73. See pp. 264 and 268 above, as well as fig. 5.23.
74. Upper elevation: 138.160 m; lower elevation: 137.190 m; average thickness: 80 cm.
75. On the shape of the coffin, see Cotelle-Michel 2004, 270, III-A-3.

Fig. 5.34: View (to north) of coffin (inv. 17039) inside tomb 9.

in situ) with a white gypsum plaster sealant.[76] The coffin was made using mud and organic material, most likely manure.[77]

Another find that was retrieved while excavating DSU124, near the base of the coffin toward its head, consisted of two joining fragments of a small, complete cylindrical object of bronze, with one handle and lid (inv. 17038; fig. 5.37).[78] It is a beaker or miniature tankard of some sort, which had likely been placed on the coffin and then rolled to the bottom of the burial pit when the grave was filled.[79] Two additional small finds from the same unit are an ostracon

---

76. Plaster drippings can still be seen along the sides of the coffin and on its lid.
77. The material used for the manufacturing of the coffin seems rather unusual. Six oval coffins, made of ceramic, were found at the K2 cemetery at Kellis: see Bowen 2022a, 352, fig. 14.9; 353. Ceramic coffins were also excavated in the K1 cemetery at Kellis; see Hope, McKenzie, and Nuzzolo 2022, 324 fig. 13.17 (with remains of a lid similar to that in tomb 9 at Amheida); 331.
78. Height: 5.9 cm; diameter at base: 3.2 cm.
79. No precise comparisons with this type of container have been established thus far. The shape is similar to some metal inkwells not uncommon in children's burials in Roman times, especially in the western regions of the empire. Nevertheless, the hinged lid of the specimen found in tomb 9 does not exhibit the hole that is typical of this class of objects. Some cylindrical metal censers found in Egypt have hinged lids of this type, although they do not match in terms of shape: cf. Eckardt 2017, 68–107. Some lids, similar in shape, were found in 7th-century female burials in England: see Hamerow 2016, fig. d. In a funerary portrait from Er-Rubayat, dated to 200–230 CE (https://www.brooklynmuseum.org/opencollection/objects/3458), the boy is represented with a similar vessel (although without a lid) in his right hand. On the subject, see also Anderson 2021.

Fig. 5.35: View of the coffin being lifted out of the north crypt.

Fig. 5.36: Coffin (inv. 17039) from tomb 9 after conservation (photograph by B. Bazzani).

Fig. 5.37: Bronze object (inv. 17038) from tomb 9 after conservation (photograph by B. Bazzani).

(inv. 17040, dated to 327/8, 337/8, or 345/6) and five joining fragments of a complete bronze finger ring (inv. 17042).[80]

Inside the coffin was the well-preserved skeleton (FN26) of a juvenile individual about 5 years old at death (fig. 5.38).[81] The body had been laid supine, facing east, with the hands flexed over the pubic brim. No artifacts or textile fragments were found associated with the body. The human remains were surrounded by DSU138,[82] a layer of soft brownish-yellow sand mixed with scattered pottery fragments, which filled the coffin.

The coffin was placed above a layer of grayish-yellow sand (DSU136) that filled the bottom of the burial pit, also covering the lower foundation ledge of north perimeter wall F15.[83] This leveling layer was mixed with moderate amounts of mud-brick debris and charcoal, small potsherds, and numerous fragments of plaster. Nine fragments of an unidentified iron object (inv. 7043) were found within this unit. It may have been a tool used during the setting and sealing of the coffin inside the burial pit.

80. The ring consists of a thin wire with rectangular section and a central overhand knot. It was found during sifting.
81. Sheldrick 2023, 10–11.
82. Upper elevation: 138.030 m; lower elevation: 137.740 m ; average thickness: 25 cm.
83. At the elevation of 137.600 m. Tomb 9 cut through the upper ledge and (partially) the foundations of walls F13 and F59.

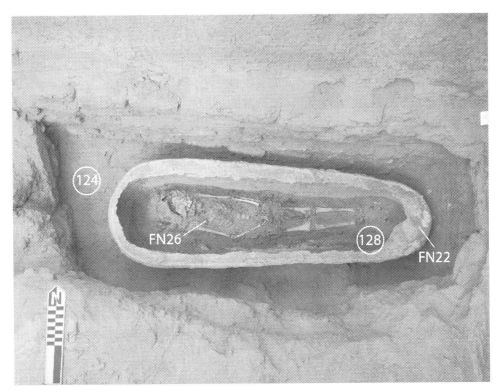

Fig. 5.38: Aerial view of human remains (FN26) inside tomb 9 (room 2).

5.3. Room 3

Room 3 is a squarish-rectangular crypt situated below the now-missing apse (room 15) at the east end of building 7 (figs. 5.1–3; 5.39). It opened onto the north and south *pastophoria* (rooms 2 and 4 respectively) via two arched doorways, which created a set of three interconnected crypts underneath the sanctuary of the church. Despite the severe erosion of building 7 in its eastern part (especially in the tripartite sanctuary), room 3 is rather well preserved, due to its location below ground level. The space, which was once covered by a barrel-vaulted roof, measures 3.23 m north-south by 3.42 m east-west and has walls reaching a maximum height of ca. 2.90 m (south wall F78, above the latest of the two floor levels identified within the room).

Features

Room 3 was accessed from the crypt below the south *pastophorion* (room 4), through an arched doorway piercing the east half of south wall F78 (fig. 5.40).[84] The doorway is 1.67 m high, 68 cm wide, and 99 cm deep; it has a mud-brick threshold lying ca. 7 cm above floor level and receding by 2 cm from the south face of the wall. The entire doorway, including the sides and

---

84. At a distance of 26 cm from the southern end of the wall.

Fig. 5.39: Aerial view (to west) of room 3 at the end of the 2023 season.

the vaulted top, is fully coated with a layer of gray mud plaster. On the same north-south axis as this doorway, room 3 opened onto the north crypt (room 2) through another vaulted doorway built in north wall F64 (figs. 5.41–42).[85]

The perimeter walls are fully preserved, while only small portions of the north-south oriented vault (F77[86] and F102[87]) are still visible along the east and west walls of the room (figs. 5.43–44). The central part of the vault (DSU108, mixed with pottery fragments)[88] was found collapsed on the windblown sand that had accumulated inside a large robbery pit (F83),[89] which had partially disturbed the stratigraphic sequence of the room (fig. 5.41).[90] Therefore, the action of the looters must have occurred before the collapse of most of the vaulted roof.

85. See p. 254 in Sec. 5.2 above.
86. Upper elevation: 140.860 m; lower elevation: 139.240 m.
87. Upper elevation: 140.620 m; lower elevation: 139.200 m; max. extent (from top to bottom): 1.42 m.
88. Upper elevation: 140.640 m; lower elevation: 140.370 m; max. thickness: 23 cm.
89. Upper elevation: 140.500 m; lower elevation: 138.160 m; max. depth: 220 cm.
90. Clandestine excavations within areas of religious buildings that were endowed with a high degree of sacrality are attested. In churches, the apse, which is an easily recognizable feature of Christian religious architecture, was often the target of excavations by looters searching for valuable items. In Egypt, this looting activity, which centered largely on sacred spaces in temples and churches, was discussed by A. Bey Kamal (1907), who outlined the rituals to be performed in order to access the treasures hidden in archaeological sites, with a particular focus on religious buildings. A robbery pit in the apse was found in the so-called Eastern Gate church at Antinoopolis: see Grossmann 2011, 2011, p. 136, pl. IIc. A pit dug in antiquity into the floor of the apse is also attested at the fourth-century church of 'Ain el-Gedida (Dakhla Oasis): see Aravecchia 2018, 104.

Fig. 5.40: View (to south) of doorway opening from room 3 into room 4.

Fig. 5.41: View (to northeast) of doorway opening from room 3 into room 2.

Chapter 5: The Underground Funerary Crypts

Fig. 5.42: View (to south) of doorways leading from room 2 (in the foreground) into room 3 and room 4.

Fig. 5.43: View (to north) of remains of vaulted roof of room 3.

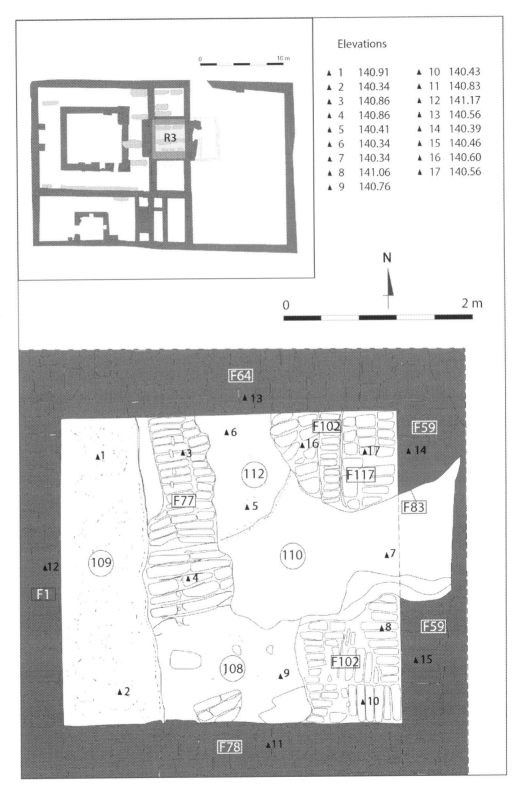

Fig. 5.44: Plan of room 3 at the beginning of excavations (drawing by S. Alfarano).

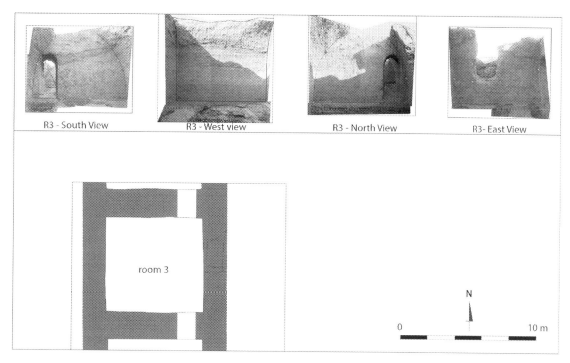

Fig. 5.45: Prospects of walls of room 3 (elaboration by L. Davighi and S. Alfarano).

Large iron-rich bricks, measuring ca. 42 by 20 by 6 cm, were employed in the construction of the vault; they were laid on edge and bonded with sandy beige mortar. The pitched brick vaulting was outlined with a thick layer of mortar and pottery sherds, and the first brick was set against north wall F64, as suggested by the slight northward inclination of the vault (fig. 5.45).[91] As documented within the robbery cut (F83) piercing east wall F59, the spring of the vault rested above a ledge (ca. 20 cm wide) of this wall, at approximately 70 cm above the upper floor level (F84) (fig. 5.41). In room 3 the wedge filling the space between wall F1 and the west spring of the vault (F77) consists of a layer (DSU107)[92] of compact sandy mortar; instead, the extant portion of the vault on its east side (F102) is covered by a different type of fill (F117),[93] built entirely with mudbricks.[94]

As in the case of the north and south crypts (rooms 2 and 4), the walls of room 3 were completely coated with a layer of undecorated gray mud plaster (with organic inclusions). No evidence of holes or marks are visible on the surface of the plaster, which was smeared down onto upper floor level F84[95] (preserved only along south wall F78). In the southeast corner of

91. As discussed in Sec. 5.2 above, with regard to the vaulted roof of room 2.
92. Upper elevation: 141.060 m.
93. Upper elevation: 140.560 m; lower elevation: 139.220 m (in cut F83).
94. Stretchers laid on bed, as visible on the north and south edges of the robbery cut. No traces are left of the platforms on which the upper floor of room 15 (the apse) was once set, as was the case for the now-missing floor of the north *pastophorion* (see description of features of room 2 in Sec. 5.2 above).
95. Upper elevation: 138.330 m; lower elevation: 138.230 m; max. thickness: 10 cm.

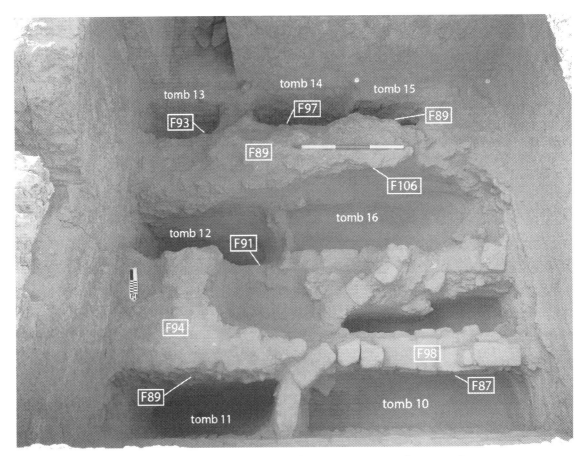

Fig. 5.46: Aerial view (to south) of tombs 10–16 in room 3 after excavation.

the room, a small portion of this floor sloped down to form a 20 cm-wide plastered channel along the east wall.[96] As in room 2, where similar features were identified at floor level, the surface of the channel still shows the fingerprints left during the smearing of the mud.

Floor F84 is made of reddish (probably iron-rich) and gray mud and its extant portions are characterized by an irregular surface (figs. 5.46–47). This walking surface lies directly on top of an earlier floor level (F94),[97] which is preserved only in the northeast corner of the room, in addition to being visible in the south profile of the cuts of two of the tombs (16 and 12) that were discovered in this crypt.[98] F94 consists of compacted gray mud, less dense than the upper floor level. Based on the stratigraphic sequence that was exposed in the cut of tomb 12, F94 was laid out directly on a foundation fill of yellow sand (DSU155) and on a compact leveling layer that was also found in room 4 (DSU162) and room 2 (DSU161).[99]

---

96. This feature was also attested in room 2 to the north of the central crypt: see Sec. 5.2 above.
97. Upper elevation: 138.230 m; max. detected thickness: 7 cm; unexcavated.
98. See Sec. 5.3.1 below.
99. This leveling deposit was only documented in section in room 3 and was not numbered.

Chapter 5: The Underground Funerary Crypts

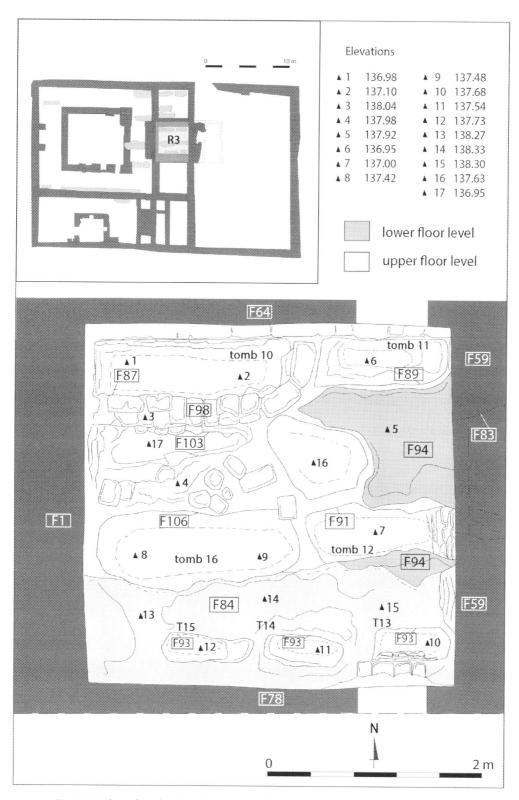

Fig. 5.47: Plan of tombs 10–16 in room 3 after excavation (drawing by S. Alfarano).

Fig. 5.48: Detail of foundations of room 3's north wall (F64) inside tomb 11.

Fig. 5.49: Detail of foundations of room 3's east wall (F59) inside tomb 12.

Both floors F84 and F94 were cut by seven burials (tombs 10–16, discussed below) and by a large pit (F95),[100] which was dug in antiquity in the middle of room 3 (figs. 5.46–47). The pit cut through tombs 10, 12, and 16 and may be associated with the robbery excavations that took place after the abandonment of the church.[101]

The foundations of north wall F64[102] were fully exposed within the burial cuts of tombs 10 and 11. The wall shows a ledge protruding by about 16 cm and consisting of stretchers for a total of eight courses; the lowest is made of mudbricks not bonded with mortar, lying on their long narrow side and placed directly on the foundation sand (DSU155) (fig. 5.48).[103] The foundations of east wall F59,[104] partially visible in tombs 11 and 12, were exposed to a maximum height of eight courses, consisting of stretchers (fig. 5.49).[105] Since F59 was a load-bearing

100. Upper elevation: 138.270 m; lower elevation: 137.770 m; max. depth: 50 cm.
101. Including the digging of pit F83 mentioned above.
102. Upper elevation: 140.985 m; lower elevation: 137.600 m.
103. At an elevation of 137.040 m.
104. Upper elevation: 140.460 m; lower elevation: 136.950 m.
105. The lowest recorded elevation is 136.950 m; the original bottom of the wall was not exposed.

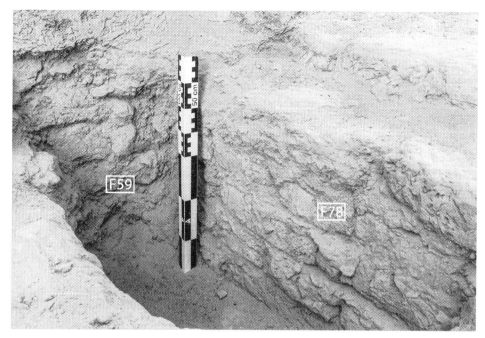

Fig. 5.50: Detail of foundations of room 3's south wall (F78) inside tomb 13.

wall, which enclosed building 7 to the east and was probably built on the slope of the hill, its foundations were deeper than those of partition walls F64 and F78. No ledge was observed in the exposed part of wall F59, but it is possible that it was cut and removed during the excavation of the burial pits. The foundations of the south wall (F78)[106] were only partially revealed inside tomb 13; they include a ledge that protrudes by ca. 16 cm and is visible for a maximum of five courses consisting of headers and stretchers (fig. 5.50).[107]

The foundations of west wall F1[108] were uncovered along the western sections of tombs 16 and 10, as well as pit F103 (fig. 5.51).[109] They are visible for a maximum of eight courses of mudbricks, laid out as stretchers. No foundation ledge was identified; it was probably cut during the digging of the burial pits. Puzzlingly, in the west profile of pit F103 (between tombs 16 and 10), only four courses of the wall are visible below floor level, with no lower courses extant.[110] It is unclear whether F1's foundations had different heights.[111] Certainly, the wall had a deeper foundation on its northern portion, as documented in test trench 2 and in the pit of tomb 6 inside room 2.

106. Upper elevation: 140.830 m; lower elevation: 137.880 m.
107. The lowest elevation that was reached during the excavation is 137.880 m.
108. Upper elevation: 141.170 m; lower elevation: 136.960 m.
109. Upper elevation: 137.770 m; lower elevation: 136.950 m; max. depth: 73 cm. The pit has an elongated shape, measures 38 cm north-south by 150 cm east-west, and slightly slopes towards the flat bottom. It was not associated with the excavation of a burial, but more likely with the looters' activity that took place inside the room.
110. At the elevation of 137.360 m.
111. Only an investigation of the foundations of wall F1 along its west side (beneath the floors of room 1's east aisle) could help shed light on these discrepancies.

Fig. 5.51: Detail of foundations of room 3's west wall (F1) inside tomb 10.

Stratigraphy and finds (figs. 5.52–53)

Room 3 was filled by a sequence of layers of windblown sand and debris. Excavations inside the crypt revealed that the central portion of the church's east side was disturbed by looters after the abandonment of the building, as attested by the large pit (F83; see above) that was dug into room 3 following the collapse and erosion of the apse (room 15). For this reason, the original stratigraphy inside the room was disturbed down to the earlier floor level of the room.[112] The looters' digging also affected the mud-brick superstructures and/or the upper levels of the fills of some tombs that were found in room 3.

Due to time constraints, the investigation of room 3 in 2013 was limited to the identification of DSU16,[113] a sub-surface layer of yellow sand, mixed with pottery fragments, mud-brick debris, and a few pebbles, that filled the crypt. This unit was not removed until 2023,

---

112. In addition to partially damaging the east perimeter wall (F59).
113. Upper elevation: 141.080 m; lower elevation: 140.340 m.

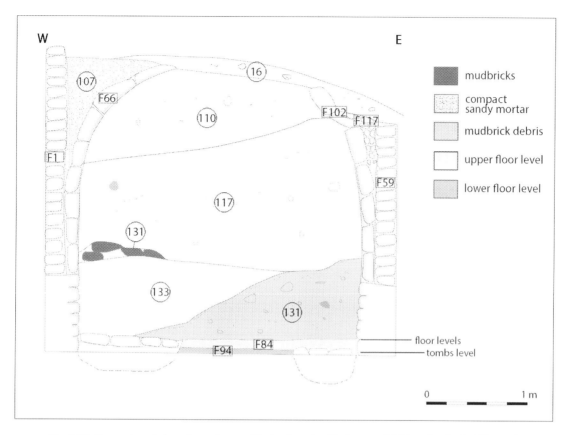

Fig. 5.52: Reconstructed section of room 3's stratigraphy (facing north) (drawing by S. Alfarano).

when its lower portion was arbitrarily assigned a different number (DSU110)[114] in order to distinguish it as an underground room's fill.[115] DSU110 consisted of soft yellow windblown sand and contained a few inclusions, such as mud-brick debris and fragments of pottery, plaster, and charcoal. It is likely that the debris resulted from the collapse of the vault and of the structures of the upper floor (inside the apse/room 15). In the northeast quadrant of room 3, DSU110 was more compact, due to a higher concentration of mud-brick fragments; for this reason, this part of the unit was assigned a different number (DSU112) (figs. 5.44; 5.54).[116] In the eastern edge of cut F83, where it partially destroyed vault spring F102 and wedge F117, the yellow sand abutted a wall collapse (DSU172)[117] with the mudbricks still bonded and decorated with painted plaster.[118]

---

114. Upper elevation: 140.410 m; lower elevation: 139.820 m; average thickness: 50 cm.
115. The upper portion (labeled DSU16) was assigned to the stratigraphy of room 15 (almost completely disappeared) above room 3.
116. Upper elevation: 140.340 m; lower elevation: 139.900 m; max. thickness: 44 cm.
117. Upper elevation: 140.350 m; lower elevation (in cut F121): 139.600 m; max. thickness: 73 cm.
118. DSU172 is discussed in Sec. 5.3.2 below (about test trench 4).

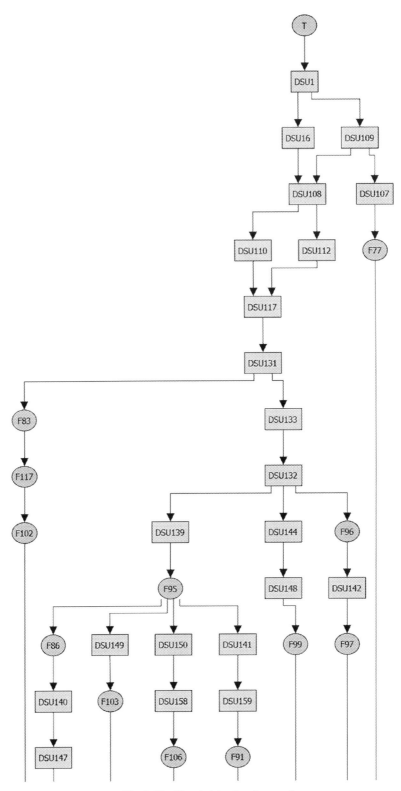

Fig. 5.53a: Harris Matrix of room 3.

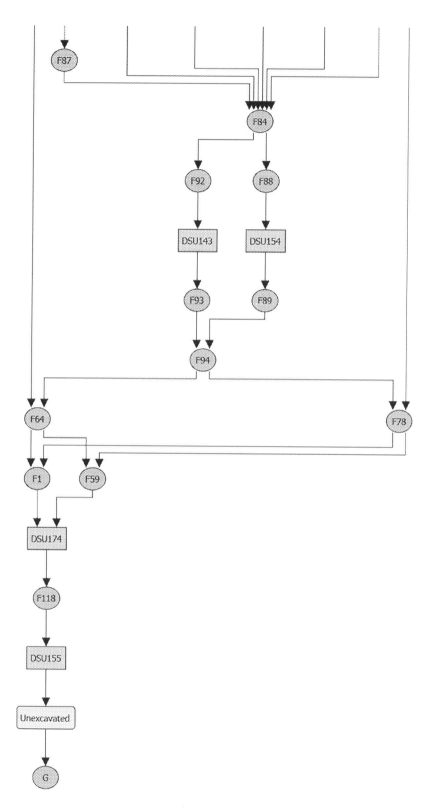

Fig. 5.53b: Harris Matrix of room 3.

Fig. 5.54: View (to north) of DSU110 and DSU112.

Below DSU110, another deposit, consisting of silty sand (DSU117),[119] filled pit F83 that had been cut by looters. It was documented as a different unit because of its dark yellow color, the presence of more inclusions of pottery fragments and mud-brick debris, and the large number of fragments of painted plaster that were found within it.[120] A few whole bricks

---

119. Upper elevation: 139.920 m; lower elevation: 138.710 m; max. thickness: 110 cm. To verify the relationship between this collapse and others (DSU170–171) that were visible on the surface to the east of room 3, test trench 4 was excavated (see Sec. 5.3.2 below). The painted plaster was restored and left *in situ*, then backfilled with sand at the end of the 2023 season.

120. Minor concentrations of painted plaster fragments have also been documented on the bottom of the upper layers (DSU 110, 112). Two fragments of a wooden object with five faces preserved were also gathered within this unit (during sorting); the first is decorated with an openwork geometric motif representing rhombuses, while the second has one side decorated with three incised lines and five hollows carved into the wood, possibly depicting two acanthus leaves. Traces of white plaster are visible all over the two fragments. Similar objects were found in DSU132 (inv. 17047; see below) and during the 2012–2013 excavations in rooms 1 and 2 (inv. 15847 and 16122); they were probably parts of decorative elements (of door lintels or furniture?) inside the church.

Fig. 5.55: View (to south) of a cluster of mudbricks (DSU131) in the southwest corner of room 3. The limestone block belongs to DSU117.

(probably from the digging of pit F83 by looters) and a limestone block,[121] measuring 42 by 32 by 19 cm and with traces of white mortar, were also found during the excavation of this unit.

DSU117 was found on top of a cluster of mudbricks (DSU131)[122] located in the southwest corner of room 3, against walls F1 and F78 (fig. 5.55).[123] The concentration of mudbricks likely resulted from the dismantling of structures by the looters who dug pit F83, cutting through the stratigraphy down to floor level in the western half of the room.[124] Sand DSU117 and mud-brick debris DSU131 covered a deposit of compacted dark-yellow sand (DSU133),[125] which was mixed with a moderate quantity of mud-brick debris and fragments of pottery, plaster, and charcoal. In the eastern half of the room, DSU117 also covered a compact layer of mud-brick debris (DSU132).[126] The unit was mixed with small pottery, mudbricks, and fragments

121. The block likely originated from the temple area (i.e., Area 4).
122. Upper elevation: 139.210 m; lower elevation: 138.620 m; average thickness: 40 cm.
123. Upper elevation: 138.810 m; lower elevation: 138.500 m; max. thickness: 31 cm. DSU133 partially lay below DSU131, too.
124. On the basis of the bricks' dimensions, the layer may have originated from the destruction of part of east wall F59, thus resulting into an accumulation of waste material.
125. Upper elevation: 138.810 m; lower elevation: 138.500 m; max. thickness: 31 cm.
126. Upper elevation: 138.720 m; lower elevation: 138.060 m; max. thickness: 70 cm.

of gray and white plaster.[127] A few small finds were retrieved, consisting of a fragmentary and illegible Roman coin (inv. 17041), an incomplete carved wooden object (inv. 17047),[128] and one fragment of a jar stopper (inv. 17046) made of mud plaster.[129]

DSU132 accumulated in the northeast corner and along the east wall of the room, sloping from northeast to southwest. It possibly consisted of waste material from the looters' activity, mixed with the materials from the occupation level above floor F84.[130] Indeed, below pit F83, excavations revealed evidence of another robbery cut (F95), which had caused the destruction of most of floors F84 and F94 in the central and north-western areas of the room. F95 was filled by DSU139,[131] which consisted of yellow sand mixed with small amounts of mud-brick debris, charcoal, plaster, and small potsherds. The looters who dug pit F95 also partially destroyed the superstructures of some tombs, as well as the uppermost part of their burial fills.[132]

The earlier floor level (F94) was laid directly on foundation sand DSU155[133] and, in the eastern portion of the room, on a layer of compacted yellow sand that was exposed on the south wall of tomb 12's cut (F91) (fig. 5.56). Likely, this preparation layer had been deposited to partially level the east slope of the hill before the construction of the church.

In addition to the seven burials that were found in room 3 (discussed in Sec. 5.3.1 below), an additional pit (F103) was investigated between tombs 16 and 10; as mentioned earlier, it did not host human remains, but was more likely associated with looting activity that took place inside this room. This pit was filled by a unit (DSU149)[134] of loose yellow sand, mixed with small potsherds, scattered mud-brick debris, and fragments of charcoal.

Finally, it is worth mentioning in this section that the excavation of some tombs in room 3 (especially tomb 16)[135] exposed backfill material consisting of gray sand and inclusions such as pottery fragments, slag, ash, mud-brick debris, and charcoal; the composition of this soil suggests that the foundation trenches (from which the fill of the burials most likely originated) were filled with topsoil coming from nearby industrial areas, which were preliminarily surveyed in 2023.[136]

---

127. The gray plaster fragments were rough and probably originated from the facing of the vault. The medium-sized fragments of white plaster bore some impressions (perhaps of wood).

128. Similar to fragments found in another unit (DSU117) inside room 3 and, in previous seasons, also in rooms 1 and 2; see n. 120 above.

129. The stopper has a roughly conical shape, with three rectangular stamps partially preserved on the exterior, as well as the impression of a vine leaf on the inner side.

130. According to C. Caputo (personal communication, January 2023), some of the pottery fragments found in this layer match others that were found in the first occupation level (DSU138) on upper floor F85 in room 4 (see Sec. 5.4 below).

131. Upper elevation: 138.080 m; lower elevation: 137.630 m; max. thickness: 43 cm.

132. As in the case of tombs 10, 12, and 16; see Sec. 5.3.1 below.

133. Upper elevation: 137.980 m; unexcavated in room 3. See Sec. 5.4 below.

134. Upper elevation: 137.770 m; lower elevation: 136.950 m; max. thickness: 73 cm.

135. Discussed in the following section.

136. C. Caputo, personal communication, January 2023.

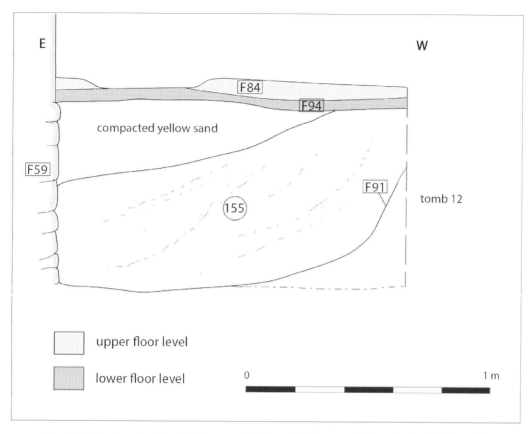

Fig. 5.56: East-west section (facing south) of tomb 12 in room 3 (drawing by S. Alfarano).

5.3.1. Tombs 10–16 in Room 3

Tombs 10–16, all oriented east-west, were found tightly packed inside the central crypt (figs. 5.46–5.47; 5.57). All graves were found sealed, with the human remains intact and *in situ*, although the superstructures and upper levels of the tombs' fills were partly disturbed due to looting activity. Two of the burials (10 and 16) abut the west wall (F1) along their western edges. Tomb 12 is placed against the middle of east wall F59, while tombs 13–15 are lined up against the south wall (F78) of the room; in particular, tomb 13 lies in front of the doorway that allowed access to the south crypt. Finally, tomb 11 was identified in the northeast corner of room 3, facing the door opening onto room 2 to the north. The seven graves cut through the two pre-existing floor levels that were documented inside room 3. Significantly, tombs 11 and 13 were dug only through the earliest floor level (F94), while tombs 10 and 14–15 were created after the later floor (F84) had already been laid out. This points to the existence of two burial phases, as attested in room 2. Concerning tombs 12 and 16, it was not possible to ascertain into which floor level (or levels) they cut, due to the removal of the floors (as well as the upper parts of the two graves) resulting from the digging of pit F95 by looters.

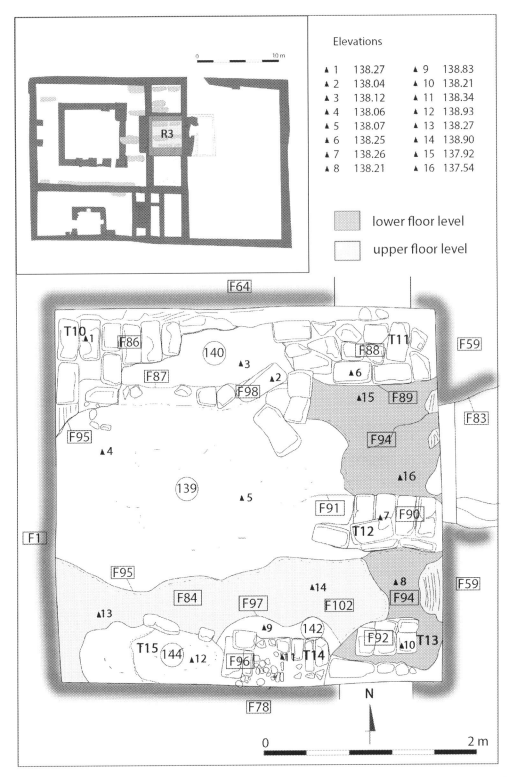

Fig. 5.57: Plan of tombs 10–15 before their excavation (drawing by S. Alfarano and L. Davighi). The outline of tomb 16 is hidden by the fill (DSU139) of pit F95.

Tomb 10 was found in the northwest corner of the room, abutting the north and west walls (F64 and F1 respectively; figs. 5.46–5.47; 5.57–5.59). The burial pit (F87)[137] has a rectangular shape and measures 42 cm north-south by 180 cm east-west. Unfortunately, tomb 10 was somewhat damaged by the digging of pit F95 by looters, who removed the floors and part of the superstructure that covered it (F86) (fig. 5.58).[138] The preserved portion of the superstructure (measuring 70 cm north-south by 110 cm east-west) consisted of both fragmentary and complete mudbricks;[139] these were laid out (on bed) in two parallel rows, which formed a rectangular feature above the burial pit. The south side was strengthened by a short mud-brick wall (F98)[140] that was preserved to a height of six courses (figs. 5.59–61). The mudbricks were laid out in alternating rows of headers and stretchers;[141] the wall was built directly on foundation sand and was partially destroyed by looters' pit F95.

The burial pit was filled by a layer of yellow sand (DSU140)[142] mixed with mud-brick debris, pottery fragments, animal bones, charcoal, and slag; one fragment of a conical stopper (inv. 17052) was found within this unit. The matrix of DSU140 hints at the fact that the pit was backfilled with material previously removed (during the excavation of the tomb) from the foundation trenches of walls F1 and F64.[143]

At a depth of ca. 50 cm, the excavation of the burial revealed a complete and well-preserved skeleton (FN43) of an elderly woman of about 50–65 years old at death (fig. 5.62).[144] She was laid supine, facing east, with the right hand flexed over the right pubic bone, while the left hand was placed behind the lumbar spine. Evidence of textile was found in the form of a band around the upper skull and over the eyes. A preliminary analysis of the human remains pointed to a sedentary lifestyle and a comparatively refined diet. The deceased was laid directly on top of DSU147,[145] a unit (20 cm thick) of compacted mud-bricks debris and fragments of plaster, likely spread to level the bottom of the pit.

Tomb 11 lies to the south of tomb 10, in the northeast corner of room 3. It abuts the north and east walls (F64 and F59 respectively) and fills the space in front of the doorway leading into the north *pastophorion* (figs. 5.46–5.47; 5.56). The burial pit (F89),[146] rectangular and measuring 44 cm north-south by 125 cm east-west, was cut into lower floor F94, narrowing down ca. 25 cm towards the bottom. It was sealed by mud-brick superstructure F88,[147] which measured 54 cm north-south by 150 cm east-west and was made of both fragmentary and complete mudbricks, arranged on bed and on edge to form a rectangular outline. The west edge of the superstructure may have been partially removed by robbery cut F95.

---

137. Upper elevation: 138.040 m; lower elevation: 136.980 m; max. depth: 97 cm.
138. Upper elevation: 138.270 m; lower elevation: 138.030 m; max. thickness: 24 cm.
139. Average measurements of the bricks: 35 by 20 by 7 cm.
140. Upper elevation: 138.130 m; lower elevation: 137.590 m; max. height: 54 cm.
141. Bricks varied in size from 27 by 17 by 10 cm to 35 by 18 by 8 cm.
142. Upper elevation: 138.130 m; lower elevation: 137.180 m; max. depth: 91 cm.
143. The foundation courses of the walls are visible along the west and north sections of the pit.
144. Sheldrick 2023, 11–12.
145. Upper elevation: 137.220 m; lower elevation: 136.980 m; average depth: 20 cm.
146. Upper elevation: 138.020 m; lower elevation: 137.070 m; max. depth: 93 cm.
147. Upper elevation: 138.260 m; lower elevation: 138.010 m; max. thickness: 25 cm.

Fig. 5.58: View (to north) of mud-brick superstructure F86 (partially missing) above tomb 10.

Fig. 5.59: View (to west) of tomb 10.

Fig. 5.60: View of southwest corner of burial pit F87, showing east-west wall F98.

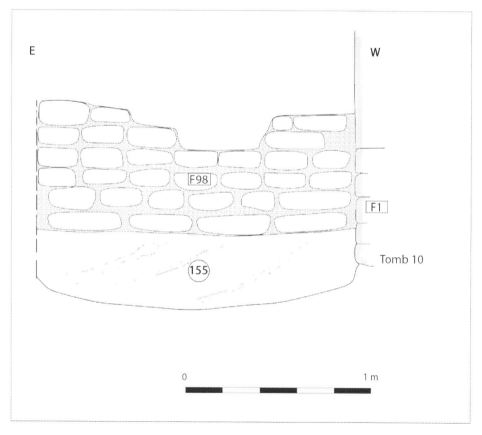

Fig. 5.61: Profile (looking south) of wall F98 (inside pit F87 of tomb 10) (drawing by S. Alfarano).

Fig. 5.62: Aerial view (to west) of human remains (FN43) inside tomb 10 (room 3).

The pit of tomb 11 was filled by dark-yellow sand (DSU154),[148] with inclusions consisting of mud-bricks debris, pebbles, small potsherds, animal bones, and fragments of charcoal and slag.[149]

At a depth of ca. 90 cm, tomb 11 hosted the well-preserved remains (FN49) of a small child, who was about 6 years old (± 24 months) at death.[150] The body was laid supine, facing east, with the head propped up against the western wall of the grave, the arms and hands crossed over the pelvic area, and the feet pressed flat against the eastern wall of the pit (fig. 5.63).[151] No traces of textiles or grave goods were found.

Tomb 12 was excavated in the central area of room 3, against east wall F59 (figs. 5.46–5.47; 5.57). The burial pit (F91),[152] rectangular in shape and measuring 52 cm north-south by

148. Upper elevation: 138.020 m; lower elevation: 137.070 m; max. depth: 93 cm.
149. As in the case of tomb 10, the unit seems to have originated from the fill of the foundation trenches of the adjacent walls (F64 and F69 in the case of tomb 11). The foundation courses of the two walls are visible along the north and east interfaces of the cut.
150. Sheldrick 2023, 12.
151. The skull was broken, but soil in the surfaces of the fracture shows that the breakage occurred in the grave (albeit long before excavation).
152. Upper elevation: 137.060 m; lower elevation: 136.950 m; max. depth: 110 cm.

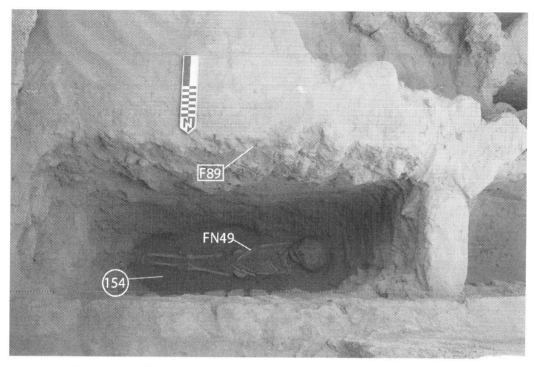

Fig. 5.63: View (from above) of human remains (FN49) inside tomb 11 (room 3).

135 cm east-west, seems to have cut through F94, the earlier floor of the crypt. It was originally covered by a mud-brick superstructure, no longer preserved due to looting activity and, in particular, the digging of pit F9, which partially affected the tomb's uppermost level (but left the human remains intact). The pit, which slightly narrowed down towards the bottom, was filled by DSU141,[153] a layer of dark yellow sand mixed with mud-brick debris, pottery fragments, pebbles, and a moderate amount of charcoal; an ostracon (inv. 17049), consisting of two lines of Greek (without date) written in black ink, was gathered within this unit. The lowermost part of the fill was distinguished as DSU159,[154] in order to document the soil surrounding the human remains as a separate unit.[155]

A complete and well-preserved skeleton (FN47) was found at a depth of ca. 70 cm. The body, which belonged to a young child about 8 years old (± 24 months), was laid supine, in an S-shaped position, with the head propped up against the western edge of the pit, facing east, and the arms and hands crossed over the pelvic area (fig. 5.64).[156] No grave goods or textile remains were found associated with the body of the deceased.

153. Upper elevation: 138.090 m; lower elevation: 137.000 m; max. depth: 107 cm.
154. Upper elevation: 137.060 m; lower elevation; max. depth: 6 cm.
155. The layer was more brownish in color and had fewer inclusions than the upper part of the tomb's fill. The discovery of debris in the two fills suggests that the pit was backfilled with material originally cut from the foundation trench of east wall F59 and, in part, its foundations (which are visible along the east interface of the tomb's cut).
156. Sheldrick 2023, 12–13. The skull was broken, but it seems that the damage occurred in the grave, long before the human remains were exhumed.

Fig. 5.64: View (from above) of human remains (FN47) inside tomb 12 (room 3).

Tomb 13 was dug in the southeast corner of the central crypt, against the east and south walls (F59 and F78, respectively) and in front of the passageway between rooms 3 and 4 (figs. 5.46–5.47; 5.57). The burial pit (F93),[157] rectangular in shape and measuring 30 cm north-south by 70 cm east-west, cut through the room's earlier floor (F94) and was partially covered by the later one (F84). The burial was sealed by a mud-brick superstructure (F92),[158] which measured 30 cm north-south by 75 cm east-west (fig. 5.65). The superstructure consisted of both fragmentary and complete mudbricks, laid on bed in two rows that marked the rectangular outline of the tomb.

The burial pit was filled by a deposit of brownish-yellow sand (DSU143),[159] with few inclusions such as mud-brick debris, pottery fragments, and pebbles.[160] At the elevation of about 137.900 m, the burial revealed a complete, well-preserved skeleton (FN40) of a child about 6 months old (± 3 months) at death (fig. 5.66).[161] The body was laid supine, facing east, in an S-shaped position, with the head touching the west wall of the pit, the knees slightly bent

---

157. Upper elevation: 138.340 m; lower elevation: 137.880 m; max. depth: 70 cm.
158. Upper elevation: 138.390 m; lower elevation: 138.190 m; max. thickness: 7 cm.
159. Upper elevation: 138.340 m; lower elevation: 137.800 m; max. depth: 70 cm.
160. The fill's number was not changed near the bones, since the skeleton lay directly on the bottom of the burial.
161. Sheldrick 2023, 13.

Fig. 5.65: View (to south) of superstructure F92 of tomb 13 (room 3).

and the feet pressed against the east edge of the cut. The arms and hands were crossed over the pelvic area.

To the west of tomb 13, along the south wall (F78) of the crypt under the apse, is tomb 14 (figs. 5.46–5.47; 5.57). The burial pit (F97)[162] of this grave, oval-shaped and measuring 28 cm north-south by 73 cm east-west, seems to have been cut into the room's upper floor (F84). The grave was undoubtedly dug at the same time as tomb 15 to the west, since the pits of the two burials are partially continuous (fig. 5.67).

The pit of tomb 14 was completely covered by mud-brick superstructure F96[163] (40 cm north-south by 94 cm east-west). This feature was made of both fragmentary and complete mudbricks laid irregularly on edge, with a complete mudbrick set on bed and defining the western edge of the superstructure (fig. 5.68).

The fill of tomb 14 was DSU142,[164] a layer of brownish-yellow sand mixed with moderate amounts of mud-brick debris, pottery fragments, charcoal, and slag. At a depth of ca. 60 cm within the burial pit, excavations revealed a complete and well-preserved skeleton (FN41) of a 5-year-old child (± 16 months) (fig. 5.69).[165] The body was laid supine, facing east; it had been placed in the grave with the knees flexed, to fit into the small grave. The arms and

162. Upper elevation: 138.350 m; lower elevation: 137.540 m; max. depth: 81 cm.
163. Upper elevation: 138.500 m; lower elevation: 138.340 m; max. thickness: 15 cm.
164. Upper elevation: 138.270 m; lower elevation: 137.540 m; max. depth: 73 cm.
165. Sheldrick 2023, 13–15.

Fig. 5.66: View (from above) of human remains (FN40) inside tomb 13 (room 3).

the hands were extended along the sides of the body. The tomb did not contain any grave goods; no traces of textiles were found associated with the remains of the child.

Tomb 15 was found near the southwest corner of room 3, along south wall F78 and in line with tombs 14 and 13 further east (figs. 5.46–5.47; 5.57). The oval-shaped burial pit (F99)[166] measures 26 cm north-south by 86 cm east-west, cutting through lower floor F94 and (seemingly) upper floor F84.[167] As mentioned above, tomb 15 was cut in phase with adjacent tomb 14.

No evidence of a mud-brick superstructure was found on top of the grave; nevertheless, it is possible that the original covering was destroyed by robbery excavations that also damaged the stratigraphy and floors of room 3. The fill of the burial consisted of clean brownish-yellow sand (DSU144),[168] mixed with a very small quantity of mud-brick debris and small potsherds. The lowermost part of the layer was distinguished as DSU148,[169] in order to document the soil around the human remains separately. At a depth of ca. 52 cm was an intact skeleton (FN42), belonging to a child about 18 months old (± 6 months) (fig. 5.70).[170]

166. Upper elevation: 138.370 m; lower elevation: 137.730; max. depth: 64 cm.
167. The poor condition of the upper floor around tomb 15 makes it difficult to establish its relationship with the burial.
168. Upper elevation: 138.370 m; lower elevation: 137.710 m; average depth: 60 cm.
169. Upper elevation: 137.750 lower elevation: 137.730 m; average depth: 2–3 cm.
170. Sheldrick 2023, 15.

Chapter 5: The Underground Funerary Crypts

Fig. 5.67: View (to east) of burial cuts F97 of tomb 14 (in the background) and F99 of tomb 15 (in the foreground).

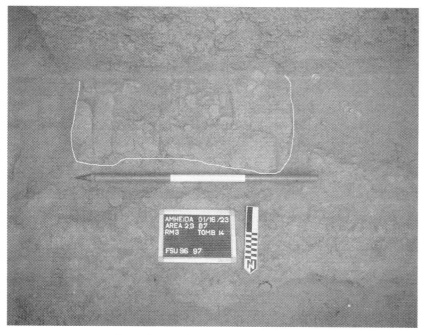

Fig. 5.68: View (from above) of superstructure F96 of tomb 14 (room 3).

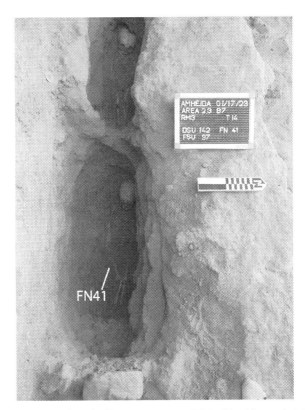

Fig. 5.69: View (from above) of human remains (FN41) inside tomb 14 (room 3).

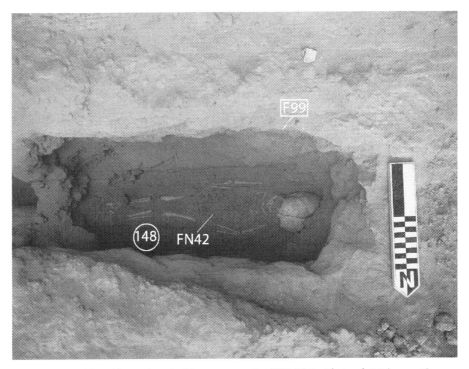

Fig. 5.70: View (from above) of human remains (FN42) inside tomb 15 (room 3).

Fig. 5.71: View (to west) of burial cut F106 of tomb 16 (room 3).

The body was laid supine, facing east, in an S-shaped position in order to fit within the small grave. The arms were stretched along the body, with palms resting on the pelvic area. The human remains were not associated with any grave goods and no textiles were preserved.

Tomb 16 is located along west perimeter wall F1 in the central area of room 3. The burial pit (F106)[171] is ovoidal in shape and measures 63 cm north-south by 187 cm east-west, reaching the maximum depth of 64 cm (figs. 5.46–47; 5.57; 5.71). The pit narrows down by about 18 cm towards the bottom, cutting through both floor levels F84 and F94 and the foundation trench (F118)[172] of west wall F1, filled by DSU174 (fig. 5.72).[173] The grave was partially disturbed by the excavation, in antiquity, of pit F95 by looters, who removed the tomb's superstructure and (likely) part of the edge that marked the northern boundary of the cut.[174] However, the digging of the pit did not damage the deeper layers of the grave, leaving the human remains intact and *in situ*.

171. Upper elevation: 138.020 m; lower elevation: 137.420 m.
172. Upper elevation: 138.200 m; lower elevation: 137.420 m. The foundation trench is visible along the south side of the pit.
173. Upper elevation: 138.200 m; lower elevation: 137.420 m.
174. At the time of the excavation, loose bricks were found immediately to the north of the tomb, in the fill of the robbers' pit.

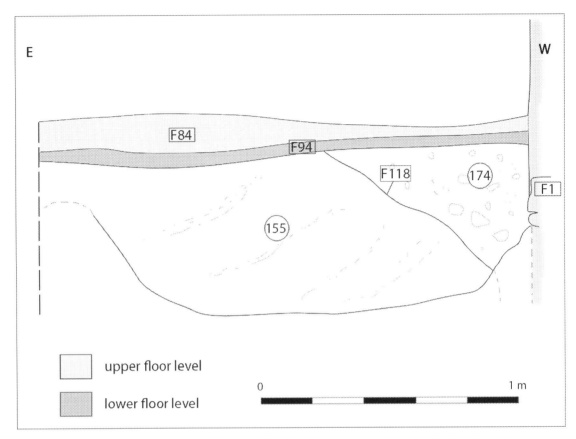

Fig. 5.72: East-west section (facing south) of tomb 16 in room 3 (drawing by S. Alfarano).

The tomb's pit was filled by DSU150,[175] a layer of brownish-yellow sand mixed with some pottery fragments, mud-brick debris, and charcoal. The lowermost part of the fill, surrounding the human remains at the bottom of the pit, was excavated as DSU158.[176] The unit consisted of loose dark yellow sand with scattered inclusions of pottery sherds, mud-brick debris, and charcoal. It is likely that the pit was (at least partially) backfilled with materials originally from the fill of the foundation trench of wall F1.

At a depth of about 46 cm was the complete, well-preserved skeleton (FN47) of a middle-aged woman of about 40–50 years old at death (fig. 5.73).[177] The body was laid supine, facing east, and slightly flexed at the hips. The right forearm was placed over the right pubic bone; the left elbow was slightly flexed, and the left hand lay over the lower pelvic cavity. The skull preserved the remains of her long hair braided and gathered into a bun, and (perhaps) the remains of a cloth hairband.

175. Upper elevation: 138.020 m; lower elevation: 137.520 m; max. depth: 50 cm.
176. Upper elevation: 137.600 m; lower elevation: 137.420 m; max. depth: 14 cm.
177. Sheldrick 2023, 15–16.

Fig. 5.73: View (to west) of human remains (FN47) inside tomb 16 (room 3).

5.3.2. Test Trench 4 to the East of Room 3

Test trench 4 was excavated in 2023 to the east of room 3, within the enclosed space (courtyard? Cemetery area?) of building 7 (figs. 3.2; 5.74). The aim was to investigate the relationship between the collapse unit with evidence of painted wall plaster (DSU172), which was found in the robbery cut (F83) piercing the east wall of room 3, and other collapses visible on the surface in the proximity of the central crypt, as well as the crypt's stratigraphy. The area selected for test trenching was roughly rectangular in shape and measured 3.9 m north-south by 5 m east-west. Digging was carried out only for a few days at the end of the 2023 season.[178] Only extensive excavations within the large rectangular enclosure visible to the east of building 7 will serve to clarify the stratigraphy, construction history, and possibly the function(s) of this large area adjacent to the church.

---

178. The lowest elevation reached inside the trench was 139.370 m.

Fig. 5.74: View (to south) of test trench 4.

Features and stratigraphy (figs. 5.75–76)

As mentioned earlier, the portion of wall decorated with painted plaster (DSU172),[179] which was retrieved inside robbery pit F83 within the test trench, likely resulted from the collapse of the upper section of the church's perimeter walls. No clear pattern could be discerned in the decoration, which is in shades of yellow, brown, and gray (fig. 5.77). At first, this portion of wall with plaster appeared to be *in situ*, but as the excavation progressed, windblown sand[180] was found underneath the lowest course of mudbricks. It is possible that this cluster of mudbricks once belonged to one of the walls of the now-missing apse above ground.

Within the area where DSU172 was found a surface layer of windblown sand (DSU166)[181] was removed against the east wall of the central crypt. This unit, which was mixed with abundant pottery fragments, mud-brick debris, cobbles, and ash pockets,

---

179. Upper elevation: 140.350 m; lower elevation (in cut F121): 139.600 m; max. thickness: 73 cm.
180. DSU175, described below.
181. Upper elevation: 140.490 m; lower elevation: 139.800 m; max. thickness: 50 cm.

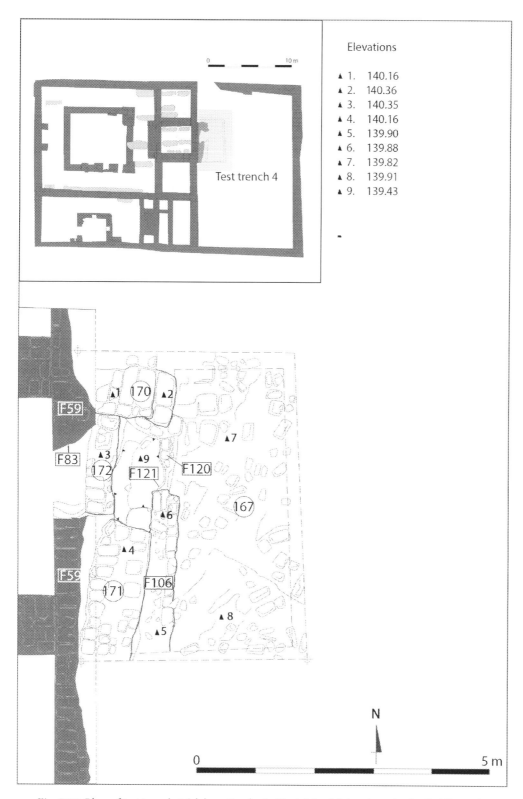

Fig. 5.75: Plan of test trench 4 (elaboration by L. Davighi; additional tracing by S. Alfarano).

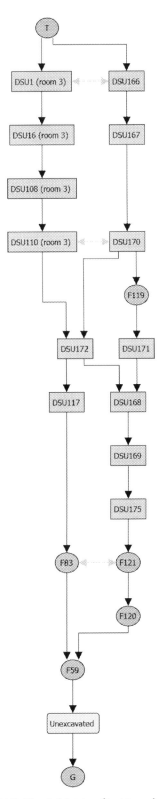

Fig. 5.76: Harris Matrix of test trench 4.

Fig. 5.77: View (to east) of collapsed wall with painted plaster (DSU172) in test trench 4.

partially concealed several collapse layers. Two of them (DSU170 and DSU171) consisted of clusters of bricks still bonded together, located immediately to the east of F59 (the east wall of room 3), to the north and south of F83 and DSU172 respectively. DSU170,[182] oriented east-west, was made of headers and stretchers bonded with a thick layer of beige compact mortar. DSU171[183] was instead oriented north-south and thus parallel to the east perimetral wall of the church (F59). It consisted of four preserved layers of alternating headers and stretchers bonded using gray compact mortar and extended south of the test trench in a seemingly irregular pattern.

Excavations carried out to the east of DSU171 exposed F119,[184] a north-south oriented rectangular feature, measuring 48 cm north-south by 272 cm east-west.[185] F119 consists of a row of mud-brick stretchers, with the space between it and DSU171 filled with brownish-yellow sand and mud-brick debris.[186] It is possible that this structure was built abutting part of the collapse of the east wall of the church (F59). Therefore, it can be associated with a post-abandonment phase of occupation of Area 2.3.

182. Upper elevation: 140.270 m; lower elevation: 140.010 m; max. thickness: 15 cm.
183. Upper elevation: 140.460 m; lower elevation (in robbery pit F121): 139.650 m; max. thickness: 70 cm.
184. Upper elevation: 139.920 m; lower elevation: 139.600 m; average thickness: 24 cm.
185. The feature seems to continue south of the test trench.
186. This fill, as well as the adjacent mud-brick feature, were not fully investigated in the 2023 season.

F119 partially lies above DSU168,[187] a sand layer that was exposed immediately to the east within the test trench. The unit, slightly sloping from west to east, was made of compacted brownish-yellow sand mixed with numerous pottery sherds, abundant mud-bricks debris and charcoal, and a few pebbles. The only small find from test trench 4 was retrieved in this unit; it is a Greek ostrakon (inv. 17077) broadly dated to the late third/mid-fourth century. The upper interface of DSU168 was darker and more compact than the lower part and may have possibly been a walking surface in phase with F119, and so to be associated with a phase of post-abandonment use of the area east of the church.

F119 was found partially below DSU167,[188] excavated to the east of DSU170 and DSU171. This unit, which extended throughout the test trench, sloping down from west to east, consisted of mud-brick fragments and debris mixed with a few fragments of choroplastic and yellow sand, which had accumulated following the collapse of the church's walls.

The robbery pit (F83), which was cut through the east wall (F59) and the vault of room 3, extended in the area of test trench 4, where it was identified as F121.[189] This cut seems to have damaged F120, a north-south oriented feature located east of wall collapse DSU172, along the church's east wall (F59). F120, which measures about 150 cm north-south by 28 cm east-west and has a max. height of 38 cm,[190] consists of two courses of mudbricks bonded with fine and compacted dark beige mud mortar. This structure, as well as its relationship with the other features identified in the test trench, are unclear.

Within the test trench pit F83 was filled by a layer (DSU169)[191] of collapse material (mud-brick fragments and debris, mixed with a few pottery sherds and loose yellow sand, as well as a few fragments of choroplastic). The removal of this unit, which may have resulted from the partial destruction of F120 when the cutting of the robbers' pit took place, revealed DSU175.[192] This deposit, which was not fully excavated, consisted of loose yellow sand with very few inclusions, such as small fragments of pottery and painted plaster.[193]

A study of the stratigraphy inside test trench 4 allowed the identification of three collapse episodes and two phases of occupation/reuse of the area east of the church. The relationships among the collapse units that were identified (DSU167 and DSU170–172) are not completely clear; nevertheless, they seem to have collapsed at different times after the abandonment of the church. The relative chronology seems to suggest that DSU170 was the last to fall on DSU167, which must have already been in an advanced phase of disintegration. Preceding this phase was the collapse of the north-south oriented wall DSU171. Afterwards, the area was used for some time, as suggested by the construction of feature F119 and the use of DSU168 as

---

187. Upper elevation: 139.770 m; lower elevation: 139.370 m; average thickness: 25 cm.
188. Upper elevation: 140.320 m; lower elevation: 139.500 m; max. thickness: 65 cm.
189. Upper elevation: 139.650 m. The visible edges of F121 measure 163 cm north-south by 86 cm east-west.
190. The feature was not fully excavated and documented, so its measurements refer only to the part of F120 that was exposed in 2023.
191. Upper elevation: 140.050 m; lower elevation: 139.870 m; max. thickness: 20 cm.
192. Upper elevation: 139.650 m; lower elevation (at the end of the 2023 season): 139.430 m; max. thickness: 22 cm.
193. The unit equals DSU117 excavated in room 3.

a walking surface. At some point, a large pit (F83+F121) was cut by robbers into room 3 and extending over the area immediately to the east of the central crypt. The pit was then followed by the collapse of DSU172 (the portion of wall with traces of painted plaster).

5.4. Room 4

Room 4 is located at the southeast corner of building 7, directly below room 16 (the now-missing south *pastophorion*) with which it shares all perimeter walls (figs. 3.92–94; 5.1–3). The space measures 3.50 m north-south by 3.30 m east-west and has walls reaching a maximum height of ca. 2.90 m (south wall F13, above the latest of the two floor levels identified within the room). Even though the sanctuary at the east end of building 7 (rooms 14–16) is almost completely lost (due to human activity and/or natural elements), room 4 is remarkably well preserved, with only part of its barrel-vaulted roof missing. This space can be interpreted as a vestibule for rooms 2–3 (the north and central crypts); indeed, the trapdoor (F82)[194] that was identified in the northwest corner of room 4's vaulted roof provided the only access from the church's ground level (via room 16) into the underground crypts. From within room 4 a door piercing the north wall (F78) would have allowed access onto room 3 to the north and, via another doorway in the north wall of room 3, onto the north crypt (room 2; fig. 5.78). The absence of burials inside the south crypt, combined with the discovery of several complete and fragmentary ceramic pots associated with the room's two floor levels (F85 and F107),[195] suggests that this space may have been used for the storage of vessels and/or funerary preparations and rituals.

Features

The walls of room 4, whose structural relationships to each other are hindered by their mud-plaster coating, consist of: F78[196] to the north; F59 to the east;[197] F13 to the south;[198] and F1 to the west[199] (fig. 5.79). As mentioned above, they are completely preserved, while only small portions of its barrel-vaulted roof (oriented north-south) were found *in situ*:

---

194. Discussed below.
195. See section below.
196. Upper elevation: 141.260 m; lower elevation: 138.250 m. The wall seems to abut both the east and west walls of the crypt.
197. Upper elevation: 140.690 m; lower elevation: 138.350 m. F59 is the east wall of the sanctuary (and underground crypts), as well as of the entire building 7.
198. Upper elevation: 141.390 m; lower elevation: 138.430 m. F13 is also the south perimeter wall of room 1 further west. Within room 4 F13 seems to be bonded with the east and west walls (F59 and F1, respectively).
199. Upper elevation: 141.250 m; lower elevation: 138.270 m. F1 is also the east boundary of room 1/west boundary of the sanctuary and underground crypts.

Fig. 5.78: Partial view (to northwest) of room 4, showing the doorway opening onto room 3 to the north and (in the background) the doorway leading into room 2.

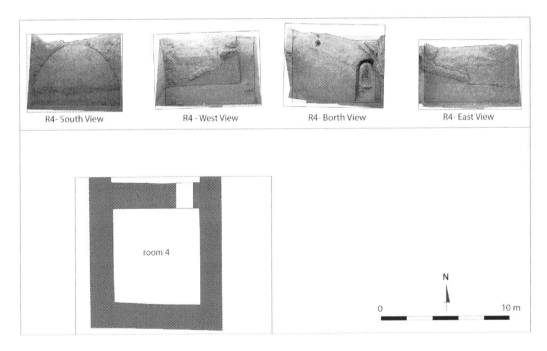

Fig. 5.79: Prospects of walls of room 4 (elaboration by L. Davighi and S. Alfarano).

these include F104,[200] at the north and south ends of east wall F59, and F105[201] along west wall F1 (largely hindered by DSU113, discussed below)[202] (figs. 5.80–81). Large black chinking sherds, visible in the upper part of south wall F13, mark the top curvature of the vault, which is itself now missing (fig. 5.82).

In the northwest corner of the wedge behind north vault spring F105, a rectangular opening led into a vertical shaft (F82),[203] measuring 70 cm north-south by 100 cm east-west and leading into room 4 (figs. 5.83–84). The shaft's west and north sides correspond to the room's northwest corner, while its south edge cuts through wedge DSU113. To the east, the shaft opened into the room, with the exception of its highest elevations where a few courses of mudbricks supported a lintel on which the vault was probably resting.[204] No recesses were documented within the north and west walls of the crypt (F78 and F1) that would have facilitated the descent into the crypt;[205] therefore, a long ladder was most likely used. Traces of recesses around the top of the shaft point to the use of a wooden trapdoor to close the opening when not in use (figs. 5.85–86).

All perimeter walls were coated with undecorated mud plaster, with no evidence of holes or marks on the walls pointing to the existence in antiquity of shelving or other wall-installations. Along the south wall (F13), a slightly dark band was noticed running horizontally through the entire length of the wall in its lower part (fig. 5.82). In proximity to this feature were found the remains of a wooden (palm) beam, within room fill DSU134[206] at the elevation of 139.170 m (fig. 5.87). One possibility is that the beam was placed against the wall when a wooden frame was set up for the construction of the vault. After work was completed, the beam may have been left *in situ* and perhaps repurposed.

Two floor levels of compacted clay, thick and leveled, were detected within room 4. They hindered a protruding ledge at the bottom of south wall F13, which was part of its foundations (fig. 5.82).[207] The upper floor (F85)[208] displayed circular finger marks on the surface of the compacted mud, undoubtedly associated with the construction phase of the floor (fig. 5.88).

200. Upper elevation: 140.760 m; lower elevation: 138.930 m; max. preserved height: 183 cm.
201. Upper elevation: 140.860 m; lower elevation: 139.180 m; max. preserved height: 168 cm.
202. The fill of the wedge between the west wall and the vault's spring consists of compacted mud and mudbrick debris. On the upper surface, concretions are evidence that the layer was exposed to natural elements for a long time. In room 4 it was impossible to ascertain if the wedge between the vault and the east wall was built with mudbricks (as in rooms 2 and 3).
203. Upper elevation: 141.160 m; lower elevation: 138.390 m; max. depth of the vertical shaft: 277 cm.
204. Similar trap doors were found in the houses and granaries at Karanis and Soknopaiou Nesos. They were used to gain access to the cellar underground and were usually set in the corners of rooms so that people could use footholds cut in the walls of the lower rooms: S. Alfarano (personal communication, January 2023); cf. Husselmann 1979, 39. In the crypt at Amheida, however, no recesses were documented within the north and west walls of the crypt (F78 and F1) that would have facilitated the descent; therefore, a ladder was most likely used. According to Grossmann (2002, 133), in the last quarter of the fourth century, the underground tomb of Abu Mina was accessible via a trapdoor and a shaft later replaced by stairs following the construction of the large church complex to facilitate the pilgrims' visit of the saint's relics.
205. Only one rectangular hole was documented in wall F1 that may be linked with the use of the shaft, but it is unclear what function it had, especially in the absence of other similar recesses.
206. See the section below.
207. The three uppermost courses of the ledge in English bond were exposed during the excavations.
208. Upper elevation: 138.510 m; lower elevation: 138.390 m; max. thickness (as visible in exposed section): 12 cm.

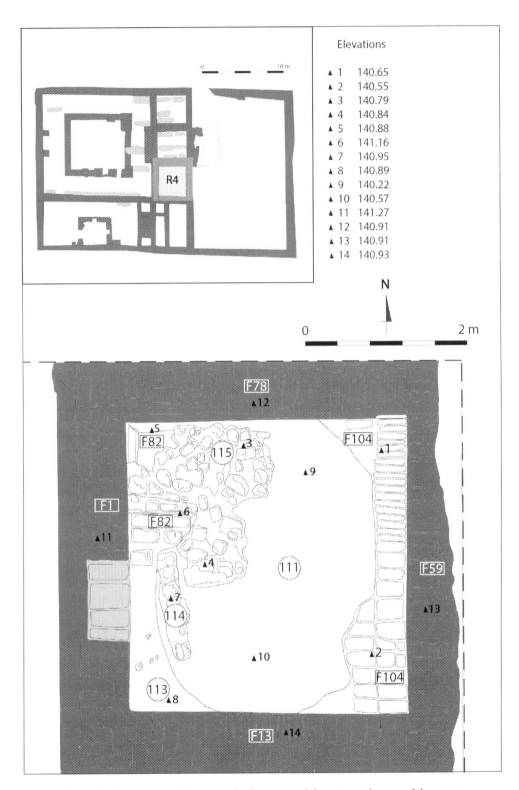

Fig. 5.80: Plan of room 4 showing the features and deposits at the top of the crypt (elaboration by L. Davighi and S. Alfarano).

Fig. 5.81: View of west wall F1 of room 4, showing remains of vault segment F105.

Fig. 5.82: View of south wall F13 of room 4, showing the curvature of the original barrel-vaulted roof.

Fig. 5.83: View (to southwest) of room 4's west wall, showing the shaft (F82) that once led from the church's ground floor into the underground crypts.

Fig. 5.84: View (from above) of shaft F82.

Chapter 5: The Underground Funerary Crypts 325

Fig. 5.85: View (from above, to southeast) of shaft F82.

Fig. 5.86: Hypothetical reconstruction of room 16 (view to northwest), showing the trapdoor leading into the underground crypts (by C. Ullendorff).

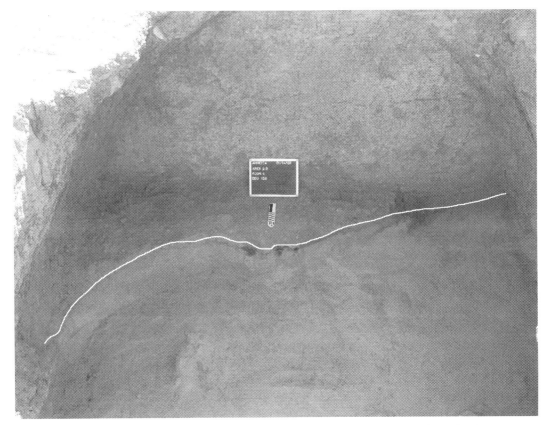

Fig. 5.87: View (to south) of DSU120 and (below) DSU134 with visible remains of wooden fragments.

The floor along the walls of the room displays imprints with a more linear pattern. These marks form a band about 20 cm wide and slightly lower than the rest of the floor. These features, which are attested also in rooms 2 and 3, may have facilitated the process of cleaning the floors of the crypts (for example, following a new deposition or in the context of a funeral rite). Floor F85 was made of mud mixed with several potsherds, some of which joined to create more complete vessels. A small, shallow, and roughly circular pit (F101)[209] was cut into this floor in the south part of the room, approximately in the middle of it; its sand fill (DSU146) was only partially removed.[210] The lower floor F107[211] was laid on top of a layer of compacted sand (DSU162), belonging to the fill of the foundation trenches of the room's walls (fig. 5.89).[212] A number of roughly circular impressions in the mud were detected on this floor in the southeast corner of the room (fig. 5.90). Four of these impressions were clearly discernible and were found in context with several complete and fragmentary ceramic vessels, which may have been used for storage within the crypt.

209. Upper elevation: 138.420 m; lower elevation: 137.290 m; max. thickness (excavated): 113 cm.
210. See section below.
211. Upper elevation: 138.420 m; lower elevation: 138.330 m; max. thickness (as visible in exposed section): 9 cm.
212. See section below for a discussion of DSU162.

Fig. 5.88: View (from above, to west) of upper floor F85 in room 4.

In the west half of room 4 the removal of floor F107 exposed the rectangular foundation trench (F114)[213] of west wall F1. It measured 260 cm north-south by 140 cm east-west and was filled by DSU153.[214]

Stratigraphy and finds (fig. 5.91)

The uppermost level of room 4's stratigraphy consisted of a thick layer of clean windblown sand (DSU111),[215] with only a few scattered potsherds as inclusions (fig. 5.80). One Greek ostracon (inv. 17019, dated to 294/5 or 316/7 on the basis of regnal years) and one coin (inv. 17024, possibly dated to 364–378 CE), were found within this unit. Below DSU111 excavations in the northwest corner of the south crypt revealed a medium-size mud-brick layer (DSU115),[216]

213. Upper elevation: 138.490 m. The trench remained unexcavated.
214. Discussed in the section below.
215. Upper elevation: 140.660 m; lower elevation: 139.800 m; max. thickness: 85 cm.
216. Upper elevation: 140.790 m; lower elevation: 139.760 m; max. thickness: 103 cm.

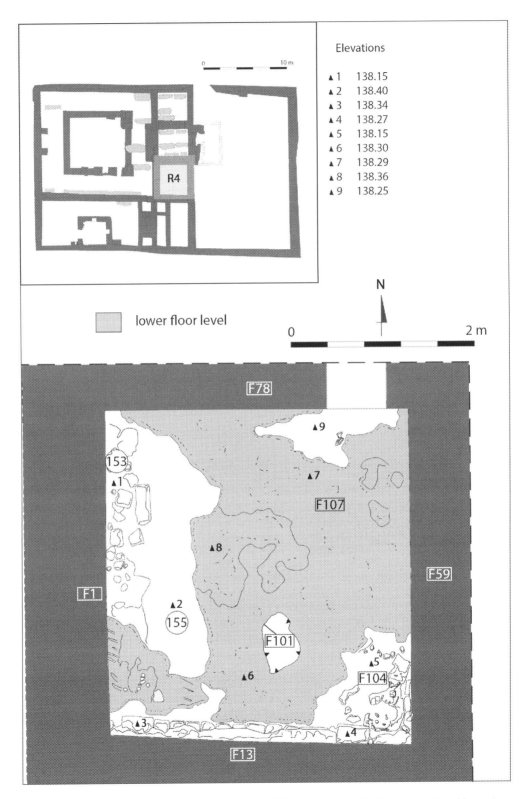

Fig. 5.89: Plan of room 4 showing lower floor F107 (elaboration by L. Davighi and S. Alfarano).

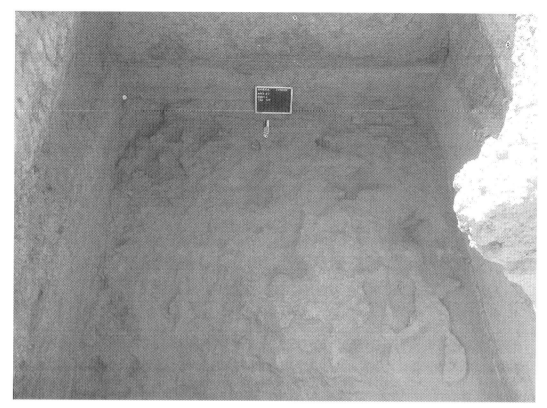

Fig. 5.90: View (from above, to south) of lower floor F107 in room 4, showing circular imprints in the southeast corner.

which likely originated from the collapse of the west wall of room 16 (at the church's ground level) (fig. 5.80). In addition to some potsherds, a few small finds were gathered during the investigation of this unit: four illegible coins (inv. 17018, 17020–17021, and 17023) and one Greek ostracon (inv. 17022, a well tag dated to 286/7). DSU115 extended above trapdoor and shaft F82 and, in part, above the north end of a layer of compacted mud (DSU113),[217] located in the southwest corner of room 4 (fig. 5.80). This was an artificial deposit in the shape of a wedge, which filled the space between the vault and the west wall (F1) of the crypt.

Beyond DSU115, no evidence of other collapses from room 16 was detected inside the south crypt. The removal of DSU111 revealed also DSU118,[218] a natural deposit of clean yellow sand that had accumulated throughout room 4 after the collapse of a large vault. Several small finds were gathered within this unit, including seven bronze coins (inv. 17025, dated to the second half of the fourth century CE; inv. 17037, a *maiorina* struck under Constantius II in 355–361; inv. 17026, dated from the second half of the fourth century to the early fifth century; inv. 17030–17031, complete but illegible; inv. 17028, fragmentary and broadly dated to the second half of the fourth century CE; and inv. 17029, illegible).

217. Upper elevation: 140.890 m; lower elevation: 139.850 m; max. thickness: 104 cm (not excavated).
218. Upper elevation: 140.400 m; lower elevation: 139.400 m; max. thickness: 50 cm.

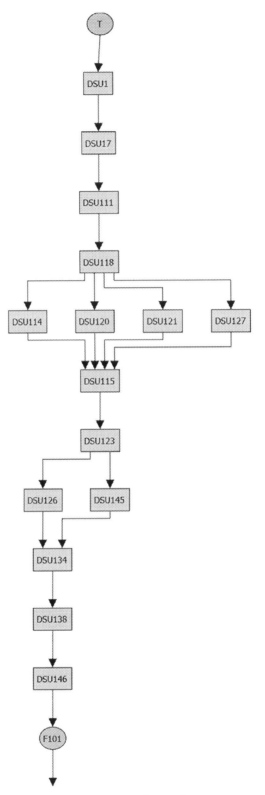

Fig. 5.91a: Harris Matrix of room 4.

Chapter 5: The Underground Funerary Crypts

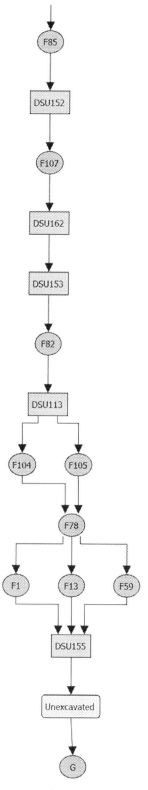

Fig. 5.91b: Harris Matrix of room 4.

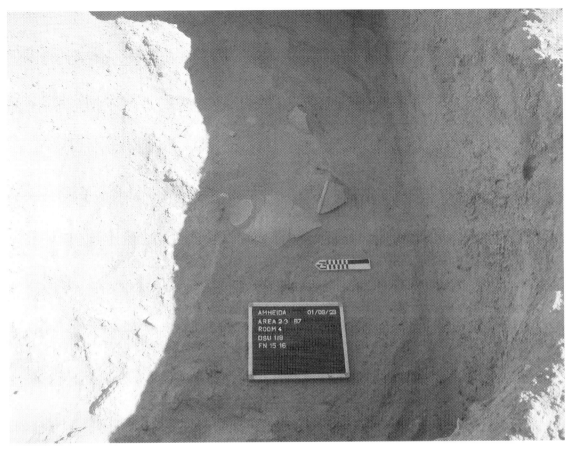

Fig. 5.92: Half-complete basin (inv. 30538) with coin attached to it (inv. 17037), found within DSU118 in room 4.

A half-complete basin (inv. 30538) was also found within DSU118, with one of the above-mentioned coins (inv. 17037) attached to the outer surface of the vessel (figs. 5.92–93). All of these objects were found in proximity to south wall F13, toward its middle, and were concentrated in the lower part of the unit.

The removal of DSU118 exposed the remains of the vault's collapse, which seems to have occurred as one episode. The mudbricks were found still bonded, with the vault's original structure and profile still recognizable.[219] However, since the vault did not fall onto a flat surface, it broke in two halves (DSU120 to the south and DSU121 to the north) (fig. 5.94). DSU120[220] fell to a lower elevation than the north one, coming to rest on a layer of sand (DSU134)[221] that had accumulated inside the room after it was abandoned, but before collapse episode of DSU120+DSU121. The northern part of the collapse (DSU121)[222] was found at

219. Even the chinking sherds were still in place between the bricks.
220. Upper elevation: 139.750 m; lower elevation: 139.010 m; max. thickness: 54 cm.
221. Upper elevation: 139.470 m; lower elevation: 138.380 m; max. thickness: 109 cm.
222. Upper elevation: 140.360 m; lower elevation: 139.470 m; max. thickness: 61 cm.

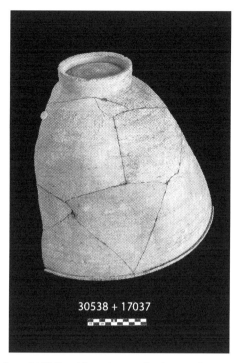

Fig. 5.93: Half-complete basin (inv. 30538) with coin attached to it (inv. 17037), from DSU118 in room 4 (photograph by B. Bazzani).

a higher elevation, steeply inclined from north to south. This section was found above the collapse of part of room 16's west wall (DSU126)[223], which had already tumbled into room 4 through the trapdoor and shaft F82 (figs. 5.95–96). As DSU126 fell through the rather small opening of the trapdoor, it maintained a very steep inclination from west to east and southeast. It was very narrow at the top, where it accumulated up to the trapdoor, and substantially wider at the bottom, stretching to the northeast corner of the room. The stratigraphic relations between vault collapses DSU120+DSU121 and wall collapses DSU115 and DSU126 suggest that it was the collapse of room 16's west wall that caused the collapse of room 4's barrel vault. The south half of the vault collapse (DSU120) was covered by sand rather quickly, whereas the north half (DSU121) and wall collapse DSU115 remained exposed to the elements for some time, as attested to by hard concretions that covered the surface of the mudbricks. At the time when the various episodes of wall and vault collapse took place, the room must have already been abandoned, as pointed to by DSU134, the above-mentioned layer of clean sand (below DSU120 and DSU126) that had accumulated throughout the room, especially in its southern half. The sand must have found its way into room 4 via its trapdoor and shaft, which was, at that point, not yet blocked by any collapsed bricks.

---

223. Upper elevation: 140.300 m; lower elevation: 138.440 m; max. thickness: 73 cm.

Fig. 5.94: View (to south) of vault collapse DSU120+DSU121 in room 4.

DSU134, which was mixed with moderate quantities of potsherds and plaster fragments, was found immediately above the occupation level (DSU138)[224] associated with the upper floor (F85) of room 4. DSU138 consisted of dusty and dark-yellow sand mixed with numerous potsherds, most of which could be joined into complete or almost-complete vessels. Numerous small finds were retrieved while excavating this unit, including four fragments of iron nails (inv. 17053); two bronze coins, one (inv. 17051) illegible and the other (inv. 17050) a *maiorina* dated to 351–361 CE; and two complete vessels (FN35 and FN39), which were found near the northwest corner of the room.

The removal of DSU134 exposed upper floor F85 and, beneath it, an occupation layer (DSU152)[225] associated with lower floor F107. DSU152 was mostly preserved in the southeast corner of room 4 and along south wall F13. Its matrix was similar to that of the occupation layer of the upper floor: it contained numerous joining fragments of ceramic pots,

---

224. Upper elevation: 138.610 m; lower elevation: 138.510 m; max. thickness: 10 cm.
225. Upper elevation: 138.400 m; lower elevation: 138.300 m; max. thickness: 10 cm.

Chapter 5: The Underground Funerary Crypts

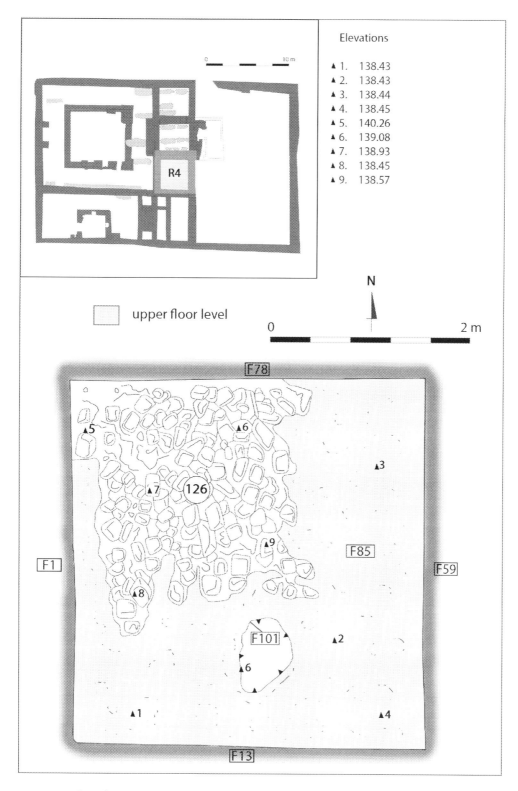

Fig. 5.95: Plan of room 4 with wall collapse DSU126 (elaboration by L. Davighi and S. Alfarano).

Fig. 5.96: View (to west) of wall collapse DSU126 in room 4.

as well as a complete vessel (FN45). Floor F107 was laid out on top of DSU162,[226] a deposit of compact sand and debris that partially filled the foundations of room 4 (and was also identified in the foundations of rooms 2 and 3 to the north) and seems to have been used as a leveling layer (to flatten the area of the hill on which the church was built) (figs. 5.97–98). Under this unit was DSU155,[227] a layer of clean sand that formed the foundation fill of the three crypts. Along west wall F1, abutting (and above) DSU155, was a unit of mud-brick rubble (DSU153),[228] mixed

226. Upper elevation: 138.270 m; the unit was not excavated.
227. Upper elevation: 138.240 m; the unit was not excavated.
228. Upper elevation: 138.400 m; lower elevation: 137.980 m; max. thickness: 42 cm.

Fig. 5.97: View (from above, to south) of room 4 at the end of the excavations.

with pottery fragments, that filled the foundation trench (F114) of F1. Finally, the small and roughly circular pit (F101) that was documented in the south half of the room was filled by an accumulation of clean windblown sand (DSU146).[229]

5.5. Building 7 as a Funerary Church

The identification of building 7 as a funerary church, already established during the 2012–2013 excavations, was further supported by the investigation in 2023 of the thirteen tombs discovered in the underground crypts below the sanctuary. The distribution of the burials shows a preference for the crypt under the apse (room 3) (fig. 3.2); here, the entire surface of the room at floor level was used for the deposition of seven burials (tombs 10–16), which also occupied the space in front of the doorways opening onto the north and south crypts (rooms 2 and 4 respectively).

229. Upper elevation: 138.420 m; lower elevation: 138.290 m; max. thickness: 13 cm.

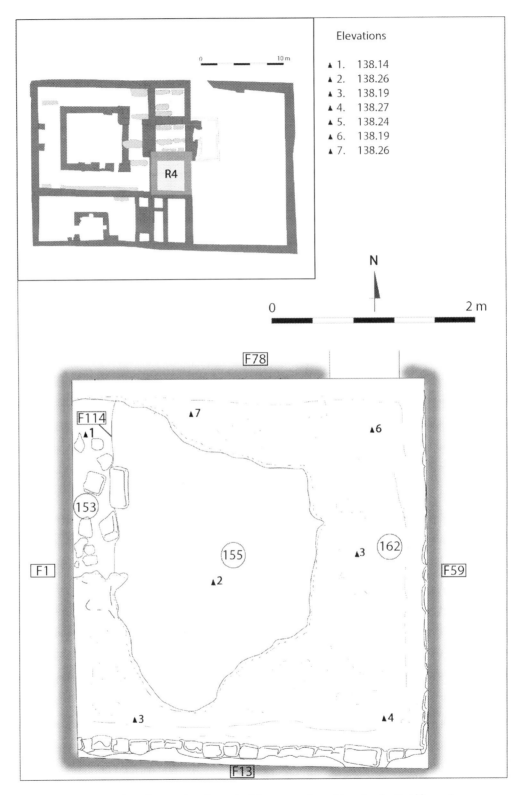

Fig. 5.98: Plan of room 4 at the end of the excavations (drawing by S. Alfarano).

Another prominent location for burying the dead in building 7 was the east return aisle in room 1, where four tombs (2–4 and 17) were placed facing the apse. Four other depositions (tombs 6–9) were found in the crypt (room 2) under the north *pastophorion*, but here not all space was used for funerary depositions (as was instead the case in room 3). Finally, two burials were exposed (in isolation) in building 7, one (tomb 1) in the northwest corner of room 1 and the other (tomb 5) in the south annex of the complex (room 6), adjacent to the south wall of room 1.

Inside room 1 three tombs (1, 4, and 17) were of adult males, while two (2 and 3) hosted the remains of female individuals, one of whom (2) was teenaged and the other (3) adult. A young adult female was buried in tomb 5 inside the south annex (room 6) of building 7. Therefore, it is apparent that these areas of the church were intended for the burial of adult (or young-adult) individuals. In the north crypt (room 2), the distribution seems more varied: out of four burials, one (tomb 6) is of an adult male, one (tomb 8) of an adult female, one (tomb 7) of a juvenile female and one (tomb 9) of a five-year-old child. In the central crypt (room 3), located under the apse, only two graves (tombs 10 and 16) were of adult female individuals, with the remaining five containing the remains of infants and children, ranging from six months to eight years of age. Therefore, out of the seventeen bodies exhumed between 2012 and 2023, only four belonged to adult males.[230] What is more remarkable is that inside the three crypts, located below the sanctuary and thus likely desirable spaces for Christian interments, only one grave (tomb 6 in room 2) was found belonging to an adult male. Even more striking is that the crypt (room 3) below the apse, generally assumed to be the location for particularly important members of the local clergy like bishops and priests, if not martyrs and saints, did not host a single burial of an adult male. Rather, the analysis of the human remains from building 7 points to the crypts as having been the preferred burial places for children and infants and (in lesser measure) for adult women. Due to the paucity of comparable data from contemporary funerary churches and crypts, it is difficult to draw conclusions on the hierarchy of burials in the church at Amheida or (more broadly) in early Christian churches of Egypt.[231]

As discussed in Chapter 3, the six burials that were excavated in the church complex (rooms 1 and 6) were not associated with any funerary goods; the same was attested in relation to the thirteen burials that were investigated in the underground crypts (more specifically, rooms 2–3) in 2023.[232] The placement of all burials inside building 7 (including the church, annex, and crypts below the sanctuary), as well as their east-west orientation, undoubtedly point to the Christian affiliation of the deceased. While the east-west orientation of the bodies is not exclusively typical of Christian burials, most Christian interments point to this as a common practice. Likely, the idea behind it is that the deceased, with their feet lying to the east and their head to the west, would have been able to face the Son of Man rising from the East at the time

---

230. In building 7, 41% of the deceased buried there were women, 35% were infants or children (sex undeterminable), and only 24% men.

231. See below in this section (as well as in the following Sec. 5.5.1) for a more in-depth discussion of burials and human remains from building 7 in relation to questions of gender, identity, and social hierarchy. In terms of family relationships among the individuals buried inside the church, only genetic analysis could provide answers.

232. With the exception of the small bronze cup with lid (inv. 17038) that was retrieved from tomb 9 in room 2.

of resurrection.²³³ Thus, the arrangement of Christian burials is to be understood as reflecting the concept of the *parousia*, or the Second Coming of Christ, associated with the rising of the deceased from their tombs.²³⁴

The mud-brick superstructures, laid out to seal some of the graves, reflect a practice already documented in all tombs within room 1 (with the exception of tomb 1, which was found unsealed). As discussed in a previous chapter, this custom is widely attested in cemeteries of the Great Oasis and beyond.²³⁵

Of the 17 graves that were detected and excavated in the church and in the underground crypts (rooms 2–4), only two contained coffins, one rectangular in shape and made of wood (tomb 17 in room 1) and the other roughly oval and built with mud and organic material (likely manure) (tomb 9 in room 2). It is impossible to know if the presence of coffins is an indicator of higher status of the individuals buried in them. Tomb 17 belonged to an adult male, who was buried in a prominent location within the church, i.e., right in front of the platform (F19) leading onto the apse; a child was buried inside tomb 9, which was located in the underground space (room 2) below the north *pastophorion*, also an important location for Christian burials inside the church. All that can be remarked upon here is that a similar paucity of coffins is also attested in Christian cemeteries from the region.²³⁶

As mentioned in the previous section, a small cooking pot containing the remains of an unidentified substance, as well as a few fish bones (inv. 30129), was discovered at floor level in the northeast corner of the north crypt, immediately to the east of tomb 6. Traces of aromatic plants (FN59) were also detected on the superstructure of tomb 6, in the northwest corner of the crypt.²³⁷ Both the vessel and the plants were likely used during a funerary rite and/or left as grave offerings. Ceramic vessels, including the type of small jar found in the north crypt at Amheida, were gathered from several tombs at the cemeteries of nearby Kellis.²³⁸ It was stated in an earlier chapter that the use of plants as grave offerings is also widely attested at Kellis.²³⁹ Sprays of rosemary and myrtle were discovered within numerous graves of the Kellis 2 cemetery.²⁴⁰ Similar bouquets were also found in West Tomb 1, within the cemetery located in Enclosure 4 at the same site.²⁴¹ Further evidence for the use of floral garlands and bouquets

---

233. Davies 1999, 199; Bowen 2003b, 169; Fox and Tritsaroli 2019, 109.

234. Marinis 2009, 161; Kuryakakis 1974, 55–56. On the orientation of Christian burials in Egypt, but reflecting a practice adopted throughout the Mediterranean world, see Bowen 2019, 375; Heikkinen 2011, 110–11. Cf. Rahtz 1978 regarding slight discrepancies in the orientation of burials, depending on the time of the year when the interments took place. It must be remarked that evidence exists for a significantly different orientation of the deceased in early Christian burials from the Mediterranean region, such as Cyprus: see Fox and Tritsaroli 2019, 109.

235. See Sec. 3.4 above, esp. pp. 133–37, n. 185–86.

236. Such as at Kellis (K2 cemetery), El-Deir, or the pit graves at El-Bagawat: see Bowen 2022a, 354.

237. Evidence for the use of plants in funerary rituals and/or as offerings was found also during the excavation of tomb 4 in room 1: see Sec. 3.4 (p. 131).

238. Birrell 1999, 38 and 41; Bowen 2003b, 175–77; Hope and McKenzie 1999, 56 and 59, pl. 6. For comparative evidence from Dush (Kharga Oasis), cf. Dunand et al. 1992, 237–41; pls. III–IV and 76–86.

239. See Sec. 3.4 (p. 131, n. 174).

240. Bowen 2003b, 168; Bowen 2012a, 361; Bowen 2019, 375–77; Hope and McKenzie 1999, 56; Thanheiser 1999, 89. P. Sheldrick reported that the excavation of one of the burials, which held the remains of a child, revealed a rosemary garland placed around the body (Sheldrick 2008, 138).

241. Bowen 2003b, 176; Bowen 2019, 375–77.

in funerary assemblages was discovered at the necropolis of Dush, in Kharga Oasis.[242] Flowers and plants were placed with the bodies of the deceased and on top of the tombs above floor level.[243] The herbs that were identified included rosemary, thyme, myrtle, and marjoram; they were likely chosen because of their aromatic qualities, as well as because they were easily found in the area.[244] The significance of flowers and plants in a ritual context, including a possible reference to renewal and regeneration, is thus apparent.[245]

Archaeological evidence is scanty at best regarding the nature of the liturgical practices that were carried out inside the church of Amheida. However, what is undeniable is that the presence of burials in the church, as well as in the underground crypts, suggests that building 7 served, at least at some point (if not from the very beginning, as the existence of the crypts themselves suggest), as a funerary church. Certainly, it remained in use after the deposition of the burials near the sanctuary, since the mud-brick coverings of the pits were sealed by a floor that extended throughout the eastern half of the nave and side aisles.

The association of a church with funerary practices in the fourth century is well attested in Dakhla. One example is the church at Deir Abu Matta, the only triconch basilica known from the oasis (fig. 2.5).[246] Several burials were discovered since 1979 at this site, in the area to the north and west of the church as well as inside it. Most of the graves within the church were found disturbed, with the exception of a child's burial, and all of them, including the interments outside the basilica, were dated to a post-abandonment phase of the site in the late seventh century.[247] Notwithstanding the relatively late date, the fact that the pits were dug inside the abandoned church, as well as in its proximity, suggests that the place was still important to members of the local community even after it ceased to be in use.[248] On the other hand, as a hiatus seems to have existed between the abandonment of the church and the creation of the cemetery, it is difficult to establish if the church itself was used for funerary and commemoration rituals before it was abandoned.

The West Church of Kellis is another church in Dakhla that may also have been associated with funerary practices and is contemporary with the church of Amheida (fig. 2.4).[249] Two burials, both oriented to the east, were discovered in 2000 in the proximity of the sanctuary, at the east end of the church. One grave, containing the remains of an adult male, was found to the north of the stepped platform leading into the apse; the other, of an infant, had been dug along the south side of the *bema*, very close to the area of the sanctuary.[250] More

---

242. Dunand et al. 1992, 252; 259–60; pls. 92–93.
243. The latter may have been the case for the plant remains inside the north funerary crypt at Amheida.
244. Dunand et al. 1992, 252; 259. It is possible that herbs and flowers were used to lessen the strong smell of decaying bodies, as in this period corpses were buried with their viscera and, in many cases, were only minimally treated (if at all): see Dunand and Letellier-Willemin 2019, 246–47. On the changing customs regarding the treatment of bodies, see also Dunand 2007, 176–82.
245. Dunand et al. 1992, 252.
246. Bowen 2008; Bowen 2009; Bowen 2012b. See also Sec. 2.1.1.
247. Bowen 2019, 377.
248. Bowen 2019, 377.
249. See Sec. 2.1.1.
250. Hope 2003, 244–52; Molto et al. 2003, 347; 349.

graves were discovered in the immediate proximity of the West Church, suggesting that the building was likely connected with funerary rituals.[251]

It is known that official legislation, both ecclesiastical and imperial, prohibited the interment of bodies within intramural churches (including Theodosius' edict of 381).[252] Nevertheless, there is evidence suggesting that the custom of burying the deceased inside these churches was tolerated, if not accepted, throughout the Mediterranean region in late antiquity.[253] Thus, notwithstanding the existence of such legislation, it seems that common practice was another matter and reflected a disregard, in several instances, of such regulations.[254] With regard to the evidence from Dakhla, it may be difficult to categorize the West Church at Kellis or the church at Amheida as "intramural." Admittedly, the former is located at the west limit of the inhabited site, in close proximity to several tombs and mausolea; therefore, it may be reasonable to interpret this building as a "cemetery" church. However, it is not fully detached from the settlement and does not lie in an isolated site; rather, it seems part of the urban fabric of the town, even if at its edges. As for the church at Amheida, the plan of the city suggests that the church is located at the east end of the ancient settlement; however, no evidence has yet been detected pointing to the fact that building 7 was erected in a cemetery; it seems that the church had rather been built within the city, albeit at its east end and in a higher, more prominent location.[255]

The discovery of burials inside the church of Amheida raises important questions that are key to our understanding of Christian funerary architecture in Egypt. Some of these questions are: what characterizes a funerary church in late antique Egypt, in terms of both layout and use? Did it host only regular liturgical services or also ritual meals and commemorations by the relatives of the deceased? Also, who were the individuals buried inside the church at Amheida? Certainly, any assumption that the area closer to the sanctuary might have been reserved for important adult individuals, possibly members of the local clergy, does not fully

---

251. Bowen 2002, 81; Bowen 2022a, 358–62. Cf. Sec. 2.1.2 for further bibliography. For a summary of bioarchaeological investigations on the human remains from the church and adjacent burials, cf. Dupras, Wheeler, Williams, and Sheldrick 2022, 373–75. Evidence of human remains was also found, by G. E. Bowen and C. A. Hope, within the collapse of another church in Dakhla, located at the site of Deir el-Malak in the proximity of the modern village of Masara. The dating of this church is still debated, but it is certainly later than the fourth-fifth centuries: cf. Bowen and Hope 2019a, 422–23. Although the building still awaits to be fully investigated, the presence of human bones points to the existence of isolated burials, or a cemetery, that may have been associated with the church itself (Bowen and Hope 2019a, 429). A preliminary report on the church is Mills 1981, 184–85.

252. *Cod. Theod.* IX.17.6 (fourth century; cf. Mommsen and Meyer 1905, 465–66). Later legislation, including *Cod. Just.* I.2.2 (sixth century) and *Basilika* 5.1.2 (ninth century; cf. Scheltema and van der Wal 1955, I:125), reiterated this prohibition.

253. Marinis 2009, 150–51. See also Fox and Tritsaroli 2019, 108. According to Grossmann, exceptions to the ban on church interment would have likely been made only for members of the clergy and individuals of high status: see Grossmann 2002a, 128.

254. It is necessary to allow for the possibility that some intramural churches might have not been so at the time of their foundation (as in the case of the memorial church of Bishop Ambrose of Milan: see Grossmann 2014, 107, after Volp 2002, 117). Grossmann believes that the available evidence from Egypt, as well as the broader Mediterranean region, rather supports an overall adherence to the legislation against intramural burials (see Grossmann 2014, 109).

255. See also Sec. 7.5 below.

stand against the available evidence.[256] As discussed earlier on, anthropological studies carried out on the human remains from building 7 show that people of both sexes and of all ages, including at least one female adolescent, were buried inside the church, even in prominent locations near the sanctuary and in the crypts.[257] One cannot rule out the possibility that individuals who clearly were not members of the local clergy might have still been related to them, thus benefiting from some privileges after death.[258]

It is clear that burial inside the church complex of Amheida was not solely reserved for adult male Christians.[259] However, it is not possible to speculate if the female individuals interred there held particular responsibilities in the local Christian community. In fact, there is no documentary evidence shedding light on this topic with regard to fourth-century Dakhla.

Who, then, would have been the beneficiaries of burial and funerary rites inside the church at Amheida (and perhaps other churches in Dakhla)? Did these deceased, male and female, adult, adolescents, and even infants (as was also the case in the West Church at Kellis), belong to the families of wealthy and influential Christians, who were also benefactors of this particular church and might have wished to be buried inside it after death? This seems to be a reasonable assumption, supported by the fact that the custom of interring members of local Christian elites inside churches is attested elsewhere in Egypt.[260] Preliminary analysis on the thirteen bodies discovered in 2023 revealed that the teeth of most individuals had suffered less attrition: this points to the consumption of a higher grade of flour, milled without grit. Also, the lack of evidence of patellofemoral arthritis, which is often detected in individuals who squat

---

256. Fox and Tritsaroli (2019, 110, after Marinis 2009, 156) list religious hierarchy as a factor dictating the location of graves in churches of the Eastern Mediterranean, with clerics buried in the sanctuary and laymen or monks in front of it. However, the primary sources cited by Marinis seem to concern more with the placement of the deceased during their funeral rites, rather than their burial. On the area of the sanctuary, and its immediate vicinity, as the likely location of burials for members of the higher clergy, cf. Grossmann 2002a, 128.

257. See Aravecchia et al. 2015, 33–34. Additional evidence from Dakhla (noted above) is the infant's burial discovered in close proximity to the apse in the West Church at Kellis.

258. Aravecchia et al. 2015, 39.

259. A rather different situation is attested at the cemetery church excavated at Kom el-Ahmar near Sharuna, north of Minya. The church, seemingly built over the remains of a local saint, hosted numerous burials within it, but they were all male; apparently, women and children were interred outside the church: Grossmann 2002a, 131; 428–29; Grossmann 2014, 102.

260. Grossmann 2002a, 127–32. In Constantinople important individuals, like members of the imperial family or bishops, were buried in churches, notwithstanding the official prohibition against interments *intra urbem*; however, even the graves of prominent people were located mostly in parts of the church (such as the narthex or the side aisles) that were farther from the liturgically most significant area of the sanctuary: see Marinis 2009, 151. Based on the evidence from Constantinople and Greece, Marinis interprets the prohibition against intramural church interments as referring only to the "liturgical center" of churches, consisting of the sanctuary and the *bema* (Marinis 2009, 152). This reading is only partially supported by archaeological evidence from Egypt and particularly Dakhla, although one must bear in mind that the examples cited by Marinis are significantly later than those from Dakhla. On the one hand, tombs 2 and 4 in the Amheida church were located to the side of the stepped platform that led onto the apse, thus leaving the central nave free; on the other hand, one burial inside the West Church at Kellis was also placed to the side of the *bema*, but right in front of the apse, therefore in a very central position. According to Bowen (2003b, 177), the West Church resembles the "apse" tombs at Oxyrhynchus, where bodies were often buried in front of the sanctuary; admittedly, the latter are tombs and not churches, although Grossmann (2002a, 337) believes that at least one of them (tomb 42) was in use as a funerary church. On the "apse" tombs, see Petrie 1925, 16–17, pls. XLI and XLV.

for prolonged periods of time in their life, suggests that the people buried in building 7 had a sedentary and relatively privileged life.[261] More in-depth study of the human remains from building 7 is forthcoming; it will hopefully shed more light on the age, gender, pathologies, and possible causes of death of the individuals buried in the church complex, including the crypts. Currently, it is not possible to move beyond mere guesswork as regards the identities of those buried in the church or their socio-economic status in late antique Amheida.[262]

A related question concerns the reason (or reasons) why the bodies were laid to rest in the church and the crypts, rather than in a tomb (or a family mausoleum) in the necropolis to the south of the city, or even in the nearby mortuary complex, which was associated with an (earlier) pyramid tomb structure.[263] The issue at Amheida is that the necropolis has not yet been investigated; therefore, it is unknown if this cemetery hosted the remains of both Christian and non-Christian citizens, or if it was used exclusively by those adhering to one religious tradition or another. It is also impossible to speculate if Christians might have buried their dead in the necropolis at an earlier stage, but subsequently began to choose locations closer (or within) the city, a phenomenon attested elsewhere in Egypt and beyond from the end of the fourth century.[264] Unfortunately, the lack of data prevents any easy assumption about the existence of separate Christian cemeteries at Amheida, or more generally about Christian burial customs at the site during the fourth century.

A thorough reflection is also needed on how sacred space was used in funerary churches. Ancient sources, such as the third-century *Didascalia Apostolorum*, offer insights on Christian burial practices, including the preparation of the body, its interment in the context of rituals that included the Eucharist, as well as gatherings of friends and family at the grave of the deceased for prayers and the consumption of food.[265] These rituals would have often taken place in cemeteries, including churches that began to appear in Christian necropoleis by the second quarter of the fourth century.[266] Nevertheless, one has to assume that the same could very well have taken place inside intramural churches.[267] The *mastabas* inside the church of Amheida could have accommodated several people who might have assembled for different purposes,

---

261. Sheldrick 2023, 18.
262. On this subject, see also Sec. 5.5 below, esp. pp. 343–45. Information about the possible occupation of one of the individuals buried inside the church (in tomb 1) is discussed by T. Dupras in Aravecchia et al. 2015, 38.
263. On the Roman pyramid, see Warner 2012. See also Kaper 2015.
264. Grossmann 2014, 93; Davies 1999, 193. The practice of burying the deceased inside, or in close proximity to, churches in cities and villages is attested not only in Dakhla and Egypt, but throughout the Mediterranean world in late antiquity. Fox and Tritsaroli (2019, 109) see the practice of intramural burials taking place especially since the late sixth century.
265. Davies 1999, 199. See also Yasin 2005, 447–51.
266. Grossmann 2014, 93. According to Grossmann, the function of these cemeterial churches would have been similar to that of private or family chapels, that is to say, to provide a venue for the commemoration of the deceased, but on a larger scale.
267. Stewart-Sykes 2009, 255 (*Didascalia Apostolorum*, Ch. 6, Sec. 6.22).

perhaps the commemoration of the dead including ritual meals (the so-called *refrigerium*).[268]

It is difficult to arrive at definitive answers to these questions, certainly with regard to the church of Amheida, due to the overall lack of funerary goods inside the tombs that were investigated. Nevertheless, these are questions worth asking and testing against all kinds of evidence, in an attempt to learn more about the life—and death—of the Christian community that lived at Amheida in the fourth century.

5.5.1. Crypts in Early Christian Churches of Egypt

The discovery of three underground funerary crypts makes the Amheida church an exceptionally important case study, with the potential to make a significant contribution to the study of Christian funerary architecture, as well as of Christian burial customs, in late antiquity. These are the first known crypts associated with a church to have been found in the region of the Western Desert, and their fourth-century dating makes them the oldest of any other known crypts throughout Egypt.[269] Indeed, relatively little is known of underground crypts or their functions in early Christian architecture in Egypt. In this section I provide an overview of the available evidence.

According to A. Grabar, the term "crypt" was used by ancient Greeks to designate underground vaults, but it does not seem to have been adopted by Eastern Greek-speaking Christians to designate the underground spaces of their funerary monuments or martyrs' mausolea. Conversely, it was widely adopted in Western Christian architecture, which likely borrowed it from Roman architects.[270]

Generally, early Christian crypts were characterized by their association with relics; therefore, they maintained a strong funerary connotation, seemingly modelled on pre-Christian funerary *hypogea*.[271] With regard to Egypt, we know of chapels built above crypts

---

268. The Roman feast calendar informs us that the memorial meal was celebrated on the occasion of the deceased's birthday, as well as on specific days following their death: see Volp 2002. Other features, distinctly associated with banquets, are attested in late antique funerary contexts. For example, several *stibadia*, or semi-circular banquet beds, can be seen in a large building (no. 180, in the past interpreted as a church) located at the late antique Christian cemetery of El-Bagawat (Kharga Oasis): see Cipriano 2008, 74–83, who includes *comparanda* from North Africa. Grossmann believed the building, which shows different phases of construction, to be of non-Christian origin: see Grossmann 2002a, 318–19; Grossmann 2014, 93; 106–7, fig. 15. Another example at El-Bagawat is the *stibadium* in the courtyard of mausoleum 18, dated to the second half of the fifth century (Cipriano 2008, 68–69, fig. 38). In time, funeral banquets seem to have degenerated and lost their original meaning, as St. Augustine frequently complained (Aug., Conf. VI, 2), and the ecclesiastical authorities began to oppose these practices. The hostility towards these rites continued in the 6th century, as attested in the Theodosian Code (*CTh*. XVI 10, 19, 3); a prohibition of these celebrations was discussed at the Council of Tours in 567 and later at the Council of Braga. Cf. Spera 2005, 5–33, De Santis 2008, 4531–54.

269. According to Grossmann, the archaeological evidence of intramural churches with crypts does not predate the end of the fourth century: see Grossmann 2014, 93.

270. Grabar 1972, Vol. 1, 436–37.

271. See Grabar 1972, Vol. 1, 437, which includes a discussion of the basic layout and function of the rooms forming these early Christian crypts. On the different types of crypts in churches from the Eastern and Western Mediterranean, see pp. 437–87.

hosting private burials from cemeteries at El-Bagawat, Abu Mina, and Atripe.[272] Crypts begin to appear within intramural churches by the end of the fourth century, with the purpose of hosting relics of saints and martyrs. However, the evidence for crypts in these early Christian churches, both intra- and extramural, is not very abundant.[273] Among the ones that are known is the crypt under the *martyrion* (or Tomb Church) at the pilgrimage site of Abu Mina.[274] The *martyrion* was erected over the tomb of the famous Egyptian saint Menas, who was buried in a pre-existing *hypogaeum* (part of a pre-Christian necropolis).[275] The crypt underwent different phases of remodeling in the fifth and sixth centuries. In its latest phase it was accessible via two sets of stairs; these had likely been built to regulate the flow of pilgrims to the tomb, where the relics of Saint Menas would have been kept within an *arcosolium* (semi-domed niche).[276] Also at Abu Mina are two rectangular burial crypts situated in the apse of the Great Basilica.[277] They were dug into the ground and seem to be contemporary with the second phase of the church, dating to the sixth century.[278] According to Grossmann, these burials would have likely hosted individuals of a high status, more precisely members of the high local clergy.[279]

A crypt believed to have hosted the remains of the Egyptian martyr St. Epimachus was excavated at a necropolis at Tell el-Makhzan, to the east of Pelusium in North Sinai.[280] In its original phase, possibly dating to the fourth century, it was part of a self-standing burial chapel built above ground. The chapel was then incorporated into a church built against its west wall (fig. 5.99). The latter was equipped with a large underground crypt, which extended below the central nave and side aisles. Burials were also detected in the area of the sanctuary, immediately to the west of the semicircular apse. In the sixth century, a very large basilica was built to the north of the above-mentioned church.[281] The basilica, which could host large numbers of

272. Grossmann 2014, 95–97. Worthy of note is the (possible) tomb of Shenoute that was found below a funerary chapel at the White Monastery (thus, in the context of a monastic site rather than a cemetery): see Bolman, Davis, and Pyke 2010.

273. Grossmann 1991a, 208; cf. also Grossmann 2010, 165; Grossmann 2014, 106–7.

274. The *martyrion* was built in difference phases, beginning in the first half of the fifth century, and continuing until the ninth century: for a summary of the archaeological evidence from the area of the *martyrion*, see Grossmann 1998b, 281–86; Capuani 1999, 52; McKenzie 2007, 290 (after Grossmann 1989, 23 n. 30); Grossmann 2014, 104–5. It should be noted that, according to literary sources, an early memorial church at Abu Mina was consecrated in 375, when the body of St. Menas was moved to the crypt: see McKenzie 2007, 290 (after Drescher 1946, 144–45). Cf. also Ward-Perkins 1949, 32.

275. Grossmann 1998b, 282 (after Kaufmann 1910, 71–76) and Grossmann 2014, 104–5. Since the "tomb church" was erected in a pre-Christian cemetery, the interment of Saint Menas in this area during the fourth century would not have contravened any legislation against intramural burials: see Grossmann 2014, 109. In general, early Christian crypts that were easily accessible, as well as equipped with features to help regulate the flow of visitors, may be more securely identified with burial places of saints and martyrs (although the memory of who these holy men were has been lost in the case of many *martyria*): see Grossmann 2002a, 132; 134–35.

276. Grossmann 1998b, 286. Cf. also Grossmann 2002a, 133.

277. Kaufmann 1910, pl. 59; Wace et al. 1959, 27; Grossmann 2002a, fig. 20.

278. Grossmann 2014, 109. A third burial was found in the same area of the apse but seems to have been dug at a later stage. According to Grossmann (2002, 134), the fact that no other burials *ad martyrem* were found in the area of the Great Basilica and of the "tomb church" points to an effort, by the administrators of the pilgrimage center, to curtail the practice of intramural burials at Abu Mina.

279. Grossmann 2002a, 129; Grossmann 2014, 109.

280. Bonnet, El-Samie and Talha 2005; Grossmann 2014, 100–1; 103, fig. 11.

281. Bonnet, El-Samie and Talha 2005; Grossmann 2002a, 129; fig. 89.

pilgrims visiting the *martyrion* of St. Epimachus, also included a crypt, located below the chapel at the southeast corner of the complex.[282]

Excavations at the site of Pelusium revealed a circular church, dated to the fifth century, with a crypt located at its west end and accessible via two stairways.[283] The relatively small size of the crypt points to the existence of just one burial, although the identity of the deceased (a holy person?) is unknown.[284]

A sealed individual tomb, rather than a proper crypt and thus inaccessible, was found lying below the area of the altar (now missing) in the late fifth- or sixth-century "bishop's church" at Pharan, in the Sinai Peninsula. As the name of the church suggests, it is believed that the grave, located in a particularly prominent location, might have belonged to the founding bishop of this basilica.[285]

Underground burial chambers are also attested, albeit in small numbers, in churches situated along the west Mediterranean coast of Egypt; in particular, one crypt was discovered at ʿAin Makhura, to the west of Abusir, in the area in front of the sanctuary of the central church, perhaps dated to the sixth century.[286] Two crypts were also investigated in the area of the sanctuary at the sixth-century basilica of Marea, to the southwest of Alexandria.[287]

A funerary crypt also exists inside the church at the monastery of St. John the Little in Wadi al-Natrun.[288] Currently, the entrance is in the central nave of the church, in close proximity to the apse. It once led to a set of at least two rooms, one to the west, which bore a graffito with the name of John and was filled with earth in antiquity, and another to the east, which had niches piercing the south and east walls and was subject to alterations, including a new vaulted roof.[289] Grossmann compared the latter space to fifth-century cells from the monastic site of Kellia and hypothesized that this could also be the earliest dating of the underground rooms at St. John the Little.[290] If this is the case, the construction of the crypt may belong to an earlier phase than that of the church in which it was found, since the chronology of the entire site has been established as ranging from the sixth to the thirteenth century.[291] The alterations that were

282. According to Grossmann (2002, 129), the crypt might have held the burial of the church's donor.
283. Grossmann and Hafiz 1998, 177–79; pl. 16a; Grossmann 2002a, 134; fig. 88.
284. Grossmann 2014, 109.
285. Grossmann 1998a, 59; Grossmann 2002a, 129, figs. 97–98. The tomb was heavily disturbed; some bones were discovered in another hole dug into the floor of the apse, perhaps associated with the reburial of human remains from the previously mentioned tomb (Grossmann 1999–2000, 155).
286. The chamber contained four burials, but based on its relatively small size, it might have been originally intended for a single interment: see Grossmann 2002a, 129; fig. 6. See also Capuani 1999, 47.
287. Szymańska and Babraj 2003, 59. A later construction, in the area of Old Cairo, is the Church of St. Sergius, dated to the late seventh/early eighth century but heavily restored in subsequent centuries. Below the sanctuary of the church is an underground crypt, which is not associated with burials: it was instead built to memorialize the location where the Holy Family would have stayed on their journey through Egypt: Grossmann 1991a; Grossmann 2002a, 135; Gabra 1993, 118–21; Capuani 1999, 107–8.
288. Brooks Hedstrom et al. 2010, 219, fig. 2. On recent work at the site, carried out by a Yale mission directed by Stephen J. Davis, cf. also Davis et al. 2012.
289. Samuil and Grossmann 1999, 361. The discovery of the graffiti, as remarked by the authors, is not sufficient evidence to suggest that this crypt was originally the cell in which John Kolobos (the Little) resided.
290. Samuil and Grossmann 1999, 361.
291. The chronological range was based on pottery collected during a surface survey, which was carried out at the site in 2006: cf. Brooks Hedstrom et al. 2010, 218.

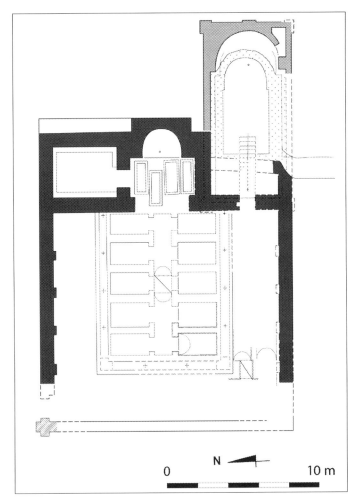

Fig. 5.99: Plan of the church with crypts at Tell el-Makhzan, near Pelusium (after Grossmann 2014, 103, fig. 11; tracing by C. Fosen).

made in the east room of the crypt, with its new vaulted roof, may be contemporary with the construction of the church.[292] Rooms 2–4 at Amheida seem to be about a century earlier than the crypt at St. John the Little. Furthermore, they appear to differ in terms of their function: whereas the funerary nature of rooms 2–4 is beyond doubt, no evidence of burials or human remains was detected inside the crypt at St. John the Little.[293]

Additional evidence of early Christian churches with crypts can be found at Hermopolis Magna in Middle Egypt. An underground space lies below the east apse of the large basilica, dating from the mid-fifth century; the crypt was once accessible from the church via a flight

---

292. Samuil and Grossmann 1999, 361.
293. Samuil and Grossmann 1999, 361.

of steps, a corridor, and an antechamber.[294] Investigations at the south church of Hermopolis Magna, dated to the first half of the fifth century, also revealed a crypt, which combined an alcove for the remains of a deceased (a saint or a bishop according to Grossmann) and a small area for prayers.[295]

Another crypt was excavated by S. Donadoni at a fifth-century church near the so-called "Eastern Gate" of Antinoopolis (fig. 5.100).[296] The crypt is placed in the area of the sanctuary, in front of the now-disappeared apse, and therefore in a different location from that of the crypts in the Amheida church. Both churches housed tombs in the proximity of their crypts. The human remains from Antinoopolis consisted largely of women, in addition to two men and a child.[297] The burial pits from the same church were sealed with stones that were taken from the church and then covered with earth, suggesting that the tombs postdate the abandonment of the church.[298] This echoes what was seen by G. E. Bowen in the church of Deir Abu Matta in Dakhla.[299] Instead, the graves inside the church at Amheida were most likely dug when building 7 was still in use, since they were sealed and hidden below later floor levels of compacted clay.

On the basis of the evidence presented above, Grossmann classified burials inside known church crypts into two groups, namely those of martyrs or saints and those of members of the local élite or clergy, who were buried in proximity to an individual who had attained martyrdom and/or sainthood, in order to gain their intercession.[300] One example of the former is the above-mentioned church from Antinoopolis, where the crypt may have hosted the tomb of an important saint, while the graves inside the nave likely belonged to individuals who wished to be buried near the tomb of that particular holy man.[301] In theory, one might be tempted to recognize a similar situation at Amheida and identify the burials in room 1

---

294. The crypt, which incorporated features of an earlier Ptolemaic temple, was labeled by Grossmann as a Bischofsgräber: Grossmann 2002a, 129; figs. 59–60. See also Grossmann 2014, 109. Previously, Wace et al. (1959, 23–27) had put forth three possibilities for the use of the chapel, namely, that it was a confessional crypt, a repository of martyrs' relics, or a burial vault for the basilica's founder and other important benefactors.

295. Bailey and Grossmann 1994, 49–71, fig.5; Grossmann 2002a, 135; fig. 58; Grossmann 2014, 108–9.

296. Uggeri 1974, 37–67, fig. 14, pls. 18–21; Grossmann 2010, esp. 166–69.

297. Grossmann 2010, 169.

298. Grossmann 2010, 170.

299. As noted above, the burials inside the church of Deir Abu Matta were dug after the church was no longer in use, although the religious significance of the site would almost certainly not have been lost on the local Christian community.

300. Grossmann 2002a, 128; 131. See Grabar 1972 about *martyria* in early Christian architecture; with regard to Egypt, the author detected close typological connections between triconch basilicas and *martyria* from Palestine (Vol. 1, 384–85). On church interments as markers of social status, including clergy, see Yasin 2005, 446. See Rose 2013, 37–38 on the belief, common among early Christians, in the power of martyrs and saints to protect and benefit the deceased.

301. Grossmann 2010, 169. Grossmann believed the crypt to be too small for a proper burial; however, it could have hosted relics in a small niche piercing the east wall: see Grossmann 2002a, 135; Grossmann 2014, 107–8. Another striking example is offered by a church, mentioned above, that was discovered at Kom el-Ahmar, north of Minya (see n. 259); one must note, however, that many of the graves found at the site, as well as the underground vaulted burial associated with a saint's or martyr's interment, belonged to an area that was only later incorporated into the five-aisled basilica: cf. Grossmann 2002a, 131. Therefore, the crypt predates the erection of the church at Kom el-Ahmar, while at Amheida church and crypt belong to the same construction episode.

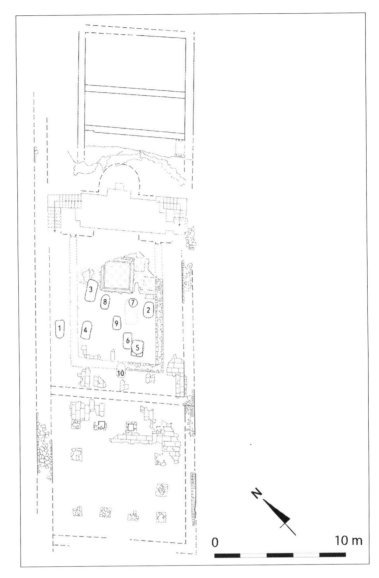

Fig. 5.100: Plan of the church at the "Eastern gate" of Antinoopolis, including the burials in the nave (after Grossmann 2010, 175, fig. 2; tracing by C. Fosen).

as those of individuals who venerated one or more of the deceased interred in the crypt.[302] However, there is no evidence to substantiate or reject such a hypothesis; more crucially, the archaeological evidence for Amheida paints a radically different picture, suggesting that most, if not all, of the individuals buried in the underground crypts were lay people, even if in some way privileged ones.[303]

302. Based on Grossmann's classification, it is also possible that one or more of the individuals interred in the crypt might have been followers of the holy man (or men) buried in the same underground space, most likely members of the clergy: see Grossmann 1991a, 208.

303. On the topic, see Török 2005, 171–73.

Furthermore, even in the presence of the tomb of a martyr or saint, one could argue that elite individuals might have wanted to be buried inside a church, including a crypt, not to be close to the tomb of a saint or martyr, but out of some "soteriological" desire to benefit from prayers and the celebration of liturgies by the living, thus independently from the existence of a "holy" tomb within a particular church.[304] If no martyr or saint had been buried in the crypts at Amheida, the question would then arise if there existed any perceived difference, in terms of prestige, between interments in the nave or aisles and those inside the crypts. One may posit that members of the higher clergy, who belonged to that church, would have been buried below the apse and the north *pastophorion* (or both *pastophoria*?), while local benefactors and their families would have been interred within room 1, that is, in a prestigious location but not in the area of the sanctuary.[305] Again, as discussed in Sec. 5.5 above, the evidence from Amheida does not point to the crypts (including room 3 below the apse) as the privileged location for burials of clergy; also, no evidence is available, either archaeological or documentary, concerning the identity of the deceased whose remains were investigated inside rooms 2 and 3. Therefore, given the data currently available, this discussion must remain essentially speculative.

304. Marinis 2009, 165–66. This reflects the beliefs of the time and is attested by primary sources, which highlight the wish of the deceased to garner special intercession, by means of the prayers of the living, on the occasion of the Second Coming of Christ: see Grossmann 2014, 93, based on Augustine's *De cura pro mortuis gerenda* (18, 22; cf. Zycha 1900, 658–59 and, for a commentary on this passage, Rose 2013, 30–37). Closeness to the sanctuary, and particularly to the area of the altar where the Eucharistic rites were performed, would have mattered considerably to the individuals who wished to be buried in a church: see Grossmann 2002a, 130–1. On the other hand, the position of a martyr's or saint's burial within a church was not necessarily bound by proximity to the altar, as the deceased would have had no need of intercessory prayers and rituals due to his holiness: see Grossmann 2002a, 136.

305. According to A. M. Yasin (2005, 447), evidence from North Africa, more specifically Tunisia, suggests that the apse and the central nave of early Christian churches were ideal locations for clerical burials. Cf. also n. 256 above. On church regulation concerning the burials of presbyters in the apses of churches from the second half of the fourth century, see Kötting 1984 and Duval 1988.

Chapter 6

The Painted Ceiling of the Church*

6.1. Introduction

As discussed above in Chapter 3, excavations inside room 1 revealed a rather limited stratigraphy, due to wind erosion and/or human intervention. Nevertheless, some evidence was found for the now-collapsed walls of the church. Based on the fragments that were retrieved, the walls were mud-brick features originally covered with mud plaster and, over it, a thin layer of white gypsum plaster.[1] No ornamentation was detected, suggesting that the four walls of the church were most likely white. The only exception is a large fragment of a corner of a wall (inv. 15756) found in room 1 during the investigation of DSU10 (fig. 6.1).[2] The plaster was painted in yellow and bore a decoration of parallel red lines on one side of the corner (presumably facing the east aisle), with shorter diagonal strokes painted in red and black. Considering that the fragment was discovered in the area facing the sanctuary, it is possible that it was once part of the no longer extant entrance into the apse (defined by the remains of engaged semi-columns F2 and F12).[3] Although not formal ornamentation, it is worth noting here that at least two graffiti and one roughly incised inscription were discovered in a large patch of wall plaster (FN82) (fig. 6.2).[4] The graffito was executed in a small, practiced hand and reads *ho theos* or "God"; its meaning here and what if any relationship it bears to the other inscriptions is still being studied.

Even though the walls of the church were seemingly white and left undecorated—certainly within room 1—a thoroughly different treatment is noticeable with regard to its ceiling. Thousands of plaster fragments, both small and large, were discovered throughout room 1 at floor level (fig. 6.3). Undoubtedly, these point to the existence of a flat ceiling in antiquity. Indeed, several of these pieces were found still adhering to a thick layer of mud bearing the imprints of palm ribs (fig. 6.4). A flat roof—unadorned or with painted decoration

---

* This chapter is based and builds on Aravecchia 2020b.
1. To be contrasted with oasite domestic architecture, in which one often finds whitewash around particular features, such as niches.
2. For a discussion of this unit, see Sec. 3.2 above.
3. Or it may have belonged to a structural element originally supporting the painted roof.
4. These will be discussed by D. M. Ratzan in a chapter that will be published as part of the companion volume.

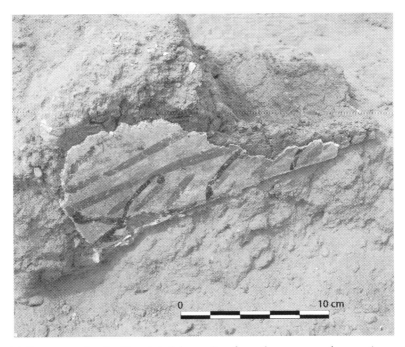

Fig. 6.1: Fragment of wall with painted decoration from the area near the apse (room 15).

Fig. 6.2: Large patch of wall plaster (FN82) from room 1, with traces of graffiti and inscriptions (line drawing superimposed).

on the inside—may draw inspiration from secular architecture.[5] It is also well attested in early Christian buildings. The church of ʿAin el-Gedida (Dakhla Oasis), dated to the early fourth century, was built with a vaulted ceiling,[6] but there is also abundant evidence elsewhere in

---

5. Warner 2018a, 459.
6. Possibly adapted (at least in its eastern half) from a pre-existing structure with a vaulted roof.

Fig. 6.3: Dorothea Schulz working on fragments of collapsed painted ceiling in room 1.

Dakhla for fourth-century Christian churches with flat roofs. Three well-known examples were found at Kellis. One is the Western Church, where traces of a collapsed flat roof, consisting of palm beams and ribs tied together with ropes, were discovered at floor level.[7] The Small East Church likely had a flat-roofed nave, while the apse was topped with a dome (*cupola*) and the two side rooms (*pastophoria*) were vaulted.[8] The walls of the Large East Church are not preserved to a sufficient height to know what kind of roof covered the building. However, a few palm beams were found in the stratigraphy of the church, thus pointing to the existence of a flat roof.[9] In the nearby Kharga Oasis, traces of a flat roof were detected in the debris of the so-called "Stone Church." Unfortunately, the archaeological remains of several other churches in the area do not offer enough information on what kind of ceiling originally covered them.[10]

7. Bowen 2002, 77.
8. Bowen 2003a, 158.
9. Bowen 2002, 67. Grossmann (2007, 107) suggested, instead, that the Large East Church was one of the first examples of churches in which a flat ceiling had been abandoned in favor of a saddleback roof. The church at Deir Abu Matta, located in Dakhla Oasis and recently dated to the fifth century (based on recent work carried out at the site) bears some evidence of a flat roof (now collapsed), at least in the area above the church's side aisles: see Winlock 1936, 24, also cited in Bowen 2012, 434.
10. Warner 2018a, 458.

Fig. 6.4: Large fragments of collapsed ceilings in the church's east and north aisles, with imprints of palm ribs still visible.

While the evidence for early Christian places of cult built with flat ceilings is relatively abundant, what is thus far unique to the church at Amheida is that it provides the clearest evidence for a painted flat ceiling in 4th-c. Christian architecture in Egypt.[11]

11. Cf. p. 367 and n. 52 below for recently-reassessed comparative evidence from the Large East Church at Kellis.

6.2. Excavation and Conservation of the Fragments

The study, collection, and conservation of the numerous pieces of painted plaster, found in DSU 5, 10, and 19 (with smaller quantities recovered from DSU 1, 3–4, and 6) took place after the entire surface of room 1 was divided into quadrants. This strategy was deemed necessary, as several fragments were found in the context of depositional units that spread throughout a large area. The aim was to allow excavators to retrieve information on the location of each fragment at floor level, and thus to reconstruct, with a higher degree of probability, its original placement before the collapse of the ceiling.

Different approaches were considered and used based on the condition and size of the fragments. Thousands of small pieces of painted plaster were collected on wooden trays,[12] then photographed and documented; finally, they were placed in cloth bags and carefully reburied in the proximity of their original place of discovery. As for larger fragments, they were first consolidated *in situ* by Bahaa Gomaa and Dorothea Schulz.[13] Solutions of Paraloid B72 (5%, 7%, and 10%) in acetone were used as part of the consolidation treatment, following preliminary cleaning with a soft brush. Gauzes were then applied and, once dry, the fragments were removed and a 15–20% Paraloid solution was applied to their undersides. Even though most patches of plaster were removed after consolidation, some large fragments, located in the southwest sector of the nave, were deemed to be too deteriorated for safe removal; they were therefore consolidated and documented but left *in situ* and subsequently re-buried.[14]

It is certain that most of the ceiling of room 1, both in the nave and in the north and south aisles (as well as in the east return aisle facing the sanctuary), was painted. However, not much is known about the area of the apse and of the north and south *pastophoria*. In Chapter 3, it has been discussed how the room to the north of the sanctuary (room 14) had completely disappeared, because of environmental or human factors, leaving only the superstructure (vault) of the north underground crypt (room 2). However, the excavation of the crypt itself, which took place in 2013, revealed a small number of finds that may be tentatively assigned to the context of room 14 at the church's floor level. Among these finds were fragments of white liquid mortar, with impressions of chisel marks, as well as fragments of painted plaster.[15] Their discovery in the fill of the crypt, which is completely undecorated, is likely due to the collapse of the upper part of the vault. It is through this hole that material from the room above (i.e., the north *pastophorion*) may have found its way into the crypt. It is unknown if the fragments of painted plaster recovered inside the north crypt were part of the wall or ceiling decoration inside the *pastophorion*. However, based on the evidence for white wall plaster inside room 1, it is more likely that these fragments were once part of the now-disappeared ceiling of the service room.

---

12. Sixty-six in total.
13. Mr. Gomaa is a conservator affiliated with Dakhla's local Antiquities Inspectorate; Ms. Schulz is a member of the Amheida archaeological team and was in charge of the process of conservation and documentation of the fragments of painted plaster from the church in 2012. I am especially grateful to her for her significant contribution.
14. Each of these patches was protected with cloth, then covered with clean sand.
15. Recovered as part of DSU103: cf. Sec. 3.3 above.

As for the apse and south *pastophorion* (rooms 15–16), the survey suggested that the two rooms completely disappeared. The excavation in 2023 of crypt 3 (below room 15) led to the discovery of a moderate number of fragments of painted plaster, which may have originated from the collapse of the apse above. No evidence of painted plaster was retrieved during the investigation of room 4 (south *pastophorion*) underneath room 16.

6.3. The Polychrome Decoration of the Ceiling

The study of the substantial remains of painted plaster, which were found in the church's debris, allowed for a reconstruction of the overall decorative program of the ceiling, although not in its full extent. In fact, data were missing from several areas within the church, especially in the west sector where human intervention, or more likely wind erosion, was particularly harsh.[16] More specifically, an adequately broad understanding is available of the different schemes that once decorated the underside of the roof in the central nave; less conclusive evidence exists to verify if the same type of geometric ornamentation was used to adorn the ceiling over the north and south aisles.

Both the larger patches and smaller fragments of painted plaster display a wide range of geometric shapes, combinations, and colors. A number of fragments were found that are decorated with a pattern of yellow, dark yellow, and purple bands (figs. 6.5–6). A dark yellow wavy line, with light yellow dots, fills the broad purple strip; it is perhaps to be understood as a schematic representation of a tendril, with leaves or flower buds that stem from it. Both edges of the purple band are marked by narrower light-yellow strips and, farther out, dark yellow bands. It is possible that these fragments were once part of a painted frame that ran around the geometric ornamentation of the ceiling.

Most remains of the painted ceiling reveal a main decorative scheme consisting of several patterns, which are made of interlocked geometric forms. Several fragments, including large patches, show that a design of squares, triangles, and lozenges once decorated a substantial area within the ceiling of the nave (figs. 6.7–8). The squares are painted in yellow, and each encloses a four-petal rosette in black paint.[17] Triangles, which are vertically divided into two halves, one in reddish/pink color and the other in yellow, rest on the four sides of each square. Elongated lozenges (also painted in reddish/pink and yellow in alternating areas and decorated with a small black lozenge in the middle) fill the remaining area. Sets of four lozenges are joined at one end, creating four-pointed stars.

---

16. A particularly challenging task was to ascertain how the different designs were laid out within the general decorative scheme of the ceiling, i.e., how one pattern shifted from one to another. The available evidence is very scanty in this respect.

17. The pigments still need to undergo chemical analysis, which may provide useful information on minerals used, production techniques, and provenance of these colors.

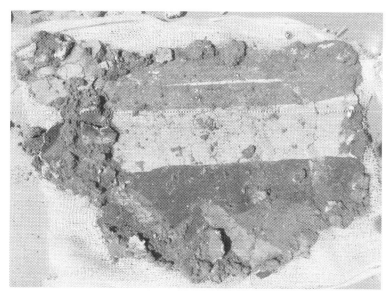

Fig. 6.5: Fragment of purple, yellow, and dark yellow band, with traces of a wavy vegetal motif.

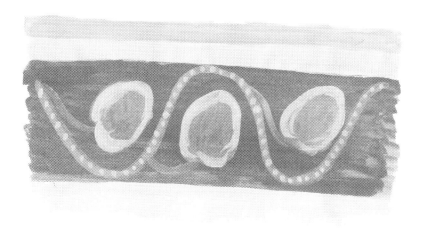

Fig. 6.6: Reconstruction of the purple, yellow, and dark yellow band motif (drawing by D. Schulz).

A different pattern, which was reconstructed based on the available evidence, comprises squatted pentagons, with three sides considerably shorter than the remaining two and filled with reddish/pink and yellow blotches (figs. 6.9–10). Surrounding the pentagons is an arrangement of lozenges, squares placed horizontally or diagonally, and triangles, all of which are, once again, filled with alternating areas in reddish/pink and yellow.[18] In the middle of each square is a smaller quadrangular shape painted in black, with parallel black lines filling the area between

---

18. Numerous fragments from the painted ceiling show traces of discoloration. In particular, yellow turned into creamy white, while pink seems to be due to the fading of the original red pigment.

Fig. 6.7: Fragment of the painted ceiling, with triangle-, lozenge-, and square-pattern.

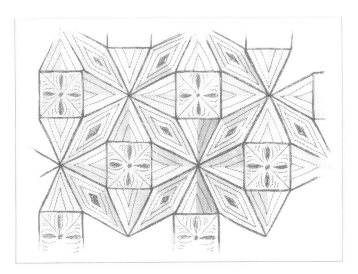

Fig. 6.8: Reconstruction of triangle-, lozenge-, and square-pattern (drawing by D. Schulz).

the latter and the outer edge.[19] The same kind of ornamentation was used in the adjoining triangles and lozenges. As for the hexagons, the same alternating colors are adopted, as well as parallel black lines that surround a schematic six-petal floral motif, located in the middle of each shape.

A third decorative scheme, for which fairly well-preserved evidence is available, is comprised of interlocked octagons, lozenges, and squares (figs. 6.11–13). As is the case with the other patterns, thick black lines define all these shapes, which are filled with parallel lines.

---

19. Parallel black lines, painted on top of reddish/pink and yellow areas, are common decorative features of all geometric shapes of the ceiling.

Chapter 6: The Painted Ceiling of the Church   361

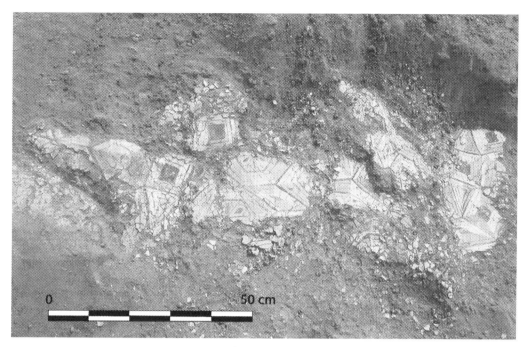

Fig. 6.9: Fragment of pentagon- and hexagon-pattern.

Fig. 6.10: Hypothetical reconstruction of pentagon- and hexagon-pattern (drawing by D. Schulz).

Fig. 6.11: Fragment of painted ceiling with octagons.

Fig. 6.12: Fragment of painted ceiling with eight-lozenge star.

The latter are superimposed to alternating areas that are painted in reddish/pink and yellow. The octagons are decorated with stylized eight-petal rosettes, drawn in black against a yellow background and placed in the middle of each shape.[20] In some combinations, the octagons

---

20. Following the custom noticed in the other patterns, the center of squares and lozenges are filled with small black square- and lozenge-designs, respectively.

Fig. 6.13: Reconstruction of pattern with octagons, squares, and eight-lozenge stars (drawing by D. Schulz).

are adjoined to each other along their horizontal and vertical sides, while squares rest on their diagonal sides (fig. 6.10). In another arrangement, lozenges are joined in groups of eight, thus forming large eight-pointed stars, while the remaining space is filled with squares of different sizes lying on all sides of octagons (fig. 6.11–12).[21]

The selection and elaborate arrangement of all these geometric shapes suggest that the original goal was to recreate the effect of a coffer design, one that was undoubtedly rather complex and is difficult (if not impossible, based on the currently available evidence) to reconstruct in its whole extent. The adoption of bright colors, used to paint areas defined by thick black lines, must have significantly enhanced the visual appreciation of the roof's geometric patterns.[22] This ornamentation would have stood in a striking contrast to the stark simplicity of the walls of the church, which were less decorated if not, as suggested above, completely white (fig. 6.14). Based on the available archaeological evidence for fourth-century Christian architecture in the Western Desert, and in particular Dakhla and Kharga Oases, churches were not extensively decorated at this time; this was certainly the case in comparison with later Egyptian examples, such as the well-known and richly decorated church of the Red Monastery at Sohag.[23]

21. Scantier evidence is available for this particular arrangement, which is, however, attested elsewhere in the region: cf. p. 367 below.
22. See MacDonald 1965, 174 on Roman painted ceilings, particularly on the visual effects of vaults' polychrome decoration. See also Roberts 1989 (esp. Ch. 3) and Bolman 2016.
23. Bolman 2006 and 2016. It should be acknowledged that churches such as the Red Monastery Church cannot be necessarily taken as representative of the full extent of church painted decoration in later centuries.

Fig. 6.14: Hypothetical reconstruction of the interior of the church at Amheida at night (by C. Ullendorff).

At the early fourth-century church complex of ʿAin el-Gedida (Dakhla), excavated in the mid-2000s, the walls of the church were coated with mud plaster and, over it, a layer of gypsum plaster, without any substantial trace of painted decoration.[24] A similar approach, which consisted of a fairly limited use of painted ornamentation, can be noticed in the treatment of the interior surfaces of the churches at Kellis, also dated to the fourth century.[25] Painted architectural features seem to have decorated only the area of the apse inside the Large East Church.[26] The apse in the Small East Church was also decorated with painted architectural elements, including columns and panels, while the rest of the room seems to have been gypsum coated and left undecorated.[27] The fairly poor remains of walls of the West Church do not show any evidence of polychromy. On the basis of the available evidence, it is reasonable to conclude that these early fourth-century churches of Egypt's Western Desert were often devoid of painted decoration on their walls, which were, in many instances, simply whitewashed.[28]

---

24. Aravecchia 2012, 399. The north wall shows traces of a small, two-line graffito, clearly not part of any decorative program: Bagnall and Dzierzbicka 2018, 532–23. The only evidence of painting within the nave were (tentatively) two feet of a largely disappeared figure, located on top of a rectangular niche in the east half of the north wall: Aravecchia 2018, 93.

25. Bowen 2002.

26. Knudstad and Frey 1999, 207–8; Bowen 2022b, 278–79.

27. Bowen 2003a, 158–61.

28. These churches were often found in rather poor condition, with their ceilings, as well as numerous courses of bricks from their walls, collapsed. Developing a knowledge of their interior decoration is therefore necessarily a speculative (if not impossible) undertaking.

One likely reason for painting these interior surfaces white was that such a light color would have contributed to brighten spaces that must have been rather dark. Indeed, in most of these buildings the main source of illumination would have been provided by oil lamps, placed in niches or on shelves, whose light would have reflected against the white walls.[29]

6.4. Discussion

The use of coffered ceilings is attested in Greece since the fifth century BCE, possibly originating from wooden models.[30] Scholars such as Pensabene see a gradual movement, already evident in the fourth century BCE, away from the "functional structure of coffers in favor of more decorative and illusionistic effects."[31] This emphasis on ornamentation is conveyed by means of new systems used in ceiling decoration, consisting of several geometric forms, including triangles, squares, hexagons, and octagons, combined either in a three-dimensional form or painted.[32] In the context of Roman art and architecture—especially in the decoration of both stucco and painted coffer ceilings, typical of Pompeian Second Style—the derivation from original wooden models is stressed by Ling, who cites several examples of coffer ceilings (either decorated in stucco or painted) from the first century BCE.[33] It seems that at this time artists adopted the same (or very similar) motifs and designs to decorate different types of surfaces, especially ceilings and floors, using various artistic media, including mosaic, stucco, and paint. In general, it was decorative schemes characteristic of coffer ornamentation that seem to have often inspired floor decoration.[34]

The popularity of this type of decoration in Roman and late antique Egypt should be understood (as suggested by Pensabene and also Cipriano) in the context of an artistic *koine* that was ultimately centered on Hellenistic Alexandrian models.[35] Among the most remarkable examples of geometric ornamentation is Tomb 2 at the Anfoushy cemetery.[36] The *hypogeum* is dated to the second-first century BCE and displays evidence of two distinct phases in the

---

29. For fenestration in early Christian churches in the northern Kharga Oasis, see Warner 2018a, 488.

30. Pensabene 1993, 108. Documentary and archaeological evidence of coffered ceilings in Egypt (both in stone and wood and also in painted imitations) is discussed, with relevant bibliography, in Whitehouse 2010, 1026. Ling (1991, 42) emphasizes the process by which coffer ornamentation, which was originally used in the context of flat ceilings, gradually came to be adopted between the second and first century BCE for the decoration of vaulted roofs in Roman domestic architecture.

31. Pensabene 1993, 108: "Ciò implica però una tendenza progressiva ad abbandonare la struttura funzionale del cassettone a favore di effetti sempre più decorativi e illusionistici, [...]." [English translation is my own.]

32. Pensabene 1993, 108.

33. Ling 1991, 42–47. Coffer ceilings in the House of the Cryptoporticus in Pompeii, in villa A at Oplontis, and in the "House of Augustus" in Rome are well-known examples.

34. Ling 1991, 48.

35. Cipriano 2008, 177; Pensabene 2001, 93. See Bolman (2006, 9–10) on the impact of Hellenistic traditions on early Christian paintings from Egypt, with a particular focus on the decorative program of the church at the Red Monastery in Sohag.

36. Venit 2002, 77–85; McKenzie 2007, 63, fig. 88.

decoration of its anteroom (room 1).³⁷ A painted geometric design was used to decorate the vaulted ceiling of this space. It consists of yellow octagons that alternate with small black squares, all these forms being outlined by polychrome (black, white, and red) lines.³⁸ Other *hypogea* with ceilings that showcase painted geometric decoration include Tomb 1 (rooms 1, 2, and 4)³⁹ and Tomb 5 (rooms 4 and 5 of Tomb 5),⁴⁰ both at Anfoushy. An additional example is from room 2 of *hypogeum* 3 located at the necropolis of Mustafa Pasha.⁴¹ Notwithstanding the generally accepted interpretation of these painted ceilings as inspired by real coffered ceilings, the possibility has been brought to scholarly attention that such geometric designs may have originated from textile patterns, in turn going back to textiles used in Macedonian burials.⁴²

The decoration of the ceilings inside Ptolemaic tombs in Alexandria may be linked typologically—if not in terms of the technique employed—to examples of architectural sculpture that also display a coffer design, even though in relief. Several of them can be found in the Graeco-Roman Museum in Alexandria and are dated to the end of the second and the beginning of the first century BCE.⁴³ These pieces, which Pensabene categorized into four different types, reveal a standard organization of coffers that are inserted in a lattice-type structure.⁴⁴ Nevertheless, with the beginning of the imperial period, the geometric forms that match those of the coffers are frequently laid out next to each other; that is to say, they are not enclosed within a frame, following an overall arrangement that is possibly inspired by floor mosaics.⁴⁵ Therefore, mosaic models may have affected not the origins of the architectural concept of the coffer ceiling, but rather some of its developments that tended towards more decorative and illusionistic effects.

Even though knowledge of decorated ceilings in Ptolemaic Egypt (as well as in later periods) is, generally speaking, more limited than for walls, we have also written sources attesting

---

37. Adriani 1966, n. 142, pl. 109; Pensabene 1993, 62, pl. 107, fig. 1005, pl. 117, figs. 1–2; Venit 2002, 80–82.

38. The painting of the vaulted ceiling is likely to be ascribed to the first phase of the decorative program executed inside this tomb: Venit 2002, 81. See also Adriani 1952, 68.

39. Tomb 1 is dated to the second century BCE (Adriani 1966, 192; Venit 2002, 77). The same pattern of large yellow octagons and small black squares, already noticed in Tomb 2, was used also in the decoration of the vaulted ceiling of rooms 2 (the burial room) and 4 (Venit 2002, 76–77). A geometric scheme of lozenges, inscribed in rectangles and outlined by polychrome bands, ornates the vault of room 1 (Venit 2002, pl. I). A very similar pattern can be seen in Roman art, in both the context of ceiling decoration and floor mosaics, during the first century BCE: see Ling 1991, 48–49.

40. A geometric design of lozenges inscribed in rectangles, very close to that found in room 1 of tomb 1, was used to decorate the vaulted ceiling of room 4 (Venit 2002, 88; pl. III). The design of the roof of room 5 is made of hexagons, which are defined by polychrome lines on white background (Venit 2002, 89).

41. The dating of *hypogeum* 3 is the first half of the third century BCE: Venit 2002, 65. See also Adriani 1936, 54. Venit (2002, 76) sees the geometric patterns used to decorate the ceilings in these Alexandrian tombs as typical of the Greek zone style. On this style, see also Ling 1991, 12–14 and Whitehouse 2010, 1022–23. According to Pensabene (2001, 93–94), the decoration in a chapel of Mausoleum 25 at El-Bagawat is suggestive of these earlier Alexandrian designs, especially in the painted *hypogea* of the Anfoushy necropolis. See also Zibawi 2003, 25, according to whom a strong similarity can be noticed between the same decorated ceiling at El-Bagawat and Tomb 3 at the Anfoushy cemetery (after Barbet 1985, 23).

42. Guimier-Sorbets 2004. See also Whitehouse 2010, 1026.

43. Pensabene 1993, 108; Cipriano 2008, 177.

44. Pensabene 1993, 521–23 (cat. nos. 973–78); 575; pl. 103.

45. Pensabene 1993, 108. See also Morricone 1965, 79–91.

to the use of actual coffer ceilings (not painted imitations) in monumental architecture, including Lucan's mention of the gilded coffered ceiling in Cleopatra's Egypt.[46] What is particularly significant in this context is that a long-standing architectural design, such as that of the coffered ceiling, seems to have been in wide use in Egypt for a long period. First attested in Hellenistic Egypt, it was never abandoned in the Roman period and was adopted, by means of painted imitations, in the decoration of early Christian churches.

With regard to Dakhla, additional evidence for the adoption of this decorative style in ceiling decoration is in the context of domestic and religious architecture. A wealthy house, labeled B/3/1 and dated to the second century CE, was excavated by C. A. Hope at Kellis and revealed an elaborate decorative project, including the collapsed remains of a ceiling decoration consisting of interlocking geometric forms.[47] Among these were rectangles, octagons, and lozenges forming eight-pointed stars, which were found also in the church at Amheida. According to H. Whitehouse, who studied the decoration of house B/3/1 at Kellis, these were meant to replicate the perspective effects created by a coffered ceiling.[48] As mentioned earlier, this seems to be the case also at Amheida. However, it is noteworthy that the decorative program in the Kellis house comprised not only geometric shapes but also included busts of deities inside the octagonal frames; no figural ornamentation was added, instead, to the decorative program of the church's ceiling at Amheida. Notably, the dating of the residence is much earlier than that of the church, as is the case for many other parallels for this design in Roman art. A decorative pattern consisting of squares, lozenges, and octagons (the latter filled with figurative elements) is attested also at Amheida in the so-called "House of Serenos" (B1, chronologically closer to the church), adorning the lower east section of the north wall of room 1 (the domed reception room).[49]

Further evidence of a coffered ceiling decoration was found at Kellis in Shrine I (the *mammisi*) of the temple complex dedicated to Tutu, dated to the first–second century CE.[50] Fragments of the collapsed vaulted ceiling reveal a similar emphasis on polychrome geometric ornamentation, based on interlocked geometric forms such as octagons, squares, and lozenges, which formed eight-pointed stars.[51]

An additional piece of evidence for this type of ceiling decoration is from one of the three churches excavated at Kellis. Following the discovery of the fragments from the Amheida church's ceiling, the excavator of the Large East Church concluded that remains of painted plaster, with a geometric design, that were found during the investigation of the church may have originally decorated its ceiling.[52]

---

46. Lucan, *Pharsalia* 10.111–12, cited in Whitehouse 2010, 1026, together with Athenaeus's reference to the gilded wood ceiling of the floating palace of Ptolemy IV Philopator (Athenaeus, *Deipnosophistae* 5.205c).
47. Hope 1990, 45; 47, pl. 2; Hope and Whitehouse 2006; Hope 2015, 207–9.
48. Hope and Whitehouse 2006, 321; 324 pl. 5; Whitehouse 2010, 1026; Whitehouse 2022b, 62.
49. McFadden 2013, pl. CXXVI, fig. 6; McFadden 2015, 197, fig. 131.
50. On the temple complex, cf. Hope, Bowen and Kaper 2022. On the painted decoration of the complex, cf. Whitehouse 2022a.
51. Whitehouse 2022a, 244, fig. 10.3; 245–47.
52. Bowen 2019, 369; 373; Bowen 2022b, 279.

The scheme of eight-lozenge stars alternating with squares is attested occasionally in Third Pompeian-Style ceilings, for example on a painted vault from the House of Gaius Julius Polybius at Pompeii, dated to the third quarter of the first century CE.[53] This design may have derived from patterns common in mosaic floors of the Augustan period.[54] Over time, it inspired the decoration of vaulted ceilings and also became an exceptionally popular design in mosaic floors of later centuries.[55] The eight-lozenge star design was, in fact, utilized in many different configurations and is attested to in mosaics from all over the territory controlled by the Romans, including modern-day Italy, Germany, Turkey, Syria, Tunisia, Algeria, and Libya.[56]

Much closer to Amheida, in the neighboring oasis of Kharga, there is evidence for the adoption of a very similar design in a Christian funerary context, one also chronologically closer to the church of Amheida. Mausoleum 25, one of the larger family tombs at the necropolis of El-Bagawat, contains a chapel whose domed ceiling is decorated with a coffered scheme (fig. 6.15).[57] The design is characterized by a range of interlocking squares, lozenges, and octagons that is strikingly similar (if not in some parts identical) to that used at Amheida. The choice of colors is different (mainly based on the use of a brownish-red, golden-yellow, and black hues), which may reflect the local availability of pigments. Furthermore, the octagons contain the four-petal rosettes that are also seen at Amheida, albeit in a rather more simplified version.[58]

The edges of the painted half-dome of the chapel at El-Bagawat are marked by three bands of varying widths and colors (the same yellow, reddish, and black used in decorating the apsidal basin). These bands surrounding the geometric ornamentation are similar to the thick yellow and purple lines that likely delimited (based on the available fragments) the ceiling of the church at Amheida, despite the differing choice of colors. G. Cipriano considers the whole mausoleum as belonging to so-called "Phase II.2," broadly dated between the end of the fourth and the beginning of the fifth century CE, and therefore later (but only marginally so) than

---

53. Ling 1991, 68, fig. 69.

54. See Ling 1991, 67–68, who highlights the prominence of this Third Style trend, in contrast to the earlier adoption of forms, inspired from painted ceilings, for the decoration of floors. On geometric decoration of Roman floor mosaics in domestic contexts, and particularly their adoption to exhibit developing social dynamics (from early to late Roman Imperial houses), see Swift 2009, 27–104. At pp. 102–3, Swift distinguishes figurative decoration, which grants "the possibility of inclusion" (based on the viewer's ability to read the scene), from geometric designs, which "offer much less possibility of comprehension," and argues convincingly that the latter can be seen as "more effective agents in a patron-client relationship than figurative designs."

55. Ling 1991, 67–68. Whitehouse also pointed out that this decorative scheme on a ceiling is typologically linked to mosaic floor designs (while also being suggestive, as mentioned earlier, of a coffered ceiling): Hope and Whitehouse 2006, 321. On the relationship between floor and wall mosaics in the fourth century, see also James 2017, 157–60, esp. 158.

56. Balmelle et al. 2002, pl. 138, fig. e; pl. 146, fig. e; pl. 154, fig. b; pl. 173, figs. d–e; pl. 174, figs. a–d, f; pl. 176, figs. e–f; pl. 177, figs. a, d; Balty 1995, 335, fig. 1.

57. Fakhry 1951, 83 (pl. VI: reconstruction). See also Zibawi 2003, 24, fig. 14; Zibawi 2005, 21–25, 30–31; Cipriano 2008, 46–49 (where she also discusses the possible functions of this chapel, as well as of two mausolea in its proximity), 169–94, especially 175–77.

58. Zibawi 2005, 24. Two fragments of decorative architectural sculpture from Oxyrhynchus, found by E. Breccia and now in the Graeco-Roman Museum in Alexandria, showcase a very similar geometric scheme, with octagons surrounding rosettes: Breccia 1933, pl. XLVI, fig. 162. J. M. Harris (1960) later studied these fragments, as well as many others that had been found at Oxyrhynchus. See also McKenzie 2007, 269.

CHAPTER 6: THE PAINTED CEILING OF THE CHURCH 369

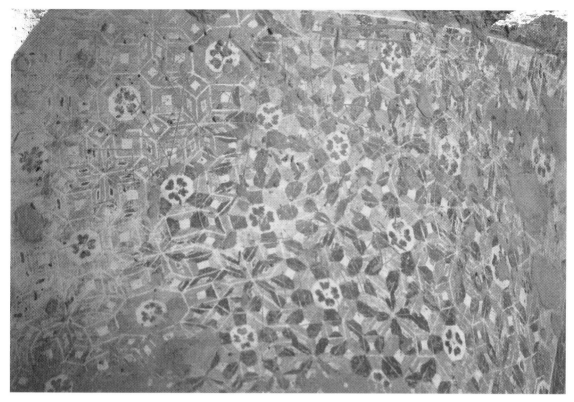

Fig. 6.15: Painted geometric decoration from Mausoleum 25 at El-Bagawat (author's photo).

the church at Amheida.[59] It is clear, however, that both the painted roof from El-Bagawat and the fragments from the ceiling of the Amheida's church stem from the same decorative style or tradition, one that was based on the use of geometric shapes to create the visual effects of a coffered ceiling. It is also evident, from these and other examples, that such a style had a long life in Egypt.[60]

In addition to the examples from Amheida and El-Bagawat, this kind of geometric ornamentation is widely attested at numerous monastic sites in Egypt, although not necessarily in the context of ceilings. Examples can be seen, for instance, among the ruins of monastic buildings that were excavated at Saqqara.[61] At the *laura* of Bawit in Middle Egypt, a wide-ranging selection of vegetal and geometric motifs was used to decorate the chapels of the local ascetics; Chapel XXXII, in particular, was once adorned with a geometric design, consisting of interlocked squares and triangles forming lozenges, that is very suggestive of one of the

---

59. Cipriano 2008, 102. See also Pensabene 2001, 93–94 on the chronology of the chapel.
60. The use of polychrome painting within Egyptian architectural ornamentation is discussed, among others, by Bolman (2006, 10) and Rutschowscaya (1986, 102). See Pensabene 1993, 108 on Egyptian coffered ceilings.
61. Saqqara: Van Moorsel and Huijbers 1981; Rassart-Debergh 1981a–b; Rassart-Debergh 1998, 29.

patterns used in the church at Amheida.⁶² This chapel also shows evidence of a more complex scheme, made of interconnected hexagons, squares, and triangles, which is, once again, found at Amheida.⁶³

This type of decoration is attested not only in Egypt but also throughout the Mediterranean region, where it was adopted from the Roman period to late antiquity.⁶⁴ Ample evidence for such an adoption of geometric forms and patterns is available at many well-known sites, including Antioch in Asia Minor, Abila and Jerash in Jordan, and, in the western Mediterranean, Aquileia. At Antioch, over 300 pavement mosaics were found (largely in domestic contexts) between 1932 and 1939, all dated to between the early second and the sixth century CE.⁶⁵ Several of these mosaics comprise figural and vegetal ornamentation, but geometric patterns often accompany and frame these motifs.⁶⁶

There are also many examples of pavements that exclusively consist of geometric forms and testify to the popular adoption of patterns that are also seen in the Amheida church. For instance, the decoration consisting of squares and triangles (as seen in figs. 6.6–7) is also found in Antioch mosaic pavements. Its use is attested between the first century BCE and the first century CE and was adopted also at Pompeii.⁶⁷ However, beginning in the early second century CE, this pattern seems to be replaced by more elaborate geometric compositions, in particular by the star made of eight lozenges.⁶⁸ At Amheida, the former motif is not supplanted by the latter, but they are both used in the same decorative program in the fourth century CE. In fact, a study of larger fragments from the collapsed ceiling reveals a complex arrangement of octagons, eight-pointed stars, squares (as well as diagonal squares), all combined within the same composition (fig. 6.12). Still within Egypt, there is further evidence for the adoption of the eight-lozenge star in early Christian art. One example is the painted ceiling of an apse inside Mausoleum 25 at El-Bagawat, mentioned earlier.⁶⁹ The same basic pattern can be observed in a capital from the fifth-century basilica at Hermopolis; here, the motif appears in the context of architectural ornamentation and attests to the popularity of this design beyond the fourth century.⁷⁰

---

62. See Clédat 1999, 30; pls. 25–26. The motif decorates the arch of a niche piercing the south wall of the chapel. It is important to notice that the painted decoration in the chapels may be later, even significantly so, than the evidence from Amheida.

63. Lucchesi-Palli 1990, 117–18; pl. 23.1, 3–4. The evidence from Bawit shows, within the overall geometric scheme, vegetal and figural motifs. These seem to be almost completely absent in the decoration of the church at Amheida, apart from the pattern of the simplified rosette.

64. Several examples come from mosaics found in Italy, France, Spain, and Tunisia: Balmelle et al. 2002, 322–23.

65. Stillwell 1961, 48.

66. For example, in the "Atrium House": Levi 1947, 15 ff. and 373. On examples from Egypt, cf., most recently, Guimier-Sorbets 2021.

67. Levi 1947, 374.

68. Two well-preserved examples are from Room 1 in the "House of Dionysos and Ariadne" and in room 1 of the "House of the Drinking Context": Levi 1947, pl. CI, figs. a–b.

69. Zibawi (2003, 23–25; 2005, 24) describes the stars as crosses.

70. Pensabene 1992, 291, fig. 25.

A particularly popular pattern in late antiquity consists of octagons and hexagons that harmoniously alternate with crosses.[71] The design is seen as a development of the above-mentioned scheme consisting of geometric shapes including eight-lozenge stars, with early examples seen in mosaic pavements in Pompeii.[72] This configuration is attested, in the context of both floor and ceiling decoration, throughout the Mediterranean region in late antiquity. One early example is the mosaic pavement of the cryptoporticus in Diocletian's Palace at Split.[73] An especially beautiful *comparandum* is offered by the mosaic vault of the ambulatory in the fourth-century church of Santa Costanza in Rome.[74] Still in the Italian peninsula, the same decorative pattern is attested in both the North and South Basilicas at Aquileia, built by Bishop Theodorus in the early fourth century.[75]

An analogous decorative scheme, consisting of polygons and crosses, is found in the decoration of the vaulted ceiling of a tomb at Abila, in Jordan, dated to the third or fourth century CE, and in the later church of Procopius at Gerasa/Jerash, dated to 526/27.[76] It is also attested to in domestic contexts, such as in the "House of the Phoenix" (late fifth century) at Antioch in Asia Minor.[77] Numerous examples of this ornamental style (from the Mediterranean region, including Egypt) display geometric shapes like octagons and hexagons, with vegetal and/or figural motifs often filling them.[78] The underside of the ceiling in the Amheida church is decorated with an equally compact scheme of interlocked geometric forms. As mentioned earlier on, the latter are lacking any figural ornamentation, but they are not empty areas filled with colors; rather, they are decorated with the same geometric shapes, painted with thin black lines, and progressively decreasing in size towards the center. Furthermore, vegetal motifs, such as four- or eight-petal rosettes, can be seen inside the octagons, as well as in some squares.

The geometric scheme of crosses and polygons was seen by Levi as an obvious borrowing of a coffered-ceiling ornamentation, which was translated, together with its strong sense of depth, into mosaic floor decoration.[79] If this was the case, the process would have to be seen as a reversal of what occurred in the fourth century, for example in the church of Santa Costanza in Rome. The mosaic decoration of the vaulted ceiling has been, in fact, understood as sharing themes and formats that ultimately derived from those of mosaic floors.[80]

71. This design is comparable in part to the arrangement found on large patches of collapsed ceiling from the church at Amheida. These fragments show octagons and elongated hexagons combined in the same design, but square crosses are absent (even though the eight-lozenge stars share the basic shape of the cross): see Zibawi 2005, 24 with regard to the design from Mausoleum 25 at El-Bagawat.
72. Stern 1958, 194, fig. 30 (also cited in Zibawi 2005, 24).
73. Dated to 305 CE. See Bulić 1929, 164, fig. 69, and Levi 1947, 412–13. This geometric scheme is attested in many other examples, mostly in the context of mosaics, that were found in areas including modern France, Italy, Great Britain, Germany, Greece, and Turkey: Balmelle et al. 2002, 278–81.
74. Levi 1947, 415; Stern 1958, 194, fig. 30.
75. Levi 1947, 413–14. See also Bertacchi 1994, 67–84, in particular figs. 67 and 71. Mosaics from both churches include figural and geometric motifs filling the octagons that flank the crosses.
76. Abila: Ling 1991, 190, fig. 208, 191. Jerash: Lucchesi-Palli 1990, 119; pl. 23, fig. 5. See also Balty 1995, 111–38 on late antique mosaics from Jordan, within the context of Near Eastern mosaic production.
77. Lucchesi-Palli 1990, 119, pl. 23, fig. 6; Stillwell 1961, 54.
78. For example, in house B/3/1 at Kellis: Hope and Whitehouse 2006, 321, 324.
79. Levi 1947, 404; Zibawi 2005, 24.
80. Leatherbury 2018, 88.

Based on the rich body of available evidence, building 7 at Amheida was purposely conceived as a church following the most current architectural and decorative styles of its times, despite being at the edge of the Roman Empire. Its builders adopted not only the layout and basic features of the basilica, but also decorative elements (chiefly the geometric decoration of the ceiling) that were popular throughout the Mediterranean region in late antiquity. One can hardly achieve a thorough understanding of the exact process by which these artistic idioms were transmitted. As has been done in other contexts,[81] one could hypothesize the existence of some form of pattern-books, which local or itinerant artists could have exhibited to their customers and then used in their work. Across the broader Mediterranean region, there are instances where exact replicas of the same mosaics were found at considerable distances from each other.[82] One possible explanation would be not only the use of pattern-books, but also the involvement of travelling artists, who would have brought along their knowledge and familiarity with artistic trends and idioms.[83] This could also pertain to other mediums such as painting. However, at least with regard to the church of Amheida, no evidence is available to support this conjecture.

Once again, with respect to the mode (or modes) of transmission of these artistic trends from the larger centers of the Nile Valley and the Delta, on one hand, and the oases of the Western Desert, on the other, conclusive answers may yet have to be found. Nevertheless, it can be reasonably assumed that it was the desire to create places that were both appealing to the eyes and spiritually uplifting, in which these desert communities could gather and worship, that may have led to the adoption of this type of ornamentation. Not only this; the Christians of the oases were also clearly aware of the trends of religious art and architecture of the early fourth century and wished to erect (and decorate) churches that were clearly identifiable as Christian, thus connecting these communities with the wider Christian world of late antiquity.

---

81. Levi 1947, 9. On the subject of pattern books, see Whitehouse 2022b, esp. 76–77.
82. Levi 1947, 9.
83. McFadden 2014, 368. On the ongoing debate about the existence and use of such pattern-books in antiquity, cf., for example, Whitehouse 2010, 1015 and Froschauer 2008, 10–11.

Chapter 7

Discussion of the Archaeological Evidence

7.1. The Development of the Church Complex

The church in Area 2.3, consisting of room 1 and the now-vanished tripartite sanctuary (i.e., rectangular apse and north and south service rooms), was built as one construction episode, in phase with the underground crypts. Other than the compact layer of mudbricks discovered at foundation level in test trench 2 (DSU30),[1] there is no clear evidence that pre-existing architectural features were razed and built over or incorporated into building 7.[2] As mentioned in Section 7.5 below, further excavation is needed in the area surrounding the church complex in order not only to clarify the topographical relationship of the church with the adjacent built environment (as well as the rest of the cityscape), but also to resolve still-standing questions of chronology.

    The construction history of the rooms in the south annex of building 7 is difficult to establish in detail. The features that are part of the staircase (i.e., walls F36, F37, F39, and flight of steps F35; cf. fig. 4.3) seem to be contemporary with the west wall of room 12 (F58), which is bonded with the south wall (F40) of building 7. In turn, F40 is bonded with walls F44 and F76, which form the east and west boundaries of the south sector. Therefore, it is certain that rooms 5–6 and 8–12 were built as part of the same construction episode. Room 7 may be a later addition to the complex within this area. Its west and east walls (F43 and F41 respectively) are bonded with the room's north wall (F42) and abut the south wall of the complex, i.e., F40. However, an abutting relationship of walls is not necessarily to be interpreted as evidence of construction phases that are chronologically distant. In other words, it cannot be ruled out that the south sector of the complex was conceived and built as one episode.

    1. See Sec. 3.3.2, esp. p. 116; cf. also figs. 3.71–73.
    2. As is the case with other fourth-century churches in Dakhla, such as the church of ʿAin el-Gedida, the Small East Church at Kellis, and the church recently excavated at ʿAin el-Sabil (see, respectively, Aravecchia 2018, 187–94; Bowen 2003a, 158–62; Bayoumy and Masoud 2019, 358). With regard to DSU30 (which was revealed in the northwest corner of building 7 at Amheida, but likely extended over a larger area below it), it is unclear if the mudbricks that formed this unit were originally part of a structure standing on the top of the hill (Area 2.3), or were brought there to level the site before the foundations of the church were laid out.

Further investigation, especially outside the south wall of building 7, is needed in order to verify this hypothesis.

A second problem of chronology is to determine if the south annex was built in phase with the church (rooms 1–4) or at a significantly later stage.[3] As with the question of the construction of the annex itself, a definitive answer, if even possible, would require further excavation in and around building 7. That said, the investigation of room 13's foundations revealed possible evidence which points to a later chronology for rooms 5–13. Within this small space, north-south oriented walls F37 and F58 abut the foundation courses of wall F13, which is the south wall of rooms 1 and 4 and forms the south boundary of the church. Excavations revealed a vertical crack running through the foundation courses of F13, in the sector between F37 and F58. The fissure was repaired in antiquity using a wooden beam that was inserted into the wall, replacing one course of bricks. The west end of this beam is concealed by the north end of F37, thus suggesting that it was inserted before F37 was built to its full height. Furthermore, this area of F13's foundations must have been exposed during the construction of the entire room consisting of spaces 11+13, as F37 and F58 share a foundation trench.[4] A layer of mortar, rich in sand, was smeared over the beam, likely to keep it in place within the foundation wall. Traces of this layer were also found against the western face of F58, suggesting that the crack in F13's foundations occurred before the construction of the south annex. It is possible that, when the south annex was built, the crack was mended by inserting the wooden beam into F13's foundations.

Building 7 shows evidence of post-abandonment reoccupation inside the south annex, particularly in rooms 7 and 9 (and possibly in room 6). In room 9, a heap of debris (DSU64) consisting of fragments of wall plaster and mud-brick rubble, as well as some sand, forms a low, elongated mound at a distance of ca. 60 cm south of wall F43. This deposit rests on a thin layer of sand (DSU63), which may have accumulated within room 9 after its abandonment and, most likely, when the flat roof of this space was no longer intact. The mound of debris seems to have suffered, along its west side, from wind erosion, which generally affected the western half of room 9, including the floor and walls. It is likely that DSU64 is a destruction deposit that accumulated in the southeast corner of room 9 after this sector of the complex (if not its entirety) had fallen into disuse. At a later stage, the layer seems to have been artificially reshaped. A large amount of debris was removed along the east wall and in the southeast corner of room 9, as well as in front of the entrance into room 7, likely to prepare this area for reuse. Following this preliminary work, a two-burner stove (F45)[5] was built against the southeast corner of room 9, abutting south wall F40 and east wall F43, both white-plastered. The west end of the stove rests above the debris layer (DSU64). The area that was cleared along wall F43, from its north end to where the stove was built, was smeared with a layer of mud plaster (F53).

---

3. This issue is touched upon also in Sec. 7.4.1 below, esp. pp. 388–89, in the context of the discussion of an ostrakon (O.Trim. 2.532) that was found in the foundation fill of room 11.

4. It is possible that the crack occurred and was already visible during the construction of the nave. This would suggest that the south annex was built shortly after, since the foundations would have not likely been visible at a later stage.

5. For a detailed description of this feature, see Sec. 4.6 above (esp. pp. 201–05).

This coating formed a sloping surface on top of DSU64 and abutted the wooden threshold in the doorway that opened onto room 7.

A second two-burner stove (F61)[6] was built against the northwest corner of room 7. The relationship of this feature with the two floor levels found inside the room cannot be established, since no traces of floors are extant in the area where the stove lies. Residues of mud plaster on the north wall (F42) and on the eastern side of the stove suggest that the walking surface around the stove was once smeared with the same plaster. Furthermore, its elevation must have been lower than that of the original floor (F63) of room 7.[7] However, it is likely that the stove was not built before floors F62 and F63 were laid out in room 7. Rather, it seems to be in phase with stove F45, which was undoubtedly built during a phase of reoccupation of this area, following, as mentioned earlier, a period of abandonment. Indeed, it appears that stove F61 was built when the floors inside room 7 were already damaged, while stove F45 was created after the accumulation of a layer of sand and debris inside room 9. Furthermore, as stoves are generally built in spaces that are open (or at least partially so), in order to allow smoke to escape, it is conceivable that the flat roofs inside both rooms 7 and 9 were no longer intact. The sand deposit (DSU63) that accumulated above the floor in room 9, but under debris layer DSU94 and plastered surface F53, further supports this hypothesis.

Another feature that may belong to the same phase of reoccupation as the two stoves and plastered surface F53 is a low rectangular platform made of bricks (F47), which is located in the southwest corner of room 6. It abuts the west wall (F41) and the south wall (F40) of this room and rests on top of its upper floor. Therefore, this platform is the latest feature to have been added within room 6 in antiquity.

7.2. A pulpit?

The L-shaped mud-brick feature (F26), which abuts the south and west sides of F11 (the easternmost pillar of the north colonnade; cf. figs. 3.4 and 3.23), was tentatively identified as the foundations of a podium (*bema*), chiefly on the basis of its location and of parallels from other fourth-century churches in the Great Oasis. This feature, consisting of a raised platform that could be accessed via a set of steps, was strategically placed in one corner of the church's central nave. The location of F26 would have allowed anyone standing on top of it a high degree of visibility, owing also to the higher elevation of the podium in relation to the nave's floor. Therefore, this feature might have served as an *ambo* (pulpit), used by a member of the local clergy to read the Scripture or to deliver a homily. Anyone sitting or standing in the nave, but also in the north and south aisle (as well as in the west return aisle and in the area facing the

---

6. See Sec. 4.4, esp. pp. 181–82; figs. 4.44–45.
7. Further investigation along wall F42 allowed us to ascertain that the remains of plaster, which are undoubtedly in phase with stove F61, are not found under F63.

sanctuary), would have been able to see and hear the preacher standing on the podium easily. The view from the side aisles would have been partial, although not completely hindered, due to the presence of the north, south, and west colonnades (cf. fig. 6.14). One should also consider the possibility that there was seating at an upper level over the rooms to the south side of the nave. This location would also have been optimal for people (perhaps women or catechumens) to attend the rites being performed in the church. However, no archaeological evidence is available to substantiate this hypothesis, other than the existence of a staircase (F35) leading to an upper level or the roof of the complex.

Ambones in Christian Egyptian churches are commonly found in the northeast corner of the nave.[8] This further corroborates the possible interpretation of F26 as a podium; significantly, it points to a continuity, in the choice of location for this type of architectural element, already from the earliest developments of Christian architecture in Egypt.[9]

A few parallels are available for this architectural feature from early Christian churches within Dakhla Oasis.[10] The fourth-century church discovered at ʿAin el-Gedida, in the proximity of Kellis, features a well-preserved, mud-brick rectangular platform, built in the central passageway that once separated the church itself from a large gathering hall to the north (fig. 7.1).[11] The top of the platform, which was originally coated with a thick layer of mud plaster,[12] was reached via three steps of different sizes that projected into the church, with no steps protruding into the adjoining hall to the north. Thus, access to this feature was exclusively from the church's nave, even though the person standing on top of the platform, against the large central passageway, would have been easily seen and heard by the people sitting (or standing) in both rooms, not just the church. At a later stage, however, the doorway was sealed off with mudbricks, for reasons that cannot now be ascertained. The new wall completely blocked the view of the stepped platform from within the gathering hall; thus, it is certain that the podium lost its original function at this stage.[13] The location of the podium in the church at ʿAin el-Gedida differs from that of F26 in the church at Amheida, but their function (and possibly their layout) may have been similar.

Excavations at the Large East Church at Kellis, which shares a remarkable number of similarities with the church at Amheida,[14] did not reveal a stepped podium built against the easternmost column of the north colonnade. Nevertheless, a stepped structure was found in this church, although in a different location, that is to say, against the inner column in the

---

8. Basilios 1991, 111–12. On the *ambo* in early Egyptian churches, cf. also Grossmann 2002a, 191–92 (193 on *ambones* in early monastic churches).

9. Albeit with some variations, as attested by some of the examples mentioned below.

10. It is worth emphasizing, once more, how the interpretation of F26 as the foundations of an *ambo* of some kind is almost exclusively based on a comparison with similarly placed *ambones* elsewhere (especially that in the church of Shams el-Din in Kharga; see the last paragraph of this section).

11. Aravecchia 2018, 93–98; Aravecchia 2022, esp. 207–9. Cf. also Sec. 2.1.1.

12. No traces of white gypsum plaster were found.

13. Although the church continued to be accessible, via a passageway in the northwest corner, from the gathering hall to the north.

14. For parallels with the church at Amheida, cf. Sec. 7.6; for a general introduction to the churches excavated at Kellis, with relevant bibliography, cf. Sec. 2.1.1. The most recent publication by the excavator of the churches at Kellis is Bowen 2023.

CHAPTER 7: DISCUSSION OF THE ARCHAEOLOGICAL EVIDENCE 377

Fig. 7.1: View (to north) of the stepped podium and of the wall sealing the central doorway inside the church of ʿAin el-Gedida.

west return aisle.[15] The feature, interpreted by Grossman as an *ambo*,[16] was associated with the scanty remains of other features, which, according to the church's excavator, make the interpretation of the stepped feature as an *ambo* more challenging.[17] Due to heavy wind erosion and/or artificial destruction, only the foundations of the west colonnade are visible in the church at Amheida; therefore, it is impossible to know if it supported a stepped structure similar to that revealed in the Large East Church at Kellis. However, the location of the stepped feature against the west colonnade of the latter would have granted a high degree of visibility to anyone standing upon it. This is in line with what was hypothesized earlier on with regard to F26 in the church at Amheida. If one considers that no other *ambones* were found in the Large East Church, the identification of the stepped feature against its west colonnade as a podium, to be used by a priest or a reader, remains quite compelling.

Another fourth-century church was excavated recently in the vicinity of Kellis at the site of ʿAin el-Sabil. This church features the unique characteristic of having two stepped podiums, located at a short distance from each other.[18] One *bema* faced the apse and was placed on the

15. Bowen 2002, 72, pl. 3, 73.
16. Grossmann 2002b, 155.
17. Bowen 2002, 73.
18. Bayoumy and Masoud 2019, 357, pl. 6. Cf. also Secs. 2.1.1 and 7.6.

main axis of the church, with steps built along the west side of the podium; unusually, it was built on top of a platform (with steps along its short north and south sides) that once allowed access from the nave onto the apse. A second *bema*, with an almost-square platform accessed via two steps, was built against the second column from the east in the north colonnade, facing the nave.[19] The location of this feature suggests possible similarities, in terms of function, with F26 in the church at Amheida (bearing in mind the above-mentioned caveats about the poor survival of F26).

The fourth-century church at Shams el-Din, located in Kharga Oasis, offers the closest parallel, in terms of the location of a stepped podium, with feature F26 in the church at Amheida.[20] Indeed, the *ambo* in the Shams el-Din basilica was built against the north colonnade's easternmost column, facing southwards onto the central nave (fig. 2.20). Even though it is impossible to know how typologically similar this *ambo* and F26 were (due to the lack of evidence above foundation level in the feature from Amheida), it seems reasonable to assume that both structures fulfilled the same function, i.e., to allow a member of the local clergy to read the Scriptures or preach from a position of greater visual prominence.

7.3. Rooms 5, 11, and 13: A Double Staircase?

The interpretation of the spaces that were labeled as rooms 11 and 13, located to the south of the church, is challenging in light of their very poor state of preservation.[21] Nevertheless, both rooms seem to have been functionally related to the adjacent staircase (room 5).[22] Indeed, the west and east walls of rooms 11 and 13 (F37 and F58, respectively),[23] the south wall of room 11 and the entire south annex (F40), as well as the west and south walls of room 5 (F36 and F39) and staircase (F35; also part of room 5), were built as part of the same construction episode (figs. 4.3; 4.78). The foundations of parallel walls F37 and F58 were laid at about the same level and the fill between them was deposited at the same time.[24]

The distance between F37 and F58 is ca. 110 cm and is equal to the width of the space between F37 and F36, which define the east and west boundaries of staircase F35 in room 5. It seems possible, if not likely, that the area above rooms 11 and 13, which in fact formed a

---

19. Bayoumy and Masoud 2019, 358. It is unclear as to the reason why two *bemata* were erected so close to each other, which is unattested elsewhere in Dakhla or Kharga; it is possible that the two mud-brick features performed different functions, but presently there is no evidence, archaeological or documentary, that can shed any light on this matter.
20. Cf. Secs. 2.3 and 7.6 for a brief description of the church, parallels with the church at Amheida, and relevant bibliography.
21. Cf. Sec. 4.8 for a detailed description of the two spaces.
22. For a discussion of the features and stratigraphy of room 5, see Sec. 4.2.
23. F37 is shared with staircase/room 5.
24. No separate foundation trenches for the two walls were identified.

Fig. 7.2: Direction (conjectural) of the staircase in rooms 5, 11, and 13.

single space,[25] also had a second flight of steps (ascending northwards). This would have been accessed from a middle landing above room 10, after climbing flight of steps F35 southwards, and would have led to an upper landing at its north end, above building 7 (fig. 7.2).

Archaeological evidence undeniably attests that square staircases, built around a central pillar, are most common in mud-brick architecture.[26] Nevertheless, parallel double staircases are also attested, especially in stone architecture.[27] At Amheida, the lower flight of steps (F35) was supported by a solid rectangular platform of mudbricks; it is possible that in room 11+13 a different solution was adopted, i.e., a suspended staircase with space for storage underneath,

25. See Sec. 4.8, esp. pp. 214–15.

26. See, for example, the fourth-century church at Shams el-Din (Kharga Oasis), which has a staircase built around a central pillar. Notwithstanding the different type of staircase, this church shares many similarities with the Amheida church; even the location of the staircase is similar, i.e., to the south of the church and accessible via a small room (see Bonnet 2004, 84, fig. 69; McKenzie 2007, 270, fig. 450).

27. For examples of double staircases in fifth- and sixth-century Christian architecture in Egypt (thus, a bit later than the staircase in building 7 at Amheida), see Grossmann 2002a, pl. 7 (west church at Ain Makhura); pls. 19–20 (five-nave basilica at Abu Mina, southeast side); pl. 22 (north basilica at Abu Mina, southwest corner outside the church); pl. 104 (east church at Abu Mina); pl. 49 (funerary church at Hawara, southwest corner); pl. 59 (basilica at Hermopolis Magna, northwest of the church); pl. 92 (south church at Ostracine).

for which several parallels are available.[28]

The south sectors of walls F37 and F58, in room 11, are coated with a layer of mud plaster for a length of about 2.40 m from the south wall. The reason why the plaster does not continue all the way to wall F57 (or even to wall F13, which is abutted by F37 and F58) is unknown. Given the fact that the plaster stops neatly at the same distance from the south along both F37 and F58, it seems clear that this is not simply due to the state of conservation of the features in this area. A possible explanation is that the space from the south face of wall 57 to the point where the plaster ends on F37 and F58 might have incorporated a cupboard or closet, which was removed at some point before or after the abandonment of the area. In mud-brick architecture of this period, the space below stairs was often filled with features such as cupboards.[29] The existence of a wooden closet of some kind in the north part of room 11 would explain not only the absence of mud plaster in that area, but also the very poor quality of wall F57's south face, as it would have been concealed from view by the cupboard. The presence of a wooden feature in this space in antiquity seems very likely. However, this reconstruction remains a conjecture, as we lack sufficient archaeological evidence. It is plausible that wall F57 was built to strengthen the stability of the foundations, as well as provide additional support for the (possible) suspended staircase in rooms 11+13, in the area where the north end of the flight of steps would have met the upper landing. Following this reconstruction, one can also hypothesize that the higher courses of F57 might have been laid in a more regular fashion on top of the currently preserved row of headers on edge. This wall would have in fact separated room 11 from room 13 to the north, with the latter space being delimited by walls F13, F37, F58 (and F57). Once again, any attempt at reconstructing the appearance of rooms 11+13 above the preserved height of the walls is nothing more than educated guesswork. Concerning F57, one must wonder about its original function; indeed, if the wall had been built to support the structural elements of a suspended staircase, its original height would have been about 3 m. This would have been a considerable height for a wall that was rather slim and, at least in its extant foundation courses, poorly constructed.

7.4. Remarks on the Chronology of Building 7

Considerations of the relative chronology of the features of building 7 (including the church and the south annex) were offered in a previous section of this chapter.[30] The evidence for

---

28. Suspended stairs, built without a solid platform underneath, are attested at 'Ain el-Gedida (staircase in room 8): see Aravecchia 2018, 130, pls. 3.61–2; 131–35. Similarly built stairs are also known elsewhere in Upper Egypt, both in antiquity and modern times. For parallels from Abu Mina, see McKenzie 2007, 294, figs. 486 (north basilica) and 487 (east church). Cf. Correas-Amador 2011 for possible analogies. At p. 16, the author describes a staircase with mud-brick steps laid on top of reed matting, which rested over beams made from tree trunks.

29. For example, room 9 (south wall) at 'Ain el-Gedida: see Aravecchia 2018, 136–39.

30. Cf. Sec. 7.1.

the establishment of an absolute chronology for the church complex is, unfortunately, not as abundant as one might have hoped. This is, as we have seen, principally the result of the very poor condition of most architectural features, heavily eroded by the natural elements and possibly human activity. Consequently, the stratigraphy that was documented inside the church was scarce, with most units not reliable and most finds having limited or no diagnostic value. The areas that revealed a more reliable sequence of (foundation) deposits include the two test trenches excavated in room 1,[31] the four sealed burial pits (tombs 2–4 and 17) in the east transverse aisles of the same room,[32] foundation deposits investigated in the south annex, especially in rooms 11, 12, and 13 (test trench 3),[33] tomb 5 in room 6 (also in the south annex),[34] as well as the three underground crypts (rooms 2–4) including the burials found within them.[35]

The pottery retrieved from the excavation of the church (rooms 1 and 2), the south annex (rooms 5–13), and the underground crypts (rooms 2–4) is consistent with ceramic material found in Area 2 at Amheida.[36] In particular, it features several utilitarian shapes that are comparable to those found in the occupational levels of house B1 (the so-called "House of Serenos"),[37] in the building to the north of it (B5, which was identified as the stable associated with B1, as well as in the latest stages of occupation of the nearby area of the baths, labeled B6. The large quantity of cooking vessels (pots, casseroles, and lids), largely made of the so-called "Christian Brittle Ware" (A11), as well as large basins and kraters,[38] all characterized by heavily blackened surfaces, points to food preparation activities. An interesting pattern in building 7's assemblage is the variety of vessels for the storage and consumption of food and liquids, such as bowls, jugs, bottles, jars, as well as table amphorae made of common local fabrics (A1, B10, A5)[39]. The diversity in shapes and size could potentially indicate a wide array of functions, with some vessels used for ceremonial purposes and others destined to personal usage. Wine consumption is further attested by the identification of fragments belonging to amphorae imported from the Nile Valley (LRA 7)[40] and flasks from Kharga (inv. 30451).[41] The most significant example of import from abroad is a fragment of a plate of African Red Slipware (A13/2.3/1/30468) dated to the late fourth–early fifth century.

---

31. Test trench 1, between the square bases of the west doorway, and test trench 2 in the north aisle (cf. Secs. 3.3.1 and 3.3.2 of this volume).

32. The human remains in tomb 1, at the northwest corner of the church, were found *in situ*, but in close proximity to surface, with most of the burial pit disappeared (and the lower half of the cut indiscernible within the surrounding foundation deposit of the north aisle).

33. Cf. Secs. 4.8 (for the stratigraphy of room 11 and test trench 3 in room 13) and 4.9 (for the stratigraphy of room 12).

34. Cf. Sec. 4.3.1.

35. Cf. Secs. 5.2.1 and 5.3.1 for the tombs in the underground crypts.

36. The following remarks are based on preliminary reports by, and personal communications with, C. Caputo and I. Soto Marín. Caputo's report on the ceramics from building 7 at Amheida is forthcoming.

37. See Caputo 2020.

38. Caputo 2020, 26–27.

39. Caputo 2020, 12; 14.

40. Caputo 2020, 38–39.

41. Caputo 2020, 84, no. 207.

In-depth comparative analysis of each vessel is yet to be undertaken. The abovementioned parallels between the shapes and types of ceramics from the church (in both foundation and occupation levels) and its crypts and those retrieved in the later levels of the House of Serenos (as well as in his nearby 'private' dump located in the area of the baths) point to the third quarter of the fourth century for the construction (and use) of the church.[42] Such dating aligns with the chronology established through the analysis of other categories of artifacts (chiefly coins and ostraka).[43]

Several of the forty-six coins retrieved in building 7 in 2012 and 2013 (plus six that were gathered on the surface of the church complex during a later visit to the site), as well as many of the twenty-one specimens collected during the 2023 season, were found in poor condition or completely illegible.[44] Some of the specimens belonged to unreliable contexts; however, a few of them came from undisturbed depositional units, largely consisting of foundation fills below floor level, or were set against walls or inside floors. Unfortunately, many of these coins remain illegible as a result of extreme deterioration. Two coins (inv. 15508–15509) were found on the threshold between room 1 (the church) and room 16 (the south *pastophorion*), below a layer of mud-brick debris (DSU13). While the first could not be read, the second was identified as a *nummus centenionalis*, struck under Constantius II in 347–348. Another specimen (inv. 15774) lay above floor F23 in the eastern half of the church's south aisle, within a unit (DSU7) that, although not sealed, consisted of very compacted mud-brick debris and formed a thin encrustation layer above the floor. Unfortunately, the coin is poorly preserved and illegible. A second bronze coin (inv. 15856), a *Spes Reipublicae* issue dated to 355–361, was also found embedded within the same floor. Inv. 15818 (a *maiorina* dated to 351–361) was found in an earlier mud floor (F27), large patches of which were detected in the eastern half of the south aisle.

The excavation of tomb 3, in the northeast corner of room 1, revealed a bronze coin (inv. 15932) in the sandy fill (DSU39) of the burial pit, which was sealed by a mud-brick superstructure (F34). The specimen was found in very poor condition and could not be read.

Numerous coins were found in the context of foundation fills below floor level in the south annex. These depositional layers largely consisted of sand and discarded material from (likely) domestic dumps. Among these specimens are: inv. 16210 (illegible) and inv. 16217 (dated to the first half of the fourth century CE) from DSU83, a thin sand layer resting on top of the remains of floors F62–63 inside room 7; inv. 16063 (struck in the fourth century CE), from DSU66 (a subsurface unit, thus a less reliable deposit, in room 11); inv. 16186 (a coin of Valens dated to 364–367), inv. 16187 (a *maiorina* minted in Alexandria in 351–361), inv. 16188 and inv. 16216 (broadly dated from the second half of the fourth century to the first half of the fifth) from DSU77 (a layer of mud-brick debris deposited in the south half of room 11 and earlier than DSU66); inv. 16099 (a *nummus centenionalis* struck under Constantius II or Constans

---

42. The appearance of Late Roman Amphora 7 provide a *terminus post quem* as the 350s. Few rare types of ceramic fragments, dated to the late third–early fourth century were recognized in units that contained chinking sherds, likely from vault collapses (C. Caputo, personal communication, January 2023).

43. For a case study (from Amheida) that highlights the correlation of texts and pottery in the dating of late Roman ceramic assemblages, see Bagnall et al. 2017.

44. A complete catalog (by D. M. Ratzan) is forthcoming in the companion volume to this archaeological report.

in 347–348), inv. 16101 (a *maiorina* minted under Constantius II in 351–361), inv. 16102 (a *maiorina* minted under Constantius II in 352–355), inv. 16189 (illegible), and inv. 16288 (a *maiorina* minted in Cyzicus in 351–361, under Constantius II), all from DSU73 (a mud-brick debris layer in room 12); inv. 16289 (dated to the second half of the fourth century/first half of the fifth) from DSU79 (the preparation layer for floor F60 in room 12).[45] A bronze coin (inv. 16047, a *maiorina* dated to 351–361) was found within the wall (F36) that separates rooms 5 and 6 in the south annex. The excavation of wall F37, parallel to F36 and dividing rooms 5 and 10 from rooms 10 and 13, led to the discovery of inv. 16225. This is a complete (though poorly preserved) bronze coin, which was found embedded in the threshold between rooms 10 and 11; unfortunately, it could not be dated. Another specimen (inv. 16212) was retrieved from the upper surface of F60, the preserved patch of floor in room 12 at the east end of the south annex. The coin is a *centenionalis* minted in Alexandria in 355–363, under Constantius II or Julianus. Four coins (inv. 16008 and 16025–16027) were found directly above floor level in room 6. Although some of them are completely or partially legible (e.g., inv. 16008 and 16025–16026), their archaeological context (DSU53) was not deemed as secure, due to its relative proximity to surface, and so they are not helpful in establishing an absolute chronology for the stratigraphy of room 6.[46]

Excavations inside the three funerary crypts (rooms 2–4), which took place in 2023,[47] revealed a limited number of small finds, including sixteen coins. Most of the specimens were illegible and were found in archaeological contexts that were of dubious or no reliability for dating purposes. The only two coins that were retrieved from a reliable stratigraphical unit (DSU138, occupation level of room 4) are inv. 17051 (illegible), and inv. 17050, a *maiorina* dated to 351–361.

The datable coins from the church (including the crypts) and the south annex span from 328 to 378 CE, with the exception of one specimen (inv. 15817) that is dated to 383–403.[48] An additional coin (inv. 15522) was found during the excavation of the church (in the western half of room 1); the specimen was dated to 114–40 BCE, thus significantly earlier than the chronological range established on the basis of the other datable coins. However, this coin was gathered from a sub-surface layer (DSU4), therefore it bears no reliable diagnostic value for the dating of the church.[49]

The datable coins that were found in reliable contexts (inv. 15509, 15855, 16047, 16186–16188, 16212, and 17050) all point to the third quarter of the fourth century with regard to the church's construction and use, with one specimen (inv. 16188, found in DSU77—a foundation fill—in room 11) that was assigned to the late fourth–early fifth century. Particularly important

---

45. This context is likely unreliable, due to the missing floor above the area of the coin's discovery and its relative proximity to surface.

46. Inv. 16008 is a *nummus* minted under Constantine in 328–329; inv. 16025 is a *maiorina* struck under Constantius II in 355–361; inv. 16026 was broadly dated to the fourth century CE; inv. 16027 is illegible. Another coin (inv. 16007), dated to 318–383, was retrieved in an unsecure context (DSU44) within the same room.

47. Room 2 (north *pastophorion*) was first excavated in 2013: see Sec. 5.2 above.

48. This coin does not come from a secure context.

49. An additional specimen (inv. 17017, dated to the first–second century CE) was collected from the surface (DSU0) of building 7 in 2023.

for dating the construction of the church is an above-mentioned coin (inv. 16187) that was found in a reliable context within room 11's foundation fill. The specimen is securely dated to 351–361 and thus provides a *terminus post quem* of 351 for the erection of building 7, or at least the southern annex.[50] Overall, the datable coins point to a construction of the church complex sometime in the second half of the fourth century, with no substantial evidence for its continued use into the fifth century (apart from traces of post-abandonment reuse, possibly by squatters, in the annex).

In addition to ostraka (discussed below), ceramics, and coins, the finds that can be linked with the occupation of the church, including room 1 (nave and side aisles) and rooms 2–4 (the crypts below the sanctuary) were relatively few. It is worth mentioning two interesting objects that were found in DSU12, the sand layer underlying a ceiling, columns, and wall collapse (DSU10)[51] in the east transverse aisle: these are inv. 15847, a fragment of worked wood that may have been part of a piece of furniture or a screen, and inv. 15848, a bone artefact with a bronze band (possibly a handle or a tool).[52] Other finds are associated with layers that formed the fill of foundation trenches or were preparatory layers below floors. Particularly rich were layers of dumped material (DSU23 and 26, as well as 4; DSU4 is a subsurface accumulation layer, although it seems to have been mixed, in its lower part, with remains of eroded DSU26). Also, DSU24, the fill of a burial pit (tomb 2) in the east aisle, may have contained mixed material from units below the floor, including DSU26. Out of 24 ostraka with assigned field numbers, 17 came from DSU4, 23–24, and 26.[53] Worthy of note is also a fragment of a terracotta figurine (inv. 15834) and a complete jar stopper (inv. 15826), both found in DSU23. Excavations in the south annex yielded a similar range of finds, including glass fragments, mud-stoppers, beads, and fragments of worked wood. Most of the small finds came from deposition units below floor level, which contained an admixture of refuse material.

With the exclusion of ceramics, coins, and ostraka, the objects that were retrieved during the excavation of the church, as well as of the south annex, are not particularly useful towards establishing a chronology of the building's construction and abandonment; what can be said, however, is that they are consistent with typologies of small finds that are found in other fourth-century contexts at the site.[54] A couple of finds, consisting of gypsum plaster decorations (inv. 14573 and 14481), deserve a particular mention. These fragments were retrieved during the excavation of the foundation fill in the west return aisle (though from an unsealed layer) and in test trench 2, dug in the north aisle of the church. Both contexts consisted of reused

---

50. No other securely dated specimens were found in sealed foundation contexts from building 7.

51. Within DSU10, one large fragment of white plaster (FN82) was retrieved with Greek inscriptions including the term *ho theos* (Greek for God); their publication (by D. M. Ratzan) is forthcoming in the companion volume to this archaeological report.

52. For more information on these small finds (as well as the others that are mentioned below), cf. the catalogs that are forthcoming in the companion volume to this archaeological report.

53. Isolated finds were from DSU5, 10, and 14, while the rest were from the surface.

54. None of the objects appears to be later than the end of the fourth century CE (M. M. S. Nuovo, personal communication, October 2022). It is also worth remarking that there are no traces of Christian symbols on any of the finds from the church complex (such as crosses or Christograms on ceramic lamps), nor is there any evidence pointing to the use of any of these objects within exclusively liturgical contexts.

CHAPTER 7: DISCUSSION OF THE ARCHAEOLOGICAL EVIDENCE

dumped material; therefore, neither piece of gypsum plaster seems to belong to any of the occupation phases of the church. More likely, they were part of discarded material originating from a domestic context, especially based on comparanda found in house B10 at Amheida and Kellis.[55]

7.4.1. The Ostraka from Area 2.3

Ostraka are an important category of objects for the dating of the church, in addition to providing the only documentary evidence from the excavation of the complex. Forty-three ostraka were retrieved in 2012 and 2013 during the excavation of the church, including room 2 (the north underground crypt), and the south annex. These were published in the second volume of ostraka from Trimithis.[56] Ten additional Greek ostraka (nine of which complete) were found during the 2023 excavation season in Area 2.3 and await publication.[57]

Several ostraka were found at, or close to, surface level or in unreliable contexts, due to the very poor level of preservation of the architectural features above ground level, as well as the lack of floors especially in the west half of the complex. The large majority of the ostraka (33) were found in room 1 (nave and side aisles), even though two of them, i.e., *O. Trim.* 2.649 and 2.730 (dated to 293/4 or 315/6 and 287/8 respectively),[58] were surface finds and therefore of no diagnostic value. Four ostraka came from the sandy surface layer (DSU1) that covered room 1 in its entirety; they therefore cannot be considered as reliable for dating purposes: *O. Trim.* 2.475, 2.488, and 2.571 (assigned to the second half of the fourth century) and *O. Trim.* 2.489 (dated to 345/6).[59] The removal of a subsurface layer (DSU4, consisting of sand mixed with numerous inclusions) located in the north and south aisles, as well as in the west return aisle, led to the discovery of ten ostraka: *O. Trim.* 2.578, 2.741, 2.743, and 2.745 (broadly assigned

---

55. Material evidence, chiefly the ceramic assemblage, from house B10 has been preliminarily dated to the late third to early fourth century CE (Bagnall et al. 2017, 201–2). The excavation of B10, however, is still ongoing and the small finds retrieved thus far await full publication; so, the chronological horizon is not yet been established. The evidence from Kellis, found in house B/3/1, was assigned to the second century (Hope 2015, 209). A third-century dating for the gypsum plaster decorations from the foundations of the church at Amheida would not be surprising, considering that they were part of material pre-dating the fourth-century foundation of the church itself.

56. Ast and Bagnall 2016.

57. These ostraka, which were examined by R. S. Bagnall, are: inv. 17010+17014 (dated to 286/7), found on the surface (DSU0) in room 2; inv. 17015 (most likely dated to 350–370), from the pit fill (DSU106) of tomb 5, excavated in room 6 within the south annex; inv. 17016 (dated to 284/5, possibly earlier), collected from the surface (DSU0) of room 4; inv. 17019 (dated to 294/5, possibly 316/7), from a layer of windblown sand (DSU111) within room 4; inv. 17022 (dated to 286/7), found in a wall collapse unit (DSU115) also in room 4; inv. 17040 (dated to 327/8, 337/8, or 345/6), discovered in the pit fill (DSU124) of tomb 9 in the north crypt/room 2; inv. 17049 (with no date in the text), from the fill (DSU141) of tomb 12 inside room 3; inv. 17054 (without date), collected during the investigation of DSU151 (a sand layer below F75, the upper floor level of room 2); inv. 17063 (with no date in the text and broadly assigned to the late third/mid-fourth century), found in DSU164 (a unit of loose yellow sand filling an irregular cut in floor F22 of room 1); and inv. 17077 (also broadly dated from the late third century to the mid-fourth century CE), from DSU168 (a layer of compact brownish-yellow sand east of wall F59 in test trench 4).

58. Ast and Bagnall 2016, 195 (*O. Trim.* 2.649); 223 (*O. Trim.* 2.730).

59. Ast and Bagnall 2016, 125 (*O. Trim.* 2.475); 130 (*O. Trim.* 2.488, 2.489); 163–64 (*O. Trim.* 2.571).

to the period 275–350); *O.Trim.* 2.635, 2.642, 2.666, and 2.732 (all possibly dated to a short period of time in the mid-280s, spanning from 284 to 287); *O.Trim.* 2.636 (dated to 295/6 or 317/8); and *O.Trim.* 2.667 (possibly dated to 291/2).[60] The archaeological context (DSU4) of these ostraka, very close to surface and thus likely contaminated, makes them of very limited use for dating the occupation history of room 1.

Another ostrakon (*O. Trim.* 2.733, tentatively dated to 287/8)[61] was found in the north aisle of the church in a unit (DSU14) that, although unreliable, must have been part of the foundation fill of room 1 below floor level. Another piece that was collected very close to surface is *O.Trim.* 2.643 (possibly dated to 285/6),[62] in a unit (DSU5) that consisted of a thin layer of ceiling collapse.

The excavation of a large test trench in the north aisle of room 1 revealed a stratigraphy consisting of floor levels and foundation fills, made of sand and ash with numerous inclusions. One of these contexts (DSU23), considered reliable as it was detected below either F21 (a lime plaster floor) or the preparation layer of the latter, contained six ostraka: *O. Trim.* 2.579 and 2.724 (broadly dated to ca. 275–350); *O. Trim.* 2.644 (possibly assigned to 286/7); *O. Trim.* 2.645 (dated to either 294/5 or 316/7); *O. Trim.* 2.646 and 2.734 (created in 296/7 or 318/9).[63] Below DSU23 was another layer (DSU26) consisting of domestic refuse, which was used to fill the foundation trench of the north aisle of the church. The excavation of this reliable unit revealed two ostraka (*O.Trim.* 2.580 and 2.735) broadly assigned to ca. 275–350.[64] The dating of the documentary evidence from DSU23 and DSU26 covers a relatively wide chronological spectrum, potentially ranging from the third quarter of the third century to the mid-fourth century. Therefore, it can hardly be used to establish a precise *terminus post quem* for the construction of room 1. A similar chronological range is shared by two ostraka (*O.Trim.* 2.637, possibly dated to 286/7, and *O.Trim.* 2.728, assigned to ca. 275–350)[65] that were found as part of the sandy fill, mixed with refuse material, of a sealed burial (tomb 3) in the northeast corner of room 1.[66] The same can be said of three ostraka retrieved during the excavation of another tomb (no. 2), located in the south half of the east aisle, immediately south of the stepped platform (F19) that once led into the apse. The ostraka, which were part of the sandy fill (DSU24) of the burial pit, are *O.Trim.* 2.647, 2.725, and 2.726 and are dated respectively to 284/5 (tentatively), 285/6 (also tentatively), and ca. 275–350.[67]

---

60. Ast and Bagnall 2016, 168–69 (*O.Trim.* 2.578); 227 (*O.Trim.* 2.741); 228 (*O.Trim.* 2.743); 229 (*O.Trim.* 2.745); 189–90 (*O.Trim.* 2.635); 192 (*O.Trim.* 2.642); 201 (*O.Trim.* 2.666); 224 (*O.Trim.* 2.732); 190 (*O.Trim.* 2.636); 201–2 (*O.Trim.* 2.667).

61. Ast and Bagnall 2016, 224.

62. Ast and Bagnall 2016, 192–93.

63. Ast and Bagnall 2016, 169 (*O.Trim.* 2.579); 221 (*O.Trim.* 2.724); 193 (*O.Trim.* 2.644, 2.645); 193–94 (*O.Trim.* 2.646); 224 (*O.Trim.* 2.734).

64. Ast and Bagnall 2016, 169–70 (*O.Trim.* 2.580); 225 (*O.Trim.* 2.735).

65. Ast and Bagnall 2016, 190 (*O.Trim.* 2.637); 222 (*O.Trim.* 2.728).

66. It is likely that at least part of the tomb's fill (labeled as DSU39) originated from the foundation fill of room 1's north aisle. This loose material may have been originally dug out when the burial pit was excavated and then reused to fill the pit after the deposition of the body.

67. Ast and Bagnall 2016, 194 (*O.Trim.* 2.647); 221 (*O.Trim.* 2.725); 222 (*O.Trim.* 2.726).

The removal of a surface layer (DSU31), consisting of windblown sand with numerous inclusions, from the south annex of building 7 revealed one ostrakon (*O. Trim.* 2.727).[68] This was broadly dated to ca. 275–350, but due to the highly unreliable context in which it was found, it cannot be considered as bearing any relevance for dating purposes.

An ostrakon was found embedded in the outer face of room 1's west wall (F14), at foundation level. The object (*O. Trim.* 2.653, dated to ca. 275–350)[69] is not particularly remarkable in terms of its content (well tag) and, although it was gathered from a reliable context, its dating is rather broad and does not provide a precise *terminus post quem* for the construction of the outer walls of the church.

The excavation of the underground crypt (room 2), below the now-disappeared north *pastophorion*, revealed only one ostrakon (*O. Trim.* 2.572), broadly assigned to the period 275–350 CE.[70] The inscribed potsherd was found in a unit (DSU102) that consisted of a wall- and vault-collapse, seemingly from the south end of the crypt's vaulted ceiling, as well as its south wall.

Taking all of the evidence from room 1 together, it is consistent with the ostraka found in the layers of material dumped to level the site before the House of Serenos (B1) was built. In particular, the prevalence of well tags bearing year numbers that cannot be later than the reign of Diocletian and the Tetrarchs, along with the presence of regnal years that must be assigned to Constantine or to the earlier part of the reign of his sons (Constantius II in the case of Egypt), led to a dating of the construction of the House of Serenos to ca. 335–345.[71] That also appears to be the *terminus post quem* provided by the ostraka for the building of the nave and its associated spaces. The evidence of the coins in the layers of material dumped before or at the time of construction, as presented above, pushes the date a bit later, into the mid-350s or even ca. 360.

Nine ostraka were retrieved in the south annex of the ecclesiastical complex (rooms 5–13). Together, they validate the chronology established by the study of the finds, especially coins and ostraka, in relation to the church and the crypts. One ostrakon (*O. Trim.* 2.503), dated to ca. 275–350, came from the surface of room 6; due to the unreliable context (DSU0) in which it was found, the object has no diagnostic value for the establishment of the chronology of room 6's use.

The best-preserved space of the south annex is room 7, whose stratigraphy consisted largely of sand and wall-collapse layers. Two ostraka, both broadly assigned to 250–350, were uncovered during the investigation of this room. One (*O. Trim.* 2.729)[72] was found in DSU68, a natural accumulation of sand below an extensive wall-collapse (DSU32); the second ostrakon (*O. Trim.* 2.502)[73] came from DSU83, a thin unit of sand deposited immediately above the floor levels of room 7. Both layers were deemed reliable and the dating of the two ostraka is in line with that of the majority of the other ostraka from building 7. It therefore appears that the

68. Ast and Bagnall 2016, 222.
69. Ast and Bagnall 2016, 196.
70. Ast and Bagnall 2016, 164.
71. Davoli 2022, 39 gives the chronology of the house.
72. Ast and Bagnall 2016, 222–23.
73. Ast and Bagnall 2016, 136.

source of most of the material dumped before building the south rooms was the same as that of the nave or at least very similar. It must also be remembered that the same source was probably, as with the House of Serenos, used as a source for chinking sherds, which can appear in collapse levels.

The investigation of the poorly preserved stratigraphy of room 9, at the west end of the south annex, revealed only one ostrakon (O. Trim. 2.782),[74] broadly assigned to 275–350 but with no diagnostic value, as it was found in a sandy fill (DSU52) immediately below the surface layer (DSU31). Further east, an ostrakon (O. Trim. 2.731, dated to ca. 275–350)[75] was detected during the excavation of an unreliable wall collapse unit (DSU67) in room 11, identified as the foundations of an upper flight of stairs parallel to F35 in room 5 (figure 4.3).[76] A more reliable context from room 11 is DSU85, which consisted of a refuse layer of sand and ash that formed part of the fill of this room's foundations. DSU85 lay below other foundation deposits (DSU76–78) and was considered a secure context. Four ostraka were found in this context, of which one (O. Trim. 2.650) was broadly dated to ca. 275–350, another (O. Trim. 2.652) to 294/5 or 316/7, and a third (O. Trim. 2.736) to 329/30 or 339/40.[77] The fourth ostrakon (O. Trim. 2.532, fig. 7.3)[78] is especially useful for establishing the chronology of the construction of the south annex. It is a complete ostrakon, consisting of six lines in Greek. It is a letter written by a certain Theotimos to his son Makarios, with a request to send a certain amount of chaff to two *officiales*. The document is precisely dated to Choiak 7 of the 6th indiction, which in the editors' view corresponds to 3 December 362.[79] The archaeological context in which this ostrakon was found consisted of domestic refuse; thus O. Trim. 2.532 might have originated anywhere in the surroundings of the church complex, or even farther. The provenance of the ostrakon is unknown.[80] However, its discovery within the foundation fill of room 11 is significant, as it provides a precise *terminus post quem* (after the early 360s) for the building of this space and, likely, of the entire south area of building 7.[81] The relative chronology of building 7's architectural features suggests that the south annex was built after the erection of room 1's south wall (F13); therefore, it belongs to the latest phase of construction. As discussed earlier on in this chapter, the temporal gap between the building of the church and that of the annex is yet be ascertained with any degree of precision. A reasonable assumption, based on the general range of finds discovered in both areas, is that it was not particularly long. The coins and ostraka do not require any temporal gap at all, even if the nave and the south rooms represent different and sequential phases of construction. Thus, the *terminus post quem* offered by O. Trim. 2.532 for the

---

74. Ast and Bagnall 2016, 241.
75. Ast and Bagnall 2016, 223.
76. See Sec. 7.3 above.
77. Ast and Bagnall 2016, 195 (O. Trim. 2.650); 196 (O. Trim. 2.652); 225 (O. Trim. 2.736).
78. Ast and Bagnall 2016, 152.
79. There is no clear evidence to date of the use of the indiction for dating at Trimithis before the middle of the fourth century, thus excluding earlier 6th indictions. A later date is not entirely excluded, but nothing clearly assignable to the indiction cycle beginning in 372 has yet been found at the site, and the handwriting is at least compatible to that in ostraka from the 360s.
80. On the reuse of dumped material in the foundation of buildings (and because of this defined as "tertiary refuse"), see Ast and Davoli 2016, 1452. On the reuse of dumped pottery as fill in foundations, see Peña 2007, 254.
81. With the possible exception of room 7: cf. Sec. 4.4.

Fig. 7.3: O.Trim. 2.532, found in DSU85 (foundation fill of room 11).

south annex is useful also for the establishment of a general chronology for the construction of the church. In particular, it supports a third quarter of the fourth century dating that was established on the basis of the numismatic evidence from building 7. This chronology assigns the construction of building 7 at Amheida to the same fourth-century chronological horizon of several other known churches in Dakhla Oasis.[82] It postdates by a few decades securely dated churches, such as the Small and Large East Church at Kellis and the church at ʿAin el-Gedida, and seems to be roughly contemporary with the West Church at Kellis and, more notably, the church recently found at ʿAin el-Sabil, which shares remarkable similarities with the church at Amheida.[83]

7.5. Building 7 within the Amheida Cityscape

The church complex in Area 2.3 was certainly an important and highly visible structure within the urban landscape of fourth-century Trimithis (fig. 1.4). This is suggested by the location of the building on the top of a hill, which is clearly visible on the modern-day topographical map

82. As well as in Kharga Oasis (see Sec. 2.3 above).
83. For a summary of these (and other) churches, including their dating, see Sec. 2.1.1 above.

of the city and was likely in existence also in antiquity. As mentioned in an earlier section, this mound on which the church was erected is located at the east end of the urban area, which might have been the case as well in antiquity. Indeed, a recent ceramic survey, carried out on a series of mounds running north-south immediately to the east of building 7, revealed that the numerous pottery sherds visible on them were mixed with abundant ceramic and metal slag.[84] Thus, it is possible that these mounds were the location of industrial installations, including workshops in the proximity of kilns, for the manufacturing of ceramic vessels and metal objects. According to C. Caputo, these installations would have ideally been located (at least in this case) outside the city center and on higher ground, so that the dust and smoke resulting from these industrial activities would have been kept away from the inhabited area.[85] Although the study of the area east of building 7 is still in an early phase, with a thorough topographical survey and possible test trenching yet to be carried out, its preliminary results support the assumption that the church was built at the east end of the urban center, with the area east of it not being residential in nature, but rather dedicated to industrial activities.

The location of the church on a slope may help explain the 3-meter-deep foundations that were discovered on the north, west, and south side of room 1, as well as the efforts made in antiquity to stabilize and level the ground before the building of the complex.[86] The discovery of the underground crypts below the area of the sanctuary may offer an alternative, or additional, explanation for the need of substantial foundation walls, in order to accommodate rooms below floor level at the east end of the complex. Overall, the construction of deep foundations, as well as the supply of hundreds of cubic meters of foundation fill, point to the great effort and the measures taken to erect the building in this particular location. The hill in Area 2.3, which dominated the surrounding cityscape also in antiquity, must have been, therefore, a particularly desirable location for the construction of building 7. Another example of a fourth-century church that was built in a prominent location, on higher ground than the surrounding built environment, is the one-nave basilica excavated at the hamlet of ʿAin el-Gedida, also located in Dakhla.[87] In this instance, the church did not stand in isolation, but was erected within a densely built setting. However, centrality and visibility must have still been key factors in the choice of its location. Indeed, the Christian villagers of ʿAin el-Gedida seemingly went to great lengths in order to build a basilica-type church in the middle of the hamlet's main mound. This choice showcased a deliberate effort in dealing with considerable challenges, largely arising from a lack of available space for expansion in the area around the mound.[88]

The privileged setting points to the existence of a thriving Christian community in fourth-century Trimithis, with the means to secure a prime spot—surrounded by a densely-built environment, at least to the west—in which to erect a building for gathering and worship. It

---

84. The survey was conducted by C. Caputo and V. Barba Colmenero in January 2023.

85. The north-south winds blowing in the region would also have helped in this regard. These preliminary conclusions are based on a personal communication with C. Caputo (January 2023).

86. To confirm this hypothesis beyond doubt, further investigation is needed on the foundations of building 7, particularly in its east sector and outside the external walls.

87. Aravecchia 2018, 187–94. On the changes in the built landscape of ʿAin el-Gedida in late antiquity, cf. Aravecchia 2020a.

88. Aravecchia 2024.

Fig. 7.4: View (to east) of building 7; the dashed line shows the east-west oriented path possibly connecting the church complex with the city's residential sector to the west.

also suggests how the basilica type, widely attested in the oasis since the early fourth century CE, came to be seen as a powerful visual symbol of religious identity in Christian architecture. Indeed, as it seems to have been the case at ʿAin el-Gedida, Christians may have adopted this form to enhance their visibility, by transforming the local natural and built environment into a more manifestly "Christian" landscape.[89]

The location of the church may also have been of equal significance in that the entrance to the church complex faced the monumental temple—or perhaps its ruins—that was located on another hill (Area 4.1) overlooking the central zone of Trimithis further west from Area 2.3. Indeed, building 7 stood at the junction of one of two major north-south oriented streets and an east-west running one (S16+S17), which may have connected Area 2.3 with the residential area of the city and, perhaps, further west to the temple's hill (fig. 7.4).[90] One might see in this topographical arrangement, with the church built at the highest point of Area 2.3, thus enjoying a high degree of visibility over the surrounding landscape, as a visual counterpoint

---

89. Aravecchia 2024. On the emphasis on visibility in early Christian places of worship, cf. White 1990, 128–30 and Wharton 1995, 32. On the basilica form of Roman civic architecture, being adopted into Christian architecture around the time of Constantine, cf. (among others) Ward-Perkins 1954; Deichmann 1982, 40–46; Krautheimer 1986, 43; White 1990.

90. Aravecchia 2015a, 121–22. Cf. also Davoli 2019, 55, fig. 4.6; 57.

to the Egyptian temple, also built on a high mound (in fact, Area 4.1 was the highest and most central mound of the site).[91] The placement of the church on an east-west axis, extending (at least visually) all the way to the temple, may indeed be read as a conscious choice, on the part of the church's builders, to erect a Christian place of cult that was as pre-eminent, within the urban environment of fourth-century Trimithis, as the temple (or what was left of it), almost to replace the latter as the chief marker of religious identity at the site. Admittedly, this is all very speculative, as it is yet undetermined if the temple in Area 4.1 was still standing when the church was erected. What is also unknown is how many churches existed at Trimithis by the second half of the fourth century, which is most likely more than one.[92]

Furthermore, it is worth remarking that the east-west street (S16+S17) mentioned above (and only partially surveyed) connected the church complex on the hill (Area 2.3) with the baths (B6) that were identified and partially excavated further west,[93] in what may have been the late antique city center of Trimithis. It is unknown if the proximity between the two buildings, and especially the fact that they were aligned on the same east-west street, was intentional and served the needs of the same group of people that frequented both buildings. However, it is attested in late antique Egypt and elsewhere that churches were, at times, located at the edge of settlements and close to public baths, which seems to reflect the arrangement of church and baths at Trimithis.[94] Additional evidence (also from Dakhla) consists of two of the three fourth-century churches excavated at Kellis (the Large and Small East Churches), which were built in the proximity of a bathhouse.[95] Abundant evidence (both archaeological and documentary) from the Mediterranean region in late antiquity points to the apparent intersection of baths and Christianity, with baths featuring prominently in ecclesiastical complexes and sponsored by religious authorities.[96] Baths were also common features of large pilgrimage centers (for example at Deir Abu Mina). As a norm, late antique Christians do not seem to have used baths for liturgical purposes; however, they often took to them, which betrayed a lack of formal opposition to their use.[97]

Further investigation is needed outside of building 7's west wall in order to gather more information on the west entrance into the church (where north-south street S11 crosses east-west street S16+S17),[98] as well as on the church's relationship to the built landscape of the city further west, including the Roman *thermae*. Additional excavations along the north, east, and west sides of the complex will hopefully help reinforce—or perhaps challenge—the current perception of the church as a building standing in isolation at the east edge of the late antique city.[99]

91. The church and the temple were not the only buildings located on higher grounds than the rest of the city. On the visibility of other monuments, such as the Roman pyramid-tomb to the east of the church and the tower-tomb towards the north end of the site (both of which were built on hills), see Davoli 2019, 72.

92. Indeed, one may be easily tempted to speculate that a church existed near (or replaced) the temple in Area 4.1, due to the centrality and high degree of visibility of buildings on this mound. On another building, located near the southern necropolis, that is likely to be identified as a church, see p. 406 below.

93. Davoli 2015a; Davoli 2017; Davoli 2019, 63–65.

94. On the evidence from North Africa in late antiquity, see Leone 2013, 66.

95. Hope 2015, 213–14. The bathhouse is still unexcavated.

96. Sometimes operated for profit: see DeForest 2019, 199.

97. DeForest 2019, 201–2.

98. Davoli 2019, 55, fig. 4.6; 57.

99. For more considerations on future work in Area 2.3, see Sec. 8.2.

7.6. Parallels

The archaeological evidence, as discussed at length in Chapter 3 of this volume, conclusively supports the identification of building 7 at Amheida as a church of a basilica type, oriented to the east and with a central nave, two side aisles, and a west return aisle (figs. 7.5–7).[100] The raised platform along the east side of room 1 (F19) provided access to a (likely) rectangular apse,[101] which had a raised floor and was flanked by service rooms, forming a tripartite sanctuary.[102]

The rectangular shape of the apse is quite unusual in churches that are not associated with monastic contexts, with the only other known example (in Dakhla) being the church recently excavated at ʿAin el-Sabil.[103] No traces were found of the placement, in the eastern half of the church, of an altar, which would have presumably been located in the area facing the apse (immediately to the west of the stepped platform), if not within the apse.[104] All these features are relatively standard in early Christian architecture of late antique Egypt, with some features such as the west return aisle particularly common to churches throughout Upper Egypt.[105] Indeed, as summarized in Chapter 2 in this volume, ample evidence was gathered attesting to the popular adoption of the basilica type in regions as remote as Egypt's Great Oasis, where remains of churches dated since the early fourth century are especially abundant. In particular, a few known examples from both Dakhla and Kharga Oases reveal remarkable similarities with the church of Amheida. One is the Large East Church at Kellis, also in Dakhla Oasis (fig. 2.3).[106]

---

100. And, possibly, an east return aisle, which created a full ambulatory running around the central nave.

101. The lack of any evidence above the original floor level does not allow us to rule out beyond doubt a different configuration for this central room of the sanctuary.

102. On the popularity of the tripartite sanctuary, with two *pastophoria* flanking a generally semicircular apse, see, among others, Van Moorsel 1991, 552.

103. On the rectangular sanctuary as a common feature of early monastic churches in Egypt, see Brooks Hedstrom 2019, 671; Grossmann 2002a, 116. Another church, in the region of the Great Oasis, with a rectangular apse is that of Shams el-Din in Kharga (cf. n. 140 in Sec. 2.3 of this volume for essential bibliography). The archaeological record for Amheida/Trimithis—from both excavations and surveys—points to the absence of the semicircular apse, as an architectural form, in domestic architecture at the site. Davoli (2019, 79) explains the lack of the apsidal shape, remarkably common in late antique architecture, as possibly the result of a delay in its adoption at Trimithis, which was then abandoned at the end of the fourth century. Evidence from other sites in Dakhla (for example, Kellis and ʿAin el-Gedida, cf. Bowen 2002 and Aravecchia 2018) suggests that the apse was in use, at least in the context of Christian architecture, since the early fourth century. For a general discussion of the apse in early Egyptian churches, cf. Grossmann 2002a, 116–18.

104. The placement of the altar is often found inside the central rectangular sanctuary, but this is attested above all in monastic contexts. According to Grossmann, instances of altars placed inside semicircular apses are rare in non-monastic churches, with this choice seemingly dictated by lack of space. Most churches from the fifth century onwards (in Egypt as well as in Syria and Palestine) commonly featured altars in the area immediately facing the apse; cf. Grossmann 2002, 117, including n. 46 for additional bibliography on churches outside of Egypt.

105. Grossmann 2007, esp. 104–7. The west entrance is seen by Grossmann (2007, 104) as relatively unusual in the context of early Christian churches in Egypt, which more often had an entrance placed along the north or south side.

106. See Hope and Bowen 1997, 49–51; Bowen 2002, 65–75; Bowen 2022, 274–82; cf. Bowen 2023. A summary of the archaeological evidence can be found in Sec. 2.1.1 of this volume.

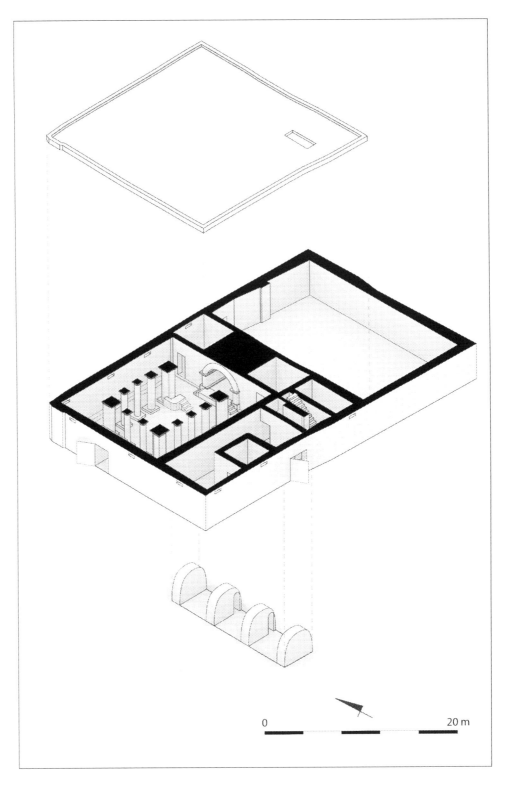

Fig. 7.5: Hypothetical isometric view of the church at Amheida (by C. Ullendorff).

CHAPTER 7: DISCUSSION OF THE ARCHAEOLOGICAL EVIDENCE

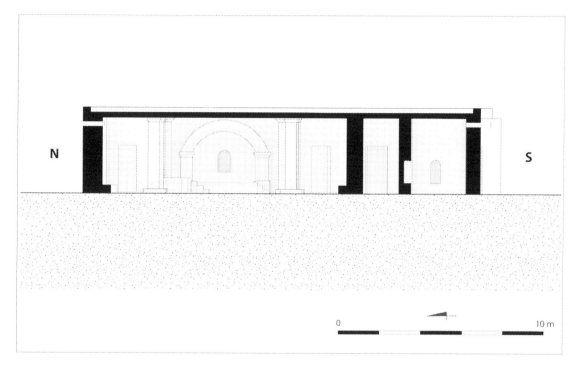

Fig. 7.6: N–S hypothetical section of the church at Amheida (by C. Ullendorff).

It is the largest of the three churches excavated at the site and its dimensions are also bigger than those of the church at Amheida. Both have, however, a very similar layout, consisting of a central nave separated by two side aisles by means of colonnades.[107] In the example from Kellis, colonnades also run from north to south, connecting the extremities of the north and south colonnades. The result is that, in addition to the north and south aisles, the space is additionally defined by a west return aisle and an east transverse aisle facing the sanctuary.

Admittedly, the poorly preserved evidence from building 7 at Amheida does not allow us to know beyond doubt if similar, north-south oriented colonnades existed in room 1. However, it is reasonable to assume, based on comparative evidence, that a colonnade, supported by foundation wall F8,[108] may have once demarcated a west return aisle. It is unknown if one or more columns existed between the two heart-shaped pillars (F11 and F3), at the east end of the north and south colonnades, respectively. The remains of foundation wall F30, running north-south between F11 and F3, were partially covered by patches of an original floor. It must also be remarked that if a podium of some kind (F26) did in fact abut pillar F11, extending

---

107. The north and south colonnades of the Large East Church consisted of six columns each, while the two colonnades in the church at Amheida, which were shorter, originally comprised five columns each.

108. Cf. figs. 3.4 and 3.19.

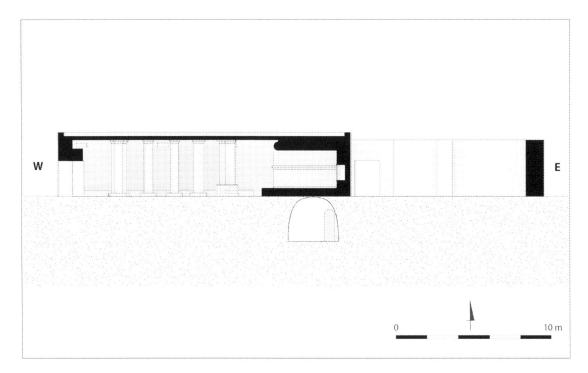

Fig. 7.7: E–W hypothetical section of the church at Amheida (by C. Ullendorff).

southwards,[109] the space for the placement of additional columns on top of F30 would have been further constrained.[110]

Both churches were accessed from the west. Three entrances pierce the west wall of the Large East Church, while remains of only one entrance were found in the middle of the west wall of room 1 at Amheida.[111] The two churches are also characterized by a remarkably similar annex of service rooms, built along the south wall, and by the existence of mud-brick benches against the inner face of the churches' walls.[112] A difference lies in the type of floor used to pave the two churches in their central naves; in the Large East Church, the central area was floored with sandstone slabs, while the entire floor in the church at Amheida (including the nave) was made exclusively of superimposed layers of compacted mud.

The two churches show similarly laid-out tripartite sanctuaries, each built against the inner face of the east wall. Both consist of a central apse (semicircular in the case of the Large East Church) flanked to the north and south by two rectangular *pastophoria* or service

109. As in the case of the church of Shams el-Din, where no east transverse aisle is attested archaeologically: cf. the discussion at p. 378 in this section.

110. It is not impossible that such columns did in fact exist. In his plan of the church at Amheida, Warner (2018a, 482, fig. 411/H) reconstructed an east transverse aisle with two columns placed between pillars F11 and F3.

111. The west wall (F14) is preserved only at foundation level; so it cannot be ruled out beyond doubt that side entrances existed to the north and south of the central doorway.

112. Evidence of such benches (F18) was found only against the south wall of the church at Amheida, due to the poor condition of the archaeological remains.

rooms.[113] In both buildings, these three spaces were accessed directly from the east transverse aisle;[114] also, the central apse had a raised floor (completely lost in the Amheida church) and was once accessed from the central nave by means of a stepped platform.[115] This feature, which is remarkably similar in the two churches, consists of a raised *bema* that is approached via a set of two steps along its north and south sides.[116] Therefore, visual access from the nave onto the apse would have still been granted by the central location of the latter, at the east end of the main axis of the church—as well as by the absence of physical barriers blocking the view in the area of the east transverse aisle. Nevertheless, physical access from the nave to the apse was not frontal; indeed, no steps lined the west side of either platform,[117] so that anyone accessing the sanctuary would have had to climb the steps along the north or south short side of the platform.[118] The presence of steps along the short sides of both platforms and, at the same time, the lack of steps alongside their west edge, was seen by Grossmann (before the discovery of the church at Amheida) as highly unusual in the context of early Christian churches.[119]

Both churches show evidence that their interior walls, as well as the colonnades were once covered in white gypsum plaster. In the Large East Church, the decoration seems to have been limited to the area of the apse, as well as the wall above its entrance.[120]

The scanty evidence of collapsed walls in the church at Amheida did not reveal any traces of decoration, with the exception of a small area with graffiti and dipinti (which would have not been part of the original decorative program).[121] As seen in Chapter 6, the only surface that would have been extensively decorated with polychrome geometric figures was the underside of the flat ceiling, now collapsed but fragmentarily preserved in the stratigraphy of the church.[122] Some evidence from the Large East Church at Kellis points to the existence of a ceiling that was also decorated with geometric shapes, in the manner documented at the church at Amheida.[123]

---

113. A door allowed direct access from the apse onto the south *pastophorion* in the Large East Church. In the case of the church at Amheida, the extremely poor state of preservation of the sanctuary does not allow to know if the central apse was directly connected with either the north or south service rooms.

114. Two mud-brick pedestals coated in gypsum plaster abut the two innermost columns of the east transverse aisle of the Large East Church: see Bowen 2002, 70. These features are missing in the church at Trimithis and have been seen as a unique architectural feature of the former: cf. Grossmann 2002b, 153.

115. F19 in room 1 at Amheida.

116. The *bema* was entirely of mudbrick in the church at Amheida, while the steps in the platform from Kellis were made of sandstone: Bowen 2002, 70.

117. Excavators at the Large East Church found traces, along the west edge of the platform, of what might have been the emplacement for a wooden screen: Bowen 2002, 70.

118. It is unclear if a sideways approach from the nave onto the sanctuary reflected particular liturgical requirements. It is archaeologically attested that contemporary churches from the Great Oasis (for example, the Small East Church and the West Church at Kellis, in Dakhla, as well as the church of Shams el-Din in Kharga) were built with apses that were accessed frontally, via platforms with steps along their west side (facing the nave).

119. Grossmann 2002b, 155.

120. Bowen 2002, 71.

121. Cf. Ratzan in the companion volume to this archaeological report (forthcoming).

122. The doorway leading onto the apse may have been decorated as well, based on a large fragment (inv. 15756), covered with a painted polychrome band, that possibly belonged to the arched top of that opening: cf. Sec. 6.1 at p. 353 and fig. 6.1.

123. Bowen 2019, 369. Cf. also p. 367 and n. 52 in Sec. 6.4 above.

Numismatic evidence from the Large East Church at Kellis places its construction in the first half of the fourth century CE;[124] thus, its chronology is somewhat earlier, albeit not significantly so, than that of building 7 at Amheida, which seems to be datable to the second half of the same century.[125]

While it is unlikely that the same people worked on the construction of the two churches, the Large East Church—or rather its layout and the type and arrangement of its features—point to a set of architectural standards that were well established in Dakhla by the middle of the fourth century CE. Those standards continued to be adopted, in the following decades, for the erection of other Christian places of cult in the region, such as at Amheida and at ʿAin el-Sabil.

The church of ʿAin el-Sabil, located in close proximity to Kellis, at the center of Dakhla, is remarkably similar to building 7 at Amheida, in terms of chronology, typology, and the adoption of certain architectural features (fig. 2.5).[126] They share the same tripartite basilica layout, with a central nave and two side aisles defined by two colonnades, as well as a west return aisle (which, in the case of the church of ʿAin el-Sabil, is marked by four columns).[127]

Access to both churches was from the west, but arranged differently; while the church at Amheida was entered from a relatively monumental entrance in the middle of the west wall (on the church's main east-west axis), two entrances were found in the church at ʿAin el-Sabil, one in the north half of the west wall and another in the southwest corner of the building, also in the west wall. The latter allowed access to the church from an opening facing a large east-west street, via a set of two rooms preliminarily identified as a vestibule and a narthex.[128]

The two churches were flanked, along the outer face of their south walls, by an annex of rooms likely serving more utilitarian functions, including food preparation. In building 7 at Trimithis, these spaces (rooms 5–13) were accessed from the south, via a doorway leading into room 6, as well as from the north, by means of a passage placed off the landing of a staircase (room 5). This was, in turn, accessed from room 1, thus allowing direct passage from the church into the south annex (cf. fig. 3.2). At ʿAin el-Sabil, on the other hand, the church and the south annex were fully separated. Access to the service rooms was either via the vestibule to the southwest of the church or, in the case of a kitchen with oven and staircase located at the east end of the annex, via a doorway placed along this room's east wall (cf. fig. 2.5).[129]

Both churches have a tripartite sanctuary at their east ends, consisting of a central apse[130] and two side rooms, although the arrangement of these lateral spaces, as well as access to

---

124. For a foundation of the church during the reign of Constantine, see Bowen 2002, 81–83, esp. 83.
125. Cf. Sec. 7.4.
126. Cf. Sec. 2.1.1 for a summary of the evidence concerning the church and its dating, as well as the available bibliography.
127. No east transverse aisle exists at the church of ʿAin el-Sabil.
128. Bayoumy and Masoud 2019, 354, fig. 1; 358. A third, narrow entrance is located in the southeast corner of the south aisle; it was once connected with a room flanking the south *pastophorion* of the sanctuary; this space was, in turn, accessed from another entrance placed further east, piercing the east wall of the church.
129. Bayoumy and Masoud 2019, 358.
130. Engaged columns marked the entrance into the apse in both churches.

them, varies between the church at ʿAin el-Sabil and building 7 at Amheida.[131] It is also worth noticing that the apse in the church at ʿAin el-Sabil is square, a shape that is attested (based on the current reconstruction) also for the apse of building 7 at Amheida.

The evidence of two fourth-century churches with squarish/rectangular apses is remarkable, when compared with most of the other known examples of contemporary churches (largely from the Great Oasis), which are generally characterized by semicircular apses. As mentioned above, rectangular sanctuaries are more commonly attested in early Egyptian churches built at monastic centers.[132] However, the evidence from ʿAin el-Sabil and Amheida suggests that rectangular apses were, if not as common as rounded ones, certainly not absent in non-monastic churches of Upper Egypt in late antiquity.

Another feature that is attested in the churches at ʿAin el-Sabil and Amheida is the mud-brick platform, coated in white gypsum, once giving access from the nave to the raised apse.[133] In both churches, there were steps leading to the top of this feature placed along the latter's north and south sides. However, while the apse in the church at Trimithis could not be accessed from the west, as there were no steps built along the west side of the platform, this was not the case in the church at ʿAin el-Sabil. As mentioned earlier, the platform facing the central room of the sanctuary is uniquely combined with a square podium that rests on top of the platform itself. The top of the *bema* was once accessed via a set of three steps ascending from the west, in line with the main east-west axis of the church.[134] The superposition of a podium, aligned on the main access of the church, on top of a platform with side steps in front of the apse is so far unattested in early churches from the region.[135] The reasons for such an unusual combination are yet to be determined.

Finally, both churches excavated at Amheida and at ʿAin el-Sabil had mud-brick benches (better preserved in the latter example), which lined the inner faces of some walls; these, as well as the columns, were coated with white gypsum plaster, with no traces of painted decoration.[136]

The remarkable similarities between the two churches extend beyond the layout and the existence in both buildings of certain architectural features such as a square apse and, possibly, a stepped podium. The church of ʿAin el-Sabil was dated by its excavators to a period following the mid-fourth century, based on a coin found in the south wall of the apse that was minted between 348 and 358.[137] A dating to the second half of the fourth century is also shared

---

131. The area adjoining the south side of the apse in the church at ʿAin el-Sabil is in fact divided into a cupboard to the east (accessible directly from the apse) and a small rectangular space to the west, opening onto the south aisle. The northern *pastophorion* extends along the entire north wall of the apse and opens onto both the north aisle and the apse. At Amheida, the two *pastophoria* were once accessed from the north and south aisles, but it is unknown if any openings existed between them and the central apse.

132. Cf. n. 103 above.

133. This feature does not appear, with the same characteristics, in other churches of the Great Oasis, with the exception of the Large East Church at Kellis.

134. Bayoumy and Masoud 2019, 358.

135. Bowen 2019, 371.

136. It is unknown if the ceiling of the church of ʿAin el-Sabil had a decoration similar to that of the roof in the church at Amheida, or if it was decorated at all (Bayoumy and Masoud 2019, 358).

137. Bayoumy and Masoud 2019, 358.

by the church at Amheida, on the basis of ceramic, numismatic, and documentary evidence (ostraka).

A third close parallel with the church at Amheida can be found at Shams el-Din in south Kharga Oasis, near Dush (Kysis) and the Darb el-Arbain (fig. 2.20).[138] The church, which is also dated to the fourth century, is similar in construction materials, size, and layout. The main room is tripartite, with a central nave and two side aisles, divided by two rows of three columns each. An additional column, placed between the westernmost column of both the north and south colonnades, was added to create a west return aisle.

No east transverse aisle is attested in the church at Shams el-Din; as mentioned earlier, it is not clear beyond doubt if this was a feature of the church at Amheida. Both basilica-type buildings were constructed as part of multi-room complexes, with smaller rooms built along the south wall of the two churches.[139] There is, however, a notable difference: while at Amheida the south rooms seem to have been secondary to the church, and likely utilitarian in function, it was only through the south annex that the church at Shams el-Din was originally accessed, with a room lined with benches likely serving as an anteroom. At Amheida, in contrast, the main access into building 7 was from the west, along the church's main axis, and the threshold placed along the south wall of room 6, at the south end of the complex, must have marked a service entrance (fig. 3.2).[140]

The churches at Shams el-Din and Amheida had mud-brick benches running along the inner faces of the walls. Also, both churches opened, at their east ends, onto a tripartite sanctuary, consisting of a centrally placed apse (rectangular in both cases)[141] flanked by two service rooms to the north and south.

The Large East Church at Kellis and the church at ʿAin el-Sabil, both in Dakhla, as well as the one at Shams el-Din, in Kharga, are in a better state of preservation than the Amheida church. Thus, they offer a more complete picture of what the church at Amheida (including the south annex) might have looked like in antiquity, before the disappearance of most features above the original floor level. What can be said, based on this comparative study, is that both the spatial arrangement and the architectural features of the church at Amheida closely match standards that were widely adopted in the region of the Western Desert, and more broadly throughout Upper Egypt, in the late Roman period.[142] Churches in the Great Oasis seem to have shared, by the mid-fourth century CE, a codified set of architectural and artistic norms (no doubt applied with local variation). However, only in part can these be seen as typical of

---

138. See Wagner 1976, 285–86; Sauneron 1976, 410–11, pl. LXXIV; Bonnet 2004, 84, fig. 69; McKenzie 2007, 270, fig. 450. See also Capuani 1999, 255, fig. 11; 256. Cf. also the evidence summarized in Sec. 2.3 of this volume.

139. Evidence was found, in the south annex of both churches, of staircases, which would have given access in antiquity to the roof (or an upper floor) of each building.

140. The presence, within the south annex at Shams el-Din, of the main (only?) entrance into the church does not rule out the possibility that the rooms flanking the vestibule might have been used for more utilitarian purposes, as in the case of the south rooms in the church at Amheida and in the Large East Church at Kellis.

141. As attested also in the church at ʿAin el-Sabil.

142. More comparanda (although not as close to the church at Amheida as the ones mentioned above) can be found in the region of the Great Oasis, especially Kharga. For an overview of the churches that were object of survey or excavation in Kharga, see Sec. 2.3; cf. also Ghica 2012 and Warner 2018a.

Christian architecture in Upper Egypt. If one looks at the available evidence (mostly from Dakhla and Kharga) with an eye to what is known from other parts of the Mediterranean world, it becomes clear how Christian architecture in Egypt's Western Desert must be seen in the context of developments that took place on a much broader scale.

Chapter 8

Epilogue

8.1. Significance of the Discovery of the Church and Funerary Crypts

The Amheida church project pursued a historical and comparative line of inquiry that attends to one of the most significant developments in the history of the Mediterranean world in late antiquity: the spread of Christianity. Though small, at the edge of empire, and poorly preserved, the Amheida church nevertheless reveals much about how new ideas and trends were transmitted, especially because of its basilica form. The site's combination of sanctuary and burial place also contributes significantly to our knowledge of early Christian ritual. Furthermore, the church's decoration is of great value to the study of early Christian art both in Egypt and beyond.

The church of Amheida had features that were relatively standard in Christian architecture of Upper Egypt in late antiquity: a central nave, side aisles, west return aisle, and a sanctuary flanked by service rooms. Several of these architectural elements support the generally accepted view that Christian basilica-type churches derive from Roman civic buildings that had the same shape. What is remarkable is that the basilica type in Christian architecture took hold in a remote oasis of the Egypt's Western Desert at roughly the same time that the first Christian basilicas were being built in Rome and the rest of the Mediterranean world. This speaks to a significantly more "interconnected" world than one might at first assume, especially considering the geographical remoteness of some of these oases.

Another important aspect of this research project concerns the evidence of painted geometric ornamentation from the collapsed ceiling of the Amheida church. What is particularly significant is that a flat roof with interior painted geometric decoration in the context of an early Christian church is (thus far) archaeologically unattested elsewhere in Egypt, with the possible exception of the Large East Church at nearby Kellis. Hence, the evidence from Amheida offers a unique avenue to study the transmission of artistic idioms and patterns in Egypt, as well as in the broader Mediterranean region, during the Graeco-Roman period and into late antiquity.

Although little is known about the nature of the liturgical practices that were once performed in the church at Amheida, the archaeological data conclusively prove that the building served as a funerary complex. This association of a Christian place of cult with funerary practices was already known in Dakhla Oasis before the discovery of this church. Nevertheless, the discovery of three underground funerary crypts makes the Amheida church an exceptionally important case study. Indeed, these spaces located below the sanctuary of the church are the earliest Christian set of funerary crypts found in Egypt. They therefore add significant data to our knowledge of Christian funerary architecture, as well as of Christian burial customs, in late antique Egypt.

As discussed in Chapter 5, a total of 17 burials were identified in the church at Amheida, including five in room 1, one in room 6, and 11 in two of the underground crypts below the church's sanctuary (four graves in room 2 and seven graves in room 3). All 17 burials were excavated and their human remains removed, but only four bodies have been thoroughly investigated, with the remaining 13 (excavated in 2023) awaiting detailed analysis.[1] Notwithstanding the numerous questions that still await answers (for example, regarding the identity of the deceased or why they were buried inside the church rather than in the nearby cemetery), data already gathered has helped to shed some light on Christian burial customs in fourth-century Dakhla. Physical anthropologists established that not only adult men (tombs 4 and 17)[2] but at least two female individuals (tombs 2–3) had been interred in close proximity to the sanctuary, i.e., the most sacred area inside the church.[3] Remarkably, out of the eleven bodies discovered in the north and central crypts, only one was of an adult male (tomb 6 in room 2, the north crypt), with all the remining ones belonging to adult females or juveniles, children, and infants (whose sex could not be determined). Even more surprisingly, none of the seven burials in the central crypt, located below the church's apse and thus—one would assume—of particular importance as a burial spot, belonged to an adult male. This fact suggests that the privilege of being buried in this area was not (or not exclusively) reserved for members of the clergy, or even for adult members of the congregation. Indeed, tomb 2 in room 1 (next to the entrance onto the apse) belonged to a woman who was in her mid-teens when she died; also, seven of the graves inside the north and central crypts were of individuals ranging from six month to 15 years of age.[4]

No unequivocal clues were found concerning the social status or the occupation of the four deceased individuals; nevertheless, evidence of pathological conditions, some potentially associated with military combat, was retrieved from one of the skeletons, suggesting that the individual might have been a soldier stationed in or near Amheida.[5] Of course, more work is needed, especially on the other burials that were excavated in the church at Amheida in 2023. Nevertheless, what is known has already offered us a vivid picture of a thriving Christian

---

1. See Aravecchia et al. 2015. A preliminary analysis of the 13 bodies exhumed in 2023, carried out by P. G. Sheldrick, is included in the preliminary season report. See also Sec. 5.5 and the chapter by Tosha L. Dupras et al. in the companion volume (forthcoming) to this archaeological report.

2. A third adult male was buried in tomb 1, in the northwest corner of building 7.

3. An additional female burial (tomb 5) was excavated in room 6, thus farther from the sanctuary (although not at a significant distance from it).

4. See (again) the discussion in Sec. 5.5 of this volume, including the evidence (from another church in Dakhla) for the interment of young individuals in fourth-century churches.

5. Aravecchia et al. 2015, 38.

community, comprised of men and women of different ages and (perhaps) backgrounds, but all united by the same faith and affiliated (likely in life as well as in death) with the same place of worship.

Overall, the discovery and investigation of the church in Area 2.3 at Amheida, combined with the documentary evidence gathered in other areas of the site, have also shed light on the growth of Christianity at Amheida in the fourth century. It is now clear, for instance, that by the mid-fourth century the *polis* had a Christian community with the means to choose prime locations for the construction of churches. As discussed above in Sec. 7.5 above, building 7 must have enjoyed a high degree of visibility from different areas of the city and therefore offered a commanding view over the surrounding built and natural landscapes.[6] This shows how Christianity had become, by the early fourth century, a key element of the religious landscape even in this remote oasis of the ancient world.

Finally, the significance of this project lies also in its interdisciplinary character. This publication was created with the goal of being relevant not only to archaeologists working on early Christianity, but also to historians and art historians of the Mediterranean region in late antiquity, as well as socio-cultural anthropologists who study the development of religious and cultural phenomena in antiquity. The results of our investigation, particularly on the effects of Christianity's spread on the pre-existing built environment, as well as the socio-cultural and religious milieu of late antique Egypt, will hopefully be of interest to scholars studying religions in other geographical, chronological, and cultural contexts.

8.2. Considerations for Future Work in Area 2.3 (and Beyond)

The goal of future excavation seasons in Area 2.3 is to gather much-needed information on the topographical relationship of the church complex with the surrounding built environment. New excavations will hopefully allow us to increase our knowledge on the urban fabric of this sector at the east end of the city of Amheida, where building 7 must have been one of its most visible landmarks.

Notwithstanding the preeminent, highly visible location of the church on the top of a low hill, it is likely that the surrounding area was densely built, as suggested by the existence of walls that were partially cleared during the topographical survey. Indeed, this sector seems to have been directly connected to the rest of the city's urban fabric, by means of streets and alleys like the one that ran east-west and apparently ended at the west monumental entrance of the church. Excavations to the east of building 7 will help shed light on the large courtyard (tentatively labeled as a *kathesterion*, or space for visitors, on comparative grounds) which was surveyed to the east of the church. The investigation of this area will also allow us to determine

---

6. Centrality must have been a key factor in the decision to build a church also at other sites in Dakhla, including the agricultural hamlet of 'Ain el-Gedida: see Aravecchia 2020.

if the courtyard belonged to the church complex and, if so, how it was spatially connected to it, thus providing some answers on its function(s) in antiquity.

It is also to be expected that future fieldwork at Amheida will reveal how several more churches dotted the built landscape of the city in the fourth century, especially considering its size and local importance in late antiquity, given that other, smaller settlements like Kellis appear to have had at least three churches in use around the same time as building 7 at Amheida.[7] The results of extensive survey work that was carried out at Amheida have already raised the possibility, indeed the likelihood, that the church in Area 2.3 was not the only Christian place of cult at fourth-century Trimithis.

In 2013, investigations were conducted in the area at the west and southwest of the archaeological site, with the goal of exploring the liminal areas of the ancient city at its west and south ends.[8] Part of the cemetery (Area 6), lying in a sector to the southwest of Area 2, was investigated as part of this survey (fig. 8.1). Clusters of large rectangular rooms, of a size ranging from 5 to 17 m² and separated by narrow passageways, were identified. Although heavily eroded at their tops, the walls of these rooms in some cases still stand to the considerable height of 3 m and show evidence of painted decoration. These rooms are yet to be excavated, but it is assumed that they were used as monumental burials. At the northwest corner of Area 6 stands a cluster of buildings (in the red circle in fig. 8.1) of particular interest in this connection, as the westernmost of these was tentatively identified as a church.[9] The walls' tops are extant above ground level only in the eastern half of the room, but one cannot fail to notice striking similarities, in terms of layout, with building 7 in Area 2.3. Two colonnades, running northwest–southeast, seem to divide one large space into a central nave and two side aisles. At the east end of the room is a set of three small rectangular spaces; the one in the middle opens onto the nave, along an east-west axis, while the other two are symmetrically placed to the north and south of the central room. Overall, the spatial arrangement points to the likely identification of this building as a church with a standard basilica plan, including a (possibly) rectangular apse flanked by what may have been two *pastophoria*.

As noted above, no information is currently available on the western half of the room, since there are no walls standing above the modern-day ground level in this area. Thus, it is not possible to know if the north and south colonnades were joined, at their west ends, by a third row of columns that formed a west return aisle (as in church building 7). A rectangular room, as well as a smaller one to the west of it, were surveyed against the northeast wall of this building. At first glance, these spaces may have served as an entryway or anteroom for the church; but it is impossible to verify this hypothesis without proper excavations. These would also allow us to establish if the building was part of a larger complex, as in building 7 and other fourth-century churches in the region, and, more broadly, how the church was related spatially to—and interacted with—the surrounding built environment. The location of the basilica, erected within an area occupied by monumental tombs, is suggestive of its nature as a funerary church. The building might have been functionally associated with

---

7. Aravecchia 2015a, 130.
8. See p. 3 of the 2013 field report: http://hdl.handle.net/2451/64551
9. Davoli 2015b, 75.

Chapter 8: Epilogue

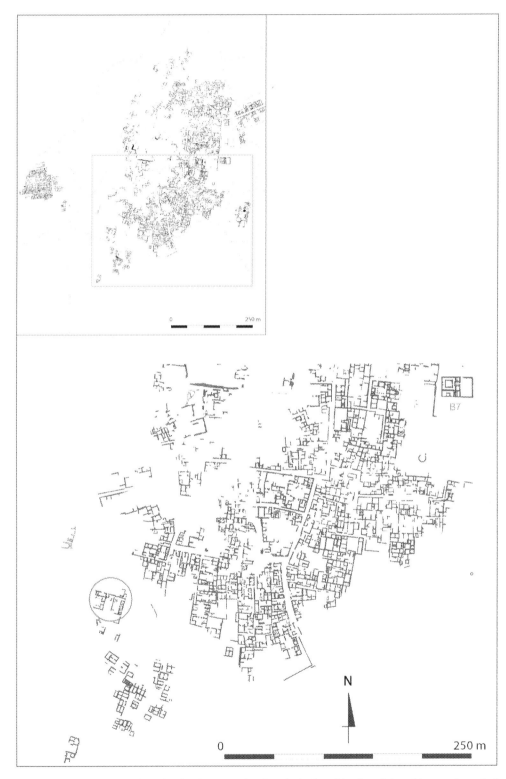

Fig. 8.1: Plan of the south area of Amheida, showing the church (B7) and (red circle) visible remains of what may be another church at the southwest edge of the site.

funerary and commemorative rituals for the deceased inhabitants of Christian Trimithis, at least those who were buried in the large cemetery to the south of the city.[10]

The list of goals for future work at Amheida/Trimithis makes it apparent that our currently available data on fourth-century Christianity at the site are far from complete. Certainly, more needs to be done, both in Area 2.3, where the church once stood, and in other sectors of the ancient city, including the (seemingly industrial) area immediately to the east of building 7, as well as the necropolis at the south end of the site. It is certainly puzzling that a large *polis* like Trimithis apparently had less, and less sizeable, churches than a smaller settlement like Kellis, whose evidence for Christian basilicas is also earlier than that from Trimithis. However, this may well simply be the result of chance discovery, with most of the ancient city still awaiting in-depth investigation.

Notwithstanding the current limitations of the evidence, an exciting picture has already started to emerge, especially following the discovery of the church and its underground crypts. It is the picture of an established Christian community, whose members must have felt part of a broader community of believers across the empire. Indeed, they desired to worship (and be buried) in a building that not only enjoyed a commanding view of the entire city, but also resembled the basilicas that were being erected (around the same time) throughout the Mediterranean region. It is our hope that this volume is only the first of many more studies on the Christianization of ancient Trimithis, a phenomenon that significantly changed both the religious and urban landscape of this important oasis city of Egypt's Western Desert.

---

10. On early Christian funerary churches, see, among others, Grossmann 2014; Grossmann 2002a, esp. 127–32; Davies 1999; Yasin 2005; Stewart-Sykes 2009; Volp 2002; Fox and Tritsaroli 2019. See also the discussion in Sec. 5.5 of this volume.

Table of Chronology[1]

Predynastic Period	to 3000 BCE
Early Dynastic Period	ca. 3000–2686
Old Kingdom	ca. 2686–2181
First Intermediate Period	ca. 2180–2040
Middle Kingdom	ca. 2040–1730
Second Intermediate Period	ca. 1730–1550
New Kingdom	ca. 1550–1069
Third Intermediate Period	ca. 1069–664
Late Period	664–332
Macedonian Dynasty	332–306
Ptolemaic Dynasty	306–30
Roman Period	30 BCE–282 CE
Late Roman/Late Antique/Byzantine Period	
Diocletian	284–305
Diocletian in Egypt	298
The Great Persecution	303–313
Constantine I	306–337
Licinius	308–324
Athanasius bishop of Alexandria	328–373
Constantine II	337–340
Constans	337–350

1. Partially adapted from Bagnall 2021.

Constantius II	337–361
Julian ("the Apostate")	361–363
Jovian	363–364
Valens	364–378
Theodosius I	379–395
Roman Empire divided into eastern and western halves	395
Arcadius	395–408
Theodosius II	408–450
Marcian	450–457
Council of Chalcedon condemns Miaphysites	451
Leo I	457–474
Zeno	474–491
Anastasius	491–518
Justin I	518–527
Justinian	527–565
Justin II	565–578
Tiberius II	578–582
Maurice	582–602
Phocas	602–610
Heraclius	610–641
Sasanian Persians occupy Egypt	619–629

Arab Conquest 639–642

Bibliography

Abbreviations

AJA	American Journal of Archaeology
ArchCL	Archeologia classica
ArtB	The Art Bulletin
ASAE	Annales du Service des antiquités de l'Égypte
BASP	Bulletin of the American Society of Papyrologists
BIFAO	Bulletin de l'Institut français d'archéologie orientale de Caire
BMMA	Bulletin of the Metropolitan Museum of Art, New York
DOP	Dumbarton Oaks Papers
GRBS	Greek, Roman and Byzantine Studies
IFAO	Institut français d'archéologie orientale
JARCE	Journal of the American Research Center in Egypt
JEA	The Journal of Egyptian Archaeology
JFA	Journal of Field Archaeology
JLA	Journal of Late Antiquity
JRA	Journal of Roman Archaeology
JSSAE	The Journal of the Society for the Study of Egyptian Antiquities
MDAIK	Mitteilungen des Deutschen Archäologischen Instituts, Abteilung Kairo
PAM	Polish Archaeology in the Mediterranean
PBSR	Papers of the British School at Rome
ZAeS	Zeitschrift für ägyptische Sprache und Altertumskunde
ZPE	Zeitschrift für Papyrologie und Epigraphik

Adriani, Achille. 1936. "La Nécropole de Moustafa Pacha." *Annuaire du Musée gréco-romain* 2 (1933/34–1934/35).

———. 1952. "Nécropoles de l'île de Pharos. B. Section d'Anfouchy." *Annuaire* 4 (1940–1950): 55–128.

———. 1966. *Repertorio d'arte dell'Egitto greco-romano*. Serie C, Vols. 1–2. Rome: L'Erma di Bretschneider.

Anderson, Branson Dale. 2021. *A Part of the Family: Funerary Preparations for Children and Adolescents in Late Ptolemaic and Roman Egypt*. Ph.D. Dissertation: University of Memphis.

Aravecchia, Nicola. 2012. "The Church Complex of ʿAin el-Gedida, Dakhleh Oasis." In *The Oasis Papers 6: Proceedings of the Sixth International Conference of the Dakhleh Oasis Project*, edited by Roger S. Bagnall, Paola Davoli, and Colin A. Hope, 391–408. Dakhleh Oasis Project Monograph 15. Oxford: Oxbow Books.

———. 2015a. "The Church of Trimithis." In *An Oasis City*, by Roger S. Bagnall, Nicola Aravecchia, Raffaella Cribiore, Paola Davoli, Olaf E. Kaper, and Susanna McFadden, 119–30. New York: New York University Press and Institute for the Study of the Ancient World.

———. 2015b. "Other Churches in Dakhla: Kellis, ʿAin el-Gedida, Deir Abu Matta, Deir el-Molouk, ʿAin es-Sabil." In *An Oasis City*, by Roger S. Bagnall, Nicola Aravecchia, Raffaella Cribiore, Paola Davoli, Olaf E. Kaper, and Susanna McFadden, 135–48. New York: New York University Press and Institute for the Study of the Ancient World.

———. 2015c. "A Rural Settlement in the Oasis System." In *An Oasis City*, by Roger S. Bagnall, Nicola Aravecchia, Raffaella Cribiore, Paola Davoli, Olaf E. Kaper, and Susanna McFadden, 157–68. New York: New York University Press and Institute for the Study of the Ancient World.

———, with contributions by Roger S. Bagnall et al. 2018. *ʿAin el-Gedida: 2006–2008 Excavations of a Late Antique Site in Egypt's Western Desert*. Amheida IV. New York: Institute for the Study of the Ancient World and New York University Press.

———. 2020a. "The Changing Sacred Landscape of Egypt's Western Desert in Late Antiquity: The Case of ʿAin el-Gedida." *AJA* 124.2: 301–20.

———. 2020b. "Geometric Painting in Late-Antique Egypt: The Ceiling of a 4th-c. Church at Amheida (Dakhla Oasis)." *JRA* 33: 449–66.

———. 2021. "The Hamlet of ʿAin el-Gedida in Dakhla Oasis: A Late Roman *Epoikion*?" *JARCE* 57: 13–31.

———. 2022. "Catechumens, Women, and Agricultural Laborers: Who Used the Fourth-Century Hall at the Church of ʿAin el-Gedida, Egypt?" *JLA* 15/1: 193–230.

———. 2024. "Christian Identity in the Archaeological Record: Evidence from Egypt's Western Desert." In *Studies in Coptic Culture and Community: Ordinary Lives, Changing Times*, edited by Mariam Ayad, 195–217. Cairo: American University in Cairo Press.

Aravecchia, Nicola, Tosha L. Dupras, Dorota Dzierzbicka, and Lana Williams. 2015. "The Church at Amheida (Ancient Trimithis) in the Dakhleh Oasis, Egypt: A Bioarchaeological Perspective on an Early Christian Mortuary Complex." *Bioarchaeology of the Near East* 9: 21–43. Available on-line at: http://www.anthropology.uw.edu.pl/09/bne-09-02.pdf

Arveiller-Dulong, Véronique, and Marie-Dominique Nenna. 2011. *Les verres antiques du Musée du Louvre*, III, *Parures, instruments et éléments d'incrustation*. Paris: Somogy éditions d'art.

Ast, Rodney, and Roger S. Bagnall. 2015. "New Evidence for the Roman Garrison of Trimithis." *Tyche* 30: 1–4; pls. 1–3.

———, with contributions by Clementina Caputo and Raffaella Cribiore. 2016. *Ostraka from Trimithis. Volume 2: Greek Texts from the 2008–2013 Seasons*. Amheida III. New York: Institute for the Study of the Ancient World and New York University Press.

Ast, Rodney, and Roger S. Bagnall. 2019. "Land and Resource Administration: Farmers, Managers, and Soldiers in the Great Oasis." In *The Great Oasis of Egypt: The Kharga and Dakhla Oases in Antiquity*, edited by Roger S. Bagnall and Gaëlle Tallet, 105–21. Cambridge: Cambridge University Press.

Ast, Rodney, and Paola Davoli. 2016. "Ostraka and Stratigraphy at Amheida (Dakhla Oasis, Egypt): A Methodological Issue." In *Proceedings of the 27th International Congress of Papyrology (Warsaw, 29 July – 3 August 2013). Volume Three: Studying Papyri*, edited by Tomasz Derda, Adam Łajtar, and Jakub Urbanik, 1447–71. Warsaw: Journal of Juristic Papyrology.

Athenaeus, *The Learned Banqueters*, Vol. II: Books 3.106e–5. Edited and translated by S. Douglas Olson. Loeb Classical Library 208. Cambridge, MA; London: Harvard University Press.

Bagnall, Roger S. 1982. "Religious Conversion and Onomastic Change." *BASP* 19: 105–24.

———. 1993. *Egypt in Late Antiquity*. Princeton: Princeton University Press.

———, ed. 2007. *Egypt in the Byzantine World, 300–700*. Cambridge: Cambridge University Press.

———. 2015. "The Economic Landscape." In *An Oasis City*, by Roger S. Bagnall, Nicola Aravecchia, Raffaella Cribiore, Paola Davoli, Olaf E. Kaper, and Susanna McFadden, 29–33. New York: New York University Press and Institute for the Study of the Ancient World.

———, ed. 2021. *Roman Egypt: A History*. Cambridge: Cambridge University Press.

Bagnall, Roger S., Nicola Aravecchia, Raffaella Cribiore, Paola Davoli, Olaf E. Kaper, and Susanna McFadden. 2015. *An Oasis City*. New York: New York University Press and Institute for the Study of the Ancient World.

Bagnall, Roger S., and Clementina Caputo. 2021. "The Great Oasis in the Later Fourth Century." *GRBS* 61: 527–50.

Bagnall, Roger S., Clementina Caputo, Roberta Casagrande-Kim, and Irene Soto. 2017. "New Evidence from Ostraka for the Dating of 4th Century CE Ceramic Assemblages." *Bulletin de liaison de la céramique égyptienne* 27: 195–211.

Bagnall, Roger S., and Raffaella Cribiore. 2012. "Christianity on Thoth's Hill." In *The Oasis Papers 6: Proceedings of the Sixth International Conference of the Dakhleh Oasis Project*, edited by Roger S. Bagnall, Paola Davoli, and Colin A. Hope, 409–16. Dakhleh Oasis Project Monograph 15. Oxford: Oxbow Books.

———. 2015. "Other Evidence of Christianity at Amheida." In *An Oasis City*, by Roger S. Bagnall, Nicola Aravecchia, Raffaella Cribiore, Paola Davoli, Olaf E. Kaper, and Susanna McFadden, 131–35. New York: New York University Press and Institute for the Study of the Ancient World.

Bagnall, Roger S., Paola Davoli, and Colin A. Hope, eds. 2012. *The Oasis Papers 6: Proceedings of the Sixth International Conference of the Dakhleh Oasis Project*. Oxford: Oxbow Books.

Bagnall, Roger S., and Dorota Dzierzbicka. 2018. "Ostraka and Graffiti." In *ʿAin el-Gedida: 2006–2008 Excavations of a Late Antique Site in Egypt's Western Desert*. Amheida IV, by Nicola Aravecchia, 507–38. New York: Institute for the Study of the Ancient World and New York University Press.

Bagnall, Roger S., and Olaf E. Kaper. 2015. "Introduction." In *An Oasis City*, by Roger S. Bagnall, Nicola Aravecchia, Raffaella Cribiore, Paola Davoli, Olaf E. Kaper, and Susanna McFadden, 1–10. New York: New York University Press and Institute for the Study of the Ancient World.

Bagnall, Roger S., and Dominic W. Rathbone, eds. 2004. *Egypt from Alexander to the Early Christians. An Archaeological and Historical Guide*. Los Angeles: The J. Paul Getty Museum.

Bagnall, Roger S., and Giovanni R. Ruffini. 2004. "Civic Life in Fourth Century Trimithis: Two Ostraca from the 2004 Excavations." *ZPE* 149: 143–52.

Bagnall, Roger S., and Gaëlle Tallet, eds. 2019. *The Great Oasis of Egypt: The Kharga and Dakhla Oases in Antiquity*. Cambridge: Cambridge University Press.

Bailey, Donald M. 1988. *A Catalogue of the Lamps in the British Museum, III. Roman Provincial Lamps*. London: British Museum Publications.

Bailey, Donald M., and Peter Grossmann. 1994. "The South Church at Hermopolis Magna (Ashmunein): A Preliminary Report." In *Churches Built in Ancient Times: Recent Studies in Early Christian Archaeology*, edited by Kenneth S. Painter, 49–71. London: Society of Antiquaries of London; Accordia Research Centre, University of London.

Baldini Lippolis, Isabella. 2005. *L'architettura residenziale nelle città tardoantiche*. Rome: Carocci.

Ball, John. 1927a. "Problems of the Libyan Desert." *The Geographical Journal* 70/1: 21–38.

———. 1927b. "Problems of the Libyan Desert (Continued)." *The Geographical Journal* 70/2: 105–28.

Balmelle, Catherine, Michèle Blanchard-Lemée, Jeannine Christophe, Jean-Pierre Darmon, Anne-Marie Guimier-Sorbets, Henri Lavagne, Richard Prudhomme, and Henri Stern. 2002. *Le décor géométrique de la mosaïque romaine*. Vol. I: *Répertoire graphique et descriptive des compositions linéaires et isotropes*. Paris: Picard.

Balty, Janine. 1995. *Mosaïques antiques du Proche-Orient: Chronologie, iconographie, interprétation*. Paris: Les Belles Lettres.

Barbet, Alix. 1985. *La peinture murale romaine: Les styles décoratifs pompéiens*. Paris: Picard.

Barnard, Hans, Willemina Z. Wendrich, Alexandra Winkels, Jolanda E. M. F. Bos, Bethany L. Simpson, and René T. J. Cappers. 2016. "The Preservation of Exposed Mudbrick Architecture in Karanis (Kom Aushim), Egypt." *JFA* 41/1: 84–100.

Basilios, Archbishop. 1991. "Ambo." In *Coptic Encyclopedia*, edited by Aziz S. Atiya, Vol. 1, 111–12. New York: Macmillan.

Bayumi, Kamel A. 1998. "Excavations at ʿAin al Gadida in the Dakhleh Oasis." In *Life on the Fringe: Living in the Southern Egyptian Deserts during the Roman and Early-Byzantine Periods. Proceedings of a Colloquium Held on the Occasion of the 25th Anniversary of the Netherlands*

Institute for Archaeology and Arabic Studies in Cairo 9–12 December 1996, edited by Olaf E. Kaper, 55–62. Leiden: Research School CNWS School of Asian, African, and Amerindian Studies.

Bayoumy, Kamel A., and Mahmoud M. Masoud. 2019 "'Ain Al-Sabil in Dakhleh Oasis." In *The Oasis Papers 9: A Tribute to Anthony J. Mills after Forty Years of Research in Dakhleh Oasis: Proceedings of the Ninth International Conference of the Dakhleh Oasis Project*, edited by Gillian E. Bowen and Colin A. Hope, 353–66. Oxford: Oxbow Books.

Beadnell, Hugh J. L. 1901. *Dakhla Oasis: Topography and Geology*. Cairo: Survey Department.

Bertacchi, Luisa. 1994. *Basilica, museo e scavi, Aquileia*. Rome: Istituto Poligrafico e Zecca dello Stato.

Bey Kamal, Ahmed. 1907. *Livre des perles enfouies et du mystère précieux au sujet des indications des cachettes, des trouvailles et des trésors*. Cairo: IFAO.

Birrell, Michael. 1999. "Excavations in the Cemeteries of Ismant el-Kharab." In *Dakhleh Oasis Project: Preliminary Reports on the 1992–1993 and 1993–1994 Field Seasons*, edited by Colin A. Hope and Anthony J. Mills, 29–41. Oxford: Oxbow Books.

Blumell, Lincoln H. 2012. *Lettered Christians: Christians, Letters, and Late Antique Oxyrhynchus*. Leiden: Brill.

Bolman, Elizabeth S. 2006. "Late Antique Aesthetics, Chromophobia and the Red Monastery, Sohag, Egypt." *Eastern Christian Art* 3: 1–24.

Bolman, Elizabeth S., Stephen J. Davis, and Gillian Pyke. 2010. "Shenoute and a Recently Discovered Tomb Chapel at the White Monastery." *Journal of Early Christian Studies* 18/3: 453–62.

Bolman, Elizabeth S. 2016. *The Red Monastery Church: Beauty and Asceticism in Upper Egypt*. New Haven: Yale University Press in association with American Research Center in Egypt.

———. Forthcoming. "Movement and Creation: A Reassessment of Early Byzantine Visual Culture." In *Worlds of Byzantium*, edited by Elizabeth S. Bolman, Scott F. Johnson, and Jack Tannous. Cambridge: Cambridge University Press.

Bonnet, Charles. 2004. "L'église du village de Douch." In *Kysis: Fouilles de l'Ifao à Douch, Oasis de Kharga, 1985–1990*, by Michel Reddé, with contributions by Pascale Ballet et al., 75–86. Cairo: IFAO.

Bonnet, Charles, and Mohamed Abd El-Samie. 2004. "Les églises de Tell el-Makhzan: La campagne de fouilles de 2002." *Cahier de Recherches de l'Institut de Papyrologie et d'Égyptologie de Lille* 24: 15–33.

Bonnet, Charles, Mohamed Abd El-Samie, and Fathi Talha. 2005. "L'ensemble martyrial de Saint Épimaque à Tell el-Makhzan (Égypte - Nord Sinaï)." *Revue d'Histoire de l'Art et d'Archéologie* 53: 281–91.

Boozer, Anna L. 2007. *Housing Empire: The Archaeology of Daily Life in Roman Amheida, Egypt*. Ph.D. Dissertation, Columbia University.

———. 2013. "Archaeology on Egypt's Edge: Archaeological Research in the Dakhleh Oasis, 1819–1977." *Ancient West and East* 12: 117–56.

———. 2015. *A Late Romano-Egyptian House in the Dakhla Oasis: Amheida House B2*. Amheida

II. New York: New York University Press and Institute for the Study of the Ancient World.

Bowen, Gillian E. 2002. "The Fourth Century Churches at Ismant el-Kharab." In *Dakhleh Oasis Project: Preliminary Reports on the 1994–1995 to 1998–1999 Field Seasons*, edited by Colin A. Hope and Gillian E. Bowen, 65–85. Dakhleh Oasis Project Monograph 11. Oxford: Oxbow Books.

―――――. 2003a. "The Small East Church at Ismant el-Kharab." In *The Oasis Papers 3. Proceedings of the Third International Conference of the Dakhleh Oasis Project*, edited by Gillian E. Bowen and Colin A. Hope, 153–65. Dakhleh Oasis Project Monograph 14. Oxford: Oxbow Books.

―――――. 2003b. "Some Observations on Christian Burial Practices at Kellis." In *The Oasis Papers 3. Proceedings of the Third International Conference of the Dakhleh Oasis Project*, edited by Gillian E. Bowen and Colin A. Hope, 167–82. Dakhleh Oasis Project Monograph 14. Oxford: Oxbow Books.

―――――. 2008. "The Church of Deir Abu Metta and a Christian Cemetery in Dakhleh Oasis: A Brief Report." *The Bulletin of the Australian Centre for Egyptology* 19: 7–16.

―――――. 2009. "The Church of Deir Abu Metta, Dakhleh Oasis: A Report on the 2009 Excavation." *The Bulletin of the Australian Centre for Egyptology* 20: 7–36.

―――――. 2010. "The spread of Christianity in Egypt: Archaeological Evidence from Dakhleh and Kharga Oases." In *Egyptian Culture and Society: Studies in Honour of Naguib Kanawati*, edited by Alexandra Woods, Ann McFarlane, and Susanne Binder. Cairo: Conseil Suprême des Antiquités de l'Égypte.

―――――. 2012a. "Child, Infant and Foetal Burials of the Late Roman Period at Ismant el-Kharab, Ancient Kellis, Dakhleh Oasis." In *L'Enfant et la Mort dans l'Antiquité II: Types de tombes et traitement du corps des enfants dans l'antiquité gréco-romaine. Actes de la table ronde internationale organisée à Alexandrie, Centre d'études alexandrines, 12–14 novembre 2009*, edited by Marie-Dominique Nenna, 351–72. Alexandria: Centre d'études alexandrines.

―――――. 2012b. "The Church of Dayr Abu Matta and Its Associated Structures: An Overview of Four Seasons of Excavation." In *The Oasis Papers 6: Proceedings of the Sixth International Conference of the Dakhleh Oasis Project*, edited by Roger S. Bagnall, Paola Davoli, and Colin A. Hope, 429–50. Dakhleh Oasis Project Monograph 15. Oxford: Oxbow Books.

―――――. 2012c. "Coins as Tools for Dating the Foundation of the Large East Church at Kellis: Problems and a Possible Solution." In *The Oasis Papers 6: Proceedings of the Sixth International Conference of the Dakhleh Oasis Project*, edited by Roger S. Bagnall, Paola Davoli, and Colin A. Hope, 418–28. Dakhleh Oasis Project Monograph 15. Oxford: Oxbow Books.

―――――. 2017. "Christianity at Mut al-Kharab (ancient Mothis), Dakhleh Oasis, Egypt." In *The Cultural Manifestations of Religious Experience: Studies in Honour of Boyo G. Ockinga*, edited by Camilla Di Biase-Dyson and Leonie Donovan, 241–46. Münster: Ugarit-Verlag.

―――――. 2019. "Christianity in Dakhleh Oasis: An Archaeological Overview." In *The Oasis Papers 9: A Tribute to Anthony J. Mills after Forty Years of Research in Dakhleh Oasis: Proceedings of the Ninth International Conference of the Dakhleh Oasis Project*, edited by Gillian E. Bowen and Colin A. Hope, 367–80. Oxford: Oxbow Books.

―――――. 2022a. "Christian Burial Practices." In *Kellis: A Roman-Period Village in Egypt's Dakhleh*

Oasis, edited by Colin A. Hope and Gillian E. Bowen, 343–66. Cambridge: Cambridge University Press.

———. 2022b. "The Churches." In *Kellis: A Roman-Period Village in Egypt's Dakhleh Oasis*, edited by Colin A. Hope and Gillian E. Bowen, 269–88. Cambridge: Cambridge University Press.

———. 2023. *The Excavations at Ismant al-Kharab. Volume II – The Christian Monuments of Kellis: The Churches and Cemeteries*. Oxford: Oxbow Books.

Bowen, Gillian E., and Tosha Dupras. Forthcoming. "The Christian Burials at Dayr Abu Matta, Dakhleh Oasis, Egypt." *Bioarchaeology of the Near East*.

Bowen, Gillian E., and Colin A. Hope, eds. 2003. *The Oasis Papers 3. Proceedings of the Third International Conference of the Dakhleh Oasis Project*. Oxford: Oxbow Books.

———. 2019a. "The Church at Dayr al-Malak in Dakhleh Oasis." In *The Oasis Papers 9: A Tribute to Anthony J. Mills after Forty Years of Research in Dakhleh Oasis: Proceedings of the Ninth International Conference of the Dakhleh Oasis Project*, edited by Gillian E. Bowen and Colin A. Hope, 419–30. Oxford: Oxbow Books.

———, eds. 2019b. *The Oasis Papers 9: A Tribute to Anthony J. Mills after Forty Years of Research in Dakhleh Oasis: Proceedings of the Ninth International Conference of the Dakhleh Oasis Project*. Oxford: Oxbow Books.

Bowen, Gillian E., Colin A. Hope, and Olaf E. Kaper. 1993. "A Brief Report on the Excavations at Ismant el-Kharab in 1992–1993." *The Bulletin of the Australian Centre for Egyptology* 4: 17–28.

Bowman, Alan K. 1996. *Egypt after the Pharaohs, 332 BC–AD 642: From Alexander to the Arab Conquest*. London: British Museum Press.

Brand, Mattias. 2022. *Religion and the Everyday Life of Manichaeans in Kellis: Beyond Light and Darkness*. Leiden: Brill.

Bravard, Jean-Paul. 2019. "Water Resources and Irrigation in Two Oases of the Western Desert of Egypt: Kharga and Dakhla." In *The Great Oasis of Egypt: The Kharga and Dakhla Oases in Antiquity*, edited by Roger S. Bagnall and Gaëlle Tallet, 17–29. Cambridge: Cambridge University Press.

Bravard, Jean-Paul, Ashraf Mostafa, Paola Davoli, Katherine A. Adelsberger, Pascale Ballet, Romain Garcier, Lucio Calcagnile, and Gianluca Quarta. 2016. "Construction and Deflation of Irrigation Soils from the Pharaonic to the Roman Period at Amheida (*Trimithis*), Dakhla Depression, Egyptian Western Desert." *Géomorphologie: Relief, Processus, Environnement* 22.3: 305–24.

Breccia, Evaristo. 1933. *Le Musée Gréco-Romain, 1931–1932*. Bergamo: Istituto Italiano d'Arti Grafiche.

Briant, Pierre, ed. 2001. *Irrigation et drainage dans l'Antiquité. Qanāts et canalisations souterraines en Iran, en Égypte et en Grèce*. Paris: Thotm.

Brooks Hedstrom, Darlene L. 2019. "Archaeology of Early Christianity in Egypt." In *The Oxford Handbook of Early Christian Archaeology*, edited by David K. Pettegrew, William R. Caraher, and Thomas W. Davis, 665–84. New York: Oxford University Press.

Brooks Hedstrom, Darlene, Stephen J. Davis, Tomasz Herbich, Salima Ikram, Dawn McCormack, Marie-Dominique Nenna, and Gillian Pyke. 2010. "New Archaeology at Ancient Scetis: Surveys and Initial Excavations at the Monastery of St. John the Little in Wādī al-Naṭrūn (Yale Monastic Archaeology Project)." *DOP* 64: 217–27.

Bulić, Frane. 1929. *Kaiser Diokletians Palast in Split*. Zagreb: Matica Hrvatska.

Cailliaud, Frédéric. 1826–1827. *Voyage à Méroé: au fleuve Blanc, au-delà de Fâzoql dans le midi du royaume de Sennâr, à Syouah et dans cinq autres oasis; fait dans les années 1819, 1820, 1821 et 1822*. Paris: Imprimerie royale.

Cailliaud, Frédéric, and Edme François Jomard. 1821. *Voyage à l'oasis de Thèbes et dans les déserts situés à l'Orient et à l'Occident de la Thébaïde: fait pendant les années 1815, 1816, 1817 et 1818*. Paris: Imprimerie royale.

Capuani, Massimo, with contributions by Otto F. A. Meinardus and Marie-Hélène Rutschowscaya. 1999. *Christian Egypt. Coptic Art and Monuments through Two Millennia*. Collegeville, Minnesota: The Liturgical Press.

Caputo, Clementina. 2014. "Amheida/Trimithis (Dakhla Oasis): Results from a Pottery Survey in Area 11." *Bulletin de Liaison de la Céramique Égyptienne* 24: 163–77.

———, with contributions by Julie Marchand and Irene Soto Marín. 2020. *The House of Serenos. Part I: The Pottery*. Amheida V. New York: New York University Press and Institute for the Study of the Ancient World.

Carandini, Andrea. 2000. *Storie dalla Terra. Manuale di scavo archeologico*. Torino: Einaudi.

Cervi, Angela 2015. "Faience Vessels." In *A Late Romano-Egyptian House in the Dakhla Oasis: Amheida House B2*, by Anna Lucille Boozer, with contributions by Douglas V. Campana, Angela Cervi, Pam J. Crabtree, Paola Davoli, Delphine Dixneuf, David M. Ratzan, Giovanni Ruffini, Ursula Thanheiser, and Johannes Walter: 341–47. New York: Institute for the Study of the Ancient World and New York University Press.

Choat, Malcolm. 2006. *Belief and Cult in Fourth-Century Papyri*. Turnhout: Brepols.

———. 2012. "Christianity." In *The Oxford Handbook of Roman Egypt*, edited by Christina Riggs, 474–89. Oxford: Oxford University Press.

———. 2020. "Earliest Christianity in the Great Oasis." In *Dust, Demons and Pots: Studies in Honour of Colin A. Hope*, edited by Ashten R. Warfe, James C. R. Gill, Caleb R. Hamilton, Amy J. Pettman, and David A. Stewart, 77–87. Leuven: Peeters.

Churcher, Charles S., and Anthony J. Mills, eds. 1999. *Reports from the Survey of the Dakhleh Oasis Western Desert of Egypt, 1977–1987*. Oxford: Oxbow Books.

Cipriano, Giuseppina. 2008. *El-Bagawat: Un cimitero paleocristiano nell'Alto Egitto*. Todi: Tau Editrice.

Clédat, Jean. 1999. *Le monastère et la nécropole de Baouit*. Cairo: IFAO.

Correas-Amador, María. 2011. "A Survey of the Mud-Brick Buildings of Qena." *Egyptian Archaeology* 38: 14–16.

Cosyns, Peter 2011. *The Production, Distribution and Consumption of Black Glass in the Roman Empire during the 1st – 5th Century AD. An Archaeological, Archaeometric and Historical Approach*. Ph.D. Dissertation, Vrije Universiteit Brussel.

Cotelle-Michel, Laurence. 2004. *Les Sarcophages en terre cuite en Égypte and en Nubie de l'époque prédynastique à l'époque romaine*. Dijon: Faton.

Coudert, Magali. 2012. "The Christian Necropolis of el-Deir in the North of Kharga Oasis." In *The Oasis Papers 6: Proceedings of the Sixth International Conference of the Dakhleh Oasis Project*, edited by Roger S. Bagnall, Paola Davoli, and Colin A. Hope, 451–58. Dakhleh Oasis Project Monograph 15. Oxford: Oxbow Books.

Cribiore, Raffaella. 2015. "Literary Culture and Education in the Dakhla Oasis." In *An Oasis City*, by Roger S. Bagnall, Nicola Aravecchia, Raffaella Cribiore, Paola Davoli, Olaf E. Kaper, and Susanna McFadden, 179–92. New York: New York University Press and Institute for the Study of the Ancient World.

Cribiore, Raffaella, and Paola Davoli. 2013. "New Literary Texts from Amheida, Ancient Trimithis (Dakhla Oasis, Egypt)." *ZPE* 187: 1–14.

Cribiore, Raffaella, Paola Davoli, and David M. Ratzan. 2008. "A teacher's dipinto from Trimithis (Dakhleh Oasis)." *JRA* 21: 171–91.

Cruz-Uribe, Eugene. 1986. "The Hibis Temple Project 1984–85 Field Season, Preliminary Report." *JARCE* 23: 157–66.

———. 1987. "Hibis Temple Project: Preliminary Report, 1985–1986 and Summer 1986 Field Seasons." *Varia Aegyptiaca* 3: 215–30.

Davies, Jon, 1999. *Death, Burial and Rebirth in the Religions of Antiquity*. London: Routledge.

Davis, Stephen J. 2004. *The Early Coptic Papacy: The Egyptian Church and Its Leadership in Late Antiquity*. Cairo: American University in Cairo Press.

Davis, Stephen J., with Elizabeth Bolman, Darlene Brooks Hedstrom, and Gillian Pyke. 2012. "Life and Death in Lower and Upper Egypt: A Brief Survey of Recent Monastic Archaeology at Yale." *Journal of the Canadian Society for Coptic Studies* 3: 9–26.

Davoli, Paola. 2011. "Reflections on Urbanism in Graeco-Roman Egypt: A Historical and Regional Perspective." In *The Space of the City in Graeco-Roman Egypt: Image and Reality*, edited by Eva Subìas, Pedro Azara, Jesús Carruesco, Ignacio Fiz, and Rosa Cuesta, 69–92. Tarragona: Institut Català d'Arqueologia Clàssica.

———. 2015a. "The Baths of Trimithis." In *An Oasis City*, by Roger S. Bagnall, Nicola Aravecchia, Raffaella Cribiore, Paola Davoli, Olaf E. Kaper, and Susanna McFadden, 76–86. New York: New York University Press and Institute for the Study of the Ancient World.

———. 2015b. "The City Plan of Roman and Late Roman Trimithis." In *An Oasis City*, by Roger S. Bagnall, Nicola Aravecchia, Raffaella Cribiore, Paola Davoli, Olaf E. Kaper, and Susanna McFadden, 61–76. New York: New York University Press and Institute for the Study of the Ancient World.

———. 2015c. "Early Remains on the Temple Hill." In *An Oasis City*, by Roger S. Bagnall, Nicola Aravecchia, Raffaella Cribiore, Paola Davoli, Olaf E. Kaper, and Susanna McFadden, 35–42. New York: New York University Press and Institute for the Study of the Ancient World.

———. 2015d. "The Natural Landscape and Its Evolution." In *An Oasis City*, by Roger S. Bagnall, Nicola Aravecchia, Raffaella Cribiore, Paola Davoli, Olaf E. Kaper, and Susanna

McFadden, 11–21. New York: New York University Press and Institute for the Study of the Ancient World.

———. 2015e. "A Sacred Necropolis." In *An Oasis City*, by Roger S. Bagnall, Nicola Aravecchia, Raffaella Cribiore, Paola Davoli, Olaf E. Kaper, and Susanna McFadden, 57–60. New York: New York University Press and Institute for the Study of the Ancient World.

———. 2017. "A New Public Bath in Trimithis (Amheida, Dakhla Oasis)." In *Collective Baths in Egypt 2: New Discoveries and Perspectives*, edited by Bérangère Redon, 193–220. Cairo: IFAO.

———. 2019. "Trimithis: A Case Study of Proto-Byzantine Urbanism." In *The Great Oasis of Egypt: The Kharga and Dakhla Oases in Antiquity*, edited by Roger S. Bagnall and Gaëlle Tallet, 46–80. Cambridge: Cambridge University Press.

Davoli, Paola, with a contribution by Nicholas Warner. 2022. *The House of Serenos. Part II: Archaeological Report on a Late-Roman Urban House at Trimithis*. Amheida VI. New York: Institute for the Study of the Ancient World and New York University Press.

Davoli, Paola. 2023. "Egyptian Houses in their Urban and Environmental Contexts: Some Case Studies of the Roman and Late Roman Periods." In *Household in Context: Dwelling in Ptolemaic and Roman Egypt*, edited by Caitlín Eilís Barrett and Jennifer Carrington. Ithaca: Cornell University Press.

Davoli, Paola, and Roger S. Bagnall. 2015. "Two Houses." In *An Oasis City*, by Roger S. Bagnall, Nicola Aravecchia, Raffaella Cribiore, Paola Davoli, Olaf E. Kaper, and Susanna McFadden, 86–104. New York: New York University Press and Institute for the Study of the Ancient World.

Davoli, Paola, and Olaf E. Kaper. 2006. "A New Temple for Thoth in the Dakhleh Oasis." *Egyptian Archaeology* 28: 12–14.

Davoli, Paola, and Olaf E. Kaper. 2015. "The Temple." In *An Oasis City*, by Roger S. Bagnall, Nicola Aravecchia, Raffaella Cribiore, Paola Davoli, Olaf E. Kaper, and Susanna McFadden, 105–11. New York: New York University Press and Institute for the Study of the Ancient World.

DeForest, Dallas. 2019. "Baths, Christianity, and Bathing Culture in Late Antiquity." In *The Oxford Handbook of Early Christian Archaeology*, edited by David K. Pettegrew, William R. Caraher, and Thomas W. Davis, 189–207. New York: Oxford University Press.

Deichmann, Friedrich Wilhelm. 1982. "Entstehung der christlichen Basilika und Entstehung des Kirchengebäudes." In *Rom, Ravenna, Konstantinopel, Naher Osten: Gesammelte Studien zur spätantiken Architektur, Kunst und Geschichte*, edited by Friedrich Wilhelm Deichmann, 35–46. Wiesbaden: Steiner.

Dell'Acqua, Antonio. 2013. "The Use of the Heart-Shaped Pillar in the Ancient Architecture: Examples and Circulation." In *SOMA 2012: Identity and Connectivity. Proceedings of the 16th Symposium on Mediterranean Archaeology, Florence, Italy, 1–3 March 2012*, edited by Luca Bombardieri, Anacleto D'Agostino, Guido Guarducci, Valentina Orsi, and Stefano Valentini, Vol. II, 1139–50. Oxford: Archaeopress.

De Santis, Paola. 2008. "Riti funerari." In *Nuovo dizionario patristico e di antichità cristiane*, Vol.

III, edited by Angelo Di Bernardino: 4531–54. Genova-Milano: Marietti 1820.

Di Castro, Andrea A., and Colin A. Hope, eds. 2015. *Housing and Habitat in the Ancient Mediterranean: Cultural and Environmental Responses*. Leuven: Peeters.

Dixneuf, Delphine. 2011. *Amphores égyptiennes : production, typologie, contenu et diffusion (IIIe siècle avant J.-C-IXe siècle après J.-C.)*. Alexandrie: Centre d'études alexandrine.

———. 2015. "La Céramique de la Maison B2." In *A Late Romano-Egyptian house in the Dakhla Oasis: Amheida House B2*, by Anna Lucille Boozer, with contributions by Douglas V. Campana, Angela Cervi, Pam J. Crabtree, Paola Davoli, Delphine Dixneuf, David M. Ratzan, Giovanni Ruffini, Ursula Thanheiser, and Johannes Walter: 201–80. New York: Institute for the Study of the Ancient World and New York University Press.

———. 2018. "La ceramique d''Ain el-Gedida." In *'Ain el-Gedida: 2006–2008 Excavations of a Late Antique Site in Egypt's Western Desert. Amheida IV*, by Nicola Aravecchia, 285–446. New York: Institute for the Study of the Ancient World and New York University Press.

Doxiadis, Euphrosyne. 1995. *The Mysterious Fayum Portraits: Faces from Ancient Egypt*. London and New York: Thames and Hudson.

Drescher, James, ed. 1946. *Apa Mena: A Selection of Coptic Texts Relating to St Menas*. Cairo: IFAO.

Drovetti, Bernardino. 1821. "Le voyage à l'oasis du Dakel." In *Voyage à l'oasis de Thèbes et dans les déserts situés à l'Orient et à l'Occident de la Thébaïde: fait pendant les années 1815, 1816, 1817 et 1818*, by Frédéric Cailliaud and Edme François Jomard, 99–105. Paris: Imprimerie royale.

Dunand, Françoise. 2007. "Between Tradition and Innovation: Egyptian Funerary Practices in Late Antiquity." In *Egypt in the Byzantine World, 300–700*, edited by Roger S. Bagnall, 163–84. Cambridge: Cambridge University Press.

———. 2019. "Changes in Funerary Structures at Kharga from 'Traditional' to 'Christian' Tombs." In *The Oasis Papers 9: A Tribute to Anthony J. Mills after Forty Years of Research in Dakhleh Oasis: Proceedings of the Ninth International Conference of the Dakhleh Oasis Project*, edited by Gillian E. Bowen and Colin A. Hope, 381–93. Oxford: Oxbow Books.

Dunand, Françoise, Magali Coudert, and Fleur Letellier-Willemin. 2008. "Découverte d'une nécropole chrétienne sur le site d'El-Deir (oasis de Kharga)." In *Études coptes X, Douzième journée d'études (Lyon, 19–21 mai 2005)*, edited by Anne Boud'hors and Catherine Louis, 137–53. Paris: De Boccard.

Dunand, Françoise, Magali Coudert, Roger Lichtenberg, Sophie Brones, and Fleur Letellier-Willemin. 2023. *El-Deir Nécropoles VI, La nécropole chretienne (nécropole Ouest)*. Paris: Éditions Cybèle.

Dunand, Françoise, Jean-Louis Heim, Nessim Henry Henein, and Roger Lichtenberg. 1992. *La Nécropole de Douch (oasis de Kharga) I*. Cairo: IFAO.

Dunand, Françoise, Jean-Louis Heim, Nessim Henry Henein, and Roger Lichtenberg. 2005. *La nécropole de Douch (oasis de Kharga) II*. Cairo: IFAO.

Dunand, Françoise, Jean-Louis Heim, and Roger Lichtenberg. 2012. "Les Nécropoles d'el-Deir (Oasis de Kharga)." In *The Oasis Papers 6: Proceedings of the Sixth International Conference of the Dakhleh Oasis Project*, edited by Roger S. Bagnall, Paola Davoli, and Colin A. Hope, 279–95. Dakhleh Oasis Project Monograph 15. Oxford: Oxbow Books.

Dunand, Françoise, and Fleur Letellier-Willemin. 2019. "Funerary Practices in the Great Oasis during Antiquity." In *The Great Oasis of Egypt: The Kharga and Dakhla Oases in Antiquity*, edited by Roger S. Bagnall and Gaëlle Tallet, 237–68. Cambridge: Cambridge University Press.

Dunand, Françoise, and Roger Lichtenberg. 2024. *Une population antique. L'oasis de Kharga et ses habitants, Égypte, IVe siècle a.C. - Ve siècle p.C.* Paris: Editions Cybèle.

Dunbabin, Katherine M. D. 2003. *The Roman Banquet: Images of Conviviality*. Cambridge: Cambridge University Press.

Dupras, Tosha L., Sandra M. Wheeler, Lana J. Williams, and Peter G. Sheldrick. 2022. "Revealing Life through Death: A Review of the Bioarchaeological Studies of Human Remains." In *Kellis: A Roman-Period Village in Egypt's Dakhleh Oasis*, edited by Colin A. Hope and Gillian E. Bowen, 367–90. Cambridge: Cambridge University Press.

Dupras, Tosha L., Lana J. Williams, Sandra M. Wheeler, and Peter G. Sheldrick. 2016. "Life and Death in the Desert: A Bioarchaeological Study of Human Remains from the Dakhleh Oasis, Egypt." In *Mummies, Magic and Medicine in Ancient Egypt: Multidisciplinary Essays for Rosalie David*, edited by Campbell Price, Roger Forshaw, Andrew Chamberlain, Paul T. Nicholson, Robert Morkot, and Joyce Tyldesley, 286–304. Manchester: Manchester University Press.

Duval, Yvette. 1988. *Auprès des saints corps et âme: l'inhumation "ad sanctos" dans la chrétienté d'Orient et d'Occident du IIIe au VIIe siècle*. Paris: Études Augustiniennes.

Dzierzbicka, Dorota. 2018. "Small Finds from ʿAin el-Gedida: Other Categories." In *ʿAin el-Gedida: 2006–2008 Excavations of a Late Antique Site in Egypt's Western Desert. Amheida IV*, by Nicola Aravecchia, 539–92. New York: Institute for the Study of the Ancient World and New York University Press.

Eckardt, Hella. 2017. *Writing and Power in the Roman World: Literacies and Material Culture*. Cambridge: Cambridge University Press.

Edmondstone, Archibald. 1822. *A Journey to Two Oases of Upper Egypt*. London: John Murray.

Emery, Virginia L. 2011. "Mud-Brick Architecture." In *UCLA Encyclopedia of Egyptology*, edited by Willeke Wendrich, Jacco Dieleman, Elizabeth Frood, and John Baines. Los Angeles: UCLA. https://escholarship.org/uc/item/4983w678

English, Paul W. 1968. "The Origin and Spread of Qanats in the Old World." *Proceedings of the American Philosophical Society* 112/3: 170–81.

Fakhry, Ahmed. 1951. *The Necropolis of El-Bagawat in Kharga Oasis*. Cairo: Government Press.

―――. 1982. *Denkmäler der Oase Dachla*. Edited by J. Osing, M. Moursi, D. Arnold, O. Neugebauer, R. A. Parker, D. Pingree, and M. A. Nur-el-Din. Mainz am Rhein: Zabern.

Förster, Frank. 2007. "With Donkeys, Jars and Water Bags into the Libyan Desert: The Abu Ballas Trail in the late Old Kingdom/First Intermediate Period." *British Museum Studies in Ancient Egypt and Sudan* 7: 1–36.

Förster, Frank, and Heiko Riemer, eds. 2013. *Desert Road Archaeology in Ancient Egypt and*

Beyond. Köln: Heinrich-Barth-Institut.

Fox, Sherry C., and Paraskevi V. Tritsaroli. 2019. "Burials and Human Remains of the Eastern Mediterranean in Early Christian Context." In T*he Oxford Handbook of Early Christian Archaeology*, edited by William R. Caraher, Thomas W. Davis, and David K. Pettegrew, 105–26. New York: Oxford University Press.

Frankfurter, David, ed. 1998. *Pilgrimage and Holy Space in Late Antique Egypt*. Leiden: Brill.

Froschauer, Harald. 2008. *Zeichnungen und Malereien aus den Papyrussammlungen in Berlin und Wien*. MPER 31. Berlin: De Gruyter.

Gabra, Gawdat, and Hani N. Takla, eds. 2020. *Christianity and Monasticism in Alexandria and the Egyptian Deserts*. Cairo: The American University in Cairo Press.

Gardner, Iain. 2020. *The Founder of Manichaeism: Rethinking the Life of Mani*. Cambridge: Cambridge University Press.

———. 2022. "Types of Christianity: History and Spread, Organization, Practices and Literature." In *Kellis: A Roman-Period Village in Egypt's Dakhleh Oasis*, edited by Colin A. Hope and Gillian E. Bowen, 289–306. Cambridge: Cambridge University Press.

Ghica, Victor. 2012. "Pour une histoire du christianisme dans le désert Occidental d'Égypte." *Journal des savants* 2/1: 189–280.

Ghica, Victor, Rhiannon Williams, Basem Gehad, Mara Elefante, Romain David, and Nicolas Morand. 2023. "The 2021 Excavation Season at Šams al-Dīn (Kharga Oasis)." *Analecta Papyrologica* XXXVI: 149–202.

Giddy, Lisa L. 1987. *Egyptian Oases: Baharia, Dakhla, Farafra, Kharga during Pharaonic Times*. Wiltshire, England: Aris and Phillips Ltd.

Gill, James C. R. 2012. "Ptolemaic Period Pottery from Mut al-Kharab, Dakhleh Oasis." In *The Oasis Papers 6: Proceedings of the Sixth International Conference of the Dakhleh Oasis Project*, edited by Roger S. Bagnall, Paola Davoli, and Colin A. Hope, 231–41. Oxford: Oxbow Books.

———. 2016. *Dakhleh Oasis and the Western Desert of Egypt under the Ptolemies*. Oxford: Oxbow Books.

Godlewski, Włodzimierz. 1990. "Polish Excavations at Naqlun (1988–1989)." *PAM* I [=Reports 1988–1989]: 29–34.

———. 1998. "Naqlun. Excavations 1997." *PAM* IX [=Reports 1997]: 77–86.

———. 2008. "Naqlun (Nekloni). Preliminary Report 2006." *PAM* XVIII [=Reports 2006]: 195–206.

———. 2010. "Naqlun 2007. Preliminary Report." *PAM* XIX [= Reports 2007]: 229–44.

Grabar, André. 1972. *Martyrium: recherches sur le culte des reliques et l'art chrétien antique*. London: Variorum Reprints.

Grimal, Nicolas. 1995. "Travaux de l'Institut Français d'Archéologie Orientale en 1994–1995." *BIFAO* 95: 539–645.

Grossmann, Peter. 1989. *Abū Mīnā I: Die Gruftkirche und die Gruft*. Mainz am Rhein: P. von Zabern.

———. 1991a. "Architectural Elements of Churches: Crypt." In *Coptic Encyclopedia*, edited by

Aziz S. Atiya, Vol. 1, 208–9. New York: Macmillan.

———. 1991b. "Bagawāt (al-): Location and Architecture." In *Coptic Encyclopedia*, edited by Aziz S. Atiya, Vol. 2, 326–27. New York: Macmillan.

———. 1991c. "Dayr Abū Mattā." In *Coptic Encyclopedia*, edited by Aziz S. Atiya, Vol. 3, 706. New York: Macmillan.

———. 1991d. "Dayr al-Malāk." In *Coptic Encyclopedia*, edited by Aziz S. Atiya, Vol. 3, 822. New York: Macmillan.

———. 1998a. *Die antike Stadt Pharan. Ein archäologischer Führer*. Cairo: Archbishopric of Sinai and the Women's Convent of Firan.

———. 1998b. "The Pilgrimage Center of Abû Mînâ." In *Pilgrimage and Holy Space in Late Antique Egypt*, edited by David Frankfurter, 281–302. Leiden: Brill.

———. 1999–2000. "Wadi Fayran/Sinai: Report on the Seasons in March and April 1985 and 1986 with Appendix on the Church at Mount Moses." *ASAE* 75: 153–72.

———. 2002a. *Christliche Architektur in Ägypten*. Leiden: Brill.

———. 2002b. "Typological Considerations on the Large East Church at Ismant el-Kharab." In *Dakhleh Oasis Project: Preliminary Reports on the 1994–1995 to 1998–1999 Field Seasons*, edited by Colin A. Hope and Gillian E. Bowen, 153–56. Oxford: Oxbow Books.

———. 2007. "Early Christian Architecture in Egypt and its Relationship to the Architecture of the Byzantine world." In *Egypt in the Byzantine World, 300–700*, edited by Roger S. Bagnall, 103–36. Cambridge: Cambridge University Press.

———. 2011. "Antinoopolis February/March 2013 Work in the so-called *Chiostro* at the Church beside the Assumed Eastern Gate." *Aegyptus* 91/IV: 127–40.

———. 2014. "Churches and Meeting Halls in Necropoleis and Crypts in Intramural Churches." In *Egypt in the First Millennium AD: Perspectives from New Fieldwork*, edited by Elisabeth R. O'Connell, 93–113; pls. 1–6. Leuven: Peeters.

Grossmann, Peter, and Mohammed Hafiz. 1998. "Results of the 1995/96 Excavations in the North-Western Church of Pelusium (Faramā-West)." *MDAIK* 54: 177–82.

Guimier-Sorbets, Anne-Marie. 2004. "Une interpretation des plafonds peints d'Alexandrie à l'époque hellénistique et au début de l'époque impériale." In *Plafonds et voûtes à l'époque antique. Actes du VIIIe Colloque international de l'Association Internationale pour la Peinture Murale Antique (AIPMA) 15–19 mai 2001, Budapest–Veszprém*, edited by László Borhy, 67–78. Budapest: Pytheas Publishing.

———. 2021. *The Mosaics of Alexandria: Pavements of Greek and Roman Egypt*. Cairo: The American University in Cairo Press.

Hadji-Minaglou Gisèle. 2020. "Architecture at al-Bagawat Cemetery." In *Christianity and Monasticism in Alexandria and the Egyptian Deserts*, edited by Gawdat Gabra and Hani N. Takla, 267–280. Cairo: The American University in Cairo Press.

Hairy, Isabelle. 2009. *Du Nil à Alexandrie: Histoires d'Eaux*. Alexandria: Editions Harpocrates.

Hamerow, Helena. 2016. "Furnished Female Burial in Seventh-Century England: Gender and Sacral Authority in the Conversion Period." *Early Medieval Europe* 24(4): 423–47.

Harding King, W. J. 1912. "Travels in the Libyan Desert." *The Geographical Journal* 39: 133–37.

Harris, Edward C. 1989. *Principles of Archaeological Stratigraphy*. London: Academic Press.

Harris, Josephine M. 1960. "Coptic Architectural Sculpture from Oxyrhynchos." *Year Book of the American Philosophical Society*: 592–98.

Hauser, Walter 1932. "The Christian Necropolis in Kharga Oasis." *BMMA* 27: 38–50.

Hayes, John W. 1972. *Late Roman Pottery*. London: British School at Rome.

Heikkinen, Deanna, 2011. "The Influence of Christianity on Burial Practices in Middle Egypt from the Fourth to the Sixth Centuries." In *Current Research in Egyptology 2010: Proceedings of the Eleventh Annual Symposium, Leiden University 2010*, edited by Maarten Horn, Joost Kramer, Daniel Soliman, Nico Staring, Carina van den Hoven, and Lara Weiss, 107–116. Oxford: David Brown Book Company.

Hellström, Bo. 1940. "The Subterranean Water in the Libyan Desert." *Geografiska Annaler* 22: 206–39.

Hope, Colin A. 1980. "Dakhleh Oasis Project—Report on the Study of the Pottery and Kilns." *JSSEA* 10: 283–313.

———. 1990. "Excavations at Ismant el-Kharab in the Dakhleh Oasis." *The Bulletin of the Australian Centre for Egyptology* 1: 43–54.

———. 1993. "Pottery Kilns from the Oasis of El-Dakhla." In *An Introduction to Ancient Egyptian Pottery*, edited by Dorothea Arnold, Janine Bourriau, and Hans-Åke Nordström, 121–27. Mainz am Rhein: P. von Zabern.

———. 2001. "Observations on the Dating of the Occupation of Ismant el-Kharab." In *The Oasis Papers 1. Proceedings of the First Conference of the Dakhleh Oasis Project*, edited by C. A. Marlow and Anthony J. Mills, 43–59. Oxford: Oxbow Books.

———. 2003. "Excavations at Ismant el-Kharab from 2000 to 2002." In *The Oasis Papers 3: Proceedings of the Third International Conference of the Dakhleh Oasis Project*, edited by Gillian E. Bowen and Colin A. Hope, 207–89. Oxford: Oxbow Books.

———. 2015. "The Roman-Period Houses of Kellis in Egypt's Dakhleh Oasis." In *Housing and Habitat in the Ancient Mediterranean: Cultural and Environmental Responses*, edited by Andrea A. Di Castro and Colin A. Hope, 199–229. Leuven: Peeters.

Hope, Colin A., and Gillian E. Bowen. 1997. "The Excavations at Ismant el-Kharab in 1995/6 and 1996/7: A Brief Report." *The Bulletin of the Australian Centre for Egyptology* 8: 49–64.

———, eds. 2002. *Dakhleh Oasis Project: Preliminary Reports on the 1994–1995 to 1998–1999 Field Seasons*. Oxford: Oxbow Books.

———. 2022a. "The Abandonment of Kellis." In *Kellis: A Roman-Period Village in Egypt's Dakhleh Oasis*, edited by Colin A. Hope and Gillian E. Bowen, 391–406. Cambridge: Cambridge University Press.

———, eds. 2022b. *Kellis: A Roman-Period Village in Egypt's Dakhleh Oasis*. Cambridge: Cambridge University Press.

Hope, Colin A., Gillian E. Bowen, and Olaf E. Kaper. 2022. "The Pharaonic and Classical Religious Complexes and the Cult of Tutu." In *Kellis: A Roman-Period Village in Egypt's Dakhleh Oasis*, edited by Colin A. Hope and Gillian E. Bowen, 203–42. Cambridge: Cambridge University Press.

Hope, Colin A., and Judith McKenzie. 1999. "Interim Report on the West Tombs." In *Dakhleh Oasis Project: Preliminary Reports on the 1992–1993 and 1993–1994 Field Seasons*, edited by Colin A. Hope and Anthony J. Mills, 53–68. Oxford: Oxbow Books.

Hope, Colin A., Judith McKenzie, and Carlo Rindi Nuzzolo. 2022. "The Traditional Cemeteries of Kellis." In *Kellis: A Roman-Period Village in Egypt's Dakhleh Oasis*, edited by Colin A. Hope and Gillian E. Bowen, 307–42. Cambridge: Cambridge University Press.

Hope, Colin A., and Anthony J. Mills, eds. 1999. *Dakhleh Oasis Project: Preliminary Reports on the 1992–1993 and 1993–1994 Field Seasons*. Oxford: Oxbow Books.

Hope, Colin A., and Helen Whitehouse. 2006. "A Painted Residence at Ismant el-Kharab (*Kellis*) in the Dakhleh Oasis." *JRA* 19: 312–28.

Husselman, Elinor M. 1979. *Karanis Excavations of the University of Michigan in Egypt, 1928–1935. Topography and Architecture. A Summary of the Reports of the Director, Enoch E. Peterson*. Ann Arbor: The University of Michigan Press.

Ikram, Salima. 2019. "The North Kharga Oasis Darb Ain Amur Survey (NKODAAS): Surveying the Tracks between the Two Oases." In *The Great Oasis of Egypt: The Kharga and Dakhla Oases in Antiquity*, edited by Roger S. Bagnall and Gaëlle Tallet, 135–51. Cambridge: Cambridge University Press.

Ikram Salima, and Corinna Rossi. 2007. "North Kharga Oasis Survey 2004 Preliminary Report: Ain el-Tarakwa, Ain el-Dabashiya and Darb Ain Amur." *MDAIK* 63: 167–84; pls. 23–24.

Isings, Clasina. 1957. *Roman Glass from Dated Finds*. Groningen: J. B. Wolters.

Iwasaki, Erina, Abdelazim M. Negm, and Salwa F. Elbeih, eds. 2021. *Sustainable Water Solutions in the Western Desert, Egypt: Dakhla Oasis*. Cham: Springer.

James, Liz. 2017. *Mosaics in the Medieval World: From Late Antiquity to the Fifteenth Century*. Cambridge: Cambridge University Press.

Jeffreys, David G. and Eugen Strouhal. 1980. "North Saqqara 1978–9: The Coptic Cemetery Site at the Sacred Animal Necropolis: Preliminary Report." *JEA* 66: 28–35.

Johnson, Mark J. 1997. "Pagan-Christian Burial Practices of the Fourth Century: Shared Tombs?" *Journal of Early Christian Studies* 5/1: 37–59.

Kajitani, Nobuko 2006. "Textiles and Their Context in the Third- to Fourth-Century CE Cemetery of al-Bagawat, Khargah Oasis, Egypt, from the 1907–1931 Excavations by the Metropolitan Museum of Art, New York." In *Textiles in Situ: Their Find Spots in Egypt and Neighbouring Countries in the First Millennium CE*, edited by Sabine Schrenk, 95–112. Riggisberg: Abegg-Stiftung.

Kaper, Olaf. E., ed. 1998. *Life on the Fringe. Living in the Southern Egyptian Deserts during the Roman and Early-Byzantine Periods. Proceedings of a Colloquium Held on the Occasion of the 25th Anniversary of the Netherlands Institute for Archaeology and Arabic Studies in Cairo 9–12 December 1996*. Leiden: Research School CNWS School of Asian, African, and Amerindian Studies.

———. E. 2012. "The Western Oases." In *The Oxford Handbook of Roman Egypt*, edited by Christina Riggs, 717–35. Oxford: Oxford University Press.

———. E. 2015. "Funerary Life: The Pyramids." In *An Oasis City*, by Roger S. Bagnall, Nicola

Aravecchia, Raffaella Cribiore, Paola Davoli, Olaf E. Kaper, and Susanna McFadden, 112–16. New York: New York University Press and Institute for the Study of the Ancient World.

Kaper, Olaf E., and Willemina Z. Wendrich. 1998. "East and West in Roman Egypt: An introduction to Life on the Fringe." In *Life on the Fringe. Living in the Southern Egyptian Deserts during the Roman and Early-Byzantine Periods. Proceedings of a Colloquium Held on the Occasion of the 25th Anniversary of the Netherlands Institute for Archaeology and Arabic Studies in Cairo 9–12 December 1996*, edited by Olaf E. Kaper, 1–4. Leiden: Research School CNWS School of Asian, African, and Amerindian Studies.

Kaufmann, Karl Maria. 1910. *Die Menasstadt und das Nationalheiligtum der altchristlichen Aegypter in der westalexandrinischen wüste*. Leipzig: Verlag von Karl W. Hiersemann.

Kimura, Reiji. 2021. "Climate Features of Dakhla Oasis." In *Sustainable Water Solutions in the Western Desert, Egypt: Dakhla Oasis*, edited by Erina Iwasaki, Abdelazim M. Negm, and Salwa F. Elbeih, 89–99. Cham: Springer.

Kleindienst, Maxine R., Charles S. Churcher, Mary M. A. McDonald, and Henry P. Schwarcz. 1999. "Geography, Geology, Geochronology and Geoarchaeology of the Dakhleh Oasis Region: An Interim Report." In *Reports from the Survey of the Dakhleh Oasis Western Desert of Egypt, 1977–1987*, edited by Charles S. Churcher and Anthony J. Mills, 1–54. Oxford: Oxbow Books.

Knudstad, James E., and Rosa A. Frey. 1999. "Kellis, the Architectural Survey of the Romano-Byzantine Town at Ismant el-Kharab." In *Reports from the Survey of the Dakhleh Oasis Western Desert of Egypt, 1977–1987*, edited by Charles S. Churcher and Anthony J. Mills, 189–214. Oxford: Oxbow Books.

Kötting, Bernhard. 1984. "Die Tradition der Grabkirche." In *Memoria. Der geschichtliche Zeugniswert des liturgischen Gedenkens im Mittelalter*, edited by Karl Schmid and Joachim Wollasch, 69–78. München: Wilhelm Fink Verlag.

Krautheimer, Richard. 1986. *Early Christian and Byzantine Architecture*. New Haven: Yale University Press.

Kucera, Paul. 2012. "al Qasr: The Roman Castrum of Dakhleh Oasis." In *The Oasis Papers 6: Proceedings of the Sixth International Conference of the Dakhleh Oasis Project*, edited by Roger S. Bagnall, Paola Davoli, and Colin A. Hope, 305–16. Dakhleh Oasis Project Monograph 15. Oxford: Oxbow Books.

Kyriakakis, James. 1974. "Byzantine Burial Customs: Care of the Deceased from Death to Prothesis." *Greek Orthodox Theological Review* 19: 37–72.

Lancaster, Lynne C. 2015. *Innovative Vaulting in the Architecture of the Roman Empire: 1st to 4th Centuries CE*. Cambridge: Cambridge University Press.

Lavan, Luke, and William Bowden, eds. 2003. *Theory and Practice in Late Antique Archaeology*. Leiden: Brill.

Lavan, Luke, Ellen Swift, and Toon Putzeys, eds. 2007. *Objects in Context, Objects in Use: Material Spatiality in Late Antiquity*. Leiden: Brill.

Leach, Eleanor Winsor. 2004. "*Doctus spectare lacunar*: Roman Ceilings in Verbal Contexts." In *Plafonds et voûtes à l'époque antique. Actes du VIIIe Colloque international de l'Association*

Internationale pour la Peinture Murale Antique (AIPMA) 15–19 mai 2001, Budapest–Veszprém, edited by László Borhy, 55–59. Budapest: Pytheas Publishing.

Leatherbury, Sean V. 2018. "Christian Wall Mosaics and the Creation of Sacred Space." In *The Routledge Handbook of Early Christian Art*, edited by Robin M. Jensen and Mark D. Ellison, 86–103. London: Routledge.

Leone, Anna. 2013. *The End of the Pagan City: Religion, Economy, and Urbanism in Late Antique North Africa*. Oxford: Oxford University Press.

Letellier-Willemin, Fleur. 2019. "Contribution of the Textiles to the Study of the Site of Al-Deir, Kharga Oasis." In *The Oasis Papers 9: A Tribute to Anthony J. Mills after Forty Years of Research in Dakhleh Oasis: Proceedings of the Ninth International Conference of the Dakhleh Oasis Project*, edited by Gillian E. Bowen and Colin A. Hope, 403–9. Oxford: Oxbow Books.

Levi, Doro. 1947. *Antioch Mosaic Pavements*. 2 Vols. Princeton: Princeton University Press.

Ling, Roger. 1991. *Roman Painting*. Cambridge: Cambridge University Press.

Lloyd, Alan B. 1979. "Coptic and Greek Inscriptions and Sealings." In *The Tomb of Ḥetepka and Other Reliefs and Inscriptions from the Sacred Animal Necropolis North Saqqâra 1964–1973*, by Geoffrey T. Martin, 102–20. London: Egypt Exploration Society.

Lucan. *Pharsalia*. Translated by Jane Wilson Joyce. Loeb Classical Library 18. Ithaca and London: Cornell University Press, 1993.

Lucchesi-Palli, Elisabetta. 1990. "Geometrische und florale Ornamente in den Wandmalereien von Bawit. Untersuchungen zu ihrer Herkunft." *Boreas* 13: 113–33; pls. 21–27.

Lythgoe, Albert M. 1908a. "The Egyptian Expedition." *BMMA* 3.5: 83–86.

———. 1908b. "The Oasis of Kharga." *BMMA* 3.11: 203–8.

MacDonald, William L. 1965. *The Architecture of the Roman Empire*. Vol. 1. New Haven: Yale University Press.

Mahmoud Masoud, D., Rodney Ast, and Roger S. Bagnall. 2021. "Two Archives of Ostraka from Ain es-Sabil." *BASP* 58: 87–134.

Mairs, Rachel 2010. "Egyptian 'Inscriptions' and Greek 'Graffiti' at El Kanais in the Egyptian Eastern Desert." In *Ancient Graffiti in Context*, edited by Jennifer A. Baird and Claire Taylor, 153–64. New York: Routledge.

Majcherek, Grzegorz. 2018. "Alexandria, Kom el-Dikka. Season 2017." *PAM* 27/1: 35–56.

Marinis, Vasileios. 2009. "Tombs and Burials in the Monastery tou Libos in Constantinople." *DOP* 63: 147–66.

Marki, Euterpi. 2002. "Τα χριστιανικά κοιμητήρια στην Ελλάδα. Οργάνωση, τυπολογία, ταφική ζωγραφική, μαρτύρια, κοιμητηριακές βασιλικές." *Δελτίον της Χριστιανικής Αρχαιολογικής Εταιρείας* 23: 163–76.

Martin, Geoffrey T. 1974. "Excavations in the Sacred Animal Necropolis at North Saqqâra, 1972–3: Preliminary Report." *JEA* 60: 15–29.

———. 1981. *The Sacred Animal Necropolis at North Saqqâra: The Southern Dependencies of the Main Temple Complex*. London: Egypt Exploration Society.

McDonald, Mary M. A. 1999. "Neolithic Cultural Units and Adaptations in the Dakhleh Oasis." In *Reports from the Survey of the Dakhleh Oasis Western Desert of Egypt, 1977–1987*, edited by Charles S. Churcher and Anthony J. Mills, 117–32. Oxford: Oxbow Books.

McDonald, Mary M. A., Charles S. Churcher, Ursula Thanheiser, Jennifer Thompson, Ines Taubner, and Ashten R. Warfe. 2001. "The Mid-Holocene Sheikh Muftah Cultural Unit of Dakhleh Oasis, South Central Egypt: A Preliminary Report on Recent Fieldwork." *Nyame Akuma* 56: 4–10.

McFadden, Susanna. 2014. "Art on the Edge: The Late Roman Wall Painting of Amheida, Egypt." In *Akten des XI. Internationalen Kolloquiums der AIPMA (Association international pour la peinture murale antique) Archäologische Forschungen* 23: 359–70; pls. 125–27.

———. 2015. "Amheida's Wall Paintings." In *An Oasis City*, by Roger S. Bagnall, Nicola Aravecchia, Raffaella Cribiore, Paola Davoli, Olaf E. Kaper, and Susanna McFadden, 193–212. New York: New York University Press and Institute for the Study of the Ancient World.

———. 2019. "The House of Serenos and Wall Painting in the Western Oases." In *The Great Oasis of Egypt: The Kharga and Dakhla Oases in Antiquity*, edited by Roger S. Bagnall and Gaëlle Tallet, 281–96. Cambridge: Cambridge University Press.

McKenzie, Judith. 2007. *The Architecture of Alexandria and Egypt, c. 300 B.C. to A.D. 700*. New Haven: Yale University Press.

Mills, Anthony J. 1979. "Dakhleh Oasis Project: Report on the First Season of Survey. October–December 1978." *JSSEA* IX: 163–85.

———. 1980. "Dakhleh Oasis Project: Report on the Second Season of Survey. September–December, 1979." *JSSEA* X: 251–82.

———. 1981. "The Dakhleh Oasis Project. Report on the Third Season of Survey. September–December, 1980." *JSSEA* XI: 175–92.

———. 1982. "The Dakhleh Oasis Project. Report on the Fourth Season of Survey. October 1981–January 1982." *JSSEA* XII: 93–101.

———. 1985. "The Dakhleh Oasis Project." *Mélanges Gamal Eddin Mokhtar* 2:125–34.

———. 1999. "Pharaonic Egyptians in the Dakhleh Oasis." In *Reports from the Survey of the Dakhleh Oasis Western Desert of Egypt, 1977–1987*, edited by Charles S. Churcher and Anthony J. Mills, 171–78. Oxford: Oxbow Books.

Molto, J. Eldon. 2002. "Bio-archaeological Research of Kellis 2: An Overview." In *Dakhleh Oasis Project: Preliminary Reports on the 1994–1995 to 1998–1999 Field Seasons*, edited by Colin A. Hope and Gillian E. Bowen, 239–55. Dakhleh Oasis Project Monograph 11. Oxford: Oxbow Books.

Molto, J. Eldon, Peter G. Sheldrick, Antonietta Cerroni, and Scott Haddow. 2003. "Late Roman Skeletal Remains from Areas D/6 and D/7 and North Tomb 1 at Kellis." In *The Oasis Papers 3. Proceedings of the Third International Conference of the Dakhleh Oasis Project*, edited by Gillian E. Bowen and Colin A. Hope, 345–63. Dakhleh Oasis Project Monograph 14. Oxford: Oxbow Books.

Mommsen, Theodor, and Paul M. Meyer. 1970–1971. *Theodosiani libri XVI cum Constitutionibus Sirmondianis*. Berlin: Weidmann.

Morricone Matini, M. L. 1965. "Mosaici romani a cassettoni del I secolo a.C." *ArchCl* 17: 79–91.

Morvillez, Eric. 1996. "Sur les installations de lits de table en sigma dans l'architecture domestique du Haut et du Bas-Empire." *Pallas* 44: 119–58.

———. 2019. "À propos du fonctionnement des installations de banquet en sigma. Nouvelles observations, entre Orient et Occident." *Antiquité Tardive* 27: 193-221.

Muhlestein, Kerry, Brian D. Christensen, and Cannon Fairbairn. 2020. "Fag el-Gamous Pottery with 'Kill Holes.'" In *Excavations at the Seila Pyramid and Fag el-Gamous Cemetery*, edited by Krystal V. L. Pierce and Bethany Jensen, 285–305. Leiden: Brill.

Muhlestein, Kerry, and Cannon Fairbairn. 2020. "Death of a Common Man." In *Excavations at the Seila Pyramid and Fag el-Gamous Cemetery*, edited by Krystal V. L. Pierce and Bethany Jensen, 93–127. Leiden: Brill.

Müller-Wiener, Wolfgang. 1963. "Christliche Monumente im Gebiet von Hibis (el-Kharga)," *MDAIK* 19: 121–40; pls. XXIX–XXX.

Murray, George W. 1952. "The Water beneath the Egyptian Western Desert." *The Geographical Journal* 118/4: 443–52.

Murray, Mary Anne, Neil Boulton, and Carl Heron. 2000. "Viticulture and Wine Production." In *Ancient Egyptian Materials and Technology*, edited by Paul T. Nicholson and Ian Shaw, 577–608. Cambridge: Cambridge University Press.

Nenna, Marie-Dominique, and Merwatte Seif El-Din. 2000. *La vaisselle en faïence d'époque gréco-romaine: catalogue du Musée gréco-romain d'Alexandrie*. Cairo: IFAO.

Nicholson, Paul T., and Ian Shaw, eds. 2000. *Ancient Egyptian Materials and Technology*, Cambridge: Cambridge University Press.

Nuovo, Marina M. S., and Silvia Prell. 2020. "The Mosaic that Never Was. Tesserae and Raw Material for an Unlaid Mosaic Floor in Trimithis (Dakhla Oasis, Egypt)." *Journal of Mosaic Research* 13: 191–217.

Osing, Jürgen. 1982. *Denkmäler der Oase Dachla: aus dem Nachlass von Ahmed Fakhry*. Mainz am Rhein: P. von Zabern.

Paprocki, Maciej. 2019. *Roads in the Deserts of Roman Egypt: Analysis, Atlas, Commentary*. Oxford: Oxbow Books.

Pearson, Birger A. 1986. "Earliest Christianity in Egypt: Some Observations." In *The Roots of Egyptian Christianity*, edited by Birger A. Pearson and James E. Goehring, 132–59. Philadelphia: Fortress Press.

———. 2007. "Earliest Christianity in Egypt: Further Observations." In *The World of Early Egyptian Christianity: Language, Literature, and Social Context*, edited by James E. Goehring and Janet A. Timbie, 97–112. Washington, D.C.: The Catholic University of America Press.

Peña, J. Theodore 2007. *Roman Pottery in the Archaeological Record*. Cambridge: Cambridge University Press.

Pensabene, Patrizio. 1992. "Architettura imperiale in Egitto." In *Roma e l'Egitto nell'antichità classica. Cairo 1989*, 273–98. Rome: Istituto Poligrafico e Zecca dello Stato; Libreria dello Stato.

———. 1993. *Elementi architettonici di Alessandria e di altri siti egiziani*. Rome: L'Erma di Bretschneider.

———. 2001. "Nota sugli archi in facciata delle cappelle funerarie della necropolis di El

Bagawat nell'Oasi di Kharga." In *The Culture of the Oasis from the Antiquity to the Modern Age. Kharga, 22–27 October 1998*, edited by Nicola Bonacasa, Maria Casini, and Ahmed Etman, 85–104. Cairo: Istituto Italiano di Cultura del Cairo.

Petrie, W. M. Flinders. 1925. *Tombs of the Courtiers and Oxyrhynkhos*. London: British School of Archaeology in Egypt.

Pierce, Krystal V. L., and Bethany Jensen, eds. 2020. *Excavations at the Seila Pyramid and Fag el-Gamous Cemetery*. Leiden: Brill.

Polci, Barbara. 2003. "Some Aspects of the Transformation of the Roman *Domus* between Late Antiquity and the Early Middle Ages." In *Theory and Practice in Late Antique Archaeology*, edited by Luke Lavan and William Bowden, 79–109. Leiden: Brill.

Rahtz, Philip A., 1978. "Grave Orientation." *Archaeological Journal* 135: 1–14.

Rassart-Debergh, Marguerite. 1981a. "Le Pitture del Convento di S. Geremia a Saqqara." *Corsi di cultura sull'arte ravennate e bizantina* 28: 255–79.

———. 1981b. "Quelques remarques iconographiques sur la peinture chrétienne à Saqqara." *Miscellanea Coptica/Acta ad archaeologiam et artium historian pertinentia* 9: 207–20.

———. 1998. "Mosaïque de couleurs." In *Palette égyptienne: de la peinture romaine au décor des monastères coptes* (*Solidarité-Orient Bulletin* 207/2): 29–30.

Reddé, Michel. 1999. "Sites militaires romains de l'Oasis de Kharga." *BIFAO* 99: 377–96.

———, with contributions by Pascale Ballet et al. 2004. *Kysis: Fouilles de l'Ifao à Douch, Oasis de Kharga, 1985–1990*. Cairo: IFAO.

Roberts, Michael. 1989. *The Jeweled Style: Poetry and Poetics in Late Antiquity*. Ithaca: Cornell University Press.

Rohlfs, Gerhard, with contributions by Paul Ascherson, Wilhelm Jordan, Karl Alfred von Zittel, and Philipp Remelé. 1875. *Drei Monate in der libyschen Wüste*. Berlin: Cassel, Verlag von Theodor Fisher. (Reprinted in 1996 in the series Africa Explorata I. Köln: Heinrich-Barth-Institut).

Rose, Paula J. 2013. *A Commentary on Augustine's* De cura pro mortuis gerenda: *Rhetoric in Practice*. Leiden: Brill.

Rossi, Corinna. 2012. "Controlling the Borders of the Empire: The Distribution of Late-Roman 'Forts' in the Kharga Oasis." In *The Oasis Papers 6: Proceedings of the Sixth International Conference of the Dakhleh Oasis Project*, edited by Roger S. Bagnall, Paola Davoli, and Colin A. Hope, 331–36. Dakhleh Oasis Project Monograph 15. Oxford: Oxbow Books.

Rossi, Corinna, and Salima Ikram. 2002. "Petroglyphs and Inscriptions along the Darb Ayn Amur, Kharga Oasis." *ZAeS* 129: 142–51; pls. XXII–XXXI.

———. 2006. "North Kharga Oasis Survey 2003 Preliminary Report: Umm El-Dabadib." *MDAIK* 62: 279–306; pls. 53–54.

———. 2013. "Evidence of Desert Routes across Northern Kharga (Egypt's Western Desert)." In *Desert Road Archaeology in Ancient Egypt and Beyond*, edited by Frank Förster and Heiko Riemer, 265–82. Köln: Heinrich-Barth-Institut.

———. 2018. *North Kharga Oasis Survey: Explorations in Egypt's Western Desert*. Leuven: Peeters.

Rutschowscaya, Marie-Hélène. 1986. *Catalogue des bois de l'Égypte copte*. Paris: Ministère de la culture, Editions de la Réunion des musées nationaux.

Rütti, Beat. 1991. *Die römischen Gläser aus Augst und Kaiseraugst*, Augst: Römermuseum.

Samuil, Bishop, and Peter Grossmann. 1999. "Researches in the Laura of John Kolobos (Wâdî Natrûn)." In *Ägypten und Nubien in spätantiker und christlicher Zeit: Akten des 6. Internationalen Koptologenkongresses, Münster, 20.–26. Juli 1996*, Vol. 1, *Materielle Kultur, Kunst und religiöses Leben*, edited by Stephen Emmel, Martin Krause, Siegfried G. Richter, and Sofia Schaten, 360–64. Wiesbaden: Reichert.

Sauneron, Serge. 1976. "Les Travails de l'Institut Français d'Archéologie Orientale en 1975–1976." *BIFAO* 76: 391–425.

Scheltema, Herman J., and Nicolaas van der Wal, eds. 1955. *Basilicorum Libri LX*. Groningen: J. B. Wolters.

Schijns, Wolf, with contributions by Olaf E. Kaper and Joris Kila. 1999. *Vernacular Mudbrick Architecture in the Dakhleh Oasis, Egypt*. Oxford: Oxbow Books.

Schild, Romuald, and Fred Wendorf. 1977. *The Prehistory of the Dakhleh Oasis and Adjacent Desert*. Warsaw: Polish Academy of Sciences.

Schrenk, Sabine, ed. 2006. *Textiles in Situ: Their Find Spots in Egypt and Neighbouring Countries in the First Millennium CE*. Riggisberg: Abegg-Stiftung.

Schulz, Dorothea. 2011. "Die neue villa des Serenus: Rekonstruktionsarbeiten in der Wüste." *Antike Welt* 2: 20–23.

———. 2015. "Colours in the oasis: the Villa of Serenos." *Egyptian Archaeology* 46: 23–26.

Sheldrick, Peter G. 2008. "The Archaeology of the Kellis 2 Cemetery." In *The Oasis Papers 2: Proceedings of the Second International Conference of the Dakhleh Oasis Project*, edited by Marcia F. Wiseman and Bruce E. Parr Bruce, 137–40. Oxford; Havertown, PA: Oxbow Books.

———. 2023. *Report on the Human Remains from B7 – Amheida*. Unpublished.

Shier, Louise Adele. 1978. *Terracotta Lamps from Karanis. Excavations of the University of Michigan, Egypt*. Ann Arbor: The University of Michigan Press.

Smith, Joyce Y., Kerry Muhlestein, and Brian D. Christensen. 2020. "Textiles and Jewelry at Fag el-Gamous." In *Excavations at the Seila Pyramid and Fag el-Gamous Cemetery*, edited by Krystal V. L. Pierce and Bethany Jensen, 186–206. Leiden: Brill.

Spaer, Maud 1988. "The Pre-Islamic Glass Bracelets of Palestine." *Journal of Glass Studies*, 30: 51-61.

Spence, Craig. 1994. *Archaeological Site Manual*. London: Museum of London.

Spera, Lucrezia. 2005. "Riti funerari e culto dei morti nella tarda antichità. Un quadro archeologico dai cimiteri paleocristiani di Roma." *Augustinianum* XLV/1: 5–34.

Starkey, Paul, and Janet Starkey, eds. 2001. *Travellers in Egypt*. London: Tauris Parke Paperbacks.

Stern, Henri. 1958. "Les mosaïques de l'église de Sainte-Constance à Rome." *DOP* 12: 157+159–218.

Stewart, Joe D., J. Eldon Molto, and Paula J. Reimer. 2003. "The Chronology of Kellis 2: The Interpretative Significance of Radiocarbon Dating of Human Remains." In *The Oasis Papers*

3. Proceedings of the Third International Conference of the Dakhleh Oasis Project, edited by Gillian E. Bowen and Colin A. Hope, 373–78. Dakhleh Oasis Project Monograph 14. Oxford: Oxbow Books.

Stewart-Sykes, Alistair, trans. and ed. 2009. *The Didascalia Apostolorum*. Turnhout: Brepols.

Stillwell, Richard. 1961. "Houses of Antioch." *DOP* 15: 45–57.

Swift, Ellen. 2009. *Style and Function in Roman Decoration: Living with Objects and Interiors*. Farnham, England: Ashgate.

Szymańska, Hanna, and Krzysztof Babraj. 2003. "Marea. Fourth Season of Excavations." *PAM* 15: 53–62.

———. 2006. "Polish Excavations in the Basilica at Marea (Egypt)." *Bulletin de la Societe d'Archéologie Copte* XLV: 107–17; pls. XI–XIII.

Szymańska, Hanna, and Krzysztof Babraj. 2007. "Marea on Lake Maryut." In *Seventy Years of Polish Archaeology in Egypt*, edited by Ewa Laskowska-Kusztal, 159–70. Warsaw: Polish Centre of Mediterranean Archaeology, University of Warsaw.

Teigen, Håkon Fiane. 2021. *The Manichaean Church in Kellis*. Leiden: Brill.

Thanheiser, Ursula. 1999. "Plant Remains from Ismant el-Kharab: First Results." In *Dakhleh Oasis Project: Preliminary Reports on the 1992–1993 and 1993–1994 Field Seasons*, edited by Colin A. Hope and Anthony J. Mills, 89–93. Oxford: Oxbow Books.

Thurston, Harry. 2003. *Secrets of the Sands: The Revelations of Egypt's Everlasting Oasis*. New York: Arcade Publishing.

Török, László. 2005. *Transfigurations of Hellenism: Aspects of Late Antique Art in Egypt, A.D. 250–700*. Leiden: Brill.

Tufnell, Olga 1984. *Studies on Scarab Seals, Volume II: Scarab Seals and their Contribution to History in the Early Second Millennium B.C. Part 1*. Warminster: Aris & Phillips.

Uggeri, Giovanni. 1974. "La chiesa paleocristiana presso la porta orientale." In *Antinoe [1965–1968]*, 37–67; pls. 18–25. Rome: Istituto di Studi del Vicino Oriente, Università degli Studi di Roma.

van Beek, Gus W. 1987. "Arches and Vaults in the Ancient Near East." *Scientific American* 257/1: 96–103.

van Moorsel, Paul. "Church Architecture in Egypt." In *Coptic Encyclopedia*, edited by Aziz S. Atiya, Vol. 2, 552–54. New York: Macmillan.

van Moorsel, Paul, and Mathilde Huijbers 1981. "Repertory of the Preserved Wall Paintings from the Monastery of Apa Jeremiah at Saqqara." *Acta ad archaeologiam et artium historiam pertinentia* IX: 125–86; pls. I–XXX.

Venit, Marjorie S. 2002. *Monumental Tombs of Ancient Alexandria: The Theater of the Dead*. Cambridge: Cambridge University Press.

Vivian, Cassandra. 2008. *The Western Desert of Egypt: An Explorer's Handbook*. Cairo: The American University in Cairo Press.

Volp, Ulrich. 2002. *Tod und Ritual in den christlichen Gemeinden der Antike*. Leiden: Brill.

Vroom, Joanita. 2007. "The Archaeology of Late Antique Dining Habits in the Eastern Mediterranean: A Preliminary Study of the Evidence." In *Objects in Context, Objects in Use:*

Material Spatiality in Late Antiquity, edited by Luke Lavan, Ellen Swift, and Toon Putzeys, 313–61. Leiden: Brill.

Wace, Alan J. B., Arthur H. S. Megaw, and Theodore C. Skeat. 1959. *Hermopolis Magna, Ashmunein: The Ptolemaic Sanctuary and the Basilica*. Alexandria: Alexandria University Press.

Wagner, Guy. 1976. "Inscriptions et graffiti grecs inédits de la Grande Oasis (rapport préliminaire, Khargeh et Dakhleh, mars et juin 1975)." *BIFAO* 76: 283–88.

———. 1987. *Les Oasis d'Égypte à l'époque grecque, romaine et byzantine d'après les documents grecs*. Cairo: IFAO.

———. 1991. "Qaṣr Nisīmah." In *Coptic Encyclopedia*, edited by Aziz S. Atiya, Vol. 7, 2038. New York: Macmillan.

Ward-Perkins, John Bryan 1949. "The Shrine of St. Menas in the Maryût." *PBSR* 17: 26–71.

———. 1954. "Constantine and the Origins of the Christian Basilica." *PBSR* 22: 447–68.

Warner, Nicholas. 2012. "Amheida: Architectural Conservation and Site Development, 2004–2009." In *The Oasis Papers 6: Proceedings of the Sixth International Conference of the Dakhleh Oasis Project*, edited by Roger S. Bagnall, Paola Davoli, and Colin A. Hope, 363–79. Dakhleh Oasis Project Monograph 15. Oxford: Oxbow Books.

———. 2018a. "Christian Architecture in North Kharga." In *North Kharga Oasis Survey: Explorations in Egypt's Western Desert*, by Corinna Rossi and Salima Ikram, 479–93. Leuven: Peeters.

———. 2018b. "The Church of Ain al-Tarakwa." In *North Kharga Oasis Survey: Explorations in Egypt's Western Desert*, by Corinna Rossi and Salima Ikram, 344–47. Leuven: Peeters.

———. 2018c. "The Church of Umm al-Dabadib." In *North Kharga Oasis Survey: Explorations in Egypt's Western Desert*, by Corinna Rossi and Salima Ikram, 236–40. Leuven: Peeters.

Wharton, Annabel Jane. 1995. *Refiguring the Post Classical City: Dura Europos, Jerash, Jerusalem and Ravenna*. Cambridge: Cambridge University Press.

White, L. Michael. 1990. *Building God's House in the Roman World. Architectural Adaptation among Pagans, Jews, and Christians*. Boston: The Johns Hopkins University Press.

Whitehouse, Helen. 2010. "Mosaics and Painting in Graeco-Roman Egypt." In *A Companion to Ancient Egypt*, edited by Alan B. Lloyd, 1008–31. Chichester, UK: Wiley-Blackwell.

———. 2022a. "Painted Decoration in the Main Temple Complex." In *Kellis: A Roman-Period Village in Egypt's Dakhleh Oasis*, edited by Colin A. Hope and Gillian E. Bowen, 243–68. Cambridge: Cambridge University Press.

———. 2022b. "Paintings from Domestic Contexts." In *Kellis: A Roman-Period Village in Egypt's Dakhleh Oasis*, edited by Colin A. Hope and Gillian E. Bowen, 57–78. Cambridge: Cambridge University Press.

Wilkinson, Charles K., 1928. "Early Christian Paintings in the Oasis of Khargeh." *BMMA* 23: 29–36.

Wilkinson, Sir John Gardner. 1843. *Modern Egypt and Thebes: Being a Description of Egypt, Including the Information Required for Travelers in that Country*. London: J. Murray.

Winlock, Herbert E. 1936. *Ed Dākhleh Oasis: Journal of a Camel Trip Made in 1908*. New York:

Metropolitan Museum of Art.

———. 1941. *The Temple of Hibis in El Khārgeh Oasis*, Vol. I. New York: Metropolitan Museum of Art.

Wipszycka, Ewa. 1996. *Études sur le Christianisme dans l'Égypte de l'Antiquité Tardive*. Roma: Institutum Patristicum Augustinianum.

Worp, Klaas A. 1995. *Greek Papyri from Kellis: I*. Oxford: Oxbow Books.

———, ed. 2004. *Greek Ostraca from Kellis: O.Kellis, Nos. 1–293*. Oxford: Oxbow Books.

Wuttmann, Michel. 2001. "Les qanāts de 'Ayn-Manâwîr (Oasis de Kharga, Égypte)." In *Irrigation et drainage dans l'Antiquité. Qanāts et canalisations souterraines en Iran, en Égypte et en Grèce*, edited by Pierre Briant, 109–35. Paris: Thotm.

Yasin, Ann Marie. 2005. "Funerary Monuments and Collective Identity: From Roman Family to Christian Community." *ArtB* 87/3: 433–57.

Youssef, Sabri. 2012. *Qanats in Dakhleh Oasis*. Paper read at the Seventh International Conference of the Dakhleh Oasis Project, 20–24 June 2012, Leiden University.

Zibawi, Mahmoud. 2003. *Images de l'Égypte chrétienne*. Iconologie copte. Paris: Picard.

———. 2005. *Bagawat: peintures paléochretienne d'Égypte*. Paris: Picard.

Zielinski, Adam K. 1999. "Conservation, Preservation and Presentation of Monuments and Objects in the Dakhleh Oasis." In *Reports from the Survey of the Dakhleh Oasis Western Desert of Egypt, 1977–1987*, edited by Charles S. Churcher and Anthony J. Mills, 183–88. Oxford: Oxbow Books.

Zycha, Joseph, ed. 1900. *Sancti Aureli Augustini: De fide et symbolo, De fide et operibus De agone christiano, De continentia, De bono coniugali, De sancta virginitate, De bono viduitatis, De adulterinis coniugiis, Lib. II. De mendacio, Contra mendacium, De opere monachorum, De divinatione daemonum, De cura pro mortuis gerenda, De patientia*. Corpus Scriptorum Ecclesiasticorum Latinorum 41. Vienna: F. Tempsky.

Index

abandonment: 1, 7, 10, 12–13, 23, 26, 34, 38, 42, 85, 90–91, 171, 182, 187, 190, 195, 202–3, 205, 207, 244, 290, 292, 317–18, 341, 349, 374–75, 380, 384

Abu Mina: 321, 346, 379–80, 392

'Ain el-Gedida: 23, 25–29, 33, 91, 283, 354, 364, 373, 376–77, 380, 389–91, 393, 405

'Ain el-Sabil: 32–33, 44, 63, 373, 377, 389, 393, 398–400

aisles: 24, 29–30, 32–33, 44, 48, 50, 52–53, 55, 62, 72, 74–76, 78, 81, 85, 87, 90–92, 94–98, 101, 105–6, 112–13, 116, 118–23, 129, 132, 137, 141, 145, 234, 257, 291, 339, 341, 343, 346, 349, 351, 353, 355–58, 375–77, 381–82, 384–86, 393, 395–400, 403, 406

Alexandria: 42, 78, 187, 240, 347, 366, 368, 382–83

altars: 45, 347, 351, 393

Amheida: *see* Trimithis

amphorae: 222, 381–82

animals: 3, 12, 22, 38, 87, 91–92, 94, 96–98, 105, 113, 115–16, 119, 121–22, 125, 128, 130–31, 133, 154–55, 157, 170–71, 185–88, 196, 205, 207, 211, 222–23, 225–27, 229, 231, 233, 241, 244, 260–61, 264, 301, 304

Antioch: 91, 370–71

apses: 22, 24, 27, 30–32, 35, 44, 48, 50, 52–53, 55, 58, 62, 66, 85, 87, 97–98, 121, 132–33, 137–38, 141, 245–46, 254, 282–83, 287, 292, 293, 307, 314, 337, 339–41, 343, 346–49, 351, 353–55, 357–58, 364, 370, 373, 377–78, 386, 393, 396–400, 404, 406

Bagawat (El-): 46, 48, 345, 366, 368–69

Bahariya (Oasis): 3

basilicas (and basilica architectural plan): 27, 29–30, 32–35, 38–39, 45–46, 48, 53, 55, 137, 145, 341, 346–49, 370–72, 378–80, 390–91, 393, 398, 400, 403, 406, 408

beads: 21, 39, 90–91, 98, 115, 154, 171, 187–88, 223, 227, 384

bemata: 33, 62–63, 341, 343, 375, 377–78, 397, 399

benches: *see mastabas*

bottles: 202, 227, 241, 381

bowls: 87, 91, 115, 171, 211, 223, 227, 244, 381
bracelets: 21, 90, 92, 105, 154, 186, 244, 261
bread: 27, 30, 33
bricks: 8, 13, 23–24, 27, 31, 33, 35, 37–39, 44, 46–48, 50, 52, 55, 57, 60, 62–63, 66, 68–70, 72–74, 76, 78, 81, 87, 90–92, 94, 97–101, 105–6, 108, 110, 112–13, 115–16, 118–19, 120–23, 125, 129–30, 132–33, 136–38, 142, 145, 147–48, 150, 154–55, 157, 159–61, 163–64, 167, 170–72, 174, 178, 181, 185–87, 189–90, 195–98, 200, 202, 205, 207–9, 211, 213, 216–17, 219, 222–23, 225–28, 231, 233–34, 240–42, 244, 249, 252, 254–55, 257–58, 260–61, 264, 268–70, 272–78, 281–82, 287, 290–93, 296–98, 301–2, 304–8, 311–12, 314, 317–18, 321, 327, 332–33, 336, 340–41, 353, 364, 373–76, 378–80, 382–83, 396–97, 399–400
bronze: 78, 81, 87, 90–92, 94, 98, 122, 128, 150, 162, 170–71, 185, 187, 196, 205, 223, 226–27, 241–42, 244, 264, 279, 281, 329, 334, 339, 382–84
burials: *see* tombs
Byzantine period: 6, 90

cancelli: 50, 55
caravan routes: 3, 5, 6, 42
ceilings: 2, 22–24, 85, 87, 91–92, 94, 96–98, 113, 115, 119, 137, 142, 158, 167, 170, 175, 187, 190–91, 195–96, 211, 213, 249, 251, 269, 353–60, 362–72, 384, 386–87, 397, 399, 403; *see also* roofs
cemeteries: 13, 26, 31, 37–39, 42, 45–46, 129, 133, 136–37, 279, 313, 340–46, 365–66, 404, 406, 408; *see also* tombs; burial; graves
ceramics: 2, 6, 9, 13, 15, 17, 19–22, 26–27, 35, 38, 57, 70, 78, 81, 87, 91–92, 94, 96–98, 101, 105, 113, 115–16, 118, 120, 122, 125, 128, 130–33, 152, 154–55, 157, 170–72, 174, 185–86, 195–97, 205, 207, 211, 213, 223, 225, 227–28, 231, 233, 236, 241, 244, 260–61, 264, 268, 272, 275, 278–79, 281, 283, 287, 292–93, 296–98, 301, 305–7, 312, 314, 318–19, 326, 334, 337, 340, 347, 381–82, 384–85, 388, 390, 400
chinking sherds/stones: 57, 78, 97, 249, 321, 332, 382, 388
Christian/Christianity: 1–2, 25–27, 29, 33, 37–43, 45–48, 52–53, 55, 131, 133, 136–37, 283, 339–40, 342–46, 348–49, 351, 354–56, 363, 365, 367–68, 370, 372, 376, 379, 381, 384, 390–93, 397–98, 401, 403–6, 408
churches: 1–2, 19–27, 29–40, 42, 44–46, 48–50, 52–58, 60, 63, 66, 70–78, 85–87, 90–92, 94–97, 99–101, 105–6, 110, 113, 116, 118–21, 132–33, 137, 141–43, 145–47, 154, 158–59, 162, 175, 182, 189, 195, 198, 208–9, 214–15, 217, 234, 236–37, 240, 245–46, 252, 268–69, 282–83, 290, 292, 296, 298, 313–14, 317–19, 321, 324, 329, 336–37, 339–51, 353–58, 363–65, 367–400, 403–8
cities: 1–2, 9–10, 12–13, 15, 17, 25, 40, 42, 57, 90, 342, 344, 390–92, 405–6, 408
clergy: 27, 40, 339, 342–43, 346, 349–51, 375, 378, 404
coins: 21–22, 27, 35, 78, 81, 87, 90–92, 94, 96, 98, 128, 150, 170–71, 185, 188, 196–97, 208, 223, 227, 240, 242, 244, 261, 264, 268, 298, 327, 329, 332–34, 382–84, 387–88, 399
    centenionales: 87, 91–92, 98, 240, 244, 382–83

maiorinae: 81, 171, 227, 244, 329, 334, 382–83
nummi: 91–92, 171, 244, 382–83
colonnades: 23, 30, 33, 44, 48, 50, 52–53, 59, 72–74, 76–79, 81, 85, 96, 98–99, 105, 106, 108, 110, 116, 118–20, 132, 375–78, 395, 397–98, 400, 406
columns: 29–33, 44–45, 48, 50, 52–53, 55, 63, 66–67, 72–74, 76–78, 80, 85, 90–91, 95, 98, 100–3, 105, 123, 137, 353, 364, 376, 378, 384, 395–400, 406
Constantine I: 171, 383, 387, 391, 398
cooking: 101, 115, 188, 207, 264, 267–68, 340, 381
Coptic (language): 22, 27, 41
crypts: 22, 24, 58, 60, 99, 121, 133, 137–38, 140–41, 145, 245–46, 248–49, 252, 254–57, 260–61, 264, 268–70, 273, 276–78, 280, 282–83, 287–88, 292, 299, 305–7, 313–14, 319, 321–22, 324–27, 329, 336–37, 339–41, 343–51, 357–58, 373, 381–85, 387, 390, 403–4, 408
cupboards: 170, 380, 399

Dakhla (Oasis): 1–3, 5–10, 21–23, 25–26, 30, 33, 35–40, 42, 44, 48, 57–58, 63, 91, 136–37, 283, 341–44, 349, 354–55, 357, 363–64, 367, 373, 376, 378, 389–90, 392–93, 397–98, 400–1, 404–5
Dakhleh Oasis Project (DOP): 7–8, 26
decoration: 2, 9, 14–15, 18, 23, 38, 46, 90, 113, 133, 269, 314, 353–54, 357–58, 363–72, 384–85, 397, 399, 403
Deir Abu Matta: 33–35, 37–38, 136, 341, 349, 355
Deir el-Malak: 35, 342
Deir Mustafa Kashef: 47, 48–49
Diocletian: 371, 387
dipinti: 41, 397
doors: 145, 149, 162, 164, 170, 187, 268, 296, 299, 319, 321, 397
doorways: 23, 27, 33, 45, 50, 52, 55, 62, 64, 68–69, 72, 92, 94, 105, 137–38, 142, 145–50, 154, 157–63, 175–76, 180, 186–87, 190, 198, 200–2, 209, 213, 216, 237, 245–46, 254, 256–57, 268, 282–85, 299, 301, 319–20, 337, 375–77, 381, 396–98
dumps and dumped material: 21, 71, 91, 108, 113, 125, 155, 171, 205, 219, 222–23, 225, 227–28, 231, 233, 239–40, 244, 382, 384–85, 387–88; *see also* middens
dunes: 3, 7, 10, 23
Dush: *see* Kysis

economy: 1, 6–8, 17, 33, 46, 344
Edmondstone, A.: 8
Edmondstone (Gebel): 3
El-Qasr: 6, 9, 12, 38
El-Muzawwaqa: 37–38, 136
epoikia: 25, 27
estates: 27

faience: 87, 91, 94, 97, 113, 115, 154, 185, 225, 227, 257, 260, 264
Farafra (Oasis): 3, 5
Fayyum: 3, 39
food preparation: 188, 381, 398
foundations: 20–21, 23–24, 33, 49, 55, 59–60, 62, 68, 70–78, 81, 85, 87, 91, 96, 99–103, 105–6, 108–13, 115–16, 118–20, 122, 132, 142, 167, 174, 198, 205, 209, 215–17, 219, 225, 227, 229, 231, 233–34, 236, 239–40, 246, 257–58, 260, 268, 272, 275–77, 281, 288, 290–92, 298, 301, 304–5, 311–12, 321, 326–27, 336–37, 342, 373–78, 380–90, 395–96, 398
furniture: 96, 170, 178, 187, 296, 384

glass: 21, 87, 90–92, 94, 96–98, 105, 113, 115–16, 119, 122, 125, 130–31, 154, 170–71, 174, 185–88, 197, 202, 205, 211, 222–23, 225–27, 229, 231, 233, 241–42, 244, 260–61, 264, 384
graffiti: 42, 55, 347, 353–54, 364, 397
graves: *see* tombs
Great Oasis: 7, 9, 25, 42, 340, 375, 393, 397, 399–400
Greek (language, culture): 7–8, 13, 17, 21, 40–41, 71, 90–91, 97–98, 113, 116, 122, 128, 163, 185, 188, 205, 207, 222, 227, 229, 261, 268, 305, 318, 327, 329, 345, 366, 384–85, 388; *see also* identity, cultural or ethnic
gypsum: 18, 23, 60, 62, 66, 68, 70, 73–74, 78, 87, 90–92, 98, 113, 116, 130, 133, 145, 159, 161, 163, 167, 170–71, 187, 189–90, 195–200, 205, 207–9, 211, 227, 233, 244, 260–61, 264, 279, 353, 364, 376, 384–85, 397, 399

hearths: 20
houses: 3, 9, 14–20, 24, 57, 90, 154, 321, 365, 367–68, 370–71, 381–82, 385, 387–88

identity, cultural or ethnic: 2, 339, 344, 347, 351, 391–92, 404
indictions: 388
industrial areas: 14, 17, 27, 298, 390, 408
inscriptions: 27, 41, 98, 353–54, 384
Ismant el-Kharab: *see* Kellis

jars: 87, 96, 222, 225, 244, 278, 298, 340, 381, 384

Karanis: 23, 154, 321
kathesteria: 141, 246, 405
Kellis; Ismant el-Kharab: 7–8, 25–27, 29–33, 37–41, 48, 63, 129, 131, 133, 136, 279, 340–43, 355–56, 364, 367, 371, 373, 376–77, 385, 389, 392–93, 395, 397–400, 403, 406, 408
Kharga (Oasis): 1, 3, 5–8, 25–26, 38–39, 42–45, 47, 52–53, 55, 57, 74, 137, 141, 340–41, 345, 355, 363, 365, 368, 376, 378–79, 381, 389, 397, 393, 400–1
kitchens: 33, 398
Kysis; Dush: 39, 44, 53–55, 340–41, 400

lamps: 91, 154, 170, 187, 226–27, 231, 241–42, 365, 384
leather: 113
letters (correspondence): 91, 388
lids: 101, 113, 278–79, 339, 381
lime: 70, 78, 91, 113, 152, 155, 164, 170–71, 176–77, 195–96, 205, 207, 211, 213, 216–17, 233, 237, 239, 252–53, 261, 386
limestone: 41, 52, 297
linen: 37, 133

magnetometry: 57
mastabas; benches: 27, 31, 33, 37, 44, 47–48, 55, 68–70, 94–95, 119, 344, 396, 399–400
metal: 21, 279, 390
middens: 20; *see also* dumps and dumped material
military: 6, 26, 404
monasteries: 26, 35, 42, 48, 52, 346–47, 363, 365
monasticism: 48
monks: 48–49, 343
mosaics: 13, 365–66, 368, 370–72
Mothis: 6, 7, 26
Mut el-Kharab: *see* Mothis

names, personal: 7–8, 40–42, 347
naves: 24, 27, 29, 31–33, 44–45, 48–50, 52–53, 55, 72, 76, 78, 81–82, 84–85, 87, 96, 98, 119, 141, 269, 341, 343, 346–47, 349–51, 355, 357–58, 364, 374–76, 378–79, 384–85, 387–88, 390, 393, 395–400, 403, 406
necropolises: 2, 9, 12–13, 37–39, 46–47, 341, 344, 346, 366, 368, 392, 408
niches: 27, 52–53, 347, 353, 365

ostraka: 21–22, 33, 35, 40, 41, 71, 87, 90–92, 97–99, 113, 116, 122, 128, 163, 172, 174, 185, 188, 205, 227, 236, 261, 268, 318, 374, 382, 384–88, 400
ovens: 27, 30, 398
Oxyrhynchus: 343, 368

paint/painted surfaces/painting: 2, 9, 14–15, 17–18, 22–24, 46, 87, 91–92, 94, 96–98, 113, 115, 119, 125, 130, 133, 170–71, 185, 187, 205, 207, 211, 227–28, 244, 260–61, 264, 269, 293, 296, 313–14, 317–19, 353–60; 362–72, 397, 399, 403, 406
palmette (motif): 90
palms (trees): 92, 94, 97–98, 131, 142, 167, 170, 172, 174, 187, 195–97, 213, 227, 321, 353, 355–56
polychromy: 358, 363, 366–67, 369, 397
panels: 15, 364

passageways: 27, 31, 72, 137, 142, 145, 158–59, 162, 164, 171, 189–91, 196, 201–2, 207, 213, 268, 306, 376, 406
pastophoria: 27, 33, 50, 52–53, 55, 58, 62, 66, 92, 94, 97, 137–38, 141, 214, 217, 237, 240, 245–46, 249, 260, 268–69, 282, 287, 301, 319, 339–40, 351, 355, 357–58, 382–83, 387, 393, 396–99, 406
pendants: 90
pigments: 358–359, 368
pits (features): 20, 34, 37–39, 46, 60, 78, 81, 85, 90–91, 98, 120–23, 125, 128–35, 145, 149, 164, 171–72, 174, 255, 257–58, 268–70, 272–73, 275–79, 281, 283, 290–92, 296–301, 303–8, 311–12, 314, 317–19, 326, 337, 340–41, 349, 381–82, 384–86
platforms: 31, 32, 44, 55, 60, 62–63, 65–66, 76, 85, 87, 98, 121, 129, 132, 137–38, 147, 161, 164, 166–67, 171, 249, 251, 260–61, 287, 340–41, 343, 375–76, 378–80, 386, 393, 397, 399
podia: 27, 375–78, 395, 399
pottery: *see* ceramics
Ptolemaic period: 6, 42, 91, 349, 366
pulpits: 74, 75, 375

qanat: 6

reuse/reused: 12–13, 42, 52, 91, 95, 97, 113, 205, 207, 277, 318, 374, 384, 386, 388,
roads: *see* streets
Rohlfs, G.: 8
Rome: 365, 371, 403
roofs: 15, 24, 27, 35, 52–53, 69, 98, 137, 142, 146–47, 159, 170, 175, 187, 190, 195, 237, 240, 249, 269, 282–83, 285, 287, 319, 323, 347–48, 353–355, 358, 363, 365–66, 369, 374–76, 399–400, 403; *see also* ceilings
ropes: 355

sanctuary: 2, 24, 33, 35, 44, 48, 50, 52, 55, 76, 78, 85, 96, 98–99, 121, 137–38, 141, 245, 282, 319, 337, 339, 341–43, 346–47, 349, 351, 353, 357, 373, 376, 384, 390, 393, 395–400, 403–4
sandstone: 5, 170, 396–97
Shams el-Din: 44, 55–56, 74, 141, 376, 378–79, 393, 396–97, 400
skeletons: 133, 174, 275, 277, 281, 301, 305–8, 312, 404
soldiers: 404
springs: 3, 5, 10
stairs/stairways/staircases: 20, 24, 30, 55, 69, 142, 146–48, 150, 152–55, 157, 159, 207–8, 215, 321, 346–47, 373, 376, 378–80, 388, 398, 400
statues: 91
stone: 13, 38, 41–42, 45, 48, 52, 62, 69, 90, 92, 162–63, 172, 187, 249, 255, 269, 349, 355, 365, 379
stoppers: 87, 91, 113, 116, 205, 222–23, 227, 229, 244, 298, 301, 384
storage: 15, 22, 96, 175, 215, 319, 326, 379, 381

stoves: 176, 181–83, 187–88, 200–2, 204–5, 207, 374–75
streets: 3, 5, 12, 27, 54, 391–92, 398, 405

temples: 10, 12, 26–27, 40–42, 44, 53–54, 283, 297, 349, 367, 391–92
terracotta figurines: 154, 384
textiles: 21, 24, 39, 91, 96, 98, 113, 115, 120, 122, 128, 131, 133, 174, 186, 223, 227, 272, 277, 281, 301, 304–5, 308, 311, 366
tombs: 2, 9, 13, 20, 22, 26, 31, 33–34, 37–39, 46–48, 60, 76, 78, 81, 85, 91, 118–37, 145, 159, 163–64, 171–75, 245–46, 252, 254–58, 260, 264, 268–82, 288–92, 298–313, 319, 321, 337, 339–51, 365–66, 368, 371, 381–82, 384–86, 392, 403–4, 406
Trimithis (mod. Amheida): 1–2, 6–13, 14–15, 17–27, 30, 33, 37–42, 44, 57–58, 69, 72, 86, 90, 133, 137, 154, 222, 245, 279, 321, 339–45, 348–51, 356–57, 364, 367–73, 376–79, 381–82, 385, 388–400, 403–8
vaults/vaulting/vaulted: 20, 24, 27, 50, 55, 90, 137, 142, 249, 250–51, 253–54, 258, 260–61, 264, 268–69, 282–83, 285, 287, 293, 298, 318–19, 321, 323, 329, 332–34, 345, 347–49, 354–55, 357, 363, 365–68, 371, 382, 387
villages: 9, 12, 26, 27, 33, 35, 37–38, 40, 52, 55, 342, 344

water: 3, 5–7, 10
weaves: 133, 275
weights: 21
wells: 5–6, 10, 71, 91, 97, 113, 122, 128, 227, 329, 387
well tags: 71, 91, 97, 113, 122, 128, 227, 329, 387
Western Desert: 1–3, 5–7, 9, 25–26, 29, 39–40, 42, 50, 136, 345, 363–64, 372, 400–1, 403, 408
windows: 52–53
wine: 6, 19, 222, 381
Winlock, H. E.: 8, 26, 33, 42, 44, 355
women: 27, 90, 174, 275, 301, 312, 339, 343, 349, 376, 404–5
wood/wooden objects: 13, 22–23, 62, 69, 91, 92, 96, 97, 105, 113, 115, 122, 128, 131, 133, 142, 145, 149–50, 154–55, 157, 161–62, 164, 170–71, 175, 177–78, 185, 187–88, 196–97, 200, 205, 207–9, 211, 213, 222–23, 226–27, 229, 231, 233–34, 237–41, 244, 249, 261, 264, 268, 296, 298, 321, 326, 340, 357, 365, 367, 374–75, 380, 384, 397